Values and Identities in Europe

Contrary to what is suggested in media and popular discourses, Europe is neither a monolithic entity nor simply a collection of nation states. It is, rather, a union of millions of individuals who differ from one another in a variety of ways while also sharing many characteristics associated with their ethnic, social, political, economic, religious or national characteristics.

This book explores differences and similarities that exist in attitudes, beliefs and opinions on a range of issues across Europe. Drawing on the extensive data of the European Social Survey, it presents insightful analyses of social attitudes, organised around the themes of religious identity, political identity, family identity and social identity, together with a section on methodological issues. A collection of rigorously analysed studies on national, comparative and pan-European levels, *Values and Identities in Europe* offers insight into the heart and soul of Europe at a time of unprecedented change. As such, it will appeal to scholars across the social sciences with interests in social attitudes, social change in Europe, demographics and survey methods.

Michael J. Breen is Chair of the European Social Survey (ESS) and Dean of the Faculty of Arts at Mary Immaculate College, University of Limerick, Ireland.

Routledge Advances in Sociology

For a full list of titles in this series, please visit www.routledge.com/series/SE0511

196 Praxeological Political Analysis
Edited by Michael Jonas and Beate Littig

197 Austere Histories in European Societies
Social Exclusion and the Contest of Colonial Memories
Edited by Stefan Jonsson and Julia Willén

198 Habermas and Social Research
Between Theory and Method
Edited by Mark Murphy

199 Interpersonal Violence
Differences and Connections
Edited by Marita Husso, Tuija Virkki, Marianne Notko, Helena Hirvonen and Jari Eilola

200 Online Hate and Harmful Content
Cross National Perspectives
Pekka Räsänen, Atte Oksanen, Matti Näsi and Teo Keipi

201 Science, Technology and the Ageing Society
Tiago Moreira

202 Values and Identities in Europe
Evidence from the European Social Survey
Edited by Michael J. Breen

203 Humanist Realism for Sociologists
Terry Leahy

204 The Third Digital Divide
A Weberian Approach to Digital Inequalities
Massimo Ragnedda

Values and Identities in Europe
Evidence from the European Social Survey

Edited by Michael J. Breen

LONDON AND NEW YORK

First published 2017
by Routledge
2 Park Square, Milton Park, Abingdon, Oxon OX14 4RN

and by Routledge
711 Third Avenue, New York, NY 10017

Routledge is an imprint of the Taylor & Francis Group, an informa business

© 2017 selection and editorial matter, Michael J. Breen; individual chapters, the contributors

The right of Michael J. Breen to be identified as the author of the editorial material, and of the authors for their individual chapters, has been asserted in accordance with sections 77 and 78 of the Copyright, Designs and Patents Act 1988.

All rights reserved. No part of this book may be reprinted or reproduced or utilised in any form or by any electronic, mechanical, or other means, now known or hereafter invented, including photocopying and recording, or in any information storage or retrieval system, without permission in writing from the publishers.

Trademark notice: Product or corporate names may be trademarks or registered trademarks, and are used only for identification and explanation without intent to infringe.

British Library Cataloguing in Publication Data
A catalogue record for this book is available from the British Library

Library of Congress Cataloging in Publication Data
A catalog record has been requested for this book

ISBN: 978-1-138-22666-1 (hbk)
ISBN: 978-1-315-39714-6 (ebk)

Typeset in Times New Roman
by Deanta Global Publishing Services, Chennai, India

To Noreen O'Loughlin, Fiachra Ó Braoin, and
Doireann Ní Bhraoin

Contents

List of Figures	ix
List of Tables	xii
Notes on Contributors	xv
Foreword	xxi
Preface	xxiii
Acknowledgements	xxv

1 **The Significance of the European Social Survey** 1
   MICHAEL J. BREEN

SECTION I
Religious Identity 15

2 **The Declining Significance of Religion: Secularization in Ireland** 17
   RYAN T. CRAGUN

3 **Religiosity and Political Participation across Europe** 36
   ANNA KULKOVA

4 **Religion and Values in the ESS: Individual and Societal Effects** 58
   CAILLIN REYNOLDS

SECTION II
Social Identity 75

5 **Work–Life Conflict of Working Couples Before and During the Crisis in 18 European Countries** 77
   MICHAEL OCHSNER AND IVETT SZALMA

6 **A Tale of Two Surveys** 100
   AMY ERBE HEALY AND SEÁN Ó RIAIN

7 **Societal-Level Equality and Well-Being** 127
   MARGUERITE BEATTIE

SECTION III
Political Identity and Security 141

8 Corruption in European Countries: A Cross-National Comparison 143
   KRISTYNA CHABOVA

9 Changing Tendencies of Youth Political Participation in Europe: Evidence from Four Different Cases 160
   DÀNIEL OROSS AND ANDREA SZABÓ

10 Untangling our Attitudes Towards Irish Citizen Involvement and Democracy: Perspectives from the European Social Survey and Implications for Higher Education 184
   AOIFE PRENDERGAST

SECTION IV
Familial Identity 199

11 Fatherhood in Russia: Fertility Decisions and Ideational Factors 201
   ALEXANDRA LIPASOVA

12 Well-Being in Married and Cohabiting Families with Children and Social Support during Economic Recession in Europe 214
   MARE AINSAAR

13 How to Measure Fathering Practices in a European Comparison? 228
   IVETT SZALMA AND JUDIT TAKÁCS

SECTION V
Methodological Issues 249

14 How Do Reluctant Respondents Assess Governmental Protection Against Poverty? 251
   HELGE BAUMANN

15 Combining Multiple Datasets for Simultaneous Analysis on the Basis of Common Identifiers: A Case Study from the European Social Survey and the European Values Study 264
   BRENDAN HALPIN AND MICHAEL J. BREEN

16 Using Mixed Modes in Survey Research: Evidence from Six Experiments in the ESS 273
   ANA VILLAR AND RORY FITZGERALD

Index 311

Figures

1.1	Trends in ESS academic publishing	5
1.2	Journals with most ESS publications	6
1.3	Most common research themes	7
1.4	Most used substantive items, social capital and political participation	8
1.5	Most used substantive items, subjective well-being, religious background, immigration and system satisfaction	9
2.1	Percentage of Americans who would not allow atheists or communists to speak in public	19
2.2	Google Ngram data on occurrences of "godless communist" phrase in English literature, 1936–2008	20
2.3	Percentage of Americans and Irish with no religious affiliation over time (GSS, EVS and ESS)	22
2.4	Change in importance of religion in lives of Irish, 1990–2010 (EVS)	23
2.5	Percentage of Irish who rarely or never attend religious service (EVS and ESS)	24
2.6	Percentage with no religious affiliation by EVS wave and cohort	25
2.7	Proportion rarely or never attending religious services by ESS round and cohort	25
3.1	Political participation index for Protestants and Orthodox Christians	38
4.1	The integrated structure of values	60
4.2	Value profile of individuals	61
4.3	Value profiles compared	62
4.4	Denominations in ESS 6	65
4.5	Denominational belonging ESS 1-6	65
4.6	Religious attendance ESS 6	66
4.7	Religious attendance ESS 1-6	67
4.8	Ranked country level residuals (u_0j) of conservation values	70
4.9	Ranked country level residuals (u_0j) of openness values	70
5.1	The difference in work–life conflict levels between 2004 and 2010 in 18 European countries by sex and country, sorted by level of increase	88

x   *Figures*

7.1	Mediation of Gini and happiness by trust	136
7.2	Mediation of Gini and happiness by fairness	136
7.3	Mediation of Gini and life satisfaction by trust	136
7.4	Mediation of Gini and life satisfaction by fairness	137
8.1	Control of corruption in post-communist countries	145
8.2	Direct experience with corruption, ESS, 2004	149
8.3	Control of corruption, pooled data	151
8.4	Scatter plot: countries with no communist past	153
8.5	Scatter plot: control of corruption and trust in other people	154
8.6	Scatter plot, pooled data: control of corruption and Gini coefficient	155
8.7	Gini coefficient in post-communist countries	156
9.1	The process of our analysis	164
9.2	Voted in last national election? (Whole population, percentage)	165
9.3	Voted in last national election? (Young people/only respondents/percentage)	165
9.4	Voted in last national election? "Yes" and "Not eligible to vote" answers (whole population, percentage)	166
11.1	Attitudes towards youngest, oldest and ideal age of becoming a father, all men (40+)	208
11.2	Statistical hindrances: male age spread in Russia versus the European Union (men 40+, 2008)	209
11.3	Statistical hindrances: timing	210
12.1	People with children in the household among 20–60-year-old persons in different European countries	217
12.2	People with children in the household and living with a partner (%) among 20–60-year-old persons in different European countries	218
12.3	Proportion of people satisfied with life in different family types in 2010 (data weighed by design weights, all countries)	220
12.4	Support for families with children and life satisfaction differences between parents with children in the household and single persons without children	223
13.1	Agreement (per cent) with the statement "When jobs are scarce, men have more right to a job than women" in 25 European countries (1990–2008)	232
13.2	Agreement with the statement "When jobs are scarce, men have more right to a job than women": mean values in 21 European countries (2004–2010)	233
14.1	Missing data mechanisms	252
14.2	The continuum of resistance	253
14.3	Interviewer performance in Germany	258
14.4	Interviewer performance in Ireland	259

14.5	The link between response propensity and attitudes towards poverty (full model)	259
16.1	Response Rates (RR1) for Studies 3, 4, and 6	286
16.2	Refusal rates for Studies 4, 5 and 6	287
16.3	Household contact rates for Studies 4, 5 and 6	288
16.4	Percentage of variables showing significant differences across modes	293
16.5	Mean costs per successful interview	301

Tables

1.1	ESS respondents, count, by country by round	4
1.2	ESS data users, by count, type and percentage	5
2.1	Religious attendance regressed (OLS) on demographic and independent variables	29
3.1	Mean values of political participation (PP) index for countries with different predominant religions in 2012 (ESS)	37
3.2	Political participation (PP) among followers of different religious traditions in 2012 (ESS)	38
3.3	Political participation index (descriptive statistics)	46
3.4	Types of political actions performed by Europeans (descriptive statistics)	46
3.5	Average rates of political participation of the Orthodox living in predominantly Orthodox and non-Orthodox countries	48
3.6A	Predominant religions in European countries	52
3.7A	Political participation rates among European countries in 2012 (ESS)	53
3.8A	Political participation and religiosity: all countries	53
3.9A	Religiosity and political participation: controlling for country predominant religion	54
3.10A	Religious services attendance and political participation among members of different religious traditions	55
3.11A	Praying frequency and political participation among members of different religious traditions	55
3.12A	Religiosity and political participation among countries with different predominant religions	56
4.1	Linear regression of conservation values	68
4.2	Linear regression of openness-to-change values	68
4.3	Multi-level model of conservation values	71
4.4	Multi-level model of openness-to-change values	72
5.1	Descriptive statistics on work–life conflict and GDP growth per capita, differences between 2004 and 2010	86

Tables xiii

5.2	Base model: multi-level fixed-effects model for work–life conflict in 2004 and 2010 respectively, no explanatory variables	88
5.3	Multi-level linear regression estimates of the determinants of work–life conflict in 2004 and 2010	89
5.4	Comparing the effect of different stress-levels at home and at work on working couples' work–life conflict	93
6.1	Goodness of fit indices, full EWCS analysis	105
6.2	Country groupings from full EWCS analysis	106
6.3	Work regimes from full EWCS analysis (6 regimes, 3 groups)	108
6.4	Goodness of fit indices, ESS variables	110
6.5	Goodness of fit indices, EWCS reduced analysis	110
6.6	Work regimes from reduced EWCS and ESS analysis	111
6.7	Inactive covariates from analysis on EWCS: work organisation	114
6.8	Country groupings from reduced EWCS and ESS analysis	115
6.9	Inactive covariates from analysis on ESS: attitudes towards welfare	117
6.10	Logistic regression predicting welfare attitudes, ESS data R2 and R5	118
6.11A	EWCS and ESS variables	123
6.12A	Country groupings from reduced EWCS/ESS merged analysis	126
7.1	Mean effect sizes for impact of social interdependence on dependent variables	130
8.1	Determinants of control of corruption (OLS regression)	152
9.1	Difference in non-electoral participation (young and adult people, index, 0–1 means, standard deviation)	170
9.2	Non-electric participation logistic binary model	172
9.3	Voted in last national election? "Yes" answer, %	174
9.4	Voted in last national election Logistic Regression Model	175
9.5A	List of variables in the analysis	181
9.6A	Statistics voted in last national election? "Yes" answer, % (Cramer's–V in all dataset and in all countries)	183
11.1	Occurrence, timing and male fertility rate: percentage of men who have a child (men 40+), average age of becoming a father and number of children (fathers 40+)	207
11.2	Attitudes towards ideal age, social age deadline of fatherhood, all men (40+)	207
11.3	Attitudes towards importance of fathering for adulthood and towards choice of childlessness, all men (40+)	208
12.1	Description of family types in 2010 (all countries, data with weights)	219
12.2	Mean life satisfaction in countries by family type in 2010	221

12.3	Satisfaction with life in different family types, results of multi-level linear regression models	222
12.4A	Number of persons from different families in a sample	227
13.1	Description of the independent variables	235
13.2	Mean values of the dependent variables: agreement with the statement: "When jobs are scarce, men should have more right to a job than women"	238
13.3	Estimates of ordered regressions	239
13.4A	Development of fathering practices related items in freely available international surveys	245
13.5A	Fathering practices related items in GGS	247
14.1	(Non)response modelling coefficients	257
14.2	Modelling coefficients of attitudes towards governmental protection against poverty	260
15.1	Mean Gamma statistics, comparing imputed attendance to observed attendance	268
15.2	Imputed religious attendance from ESS data, compared with observed attendance from EVS data, demographic variables only	269
15.3	Imputed religious attendance from ESS data, compared with observed attendance from EVS data, using also frequency of prayer	270
15.4	Mean Gamma statistics, comparing imputed attendance to observed attendance, using frequency of prayer	270
16.1	Overview of design characteristics for each study	275
16.2	Overview of design characteristics for each study: sampling	279
16.3	Average absolute error by section, mode and country	295
16.4	Significance of the difference in correlations across mode designs	296
16.5	Relative costs of fieldwork using different modes	302
16.6A	Research teams for each study	310

Contributors

Mare Ainsaar is a senior research fellow at the Institute of Social Studies at the University of Tartu (Estonia). She defended her PhD degree at University of Turku (Finland) on social policy and migration. Currently, she is also head of a unit of a social policy research group at University of Tartu. She had served as a counsellor for the Minister of Family and Population Affairs in Estonia, advising on gender, children and family issues. Her current main research interests are related to family, health policies, fertility policy and public policy on gender issues. She is the author of more than 200 scientific publications. She has been a project leader for many international projects, including the ESS in Estonia.

Helge Baumann studied social science, classical philology and empirical research methods at the Ruhr University in Bochum, Germany. In 2012, he joined the Institute for Innovation Research and Management in Bochum. He currently works as a research assistant at the Hans Böckler Foundation in Dusseldorf, Germany, where he conducts and analyses representative works councils' surveys. His research priorities comprise works councils' research and survey methodology. He is writing his PhD thesis on links between various error sources in large computer-assisted telephone interviewing (CATI) surveys, including non-response and measurement bias.

Marguerite Beattie received her bachelor's degree at the University of Virginia and is currently a postgraduate student at the University of Helsinki. While her primary research interests include subjective well-being and equality, she has also delved into health psychology in her thesis involving health behaviour change and mindfulness.

Michael J. Breen is dean of the Faculty of Arts at Mary Immaculate College, University of Limerick, Ireland. He holds undergraduate degrees from University College Dublin and the University of St. Thomas Aquinas, Rome; and a MS and PhD from Syracuse University, New York. He is currently chair of the ESS and also chair of the European Values Study (EVS) General Assembly. He is a member of the Irish Research Council's International Advisory Board and a former Government of Ireland Research Fellow. He is a director of the Irish Centre for Catholic Studies and of the Centre for Culture, Technology and Values, both located at Mary Immaculate College. A quantitative researcher, his primary research interests lie in the area of values, religious practice and social change.

Kristyna Chabova is a PhD student at Charles University in Prague, where she is finishing her final year of studies, and she has a Master of Science (MSc) in sociology from the University of Oxford. Her research is focused on corruption in post-communist countries and especially on the possible reasons why some post-communist countries have succeeded in reducing corruption while others have not. As part of her studies, she was a visiting PhD student at Hertie School of Governance in Berlin under the supervision of Prof. Alina Mungiu-Pippidi. She was also an exchange student at George Washington University in Washington, DC, and at Sciences-Po in Paris. She is associate professor at Charles University, where she co-teaches courses on data journalism, the welfare state and political sociology. At the same time, she is working as a researcher in the Academy of Science in the Czech Republic, Institute of Sociology in the Department of Value Orientations in Society.

Ryan T. Cragun is a partner, parent and sociologist of religion (in order of importance). Originally from Utah, he now lives in Florida and works at the University of Tampa. His research and writing focuses on religion, with an emphasis on Mormonism and the non-religious. His research has been published in a variety of academic journals, including *Journal for the Scientific Study of Religion, Sociology of Religion, Journal of Sex Research, Journal of Religion and Health*, and *Journal of Contemporary Religion*. He's the author of several books, including *How to Defeat Religion in 10 Easy Steps, What You Don't Know About Religion (but Should)*, and *Could I Vote for a Mormon for President?* When he's not working, he's spending time with his wife and son, cooking, watching science fiction, hiking, playing soccer or tinkering with computers.

Peter Farago is the director of the Swiss Centre of Expertise in the Social Sciences FORS and a professor at the University of Lausanne. A sociologist by formation, he has more than 30 years' experience in empirical social research, both within and outside academia. He has directed numerous scientific research projects, and he was the central coordinator and manager of the largest social-science research programme ever run in Switzerland with more than 100 projects ("*Demain la Suisse*", funded by the Swiss NSF). His research interests include social reporting, social indicators and social policy; policy and programme evaluation; and survey research methodology. He is co-editor of a volume on *Understanding Research Infrastructures in the Social Sciences* (2013, Zurich: Seismo). FORS is the leading Swiss social science research infrastructure institution responsible for several large surveys of international importance (e.g. the Swiss Household Panel, the Swiss ESS, the Swiss International Social Survey Programme [ISSP], the Swiss *Survey* of Health,

Ageing and Retirement in Europe [SHARE] and the Swiss Election Study) as well as the data documentation service, which offers hundreds of fully documented empirical datasets for use by researchers. FORS edits the Swiss Social Report and is active in cutting edge research on survey methodology. It is integrated in the global network of similar partner institutions.

Rory Fitzgerald is the director of the ESS European Research Infrastructure Consortium (ERIC) at City University London. He has been a member of the Core Scientific Team (CST) of the ESS since 2004 and became ESS director in 2012. In 2016, he was awarded a PhD in Sociology by City University London, which focused on the application of the Total Survey Error framework to cross-national surveys. He plays a leading role in the design, management and overall coordination of the ESS and directs the CST. He also works with the national coordinators in each country to ensure the effective implementation of the survey. His key expertise is in cross-national survey methodology, with a focus on questionnaire design, pre-testing and non-response. He was part of the ESS team that was awarded the Descartes Prize for excellence in scientific collaborative research in 2005. He also played a key role in developing the application for the ESS to become a European Research Infrastructure Consortium (ERIC), which was awarded in 2013. In 2016, the ESS was also given the status of a landmark infrastructure on the European Strategy Forum for Research Infrastructures (ESFRI) roadmap. In addition, Rory is the coordinator of the Horizon 2020 cluster project "Synergies for Europe's Research Infrastructures in the Social Sciences" (SERISS), which brings together the ESS, SHARE, European Values Survey (EVS), the Wage Indicator Survey and the data archive infrastructure CESSDA. This project facilitates joint methodological and strategic work in areas where cross-infrastructure collaboration can make it more effective. Prior to joining the ESS team, he worked at the National Centre for Social Research and the Gallup Organization.

Brendan Halpin is a sociologist interested in the analysis of large-scale survey data, particularly from a longitudinal point of view. After a DPhil at Nuffield College Oxford, he spent five years at the Institute for Social and Economic Research, University of Essex, home of the British Household Panel Survey, and he has worked at the University of Limerick since 2000. Current research interests include multiple imputation for life-course data; dynamic social processes in the labour market and family formation domains, including processes of educational homogamy; and methods for the analysis of longitudinal data.

Amy Erbe Healy is a quantitative sociologist currently working on the New Deals project at Maynooth University, Co. Kildare, Ireland, comparing workplace regimes in Europe. Previously, she worked in the Department of Sociology at the University of Limerick, both as a lecturer and a research associate; and as a postdoctoral researcher at Mary Immaculate College at the University of Limerick, analysing the ESS. She holds degrees from the University of Illinois Urbana-Champaign, the University of Wisconsin at Madison, and the University of Limerick. Her research focuses mainly on cross-national comparisons and change over time within a European context. She has an interest in stratification and social exclusion. Recent research has looked at secularisation theory, convergence theory vis-à-vis consumption, the impact of austerity on political legitimacy and the impact of austerity on religious belief and practice.

Anna Kulkova is a junior research fellow at the Laboratory for Political Studies and a postgraduate student in Political Science at Higher School of Economics (HSE), Russia. She holds bachelors and master's degrees in Political Science from HSE, where she specialized in Comparative Politics. Anna studies how cultural factors (especially religion) can affect both individual behaviour or value orientations and macro-level political institutions. Her previous projects focused on the link between religiosity and political participation, attitudes towards sexual minorities and nationalism. Anna's current project, "Religion and the European Welfare States: The Effect of Religiosity on Individual Redistribution Preferences" aims to identify if religion is still a powerful predictor of welfare attitudes in secularized Europe.

Alexandra Lipasova is a PhD student at the Sociology Department of the National Research University Higher School of Economics, Moscow, Russia, and she is currently working on her thesis "Fatherhood models in post-Soviet Russia: Dynamics and continuity in different social groups." She also has a degree in economics and linguistics. Her research interests comprise gender studies, familistics, parenthood, social policy, reproduction choices, discrimination, body studies and violence against women. She is the author of several articles on Scandinavian social policy, gender regimes in the developed countries and parenting practices in Russia.

Seán Ó Riain is professor of Sociology at the National University of Ireland Maynooth, where he is an associate of the National Institute for Regional and Spatial Analysis. His most recent book is *The Rise and Fall of Ireland's Celtic Tiger: Liberalism, Boom and Bust* (2014), which explores how Ireland's crisis of 2008 was caused by financialisation, the narrowing of the European integration project and the national politics of economic liberalism. Previous research includes studies of software work, comparative political economy and the institutions and politics of "network developmental states." Some of this work is published in *The Politics of High Tech Growth* (2004) and a co-edited volume on *The Changing Worlds and Workplaces of Capitalism* (2015). He is currently directing a five-year study of changing workplace bargains in Europe, particularly in Ireland and Denmark (www.maynoothuniversity.ie/newdeals/). The project is funded by a Starting Investigator grant of the European Research Council. He is an independent member of the National Economic and Social Council in Ireland.

Michael Ochsner received his PhD from the Institute of Sociology at the University of Zurich in 2014 with a thesis on the cultural differences of the effect of welfare provision on the legitimacy of the state. He works at the Swiss Centre of Expertise in the Social Sciences (FORS) at the University of Lausanne as a senior researcher in the team "international surveys," where he has been involved in the implementation of the ESS and the ISSP in Switzerland since 2013. He is currently also co-leading the Swiss part of the ERANET-RUS project "Public Attitudes to Welfare, Climate Change and Energy in the EU and Russia." From 2009 to 2014, he was a researcher in the CRUS-organized project "Developing and Testing Research Quality Criteria in the Humanities" at the Professorship for Social Psychology and Research on Higher Education at ETH Zurich, where he currently co-leads the project "Application of Bottom-Up Criteria in the Assessment of Grant Proposals of Junior Researchers in the Social Sciences and Humanities" funded by Swiss universities. He is vice-president of the EvalHum initiative, a European association for research evaluation in the social sciences and humanities.

Daniel Oross is political scientist and received his PhD in political sciences from the Corvinus University of Budapest in 2015. Since 2011, he has been a junior research fellow of the Hungarian Academy of Sciences, Centre for Social Sciences Institute for Political Sciences. In 2015, as part of the SCIEX fellowship, he spent a year at FORS Swiss Centre of Expertise in the Social Sciences in Lausanne. His research interests are political participation, youth policy and political socialization.

Aoife Prendergast is a lecturer at the Institute of Technology, Blanchardstown, Ireland. Having completed both her undergraduate (BSc, Diploma sa Gaeilge) and postgraduate studies (MA in Health Promotion) at NUI Galway, she is currently undertaking her PhD in Education, exploring practice education and supervision. Aoife has undertaken a diverse breadth of work with a variety of client groups and settings. She has substantial lecturing and training experience in both Ireland and the United Kingdom, and in a variety of roles, including National Training Projects Co-ordinator and Community Health Co-ordinator for NHS Peterborough, Cambridgeshire, the United Kingdom. She has successfully created and managed numerous innovative training and development projects in public health within diverse communities in both Ireland and the United Kingdom. In addition, Aoife was selected as the Irish representative for FESET (European Social Education Training) 2016–2018 and also as secretary for the Irish Association of Social Care Educators (IASCE) 2016–2017. She also received a Graduate Scholar for the International Aging and Society Community award in 2014 and was selected as a Community Empowerment Champion for her work in the east of England in 2010.

Caillin Reynolds is a doctoral candidate at Mary Immaculate College, University of Limerick, Ireland. His doctoral thesis concerns the changing relationship between religion and values across Europe and over time, utilising the EVS data from 1981 to 2008. His research interests include the social theory of religion and secularisation, quantifying macro-level characteristics of societies in relation to such theory and multi-level methods capable of relating these characteristics to individual level observable and latent variables. He has previously worked as fieldwork co-ordinator for the Irish section of the 2008 EVS. He holds a master's degree in Social Research Methods from the University of Limerick and a Bachelor of Arts degree (English, Sociology and Politics) from the National University of Ireland, Galway.

Andrea Szabó is a sociologist and political scientist; she received her PhD in political sciences from the Faculty of Law at Eötvös Loránd University of Sciences, Budapest, in 2009. Since 2014, she has been head of the Department for Political Behaviour at the Hungarian Academy of Sciences, Centre for Social Sciences Institute for Political Sciences. Her research interests are political protests, political sociology, voting behaviour, civil society and social integration processes.

Ivett Szalma holds a PhD in Sociology from the Corvinus University of Budapest. She currently works as a post-doctorate researcher at the Swiss Centre of Expertise in the Social Sciences (FORS). She is the Head of the Family Sociology Section of the Hungarian Sociological Association. Her research topics include childlessness, attitudes towards assisted reproduction technology, the measurement of homophobia, adoption by same-sex couples and fatherhood practices.

Judit Takács is a research chair at the Institute of Sociology, Centre for Social Sciences, Hungarian Academy of Sciences, where he is responsible for leading research teams and conducting independent research on family practices, work-life balance issues and childlessness as well as the social exclusion/inclusion of LGBTQ+ people, the social history of homosexuality and HIV/AIDS prevention. She currently works as a Seconded National Expert in Stockholm at the European Centre for Disease Prevention and Control.

Ana Villar is research fellow at the Centre for Comparative Social Surveys at City University London. She coordinates the programme of research on Mixed-Mode Methodology of the ESS and, under the Horizon 2020 SERISS project, she is leading the Cross-National Online Survey panel (the CRONOS panel). Prior to joining the ESS, she worked as a research associate at Stanford University. Ana has a doctorate in survey methodology from the University of Nebraska-Lincoln. She has published articles, chapters and conference presentations on the areas of web-survey data collection, mixed-mode data collection, cross-cultural survey research, non-response bias in telephone surveys, survey translation assessment methods, the use of interpreters in survey interviews and cross-cultural differences in response styles.

Foreword

In comparative survey research, the last 50 years can be divided in two phases: the time before the European Social Survey (ESS) came into being and the time since. The ESS was fielded for the first time in 2002, but preparations began several years earlier.

There were comparative international surveys for many decades already, and endeavours like the International Social Survey Programme, the European Values Study or the World Value Survey (to name but a few) are important and valuable data sources for the scientific analysis of social and attitudinal change. Yet, for different reasons, they lack the methodological rigour of the ESS.

The assumption that was – and still is – at the very core of the ESS is that international comparisons have to rely on strictly and in every sense comparable data with regard to question wording, translation, sampling, survey mode, data cleaning, data documentation and many other features. Additionally, there has to be context information available on every participating country in order to put results in a correct perspective. From the start, the ESS made less compromises on these issues than any other similar survey.

But there is more to the ESS: By asking each participating country to fulfil the same strict methodological standards, the ESS contributes to developing high-level scientific survey research in many European countries. And it gains much attention outside Europe as well; American and Asian scholars are among the most intensive users of ESS data.

Moreover, each round of the ESS opens up two slots for rotating questionnaire modules. These slots are allocated to scholars basing on an international open competition. In this way, research teams have the possibility of adding to the ESS standard questionnaire their preferred topics free of charge. The decision about the proposals for rotating modules is made by the Scientific Advisory Board of the ESS after a vigorous peer evaluation of all submitted proposals. The result of this procedure is a high commitment of the winning teams to work with the ESS (which supports them creating the questionnaire module) and to publish their research.

The pay-off is an impressive list of high standing scientific publications using ESS data (see europeansocialsurvey.org). Hence, it is not by mere accident that the ESS was awarded the highly esteemed European Descartes Prize for scientific research in 2005.

In sum, the ESS changed the landscape of comparative survey research remarkably. It is renowned for being scientifically demanding but at the same time highly rewarding for the research community since its data are at disposition online for all interested researchers worldwide. Thus, the ESS is a pertinent example of a research infrastructure and is therefore, rightfully, one of the few social science research infrastructures that were granted by the European Commission the status of a European Research Infrastructure Consortium (ERIC).

The ESS owes much to its founding fathers, Prof. Max Kaase and the late Sir Roger Jowell. Moreover, there are several dozens of senior scientists deeply involved with developing the ESS on the high scientific level it is known for, and there are literally hundreds of scholars forming a dedicated community doing important scholarly work with the ESS data.

This volume, edited by the current chair of the ESS, Prof. Michael J. Breen, is a landmark of such work. It unites 16 contributions by scholars from almost as many countries, including senior researchers as well as post-doctoral fellows and doctoral students. It shows the topical variety and variability of the scientific use of the ESS data in substantive and in methodological terms. Thanks to the editor and to the contributors, it is another proof of how prolific the ESS approach to comparative research is.

I am confident that the current phase in comparative survey research, and the ESS specifically, will continue to produce new insights into the dynamics of opinion and attitude formation and change. This volume contributes substantially to this scholarly debate.

Peter Farago
FORS, Switzerland

Preface

In 2010, the Irish Research Council for Humanities and the Social Sciences (now the Irish Research Council) provided funding for the fifth wave of the European Social Survey (ESS). I was appointed principal investigator for that project. The grant provided for fieldwork costs and for the necessary supports that had to be in place for such a large-scale exercise. The fieldwork was put out to a Europe-wide tender. From an initial 94 expressions of interest, the tender was eventually awarded to Amárach Research, and the data was duly collected under the very strict protocols that apply in the ESS. Then, in March 2012, the Irish dataset for ESS 5 was published along with those of 27 other European countries, and researchers across the world began using the data in their research. The data from ESS 6 and ESS 7 were published in March 2014 and May 2016 respectively. All these data are open source.

At Mary Immaculate College, we were in the fortunate position of being able to host an ESS conference in 2015, based on the first six rounds of the ESS. Researchers came from 21 countries across Europe and North America to present their work on the ESS data. This book is drawn primarily from those papers and represents a broad sample of the type of work going on across Europe today – now based on seven survey rounds – and, as we go to print, the ESS Team at Mary Immaculate College, under the leadership of Brendan O'Keeffe and Siobhán Howard, are preparing for ESS Round 8.

This book is intended for the general reader and serious scholar alike. It provides an excellent introduction to the ESS, its first chapter focusing on the nature and significance of the ESS. The remainder of the book is divided into five sections. Four of these deal with substantive themes of the ESS: religious identity, social identity, political identity and security and familial identity. The final three chapters are focused on methodology and will appeal more to those of a quantitative or statistical orientation.

The contributors to this volume have focused particularly on making their material accessible to the general reader through the use of descriptive narratives and the excellent use of graphics to help readers visualise the data under discussion. The book can, of course, be simply read cover to cover, but that is not necessary. Those unfamiliar with the ESS should start with Chapter 1. Thereafter, the book is best read in sections, which are thematically linked. Each chapter is, however, a stand-alone piece that can be read without reference to any other chapter.

For the academic community, it is hoped that this book will become a useful resource for both teaching and research. Its chapters illustrate well the kind of research that can be undertaken on ESS data, and aspiring masters or doctoral students may well find the genesis of a thesis within these pages. The chapters are also useful for researchers in providing clarity about the theory and methods used in coming to various conclusions.

Finally, I want to salute the contributors; they alone know the hours of research, analysis, writing and revision that have turned raw data into the volume you hold in your hands.

Michael J. Breen
Limerick, May 2016.

Acknowledgments

This work would not have been possible with the help of many organisations and individuals. The project was made possible in the first instance by the Irish Research Council, who have provided funding for every round of the European Social Survey (ESS) in Ireland to date. In particular, the editor acknowledges the role of Dr. Eucharia Meehan, director of the council, who has been an untiring champion of the arts, social sciences and humanities generally and of the ESS in particular.

Pivotal roles were played by the Research and Graduate School at Mary Immaculate College, who provided administrative support; Grainne O'Loughlin who organised the ESS conference; ESS post-doctoral researchers Siobhán O'Sullivan and Amy Erbe Healy; research assistants Aileen Marron and Emer Connolly; and many colleagues at Mary Immaculate College, particularly Michael Healy, Brendan O'Keeffe and Siobhán Howard.

Finally, this research is only possible because of the work of the ESS research network, its national coordinators and its various committees, and the willing respondents to the survey in every round since 2001.

1 The Significance of the European Social Survey

Michael J. Breen

Introduction

In 1988, the Standing Committee for the Social Sciences of the European Science Foundation took stock of social science datasets in Europe. They recognised that an analysis of existing datasets was required if the proposed project, Belief in Government, was to be successful, as the span was 40 years and the core questions were centred on European citizens' political orientations. It rapidly became apparent that there was no standalone dataset that provided the basis for cross-national comparisons on a time-series basis. The Eurobarometer, which started in 1973, had a very distinct orientation toward service of the European Union (EU) constituent elements and the needs of various EU bodies. The International Social Survey Program has run annually since 1984, involving, at one stage or another, some 53 nations across the globe. But neither the Eurobarometer nor the International Social Survey Program, valuable as they are, could meet the requirements envisaged by the Standing Committee for the Social Sciences in terms of a pan-European, ongoing, stable time-series survey infrastructure. In time-honoured European tradition, a committee was formed. But this was no talking shop.

History of the European Social Survey

Social scientists in Europe were swift to grasp the possibility being explored. The small committee, chaired by Max Kaase, recommended that the European Social Survey project be pursued. To this end, two further committees with distinct objective were formed: a Steering Committee to be chaired by Max Kaase, and a Methodology Committee to be chaired by Roger Jowell, with a simple objective: to establish the European Social Survey as a pan-European project, which would be rigorous, replicable, and reputable as a framework within which the attitudes, behaviours, opinions, values, and beliefs of Europe's citizens would be analysed and better understood. Both committee membership lists read like a roll of honour for European social scientists. This was serious work, undertaken by luminaries in the field. Full membership lists are given in the endnotes in this chapter.[1, 2] Ultimately, the fruit of the committees' work was the presentation of a joint proposal entitled "The European Social Survey (ESS) – a research instrument for the social sciences in Europe."

This blueprint document set out the guiding principles for the ESS: non-duplication, longitudinality, cross-national equivalence, potential for multi-level analysis, ongoing refinement of methodology, simultaneous flexibility and stability, easy and inexpensive data access and clear definitions of both population and sampling. These have been the guiding hallmarks of the ESS since its inception.

Descartes, the European Research Infrastructures Consortium and the European Strategy Forum on Research Infrastructures

The Descartes Prize for excellence in scientific collaborative research is awarded annually for outstanding scientific or technological results from European collaborative research. Its purpose is to acknowledge and showcase the finest science and scientists in Europe while demonstrating the advances that can be made through European collaboration and co-operation. The prize is open to all the sciences, including the social and economic sciences. In 2006, the European Social Survey won the Descartes Prize, the first social science project ever to do so. Speaking at the award ceremony, the late Sir Roger Jowell said

> The intention is not just to provide a snapshot, but, as survey builds upon survey, to develop a unique long-term account of change and development in the social fabric of modern Europe.... The impact of ESS on European governance could be profound. While other statistical agencies, such as Eurostat, collect rigorous data about the social and economic circumstances of EU Member States, they tend to avoid comparable statistics about cultural and political attitudes – how people think and feel about themselves and their world. The role of the ESS is to fill that gap.

Since its inception, the ESS has been filling that gap, helping Europe to better understand itself through understanding the manifold attitudes, beliefs, behaviours and values of its citizens.

Funding was always going to be an issue for such an ambitious project, given in particular the high standards demanded by the ESS and the face-to-face nature of the survey. In 2009, the Council of Europe proposed a regulation for a community legal framework for the European Research Infrastructures Consortium (ERIC). Member states wishing to establish research infrastructures with the status of ERIC would be required to apply to the commission and include a declaration from the host country that it recognized ERIC as an international organization. In 2013, after years of preparation, the ESS was awarded ERIC status in 2013, with the United Kingdom as the host country; Austria, Belgium, the Czech Republic, Estonia, Germany, Ireland, Lithuania, Netherlands, Poland, Portugal, Slovenia, Sweden and the United Kingdom as members; and Norway and Switzerland as observers. Sadly, Sir Roger Jowell had passed away suddenly at the age of 69 in 2011. He had been one of the driving forces behind the ESS and his death was an enormous loss to the initiative.

More than a decade earlier, the European Strategy Forum on Research Infrastructures (ESFRI) had been established to promote and develop large-scale research infrastructures in Europe. It published the first ESFRI "roadmap" in 2006. The ESS was listed on the first roadmap and has been included on every update since as it has gone from strength to strength. In 2016, The ESS was recognised as an ESFRI landmark . Dr. Rory Fitzgerald, Roger Jowell's successor as director of the ESS, said on that occasion

> Becoming an ESFRI Landmark is a major achievement for the European Social Survey.... It is recognition that charting stability and change in the social structure, conditions and attitudes in Europe and interpreting how the social, political and moral fabric is changing is critical for academics, civil society, policy makers and the public alike. The ESS illuminates social attitudes and behaviour on many of the key challenges facing European societies – such as immigration, climate change and energy security, democracy and health inequalities. The next steps for the ESS are to work towards full pan-European membership of the ERIC and I urge those countries outside the infrastructure to ensure that their citizens are heard on these key challenges through participation in ESS ERIC.

That goal of pan-European membership remains the aim of the ESS but will require greater investment across Europe in such key research infrastructures. The data in Table 1.1 shows precisely how difficult it is proving in practice to reach that goal. Only 15 countries have been able to field all seven rounds of the survey to date: Belgium, Denmark, Finland, France, Germany, Hungary, Ireland, Netherlands, Norway, Poland, Portugal, Slovenia, Spain, Switzerland, and the United Kingdom.

The primary, if not sole, reason for incomplete engagement with the ESS is cost. Survey fieldwork is not cheap, particularly when done according to the extremely exacting rubrics of the ESS. The additional costs of the Core Scientific Team, responsible *inter alia* for data processing, archiving, management and oversight of the ESS project, are an additional element borne by members and observers. It is regrettable that the arts, humanities and social sciences do not garner the same level of financial support from either public or private resources as do the hard sciences. That is an imbalance that must be redressed. In the interim, the ESS ERIC is profoundly grateful to the member and observer governments and research agencies whose ongoing commitment and unwavering support are the *sine qua non* of these valuable data.

The themes of the survey

While it was impossible to detail the survey themes in the early planning days of the ESS, they became clarified once the first wave questionnaire was designed. These themes have remained since the inception of the survey, while some of the individual question items may have changed in a small number of cases. Those

Table 1.1 ESS respondents, count, by country by round

	R1	R2	R3	R4	R5	R6	R7	Total
Austria	2,257	2,256	2,405				1,795	8,713
Belgium	1,897	1,778	1,798	1,760	1,704	1,869	1,769	12,575
Bulgaria			1,400	2,230	2,434	2,260		8,324
Croatia				1,484	1,649			3,133
Cyprus			995	1,215	1,083	1,116		5,941
Czech Rep.	1,360	3,026		2,018	2,386	2,009	2,148	12,947
Denmark	1,506	1,487	1,505	1,610	1,576	1,650	1,502	10,836
Estonia		1,989	1,517	1,661	1,793	2,380	2,051	11,391
Finland	2,000	2,022	1,896	2,195	1,878	2,197	2,087	14,275
France	1,514	1,818	1,986	2,073	1,728	1,968	1,917	13,004
Germany	2,997	2,870	2,916	2,751	3,031	2,958	3,045	20,568
Greece	2,566	2,406		2,072	2,715			9,759
Hungary	1,779	1,498	1,603	1,544	1,561	2,014	1,698	11,697
Iceland		579				752		1,331
Ireland	2,046	2,286	1,811	1,764	2,576	2,628	2,390	15,501
Israel	2,499			2,490	2,294	2,508	2,562	12,353
Italy	1,207	1,529				960		3,696
Lithuania					1,996	2,109	2,250	6,355
Luxembourg	1,552	1,635						3,187
Netherlands	2,364	1,881	1,889	1,778	1,829	1,845	1,919	13,505
Norway	2,036	1,760	1,749	1,549	1,548	1,624	1,436	11,702
Poland	2,110	1,716	1,721	1,619	1,751	1,898	1,615	12,430
Portugal	1,511	2,052	2,222	2,367	2,150	2,151	1,265	13,718
Russia			2,426	2,512	2,595	2,484		10,017
Slovakia		1,512	1,766	1,810	1,996	1,847	1,224	10,155
Slovenia	1,521	1,442	1,476	1,286	1,403	1,257	1,791	10,176
Spain	1,729	1,663	1,877	2,576	1,885	1,889	1,925	13,544
Sweden	2,093	1,948	2,155	1,830	1,497	1,847		11,370
Switzerland	2,038	2,141	1,804	1,819	1,506	1,493	1,532	10,801
Turkey		1,856		2,416				4,272
Ukraine		2,031	2,002	1,845	1,931	2,178		9,987
UK	2,579	1,897	2,978	2,352	2,422	2,286	2,264	16,778
Total	43,161	49,078	43,897	52,626	52,917	52,177	40,185	334,041

themes are media and social trust; politics; subjective well-being; social capital and social exclusion; religious, national and ethnic identity; immigration; health and inequality; and human values.

Research output and impact

The data of the ESS are open access and available to all via the ESS website. No national team or individual researcher has privileged access to their own dataset, and all ESS data are published *en bloc* – it is only when datasets are released in this way that they can be used for research and publication. Since its inception, some 7,115 ESS data users indicated usage as part of their ongoing doctoral dissertations. As of May 2016, there were some 93,896 registered users of the ESS data, as indicated

Table 1.2 ESS data users, by count, type and percentage

User type	Count	% of total
Student	59,898	63.8
Faculty and research	18,044	19.2
PhD thesis	7,115	7.6
Private individual	2,557	2.7
Other	1,733	1.8
Organisation (NGO)	1,666	1.8
Government	1,584	1.7
Private enterprise	1,299	1.4
	93,896	**100**

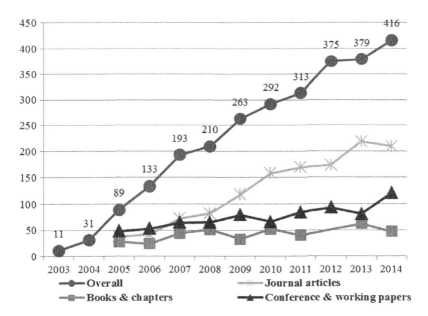

Figure 1.1 Trends in ESS academic publishing.
Source: Brina Malnar, ESS CST, University of Ljubljana.

in Table 1.2. These users have produced a substantial research output. Table 1.2 shows the outputs by type and count from 2003 to 2014 and they are represented on an annualised basis in graphic form in Figure 1.1. Figures 1.2–1.5 provide other information on ESS-based output, research themes and individual item usage.

ESS scholarship in this volume

As outlined earlier, this volume is divided into five sections, four of which are substantive and the other methodological. Each adds to the scholarship emanating from the ESS while also continuing to broaden and deepen the research derived by the ESS.

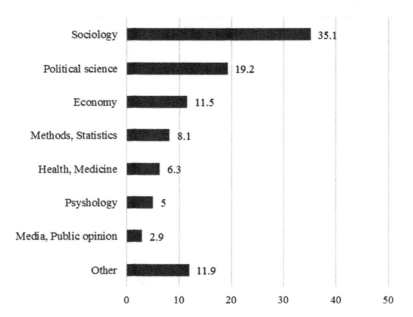

Figure 1.2 Journals with most ESS publications.
Source: Brina Malnar, ESS CST, University of Ljubljana.

Cragun looks at the related concepts of religious practice and secularization. In a European context, Ireland, Malta and Poland are recognised as the countries that exhibit the highest levels of religiosity as measured by church affiliation and levels of religious practice. The United States has been seen by some as a counter argument for secularization theory insofar as it is simultaneously exhibits high levels of development and religious affiliation. Drawing on the idea that the true beginning of secularization is seen when there is no requirement that religion be central to national or ethnic identity, Cragun postulates that the end of the Cold War in the United States and the signing of the Good Friday agreement in Ireland are such key moments. He draws on the ESS data to show how Ireland's current engagement with secularization is continuous, with the implication that so too is the decline of religiosity.

Kulkova examines the relationship between religious belonging and political participation, suggesting that religion does have an effect on the political participation of citizens insofar as members of religious communities with strong discipline are more politically active than those from communities with weaker ties. The implication is that the religious behaviour meets certain individual or group needs to varying degrees, and the stronger the religious tie, the weaker the levels of political involvement. As secularization increases across Europe, the question arises as to whether political participation will increase to meet some of the needs formerly met by religious participation and, more importantly, what

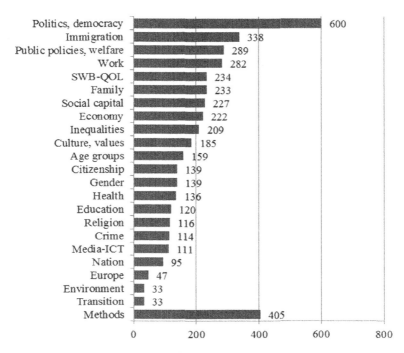

Figure 1.3 Most common research themes.
Source: Brina Malnar, ESS CST, University of Ljubljana.

political ideologies might strengthen with such increased political participation derived from previous religious adherence. This is not a trivial issue, and significant research needs to be undertaken to look at the parallels between religious and political participation.

Lastly, in this first section, Reynolds enlarges on the role of religion in Europe, focusing on the values of individuals and societies. He shows that active integration in a religious group has a significant effect on one's values, irrespective of socio-demographic variables, and that such an effect remains even allowing for age. But he also shows that the society to which an individual belongs has a significant effect on one's values. Thus, as the overall makeup of a society changes, especially in the context of ongoing secularization, the collective values held by a society are also liable to change.

One such shift in collective values is seen in research done by Ochsner and Szalma. A more modern riff on the change in family values, arising from the decline of the roles of male breadwinner and stay-at-home mother, is the rise of work–life conflict, in which couples strive for, and sometimes fail to achieve, work–life balance. The difficulties imposed by work–life conflict generated though unsocial work hours or heavy workloads were exacerbated by Europe's

8 *Michael J. Breen*

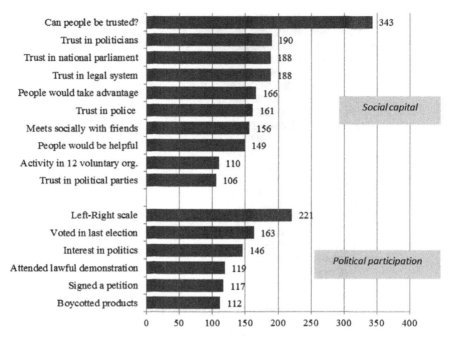

Figure 1.4 Most used substantive items, social capital and political participation.
Source: Brina Malnar, ESS CST, University of Ljubljana.

recent economic crisis, a pattern found across European countries. Having children of pre-school age and inadequate income levels are indicators of higher levels of work–life conflict, as are high levels of education and jobs that require higher level qualifications. Across Europe, the needs of the economy (as measured in terms of work) and the needs of society (as measured in terms of individual, familial and social well-being) can often be in opposition to one another. The data here provide strong markers for European policy makers in the task of maximising the outcomes for both the European economy and European society through striving to minimize the factors that lead to work–life conflict.

Healy and Ó Riain utilise the European Working Conditions Survey in tandem with the ESS to consider welfare attitudes and work regimes. In their chapter, they define typologies of work regimes in terms of work organisation, employment relationship and work schedule and analyse the relationship between work regime and welfare attitudes. In their complex analysis, they not only note the continuing importance of a class politics of income redistribution but also acknowledge the political realities in the prevention of poverty. As they put it, "the class politics of income may operate in ways that are different, overlapping, but also potentially in tension with the politics of risk in the labour market." Welfare is clearly much more important to those who are most likely to need it. As with Ochsner and

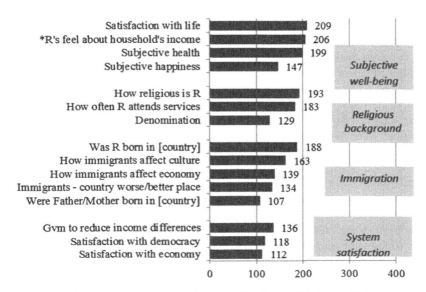

Figure 1.5 Most used substantive items, subjective well-being, religious background, immigration and system satisfaction.

Source: Brina Malnar, ESS CST, University of Ljubljana.

Szalma's work, and indeed many of the substantive papers emanating from the analysis of ESS data, there are critical indicators here for legislators and policy makers across Europe.

Beattie looks at a different measure of social well-being by demonstrating the relationship between happiness, life satisfaction and take-home income in the context of overall national wealth. She finds that happiness and life satisfaction are indeed strongly related to take-home income, irrespective of national wealth, concluding that living in a rich country may be more important, in terms of happiness and life satisfaction, than being personally wealthy because of the level of public goods and social supports. She also raises the question of how European or national social and economic policies might change if happiness were a goal with primacy over gross domestic product (GDP).

Turning to the political arena, Chabova looks at corruption across Europe. Acknowledging the low level of corruption in Europe compared to most of the world, she also states the reality of corruption within Europe, particularly in countries with a communist history, identifying such corruption as the greatest obstacle to progress and to democratization in post-communist societies. Using Protestantism as a proxy for individualism, she found that this, along with GDP and generalized trust, are associated with greater control of corruption, but that income inequality was not a factor. The political past, in particular a communist past, is a significant factor. Given that much of Europe's expansion includes many countries with former communist regimes, this is worthy of note.

Oross and Szabó turned their attention to youth participation in political life. The topic is both timely and relevant in the context of the decrease in traditional forms in political participation, including voting itself, given that the European project is driven by the concept of a participatory system in which the individual citizens directly elect both their own sovereign parliaments and the European parliament. Potentially controversially, they suggest that "compulsory voting is the most effective (intervention) in reducing the gap between adults' and young people's participation the most, both for non-electoral participation and for electoral participation." They also note that it is systemic issues rather than individual ones that most influence participation. If democracy is to flourish in Europe, such systemic issues need to be addressed across Europe.

Prendergast takes a decidedly different approach to other researchers in this volume. Using the ESS as her starting point for setting an Irish context in respect of the relationship between democracy and higher education, she sets out to look at the core issues that contextualise the data on citizens' attitudes towards democracy and citizen involvement in Ireland. Arguing that "one of the most widely accepted goals of social studies education is to produce knowledgeable and caring citizens," she argues for a change of approach in the Irish higher education system. Her final comment, that "democracy is important, it should be studied, and, for it to be meaningful and tangible, it must be fully cultivated throughout the educational experience" is beyond question. While she has set the stage for such a process in an Irish context, this chapter provides much to think about for those who wish to apply this principle in other European national contexts.

Much is made in political and social commentary of the definition of family, and there is an ongoing debate in the world of politics about "traditional family values," a debate that often presumes a particular and nostalgic vision of family. The next three papers in this volume look at aspects of family. Lipasova considers fatherhood in Russia where, as elsewhere in much of Europe, the birth rate is falling. While birth-rate studies have commonly looked primarily at female fertility, Lipasova examines the data on the lowering of male fertility rates arising from postponing fatherhood and associates this with three distinct crises: of family, of masculinity and of power. Given the cultural significance of fatherhood in Russia, this analysis raises important questions about identity, masculinity and tradition.

Ainsaar continues the family focus in her examination of the influence of children on life satisfaction, but with the additional consideration of family type. Her research leads her to conclude that partnered couples with children have several life satisfaction advantages but that these are dependent on country-level differences in terms of economic and social support. It is important to emphasise her finding that "no difference in life satisfaction of married and cohabiting people in the majority of countries was found" while also acknowledging that "official marriage seems to be the source of greater life satisfaction than cohabitation in Europe." What is unclear here is the differentiation between cause and effect, because that lies outside the realm of this particular analysis. Those who might seize on the latter quotation may well be dismayed by Ainsaar's finding that "that children in the household always contribute to the increase in life satisfaction."

This research indicates strongly the complex nature of familial structure and the inability of researchers to reduce it to absolute statements.

This section is rounded out by Szalma and Takács's research on fathering in 28 European countries, utilizing both the European Values Study (EVS) and the ESS. While these surveys are not harmonized, they allow for useful comparisons. Their focus was on traditional gender roles, and for their comparative analysis they used a statement on traditional roles as their focus: "When jobs are scarce, men have more right to a job than women." The results are intriguing. In 1990, a majority in Lithuania, Austria, Poland, Malta and Slovakia agreed with the statement, but by 2008 no country had a majority in agreement. In something of an understatement, Szalma and Takács write that "regarding traditional gender role attitudes, a significant change happened in Europe." The level of change is quite profound, and although the rate of change is differentiated across Europe, the reality of change is ubiquitous.

The final section of this volume deals with methodological issues in a trio of chapters that deal with somewhat complex issues. Baumann turns his attention to non-respondents in surveys, those individuals who refuse to respond to the survey as a whole or to an individual question. This issue often preoccupies users of survey data, who wonder what the respondent would have answered or in what way those who did not answer are different from those who did. Baumann limits his analysis to Germany and Ireland and to only one variable. It is painstaking and exacting work, and extending the analysis to multiple variables and all countries would require significant time and resources. It remains, nonetheless, critical that such work is done, given the ongoing issue of non-response in surveys generally.

Halpin and Breen also consider the issue, as did Baumann, of using the imputation of missing data but for a somewhat different purpose. Rather than focusing on the issue of non-response, they were primarily interested using common identifiers – those variables that one or more surveys have in common – to allow for the simultaneous analysis of multiple surveys on variables that might exist in one survey but not another. In this case, they used two datasets that had common identifiers but also identical variables – the ESS and the EVS – to test different models of imputing missing data. They demonstrate one potential route that provides promise for future development but requires the integration of shared variable to the greatest degree possible.

Villar and Fitzgerald report on six studies that are of immense importance to those interested in quality survey research, as the focus of the studies is the mode of data collection. The ubiquity of the internet, the change from landlines to smart mobiles, and the costs of traditional face-to-face interviewing have all contributed to a pressure to move towards mixed modes of data collection. Villar and Fitzgerald's analysis reaches an unequivocal conclusion: face-to-face interviewing remains the gold standard and, despite the expense, delivers the highest quality data.

These 16 chapters provide a series of insights into the ESS, its themes and its rigorous methodology. Taken as a whole, they are representative of the type of research that is currently being undertaken across Europe and North America by scholars from many different disciplines. As well as providing detailed insight into individual, countries and regions of Europe, they also present empirical contexts that are critical for legislators and policy makers who need to understand the complexity of Europe as well as beliefs, attitudes, opinions and behaviours as documented at the level of the individual citizen.

Challenge for the future

At the beginning of this chapter, the origins and history of the ESS were sketched out, culminating in the establishment of the ESS ERIC. The middle section showed the level of output and potential impact that has followed from the provision of ESS data as open-source material for research. Finally, the latter section showed how the chapters of this volume are indicative of the breadth and depth of ESS-based research in both substantive and methodological domains.

There is little doubt that the ESS will continue to provide both high-quality data and research output for many years to come. In that sense, the dream of the pioneers responsible for the ESS blueprint has been realised, at least partially: partially rather than fully because the ESS, unfortunately, is not run in every country in Europe – at least not yet. That dream remains, and the ESS ERIC is actively working towards its fulfilment. There are still major challenges along the way, perhaps best expressed by Max Kaase. His practical challenge, related to the mode of data collection, is resolved for now as seen in the chapter by Villar and Fitzgerald. His theoretical challenge remains. In 2008, Kaase wrote

> In the future, apart from the problem of funding already discussed, two major challenges lie ahead. The first is a challenge for researchers. With a survey covering more than twenty countries, each researcher will have to design his or her special way, embedded in good theory, of how to deal with such a large number of countries. Certainly... the proper names of countries have to be replaced in data analysis by theoretically meaningful concepts; just to compare country marginals and describe the differences and the sameness between countries will not suffice. However, the situation will become vastly more complicated and challenging as more and more rounds of the ESS will become available, permitting not only structural, but also dynamic analyses.

Kaase is, as usual, absolutely correct. He was prescient in recognising the increasing complexity and challenge as more and more survey rounds were completed and more and more countries take part. Unlike the US General Social Survey, which has been running since 1972 and is limited to a single national sample, the ESS is still very much in its infancy and draws its samples from a multitude of nations, each of which requires its own particular sampling strategy. But that was recognised by the founders *ab initio*. The ESS today is an enormous tribute to the endeavours of Roger Jowell, Max Kaase and the other perspicacious academics who brought this noble idea to fruition. Their monumental legacy is in good hands, as a new generation of both established and up-and-coming scholars engage with the ESS. This survey has already made a great contribution to Europe and will do so even more in the future. This volume provides a taste of that and an insight into some of the further contributions to be made in the decades ahead.

Notes

1 Steering Committee: Max Kaase (Chairman), Jacques Billiet, Bruno Cautrès, Henryk Domanski, Antonio Brandao Moniz, Nikiforos Diamandouros, Rune Åberg, Yilmaz Esmer, Peter Farago, Roger Jowell, Stein Kuhnle, Michael Laver, Guido Martinotti, José Ramón Montero, Karl H. Müller, Leif Nordberg, Niels Ploug, Torben Fridberg, Shalom Schwartz, Ineke Stoop, Françoise Thys-Clément, Pierre Desmarez, Niko Tos, Michael Warren, John H. Smith.
2 Methodology Committee: Roger Jowell (Chairman), Jacques Billiet, Peter Lynn, Nonna Mayer, Ekkehard Mochmann, José Ramón Montero, Willem Saris, Antonio Schizzeroto, Jan van Deth, Joachim Vogel, Max Kaase, John H. Smith.

Reference

Kaase, M. (2008). The European Social Survey – Retrospect and Prospect. In Meulemann, H. *Social Capital in Europe: Similarity of Countries and Diversity of People? Multi-level analyses of the European Social Survey 2002*. Brill: Leiden, 313–320.

Section I
Religious Identity

2 The Declining Significance of Religion
Secularization in Ireland

Ryan T. Cragun

Introduction

While relatively small in both geography and population, Ireland has played an important role in the most prominent sociological theory of religion: secularization. The basic premise of secularization theory is that modernization will reduce religiosity as people, organizations and cultures will rely less and less on religion to provide explanations for natural phenomena and succour in times of need (Cragun and Lawson 2010; Dobbelaere 2002; Gorski 2000; Wilson 2000). While the basic idea of secularization is quite broad, secularization is now a very nuanced theory (Bruce 2013). One of those nuances is that religiosity may not decline as a country or culture modernizes if religion is or suddenly becomes an instrumental or important part of identity in that culture. For example, when the importance of religion is heightened because of a conflict that involves religion, secularization may be delayed in that culture until the prominence of the conflict has waned and the salience of religion as part of one's identity declines.

It is in this context that one of the most well-known secularization theorists, Steve Bruce, has referenced Ireland (Bruce 2002). While much of the rest of western Europe has gradually secularized over the last century or so, Ireland has remained quite religious (Breen and Erbe Healy 2014; Healy and Breen 2014; Hirschle 2010; Hornsby-Smith and Whelan 1994). Bruce argued that the reason for Ireland's higher levels of religiosity compared to most of western Europe – the other prominent exception being Poland for similar, instrumental reasons – was because religion played a prominent role in the Troubles, involving the sovereignty of Ireland and the resulting conflict over Northern Ireland. While the conflict involving Northern Ireland, England and the Republic of Ireland was, at its root, political (Mitchell 2006), divisions among the parties involved were also ethnic and religious. The emphasis on religion in the conflict resulted in a heightened salience of religion as part of individuals' identities in Ireland. As Bruce (2002) argues, when and where religion has an instrumental role to play in individuals' lives, for whatever reason, secularization is unlikely to occur.

However, the level of conflict and tension in Northern Ireland has declined dramatically. While there was no definitive end date to the Troubles, many scholars have argued that the Good Friday agreement in 1998 largely brought the conflict to an end (Holland 1999). The assumption that the conflict over Northern Ireland had waned by that point could have important ramifications for secularization in Ireland. Specifically, the end of the conflict could have reduced the salience of religion in Irish identity, allowing for modernity to accelerate secularization in Ireland.

In this chapter, by examining data from several sources, I will explore the idea that Ireland has entered a phase of rapid secularization. I will begin by noting that a similar decline of religious salience in the United States of America is likely what led to the sudden increase in people no longer identifying with religion in the early 1990s. I will then look at data on religiosity in Ireland going back to the 1980s to illustrate that secularization has become more rapid since the end of the Troubles in the late 1990s. Finally, utilizing European Social Survey (ESS) data, I will illustrate that the process of secularization in Ireland is similar to the process of secularization in most other countries that are experiencing modernization, as the variables that predict declining religiosity are identical to those in other countries.

The United States and the Cold War

The idea that the salience of religion in a given culture can influence or delay the process of secularization helps to explain a number of "exceptions" to secularization around the world. As Bruce (2002, 2013) has noted, most highly developed countries have experienced a "secular transition" (Cragun and Lawson 2010; Voas 2007), resulting in low levels of religious activity, even if many people still identify with state religions in those countries (Day 2013; De Graaf and Grotenhuis 2008; Halman and Draulans 2006). But in some highly developed countries, like the United States, religiosity has not declined as rapidly as it has in other countries (e.g. France, Sweden, etc.). The two most common "exceptions" to secularization in Europe that were widely referenced during the 1990s and early 2000s were Ireland and Poland. In both countries, religious identity was intimately connected with national identity, and religion was influential in political and ethnic conflicts in those countries (Herbert and Fras 2009; Kutyło 2013). Recent research has shown that religiosity has declined in Poland following the democratic transition (Requena and Stanek 2013), which fits neatly with Bruce's nuanced version of secularization theory: the salience of religion to Polish identity has declined, allowing for people to slough off religious identities that no longer fit with their modern world views.

Another prominent "exception" to secularization that is often noted by critics of secularization theory is the United States, which, at least through the 1980s, remained somewhat more religious than many other developed countries (Norris and Inglehart 2004; Stark 1999; Stark and Finke 2000). But religion is on the decline in the United States as well (Kosmin et al. 2009; Pew Forum on Religion 2012; Sherkat 2014), and likely for the same reason that it declined in Poland – religion is no longer a salient part of national identity because an important conflict came to an end: the Cold War. In this section, I will examine how the end of the Cold War may have been necessary to allow for the rapid secularization that began in the United States in 1990.

While some prior research has noted the importance of religion in the United States as part of national identity during the Cold War (Gunn 2009; Kirby 2002; Lahr 2007), to date, very little social scientific research has examined how the end of the Cold War with the Soviet Union might have changed the salience of religion for Americans' sense of nationalism (though see Bullivant 2010 for a brief discussion of the relationship between the end of the Cold War and the rise of non-religion in the United States). While several theories have been suggested for the sudden increase in non-religion and irreligion in the 1990s (Hout and Fischer 2002; Zuckerman 2011), none, to my knowledge, have suggested that the end of the Cold War is what freed Americans to begin to secularize. I believe there was a pent-up desire among many Americans (as witnessed by the fact that roughly 60 per cent of Americans indicated that they attended religious services *less* than once a week in surveys since the 1950s; see Hadaway, Marler and Chaves 1993) to minimize the importance of religion to their identity. But the Cold War made that difficult.

Evidence for the importance of religion during the Cold War between the United States and the Soviet Union can be seen in General Social Survey (GSS) data from the United States. From 1972 to 1990, there was a strong correlation between attitudes towards atheists and attitudes towards communists among Americans ($r = .775, p < .001$), with sizable percentages of Americans not wanting representatives of either category to be allowed to speak in public (see Figure 2.1). However, after 1990, the correlation in attitudes towards these two groups diminished substantially, ($r = .085, p = .781$). As Figure 2.1 illustrates, there is a divergence in the two trend lines in the early 1990s, and while the number of those who wanted atheists to be disallowed to speak in public slowly decreased through 2006, whose who thought that communists should be disallowed to speak did not

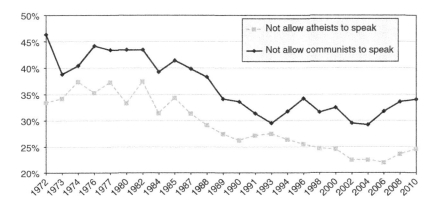

Figure 2.1 Percentage of Americans who would not allow atheists or communists to speak in public.

Source: GSS, 1972–2010.

decrease substantially during that time. This suggests a divergence of attitudes towards these two groups post 1990.

Why might attitudes towards atheists and communists have diverged post 1990? During the Cold War in the United States, communism and atheism were linked, as in the phrase "godless communists" (Gunn 2009; Lahr 2007). To be a communist also meant to be an atheist and vice versa – in the minds of Americans. The pervasiveness of the linkage between "godless" and "communist" is apparent in Figure 2.2, which presents results from Google's Ngram Viewer. Google's Ngram Viewer searches the text of books the company has scanned and plots word frequencies over time based on the year the book was published. The phrase "godless communists" doesn't occur prior to 1927, and its occurrence is not all that frequent during the 1930s, but it picks up dramatically in the United States just after the end of World War II (WWII), with the beginning of the Cold War. As the Cold War reached its final years in the 1980s, the phrase occurred very frequently; it reached a peak just as the Soviet Union collapsed and then saw another rise in the early 2000s.[1]

Even though the phrase "godless communists" has continued to be used since the end of the Cold War, Figure 2.1 illustrates that attitudes towards communists and atheists diverged somewhat around 1990 in the United States; acceptance of atheism has increased while acceptance of communism has not. While atheism and communism are not completely divorced from each other in US political ideology, it does appear as though many Americans no longer immediately associate one with the other.

Because communism was linked with atheism during the Cold War, the antipathy towards communists led to a similar antipathy towards atheists. This linkage was so significant that admitting to being an atheist during the McCarthy period in the 1950s was sufficient cause to open an investigation into an individual's political loyalties (Gunn 2009; Jacoby 2005, 2009). Of course, linking

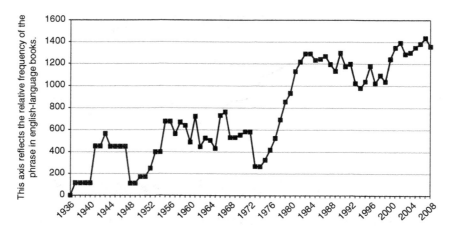

Figure 2.2 Google Ngram data on occurrences of "godless communist" phrase in English literature, 1936–2008.

the two – atheism and communism – is not required. There are and have been millions of communists who believe in God (Yang 2004, 2005). And there are millions of atheists who strongly oppose communism (Baker and Smith 2009; Pasquale 2010).

So, why were communism and atheism linked in the minds of so many Americans? The simple answer is for propaganda purposes: to create a US national identity. The Cold War was largely a war of propaganda. Both the United States and the Union of Soviet Socialist Republics (USSR) employed propaganda, spending billions of dollars to influence the opinions of their own citizens and the citizens of other countries (Hixson 1998; Staar 1991). The United States has utilized a variety of agencies for these purposes. The Advertising ("Ad") Council is an American non-profit that promotes and distributes public service announcements. The Ad Council was originally the War Advertising Council and was used specifically to mobilize Americans for the war effort. At the conclusion of WWII, the council changed its name but did not completely change its aims. The aims of the Advertising Council were and are the aims of the US government, which meant it helped with anti-communist propaganda throughout the Cold War (Hixson 1998).

The United States Information Agency, which was moved to the US Department of State's Under Secretary for Public Affairs and Public Diplomacy in 1999, was formed in 1953, after the end of WWII but at the beginning of the Cold War. When it was established, its mission was to inform and influence the public – domestically and internationally – about the interests of the United States. In short, it was designed to influence international opinion about both the United States and its enemies, chiefly the USSR. This organization was largely a pro-capitalism, anti-communism propaganda machine for the US government (Hixson 1998).

Where does religion enter into this equation? There were specific pro-capitalism propaganda campaigns by other organizations that engage in psychological warfare, like the Central Intelligence Agency's Special Activities Division (specifically the Political Action Group) and the Psych Ops divisions of the Army and Navy. But the most explicitly pro-religious campaign was the Militant Liberty campaign that was adopted by the US Department of Defense as a means of indoctrinating US soldiers as to why they should defend the US and capitalism. The campaign was the idea of John C. Broger, the founder and president of the Far East Broadcasting Company, a Christian international radio network, and it included elements of evangelical beliefs in the campaign (Sharlet 2008). While the campaign was never formally adopted, it was used throughout the military for a period in the 1950s and 1960s. It included videos that recruits were required to watch as well as wallet-sized cards that military personnel were to carry with them at all times.

And, of course, there is the clear linking of belief in God with the US government that is apparent in two notable actions that took place just after the end of WWII – the addition of the phrase "under God" to the pledge of allegiance in 1954 and the adoption of "In God We Trust" as the official motto of the United States in 1956 (replacing *E pluribus unum*, i.e. "out of many, one").

22 Ryan T. Cragun

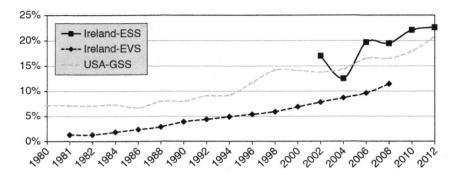

Figure 2.3 Percentage of Americans and Irish with no religious affiliation over time (GSS, EVS and ESS).

Religion and belief in God (or theism) were explicitly adopted during the Cold War as emblems of American patriotism (Gunn 2009). These emblems were aimed to counter the state-imposed atheism of communist countries. The end result was the inter-linking of atheism and communism in the minds of Americans, which only ended when the Cold War ended, in the late 1980s and early 1990s. As Figure 2.3 illustrates, the dramatic rise of the non-religious began during the 1990s, just after the end of the Cold War. The reduced salience of religiosity for American national identity allowed those who were no longer interested in religion to now openly declare their disinterest. In short, secularization was no longer hindered by religious instrumentalism.

The beginning of secularization in Ireland

Similar to the United States, religiosity in Ireland was high and religion was a prominent part of national identity when there was significant ethno-political conflict in the country. As noted above, the Troubles were not exclusively about religion, but the political tensions that divided people in Ireland often traced a Protestant-versus-Catholic religious divide (Holland 1999). As a result of this religio-ethnic division, religion was a salient component of Irish identity.

The heightened salience of religion as part of Irish identity was observable in high rates of religiosity in Ireland throughout the 1980s (Hornsby-Smith and Whelan 1994), but by the 1990s, as the conflict over Northern Ireland began to wane, and particularly by the early 2000s, when the conflict was largely resolved, the linkage between religiosity and national identity also faltered, and non-religion and irreligion began to rise (Breen and Erbe Healy 2014; Hirschle 2010).

Figure 2.4 illustrates that religion has declined in importance among the Irish since the 1980s. Data from the European Values Survey (EVS) shows that almost 50 per cent of Irish people reported that religion was "very important" to them in 1990. By 2010, that had declined to just over 30 per cent, while those

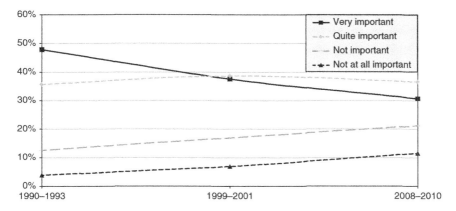

Figure 2.4 Change in importance of religion in lives of Irish, 1990–2010 (EVS).

indicating that religion was "not at all important" had increased from 4 per cent to 12 per cent, and those indicating that religion was "not important" increased from 13 per cent to 21 per cent of the population. Religion became much less salient as part of Irish identity during the 20-year period surrounding the end of the Northern Ireland conflict, and that timing results in a fairly clear picture of the rise of secularization in the Republic of Ireland.

Evidence for the timing of the onset of secularization is shown in Figure 2.3, which presents data from the EVS and ESS on the percentage of Irish people who indicated they had no religious affiliation. According to the EVS, in 1981, just 1.3 per cent of the Irish people reported no religious affiliation (see also Brown 2012). This increased slightly during the 1980s, reaching around 4 per cent of the population by 1990. Likewise, there was a slight increase during the 1990s, reaching just under 7 per cent by 2000. The ESS and EVS differ somewhat in their estimates of the percentage of people with no religious affiliation in the 2000s. According to the ESS, 17 per cent of the Irish people had no religious affiliation in 2002; this increased to 19.4 per cent by 2008. The EVS, however, puts the percentage at 11.4. Even so, ESS data suggests the exodus from religion has continued through 2012, with more than one in five Irish people now no longer reporting a religious affiliation.

A similar but clearer pattern can be observed in Figure 2.5, which shows the percentage of Irish people who never attend religious services, attend only on special occasions or attend less than once a year. Throughout the 1980s, over 90 per cent of Irish people attended religious services at least once a year, and not just for special occasions, with most of them attending once a week. But that had changed by the late 1990s, around the time the Good Friday agreement was signed. And since that point, religious attendance in Ireland has plummeted. According to the ESS, close to half of Irish people in 2012 never or only very rarely attended religious services. That is a huge difference in just a decade or so and is strongly

24 *Ryan T. Cragun*

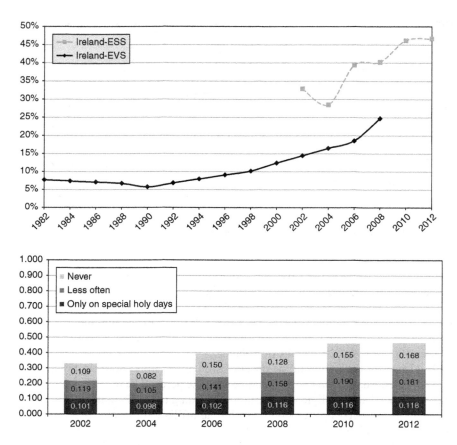

Figure 2.5 Percentage of Irish who rarely or never attend religious service (EVS and ESS).

suggestive of the onset of secularization and the declining significance of religion for Irish national identity.

While Figures 2.3, 2.4 and 2.5 provide an indication of when religion's importance for Irish national identity waned, which is, of course, a gradual process, the diminution of religiosity on identity has varied by a key demographic indicator: age. Younger people, particularly those who have come of age after the worst part of the conflict over Northern Ireland, are substantially less religious than are older generations. This is shown in Figures 2.6 and 2.7, which illustrate variations in religious affiliation and religious service attendance both by cohort (i.e. those born between certain years) and over time.

Figure 2.6 illustrates that younger cohorts were substantially more likely to have no religious affiliation than were older cohorts. As of 2012, close to one in three young Irish people born after 1979 reported no religious affiliation. Similarly, nearly one in four Irish people born between 1957 and 1979 reported

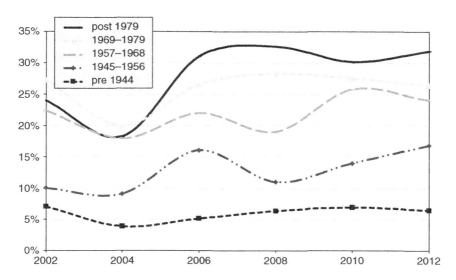

Figure 2.6 Percentage with no religious affiliation by EVS wave and cohort.

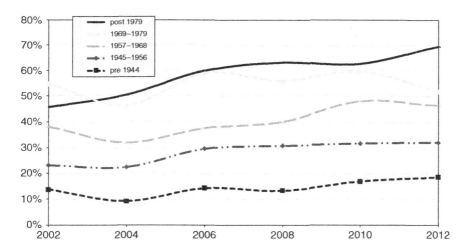

Figure 2.7 Proportion rarely or never attending religious services by ESS round and cohort.

no religious affiliation. For those born before 1944, just 6 per cent reported no religious affiliation.

Figure 2.7 is even more illustrative of cohort effects but also illustrates substantial change in religious attendance over time. Once again, the youngest generation, those born after 1979, were the least religious; close to 70 per cent reported never or very rare religious service attendance. Over the 10 years of ESS data collection, that number increased from just over 45 per cent (likely due in part to many members of that generation moving out of their parents' homes). But even among the older generations, the percentage that rarely or occasionally attended religious services increased. For those born between 1945 and 1956, just over 20 per cent rarely or never attended religious services in 2002; by 2012 it had increased by 10 per cent, to about 32 per cent.

While there was no specific point in time at which a clear transition from "religion is a salient part of Irish identity" to "religion is NOT a salient part of Irish identity" occurred, what the above discussion and corresponding data suggest is that a transition occurred during the 1990s and early 2000s in Ireland in both identity and religiosity. The significance of religion for Irish identity began to decline (see Figure 2.4). When religion was highly salient for identity, like during the 1980s, Ireland was among the most religious European countries (Hornsby-Smith and Whelan 1994). But by the early 2000s, the importance of religion in Ireland had declined, and religiosity was also beginning a rapid and steep decline. If secularization theory holds, Ireland appears to be on a trajectory towards continued religious decline, particularly as older, more religious generations are replaced by younger, less religious generations.

In summary, the theoretical explanation I have proposed for the decline of religiosity in Ireland is tied to the end of the conflicts over Northern Ireland, which resulted in a reduced significance of religion for Irish national identity. As Bruce (2002, 2013) has argued, when religion is instrumental in dealing with national conflicts, it can impede secularization. As the instrumentality of religion has waned in Ireland, so, too, has religious identity and practice. Ireland, having begun the process of divesting its national identity of religion, has now started to look like many other highly developed countries in that a growing proportion of the population – particularly younger people – reports no religious affiliation, considers religion unimportant and does not attend religious services, as I will illustrate in the next section.

The mechanisms of secularization

Scholars who study secularization have noted a number of patterns in how secularization develops (Bruce 2002; Tschannen 1991; Voas 2007, 2010). One such pattern, already illustrated above, is that younger generations tend to be less religious than older generations. In this section, I will argue that at least some of these patterns can be viewed as the actual "mechanisms" of secularization. By *mechanisms*, I mean that there are specific factors or elements of social life that function as the means of transition for the process of secularization. Just like a light switch is a mechanism that allows for the passage of electricity from a source to a destination, there are components of social life that facilitate the transition from religiosity to secularity. It is through or with the help of these mechanisms that secularization occurs.

The primary mechanism by which secularization occurs is in the transmission of religion from parents to children. While there is a fairly high degree of concordance between the religiosity of parents and children (Bengtson 2013; Bengtson et al. 2009; Cragun 2013), the concordance is never 100 per cent. By young adulthood, there is evidence, at least in the United States, that the correlation between parent and child religiosity is weaker than that between the child and his/her significant other (Arnett and Jensen 2002). Some scholars have argued that this is simply a "demographic effect" and that it is unrelated to secularization (Hout et al. 2001). Yet, the more logical explanation is that this is, in fact, a mechanism of secularization.

In any system, family included, in which something (e.g. religion) is to be transferred from one part of the system (e.g. parents) to another part of the system (e.g. children), there is a risk that the something may not make it to the receiving part of the system or could be modified in transmission. Religion is no different. Religion, a complicated and very personal phenomenon, is highly susceptible to modification and interference in the process of transferring it from parents to children. What forms might this modification or interference take? One form of interference is the growing acceptance of sexual and gender minorities around the world, but particularly in Ireland, where the citizens passed a landmark referendum in 2015 allowing same-sex couples to marry. Numerous surveys have found that young people are far more likely to accept lesbian and gay people as equal and deserving of equivalent civil rights to straight people than are older people (Barton 2012; Finlay and Walther 2003; Olson and Cadge 2002; Whitehead 2013). Religions that consider homosexuality deviant or sinful are going to be less appealing to young people who receive very different messages (i.e. interference) from other sources, like mainstream media, particularly television, movies and music stars. Parents, who have the primary responsibility for transmitting intolerant religious teachings, may feel conflicted about these doctrines themselves, resulting in them either not wanting to transmit those teachings in the first place or watering down the doctrines to make them more palatable to their children. The end result is likely to be a disconnect between the values of children and those of their parents and their parents' religion. Thus, the transmission of religiosity from parent to child can function as a mechanism of secularization: parents are unwilling or unable to convince their children to adhere to the same outdated, anti-modern values and beliefs that they were taught (Breen 2003), resulting in children who are less religious than they were.

Another possible source of interference in the transmission of religion from parents to children is a biological or psychological predisposition to religion. There is a growing body of evidence that there are genetic predispositions towards religion (Bradshaw and Ellison 2008), with some people being less interested in religion as a result of their psychology or intelligence (Kanazawa 2010), including individuals on the autism spectrum (Norenzayan 2013; Norenzayan et al. 2012). Predispositions and proclivities towards or against religion can interfere with the transmission of religion from parents to children. While there are many potential sources of interference in the transmission of religion from parents to children, the point is that this transition is one of the mechanisms of secularization.

Another well-known mechanism of secularization is education. While the relationship between education and changes in religiosity is complicated and can be quite nuanced (Johnson 1997), there is compelling evidence that education reduces orthodoxy of religious belief (Funk and Willits 1987; Uecker et al. 2007). Additionally, education has been shown to be the strongest predictor of religious decline around the world (Braun 2012). Education can serve as a mechanism of secularization by challenging previously held beliefs, by exposing students to diverse populations of people who hold different beliefs and by changing how people reason and think (Henrich et al. 2010). Thus, education can function as a mechanism of secularization.

While there are other mechanisms of secularization (Bruce 2013), I will discuss just one more: significant life changes. Prior research has noted that conversions to religion are fairly common after significant life changes, like the death of a loved one, a divorce or marriage (Gooren 2004; Rambo 1995; Stolzenberg et al. 1995). But not all life changes lead people towards religion. Some have the opposite effect, leading people away from religion. One of the most common life changes to do this is cohabitation, which, while akin to marriage in function, actually has the opposite effect on religiosity: it reduces religiosity rather than increases it. Why might this be the case? Many religions remain advocates of monogamous marriage and discourage extra-marital sex (Seltzer 2004; Uecker et al. 2007). When individuals choose to cohabit, they are violating the teachings and principles of many religions. Of course, one can argue that those who are less religious to begin with are more likely to cohabit, and that is true. But Cragun (2015; see also Uecker et al. 2007) showed that there is a causal linkage between cohabitation and declines in religiosity, likely as a result of those who choose to cohabit not wanting to feel like their lifestyle choice is somehow inferior based on the teachings of a religion. Thus, cohabitation, too, functions as a mechanism of secularization; it is a transition point at which people can and often do choose to diminish their involvement with religion.

As previously argued, the decline in significance of religion to Irish identity has led Ireland to begin to secularize at a relatively rapid pace. Prior research looking at the predictors of those who leave religion in Ireland and elsewhere has noted a number of patterns (Breen and Erbe Healy 2014; Hayes and McAllister 1995; O'Leary 2001), including the mechanisms just noted. In particular, the following variables tend to be associated with lower levels of religiosity: age (younger people are less religious), sex (males are less religious than females), marital status (married couples tend to be more religious than singles), education (those with more education tend to be less religious), and cohabitation (those who cohabit tend to be less religious than those who do not). If, as I have proposed in this chapter, Ireland is now undergoing a secular transition, we should find that all of the above variables are significant predictors of lower levels of religiosity in Ireland. Additionally, if Ireland has begun a period of rapid secularization, the passage of time itself should result in lower levels of religiosity in Ireland as the process of secularization takes place.

Table 2.1 presents the results of three regression analyses using the combined 2002–2012 ESS dataset. The dependent variable is religious service attendance.[2] As measured in the ESS, higher values on the religious service attendance variable indicate less frequent religious service attendance. Model 1 included just basic

Table 2.1 Religious attendance regressed (OLS) on demographic and independent variables

	Model 1 (N = 12,789)				Model 2 (N = 11,146)				Model 3 (N = 8,360)			
	B	SE	Beta	P-value	B	SE	Beta	P-value	B	SE	Beta	P-value
Age	−0.033	0.001	−0.357	.000	−0.025	0.001	−0.273	.000	−0.023	0.001	−0.253	.000
Sex (male = 1)	0.414	0.027	0.123	.000	0.402	0.027	0.119	.000	0.401	0.031	0.119	.000
Married (=1)	−0.289	0.028	−0.086	.000	−0.246	0.028	−0.073	.000	−0.270	0.032	−0.080	.000
Education	0.020	0.004	0.042	.000	0.003	0.004	0.006	.493	−0.003	0.005	−0.006	.577
ESS wave 2002									−0.270	0.052	−0.058	.000
ESS wave 2004	−0.113	0.046	−0.025	.015	−0.067	0.047	−0.015	.151	−0.352	0.051	−0.079	.000
ESS wave 2006	0.247	0.049	0.051	.000	0.264	0.050	0.054	.000	−0.112	0.054	−0.023	.039
ESS wave 2008	0.288	0.050	0.059	.000	0.274	0.050	0.056	.000	−0.080	0.054	−0.016	.142
ESS wave 2010	0.443	0.045	0.105	.000	0.342	0.046	0.081	.000				
ESS wave 2012	0.512	0.045	0.122	.000	0.415	0.046	0.099	.000	0.009	0.049	0.002	.847
Important to follow Tradition					0.334	0.010	0.268	.000	0.310	0.012	0.249	.000
Gays and lesbians should be free					−0.276	0.016	−0.144	.000	−0.255	0.018	−0.133	.000
Ever cohabited									0.679	0.042	0.155	.000
Constant	5.215	0.080		.000	4.775	0.093		.000	5.008	0.107		.000
R²			0.199				0.288				0.309	

Higher values = less frequent attendance.

demographic variables along with dummy variables for each wave of the ESS. In line with prior research, younger people attend religious services less frequently than do older people ($b = -.033, p < .001$). Men attend religious services less frequently than do women ($b = .414, p < .001$). Individuals who are married attend religious services more frequently than those who are not married ($b = -.289, p < .001$). Individuals with higher educational attainment attend religious services less frequently than those with lower educational attainment ($b = .020, p < .001$). The dummy codes[3] for each wave of the ESS also indicate that religious service attendance is declining year on year relative to the first year of the ESS, 2002, with the exception of 2004. The total amount of variation explained in religious service attendance in Model 1 is 19.9 per cent.

Model 2 adds two variables to the model, both of which are attitudinal variables. The first asked participants about the importance of tradition. The question was worded as follows: "Now I will briefly describe some people. Please listen to each description and tell me how much each person is or is not like you. Tradition is important to her/him. She/he tries to follow the customs handed down by her/his religion or her/his family." Response options ranged from "Very much like me" to "Not like me at all." The second question asked participants about gays and lesbians. Specifically, the question participants were asked was: "Please say to what extent you agree or disagree with each of the following statements: Gay men and lesbians should be free to live their own life as they wish." Response options ranged from "Agree strongly" to "Disagree strongly." Both variables were significantly related to religious service attendance. Individuals who do not think it is important to follow traditions attended religious services significantly less often ($b = .334, p < .001$). Likewise, individuals who support gay and lesbian freedom attended religious services less often ($b = -.276, p < .001$). The addition of these two variables increased the amount of variation explained in religious service attendance to 28.8 per cent.

Model 3 added one additional variable to the equation: cohabitation. The variable asked participants if they had ever cohabited. Individuals who had cohabited attended religious services significantly less often than those who had never cohabited ($b = .679, p < .001$). The addition of cohabitation to the model increased the amount of variation explained in religious service attendance to 30.9 per cent.

At a very basic level, the regression analyses indicate that Ireland is like most other countries undergoing a transition towards a more secular society. Males are less religious than females. Attitudes towards tradition matter for religiosity, as those who value tradition less are less religious. Importantly, the mechanisms of secularization described above are present and functioning in Ireland. The strongest predictor of lower levels of religious service attendance is age: young people are substantially less religious than older people. Likewise, attitudes towards sexual minorities also matter for religiosity even when statistically holding demographic variables like age constant, as those who have more accepting views of sexual minorities are less religious. Both of these variables suggest the transmission of religion from parents to children is faltering as young people are generally less interested in religion and find religion to be antithetical to their modern, tolerant and accepting values. Similarly, married couples are more religious than singles and more religious than cohabiting couples. These findings suggest that cohabitation is another mechanism of secularization that allows for a transition out of religion. Finally, Irish people are attending religious services less with each passing year, suggesting that Ireland is in a process of relatively rapid secularization. In short, in every respect, Ireland appears to be undergoing a secular transition.

Conclusion

Nuanced understandings of secularization theory have suggested that "exceptions" to secularization – that is, modernized countries that have not experienced notable declines in religiosity – can be explained by recognizing that religion in those countries has become instrumental and an important or significant part of national identity, often as a result of serious conflict. In this chapter, I illustrated that there is substantial support for this component of secularization theory by looking briefly at the United States and then focusing on Ireland, both of which are experiencing rapid periods of secularization. For both countries, the growth of non-religion and the decline in religious affiliation and attendance can be mapped to the time periods when the religio-ethnic related conflicts in those countries subsided. In the United States, the salience of religion for national identity ended with the end of the Cold War in 1990. In Ireland, the declining significance of religion occurred around the time the Good Friday agreement was signed in 1998. In both countries, rapid declines in religiosity followed shortly thereafter. Finally, I showed in this chapter that there are certain mechanisms that facilitate secularization, like younger cohorts being less religious than previous cohorts, as the transmission of religion from parents to children is susceptible to interference and interruption. These mechanisms have been found in other countries experiencing secularization and are observable in Ireland using ESS data. Additionally, ESS data suggest that Ireland is growing less religious and more secular with every passing year. If that trend continues, and there is no reason to think that it won't, Ireland will increasingly begin to look like its secular neighbours in western Europe over the coming decades.

Modernization generally weakens religion as it disenchants the world. As predicted by Bruce and other secularization theorists, secularization can be delayed by specific events that make religion salient to national identity, like religious conflict. However, when religion ceases to be instrumental to something like national identity, secularization begins. The end result is the declining significance of religion in society.

Notes

1 Google's Ngram data does not go beyond 2008.
2 While religious service attendance is technically an ordinal variable, it is treated here as an interval-like ordinal variable and is regressed using OLS regression. Alternative analyses using binary logistic regression (recoding religious service attendance into just two categories) and multinomial regression (recoding religious service attendance

into four categories) found nearly identical results. Thus, OLS results are presented here for simplicity in interpretation.
3 A dummy code is just a dichotomized measure, with one value being set to 1 (e.g. that year of data collection in the ESS) and all other values set to 0 (e.g. every other year of data collection in the ESS).This is a useful technique in regression analysis for indicating the presence or absence of some characteristic.

References

Arnett, J. J. and Jensen, L. A., 2002. A congregation of one: Individualized religious beliefs among emerging adults. *Journal of Adolescent Research*, 17(5), pp. 451–467.

Baker, J. O. and Smith, B. G., 2009. The Nones: Social characteristics of the religiously unaffiliated. *Social Forces*, 87(3), pp. 1251–1263.

Barton, B., 2012. *Pray the Gay Away: The Extraordinary Lives of Bible Belt Gays*, New York: New York University Press.

Bengtson, V. L. et al., 2009. A longitudinal study of the intergenerational transmission of religion. *International Sociology*, 24(3), pp. 325–345.

Bengtson, V. L., 2013. *Families and Faith: How Religion is Passed Down across Generations*, Oxford: Oxford University Press.

Bradshaw, M. and Ellison, C. G., 2008. Do genetic factors influence religious life? Findings from a behavior genetic analysis of twin siblings. *Journal for the Scientific Study of Religion*, 47(4), pp. 529–544.

Braun, C. M. J., 2012. Explaining global secularity: Existential security or education? *Secularism and Nonreligion*, 1.

Breen, M. J., 2003. Ask me another: An evaluation of issues arising from the European Values Survey in relation to questions concerning technology and transcendence. In *Technology and Transcendence*. Dublin, Ireland: The Columba Press, pp. 127–145.

Breen, M. J. and Erbe Healy, A., 2014. Secularization in Ireland: Analyzing the relationship between religiosity and demographic variables in Ireland from the European Social Survey 2002–2012. *International Journal of Religion & Spirituality in Society*, 3(4), pp. 113–125.

Brown, C. G., 2012. *Religion and the Demographic Revolution*, Boydell Press.

Bruce, S., 2002. *God Is Dead: Secularization in the West*, London: Blackwell Publishers.

Bruce, S., 2013. *Secularization: In Defence of an Unfashionable Theory*, Oxford: Oxford University Press.

Bullivant, S., 2010. The new atheism and sociology: Why here? Why now? What next? In A. Amarasingam, ed. *Religion and the New Atheism: A Critical Appraisal*. Brill Academic Publishers, pp. 109–124.

Cragun, R. T., 2015. *How to Defeat Religion in 10 Easy Steps: A Toolkit for Secular Activists*, Durham, North Carolina: Pitchstone Publishing.

Cragun, R. T., 2013. *What You Don't Know About Religion (But Should)*, Durham, NC: Pitchstone Publishing.

Cragun, R.T. and Lawson, R., 2010. The Secular Transition: The Worldwide Growth of Mormons, Jehovah's Witnesses, and Seventh-day Adventists. *Sociology of Religion*, 71(3), pp. 349–373.

Day, A., 2013. *Believing in Belonging: Belief and Social Identity in the Modern World* Reprint edition, Oxford University Press.

Dobbelaere, K., 2002. *Secularization: An Analysis at Three Levels (Gods, Humans, and Religions)*, New York: Peter Lang Publishing.

Finlay, B. and Walther, C. S., 2003. The relation of religious affiliation, service attendance, and other factors to homophobic attitudes among university students. *Review of Religious Research*, 44(4), pp. 370–393.

Funk, R. B. and Willits, F. K., 1987. College attendance and attitude-change: A panel study, 1970–81. *Sociology of Education*, 60(4), pp. 224–231.

Gooren, H., 2004. The conversion careers approach: Why people become and remain religiously active. In Annual Meeting of the Society for the Scientific Study of Religion. Kansas City, Missouri.

Gorski, P. S., 2000. Historicizing the secularization debate: Church, state, and society in late medieval and early modern Europe, ca. 1300 to 1700. *American Sociological Review*, 65(1), pp. 138–167.

De Graaf, N. D. and Te Grotenhuis, M., 2008. Traditional Christian belief and belief in the supernatural: Diverging trends in the Netherlands between 1979 and 2005? *Journal for the Scientific Study of Religion*, 47(4), pp. 585–598.

Gunn, T. J., 2009. *Spiritual Weapons: The Cold War and the Forging of an American National Religion*, Westport, Conn.: Praeger Publishers.

Hadaway, C. K., Marler, P. L. and Chaves, M., 1993. What the polls don't show: A closer look at U.S. church attendance. *American Sociological Review*, 58(6), pp. 741–752.

Halman, L. and Draulans, V., 2006. How secular is Europe? *The British Journal of Sociology*, 57(2), pp. 263–288.

Hayes, B. C. and McAllister, I., 1995. Religious independents in Northern Ireland – origins, attitudes, and significance. *Review of Religious Research*, 37(1), pp. 65–83.

Healy, A. E. and Breen, M. J., 2014. Religiosity in times of insecurity: An analysis of Irish, Spanish and Portuguese European Social Survey data, 2002–12. *Irish Journal of Sociology*, 22(2), pp. 4–29.

Henrich, J., Heine, S. J. and Norenzayan, A., 2010. The weirdest people in the world? *Behavioral and Brain Sciences*, 33(2–3), pp. 61–83.

Herbert, D. and Fras, M., 2009. European enlargement, secularisation and religious re-publicisation in Central and Eastern Europe. *Religion, State & Society*, 37(1/2), pp. 81–97.

Hirschle, J., 2010. From religious to consumption-related routine activities? Analyzing Ireland's economic boom and the decline in church attendance. *Journal for the Scientific Study of Religion*, 49(4), pp. 673–687.

Hixson, W. L., 1998. *Parting the Curtain: Propaganda, Culture, and The Cold War, 1945–1961*, New York: St. Martin's Press.

Holland, J., 1999. *Hope Against History: The Course of Conflict in Northern Ireland*, 1st edition, New York: Henry Holt and Co.

Hornsby-Smith, M. P. and Whelan, C. T., 1994. Religious and moral values. In *Values and Social Change in Ireland*. Dublin, Ireland: Gill & Macmillan Ltd, pp. 7–44.

Hout, M. and Fischer, C. S., 2002. Why more Americans have no religious preference: Politics and generations. *American Sociological Review*, 67(2), pp. 165–190.

Hout, M., Greeley, A. and Wilde, M. J., 2001. The demographic imperative in religious change in the United States. *American Journal of Sociology*, 107(2), pp. 468–500.

Jacoby, S., 2005. *Freethinkers: A History of American Secularism*, Holt Paperbacks.

Jacoby, S., 2009. *The Age of American Unreason*, New York: Vintage Books.

Johnson, D. C., 1997. Formal education vs. religious belief: Soliciting new evidence with multinomial logit modeling. *Journal for the Scientific Study of Religion*, 36, pp. 231–246.

Kanazawa, S., 2010. Why liberals and atheists are more intelligent. *Social Psychology Quarterly*, 73(1), pp. 33–57.

Kirby, D. ed., 2002. *Religion and the Cold War*, Palgrave Macmillan.

Kosmin, B. A. et al., 2009. *American Nones: The Profile of the No Religion Population*, Hartford, CT: Institute for the Study of Secularism in Society and Culture.

Kutyło, Ł., 2013. The Influence of the quasi-monopolistic religious market on religiosity in Poland: Considerations based on an economic approach. *Interdisciplinary Journal of Research on Religion*, 9.

Lahr, A. M., 2007. *Millennial Dreams and Apocalyptic Nightmares: The Cold War Origins of Political Evangelicalism*, Oxford University Press, United States.

Mitchell, C., 2006. *Religion, Identity and Politics in Northern Ireland: Boundaries of Belonging and Belief*, Ashgate Publishing, Limited.

Norenzayan, A., 2013. *Big Gods: How Religion Transformed Cooperation and Conflict*, Princeton: Princeton University Press.

Norenzayan, A., Gervais, W. M. and Trzesniewski, K. H., 2012. Mentalizing deficits constrain belief in a personal God. *PLoS ONE*, 7(5), p.e36880.

Norris, P. and Inglehart, R., 2004. *Sacred and Secular: Religion and Politics Worldwide*, Cambridge University Press.

O'Leary, R., 2001. Modernization and religious intermarriage in the Republic of Ireland. *The British Journal of Sociology*, 52(4), pp. 647–665.

Olson, L. R. and Cadge, W., 2002. Talking about homosexuality: The views of mainline protestant clergy. *Journal for the Scientific Study of Religion*, 41(1), pp. 153–167.

Pasquale, F. L., 2010. A portrait of secular group affiliates. In P. Zuckerman, ed., *Atheism and Secularity: Volume 1 – Issues, Concepts, and Definitions*. Santa Barbara, CA: Praeger, pp. 43–88.

Pew Forum on Religion, 2012. "Nones" on the rise: One-in-five adults have no religious affiliation, Washington, D.C.: The Pew Forum on Religion & Public Life. Available at: www.pewforum.org/Unaffiliated/nones-on-the-rise.aspx [Accessed June 3, 2013].

Rambo, L. R., 1995. *Understanding Religious Conversion*, Yale University Press.

Requena, M. and Stanek, M., 2013. Secularization in Poland and Spain after the democratic transition: A cohort analysis. *International Sociology*, 28(1), pp. 84–101.

Seltzer, J. A., 2004. Cohabitation in the United States and Britain: Demography, kinship, and the future. *Journal of Marriage & Family*, 66(4), pp. 921–928.

Sharlet, J., 2008. *The Family: The Secret Fundamentalism at the Heart of American Power*, New York, NY: HarperCollins.

Sherkat, D., 2014. *Changing Faith: The Dynamics and Consequences of Americans' Shifting Religious Identities*, New York: NYU Press.

Staar, R. F., 1991. *Foreign policies of the Soviet Union*, Stanford, Calif.: Hoover Institution Press, Stanford University.

Stark, R., 1999. Secularization, R.I.P. *Sociology of Religion*, 60(3), p. 249.

Stark, R. and Finke, R., 2000. *Acts of Faith: Explaining the Human Side of Religion*, California: University of California Press.

Stolzenberg, R. M., Blair-Loy, M. and Waite, L. J., 1995. Religious participation in early adulthood: Age and family life cycle effects on church membership. *American Sociological Review*, 60(1), pp. 84–103.

Tschannen, O., 1991. The secularization paradigm: A systematization. *Journal for the Scientific Study of Religion*, 30(4), pp. 395–415.

Uecker, J. E., Regnerus, M. D. and Vaaler, M. L., 2007. Losing my religion: The social sources of religious decline in early adulthood. *Social Forces*, 85(4), pp. 1667–1692.

Voas, D., 2007. The continuing secular transition. In D. Pollack & D. V. A. Olson, eds. *The Role of Religion in Modern Societies*. Routledge, pp. 25–48.

Voas, D., 2010. Value liberalization or consumption: Comment on Hirschle's analysis of Ireland's economic boom and the decline in church attendance. *Journal for the Scientific Study of Religion*, 49(4), pp. 688–690.

Whitehead, A. L., 2013. Gendered organizations and inequality regimes: Gender, homosexuality, and inequality within religious congregations. *Journal for the Scientific Study of Religion*, 52(3), pp. 476–493.

Wilson, A. N., 2000. *God's Funeral: The Decline of Faith in Western Civilization*, Ballantine Books.

Yang, F., 2004. Between secularist ideology and desecularizing reality: The birth and growth of religious research in communist China. *Sociology of Religion*, 65(2), pp. 101–119.

Yang, F., 2005. Lost in the market, Saved at McDonald's: Conversion to Christianity in urban China. *Journal for the Scientific Study of Religion*, 44(4), pp. 423–441.

Zuckerman, P., 2011. *Faith No More: Why People Reject Religion*, Oxford University Press, United States.

3 Religiosity and Political Participation across Europe

Anna Kulkova

Introduction

Political scientists have been interested in the topic of political participation in its contemporary sense since the 1950s. There were periods when political participation seemed to be understood and all its predictors identified. Nevertheless, changes in social structure, in economic and political conditions, inevitably brought changes in political participation, thus causing a revival of research interest in this topic. The list of factors that could influence political participation has been expanding constantly, from socio-demographic characteristics of the individual to interest in politics, the resources needed to take part in politics and religious factors (Brady et al. 1995; Cho et al. 2006). At least since the 1970s, religion in the United States has been perceived as a power capable of shaping citizens' political participation. Macaluso and Wanat (1979) demonstrated that electoral turnout was connected with voters' degree of religiosity: Americans who attended religious services regularly were more active *citizens* as well. Further studies revealed differences in political participation and electoral behaviour between followers of different religious traditions – not only in the United States, but also in Europe – that were considered to be much more secular (Beyerlein and Chaves 2003; Knutsen 2004; Li and Marsh 2008). Other scholars paid more attention to the degree of individual religiosity as a potential predictor of political participation and showed that religious and non-religious people behave differently regardless of their religious affiliation (Harris 1994; Jones-Correa and Leal 2001; Wald et al. 1990). Despite predictions of the classis secularization theory, religion in the twenty-first century still has an impact on individual values and behavioural patterns. Though religious attendance rates are falling, major religious traditions are still influential because they become embedded in culture. One doesn't have to attend religious services regularly to share the values of a country's predominant religious tradition because these values are transmitted through the educational system, state policy and mass media (Norris and Inglehart, 2011). In the United States, politicians are seeking support from religious voters, while in Europe, Christian–Democratic parties remain popular (Van der Brug et al. 2009).

Political participation rates vary considerably among European countries, and this may have something to do with religiosity. According to the data from the European Social Survey (ESS) 2012 (presented in Table 3.1), on average, citizens of predominantly Protestant countries performed 2.36 *different* political actions per year, while for the Orthodox Christian countries, this number fell to 1.07. These data may be misleading and reflect political characteristics of the country (such regime type or communist legacy) instead of the religious roots of differences in political participation. On the other hand, Table 3.2 suggests that followers of the Orthodox religious tradition are generally less active in politics than members of all other confessions and non-affiliated individuals. The Orthodox turn out to be far less engaged in politics than Protestants, regardless of the home country: about 34 per cent of the Orthodox performed only one political action and about 23 per cent of them performed no political actions, while the distribution for Protestants moves to the right – with higher numbers of activists (Figure 3.1). Besides individual religious factors, religion may shape political participation through country-level specifics such as the type of predominant religion or previous state–church relations. European countries are culturally close, still showing great variance in predominant religions and state–church relations experience. This makes this region a good case for comparative research.

Therefore, it becomes important to study whether religion can add something to our understanding of differences in political participation in today's Europe. Do members of different confessions differ in political participation rates, or does the main cleavage lie between religious and non-religious people, regardless of religious tradition? Does orthodoxy really lead to lower levels of political participation or is what we see the effect of political regime or communist legacy? In order

Table 3.1 Mean values of political participation (PP) index for countries with different predominant religions in 2012 (ESS)

Countries by predominant religion	PP index means
Orthodox	1.07
Muslim-Orthodox	1.19
Catholic	1.43
Jewish	1.47
Muslim	1.51
Secular	1.69
Catholic-Protestant	1.70
Protestant	2.36

Notes: PP index is an additive index of eight types of political actions performed by the individual in 2012. It varies from 0 to 7. Though almost all values are close to 1, there is a considerable difference in political activism in the Orthodox and Protestant countries. The list of countries grouped by predominant religions (Table 3.6A) and political participation rates in European countries (Table 3.7A) are presented in the appendix.

Table 3.2 Political participation (PP) among followers of different religious traditions in 2012 (ESS)

Religious tradition	PP index means
Orthodox	1.11
Muslim	1.25
Catholic	1.39
Other Christian	1.40
Jewish	1.60
Non-affiliated	1.66
Eastern religions	1.74
Other non-Christians	1.79
Protestant	2.17

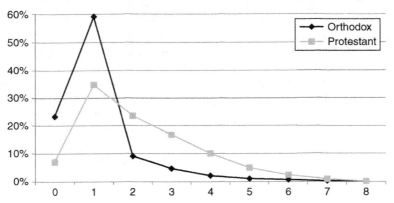

Figure 3.1 Political participation index for Protestants and Orthodox Christians.

Note: Axis X shows the number of political actions performed by individuals, while axis Y displays percentage of Protestants and the Orthodox that performed this number of actions.

to answer these questions, I will perform a statistical analysis of the interaction between religion and political participation in European countries. Using the data from ESS 2012, I will explore how political participation is affected by individual religious affiliation of the voter, by religious behaviour rates (religious services attendance and praying frequencies) and by country-level religious factors (predominant religion and previous state–church relations). The political participation index combines eight types of political actions performed by the individual during 2012. Generally, I expect to see the influence of religiosity on political participation among Europeans (H1). According to the theory, I assume that inclination to take part in politics will increase with the rise in religiosity (H2), while inter-confessional differences will be less pronounced and significant in particular countries only (H3). Finally, I expect the Orthodox religious tradition to exert a negative influence on individual political behaviour and that it will not be the effect of the regime or communist legacy.

Statistical analysis results suggest that those who pray and attend religious services are more likely to be politically active. This pattern holds for followers of all major European religious traditions and in countries with different predominant religions. On the other hand, inter-confessional differences in political participation appear weak and unstable. While there are almost no stable differences in political participation between confessions, both belonging to an Orthodox religious tradition and living in a predominantly Orthodox country exert a stable and negative effect on political participation. Additional tests suggest that there is no difference in political participation between Orthodox Christians from predominantly Orthodox states and those where they form only a minority. Consequently, it is something in a religious tradition itself that decreases political participation. The doctrine of "Ceasaro-Papism" that prescribes an integrationist approach towards the relations between church and state may be the first possible explanation of the trend. Orthodoxy and its clergy do not promote political activism because it is not a part of the religious tradition. On the other hand, members of religious communities with weaker ties are less likely to participate than those from cohesive communities. Orthodox religious communities are rather weak and unstable; there are no parishes with fixed membership. Thus, the second explanation may come from the social capital theory: weak interpersonal trust has no positive impact on political activism.

The remaining part of the paper will be organized as follows: in Section 2, I will discuss major theories linking political participation to religiosity and review the causal mechanisms through which religion may influence individual behaviour and political preferences. In Section 3, I will run an empirical analysis, while Section 4 will be dedicated to discussion.

Theoretical framework: How can religion affect political behaviour?

In order to understand how religion and religiosity are capable of shaping individual behaviour in today's Europe, it is important to focus on the individual level and to study the mechanisms that transform religiosity into differences in political participation. These differences may arise from religious doctrines and their political theologies (Beyerlein and Chaves, 2003; Grzymala-Busse, 2012; Philpott, 2007), from organizational structure of religious communities (Arruñada, 2010; Wald et al. 1990), from the degree of religiosity (Driskell et al. 2008) and, finally, from historical church-state relationships that influenced political theologies (Philpott, 2007; Roccas and Schwartz, 1997).

Religion as affiliation: Confessions differ?

The most popular understanding of religiosity equates it with belonging to a religious tradition. From this perspective, a church is regarded as a group of people who share common values and interests (Wielhouwer 2009). Major studies within the so-called sociological tradition explore the interaction between religiosity and people's attitude towards sensitive issues like abortion, education policies or electoral preferences (McTague and Layman 2009). Therefore, Catholics and Jews in the United States in recent years prefer to vote Democrat, while Republicans target Protestants and Evangelists as their core audience (Esmer and Pettersson, 2007). In Europe, despite the secularization processes, the influence of religion on party choice is not declining either; religious people are more willing to support Christian-Democrats or, in the case of an absence of such parties, the Conservatives would be their second priority (Van der Brug et al. 2009).

Religious traditions differ not only in the political preferences of their followers but also in the way that believers treat politics and political participation, whether they take part in elections, sign petitions, attend demonstrations or oppose these types of activities. For instance, American Jews and mainline Protestants are typically more active voters when compared to other confessions, and especially when compared to non-religious Americans (Wielhouwer 2009). Li and Marsh show that in Britain, Muslims and Hindu are much less eager to take part in politics than atheists and all other Christian traditions' followers, because they do not feel incorporated into society (Li and Marsh 2008).

The difference in attitudes towards social issues or towards political participation may arise from the religious doctrines that form the basis of all religious traditions. Doctrines include *political theologies* – the set of ideas that religious actors hold about political authority and justice. Therefore, doctrines can promote political participation or claim politics to be a dirty business, promote tolerant attitudes towards sexual minorities or strictly oppose social change (Philpott 2007). While Buddhists are generally less interested in politics due to their philosophy of detachment, Christians turn out to be more politically active, and in Islam, politics and religion are inseparable. In other words, different religious traditions establish different behavioural norms in all spheres of life, including politics, and their believers follow these norms. For example, American religious communities that do not support absenteeism usually "specialize" in some kind of political activism and prefer to devote their time primarily to these types of activities. A considerable amount of black Protestant communities invite local candidates to give speeches in church and raise votes to support them. Catholics organize demonstrations and lobby decisions at a local level, while Evangelists generally distribute leaflets (Beyerlein and Chaves 2003). Given this, belonging to a particular religious tradition may predispose which political actions the individuals are more likely to undertake, because they may favour activities regarded as appropriate in their religious community.

Although religious affiliation is relatively easy to measure and use in quantitative analysis, this understanding of religiosity has some limitations. Firstly, it is not always obvious how exactly religious tradition can influence people's political preferences or their inclination to take part in politics. Confessions differ not only in terms of political theologies but also in religious communities' organizational structures. Higher levels of discipline lead to political uniformity, manifesting in consolidated support for some political actions or a political party among community members. Traditionalism may influence the overall inclination of community members to take part in politics in accordance with religious doctrines. Accordingly, in the United States, Jews and mainline Protestants, whose communities are characterized by higher levels of within church cohesion, are more inclined to vote than those from less cohesive communities (Wald et al. 1990).

Previous church–state relations and political participation

The measure of religiosity understood as "belonging" is widely used as an explanatory variable in contemporary studies of political participation (Brady et al. 1995) and social policy (Alesina and Giuliano 2011). However, the opportunity to conduct a cross-country analysis using this indicator is doubtful. It is hardly correct to categorize those who are followers of the same tradition but are from different countries into one religious group and to suggest that they have a common attitude towards political participation. For example, Catholic communities in the Czech Republic and Poland differ greatly in their attitude towards political participation (Philpott 2007) and Muslim communities in countries where Muslims are only a small minority are not equal to Muslim communities in predominantly Muslim countries (Pepinsky and Welborne 2011). Though most religions claim to be transnational in their essence and to unite people from different countries, following the logic of Roccas and Schwartz, one shouldn't ignore the specifics of religiosity in particular countries. For instance, differences in state–church relations may influence local political theologies and thus predispose whether religious communities would take part in politics. The role of religion in socio-economic development can be seen from the third wave of democratization (from 1974), which was predominantly Catholic (Huntington 1993; Philpott 2007). Until the 1960s, the Catholic Church opposed democracy and democratic values because of its previous experience of confrontation with anti-clerical progressive authorities as in revolutionary France and Germany in Bismarck's time. Nevertheless, the Second Vatican Council in 1962–1965 included democratic values and human rights into its teachings, as well as declaring its separation from temporal authorities. As a result of this shift in political theology, the Catholic Church was able to become an important political actor, promoting democracy and development. Still, the Catholic Church performed differently in different European countries during the second half of the twentieth century. In Poland, the Catholic Church was in active opposition to the communist regime encouraging believers to take part in politics. As a result, after the fall of the Soviet Union, the church enjoyed mass support from the population and could influence the political behaviour of its followers. On the contrary, the Czech Catholic Church was close to the communist regime and materially depended on it. Consequently, it didn't promote participatory values among its followers and still has little impact on the behaviour and opinions of ordinary Czechs, who don't trust it. Thus, we may expect Polish Catholics to be more active in politics than those from the Czech Republic.

Roccas and Schwartz compared values of Catholics from two groups of countries: where church and state were in confrontation in the recent past (Poland, Hungary and the Czech Republic) and those that did not experience such type of conflict (Roccas and Schwartz 1997). They found that

> in countries with oppositional relations between church and state during the years that preceded data gathering (Poland, the Czech Republic, Hungary), religiosity correlates less positively with valuing conformity and security, more negatively with valuing power and achievement and more positively with valuing universalism than in countries with cordial separation of church and state (Italy, Spain, Portugal).

Similar to the Catholic Church in the Czech Republic, Eastern Orthodox churches were in close relations with the authoritarian regimes they had to live with and did almost nothing to fight for democracy. The Greek Orthodox Church supported the military junta and after its failure declared support for the new authorities. The Russian Orthodox Church has always been in close relations with the state, first during the period of the Russian Empire and later during Soviet rule. The real separation between the Russian Orthodox Church and the state has never occurred; even today, the priests are influenced by secular authorities, and in Soviet times bishops needed to get approval from secret services in order to be appointed. Thus, today, Orthodox churches in Greece and Russia but also in Ukraine, Bulgaria and Romania do not have a tradition of supporting democracy or promoting participatory values. Moreover, the Orthodox political theology generally disapproves of the whole idea of separation between church and state. According to its "Ceasaro-Papist" ideology, sacred and secular power should not be divided but should be accumulated in the same hands. In contrast to the Catholic Church, with its transnational character, Orthodox churches are divided along national borders, which leads to the prevalence of local interests and to the further integration of church and state.

Protestant movements do not form a single church with one political theology and can differ in their relations with secular authorities. For example, mainline Protestants of Eastern and Northern Europe cooperated with the state and did not promote church–state separation. On the other hand, those churches that experienced conflicts with the state and prosecution today favour radical separation and defend individual religious freedom.

Religiosity as behaviour and beliefs

The understanding of religiosity as religious behaviour stems from the works of Emile Durkheim, for whom religious rites form group solidarity and strengthen the ties between individuals in society (Wielhouwer 2009). The behavioural dimension of religiosity is operationalized through the frequency by which people attend religious services and other practical manifestations of following the rules of the religious tradition, such as praying or following dietary requirements. It is expected that people who follow religious norms are actually religious; religion is important for them, and they could be called religious. Conversely, individuals who claim to be affiliated with a religious tradition but do not follow its rules cannot be said to be religious. Proponents of this approach suggest that in a contemporary world, the main religious cleavage lies not between representatives of different confessions but between very religious people and those who are either less involved in their religious community's affairs or are non-religious (Esmer and Pettersson 2007). From this perspective, religious communities are not only communities of people with shared values (as seen from the sociological perspective) but rather agents of socialization who promote their values among their followers. Therefore, the more individuals are involved in their community's life, the more they are exposed to the community's influence (Wald et al. 1990). On the other hand, high levels of participation in community activities may imply that a person shares the community's typical values. Churches can actively engage in the electoral mobilization of their followers because they have the opportunity to convince followers to participate in politics or to vote for a particular candidate. Even if not every religious community practices political agitation among its members (confessions and countries do differ in the degree of politicization of religious communities), conservative politicians can successfully find support among religious people when sensitive issues such as reproductive rights and minorities' rights appear on the political agenda (Gershtenson 2003). Regular attendance at religious services therefore increases a person's chances of being exposed to the influence of conservative movements.

The specifics of interaction between religiosity and political participation should not be reduced to the influence that intra-communal norms exert over members' political participation. Macaluso and Wanat suggest that the necessity of regular attendance at religious services creates skills that are close to those required for being a responsible citizen as well as increasing social and political responsibility at an individual level. The most religious people pay attention to order, rites, duty and legitimacy – those psychological traits that form a sense of civic responsibility (Macaluso and Wanat 1979). On the other hand, religious participation can lead to political participation because a person gets into the habit of participating. Despite its popularity, the behavioural dimension of religiosity is constantly criticized, primarily due to the impossibility of correctly comparing religious participation between representatives of different confessions. Religions have different requirements for performing their religious rites, such as the obligation to attend religious services or to pray, and mandatory acts are not the same for a Muslim as for a Buddhist (Esmer and Pettersson 2007). While Orthodox Christians must regularly take part in sacraments, it is mandatory for Muslims to attend mosque on Friday for a sermon, but in the Buddhist tradition, attending church (khurul) is mandatory only on holidays. Moreover, in some local communities, attending church is more of a social ritual than a religious one.

Finally, if we ignore the content of religiosity and focus only on the behavioural characteristics of the individuals, involvement in the life of a religious community becomes indistinguishable from a social club's activities (like gardening) when it comes to their influence on members' political participation. In both cases, either binding or bonding social capital is formed, which can affect people's civic responsibility and their inclination to take part in politics, but this has nothing to do with religiosity (Putnam 1995).

Scholars who criticize "simple" measures of religiosity suggest focusing on beliefs instead of affiliation and quantitative manifestations of religiosity (Driskell et al. 2008; Guth et al. 2002). The beliefs that people hold are actually the most accurate understanding of religiosity. Nevertheless, beliefs are much harder to measure empirically than religious affiliation or practices.

The influence of individual religiosity on political participation can be multi-dimensional. It could be suggested that religious fundamentalism leads to political absenteeism because the religious community retires into its shell, but recent studies demonstrate that current religious conservatives actively participate in political processes, especially when sensitive issues such as abortion or gay rights are included on the political agenda (Guth et al. 2002). Therefore, supporting fundamentalist or liberal religious views will tell us nothing about the individual's inclination to participate in politics but can predispose political preferences and the type of political actions that an individual will be more likely to take part in.

Religious beliefs and modes of religious participation differ amongst confessions. This is why cross-country mass surveys often include the additional indicator of a respondent's degree of religiosity: how religious the respondents consider themselves to be, or the degree to which religiosity is important to them (Prutskova 2012). The way that this question is formulated allows the respondents to reveal their subjective attitudes towards religion, while answers may be compared between followers of different religions, regardless of their particular beliefs.

There is no perfect indicator of religiosity, which is why, from the early 2000s, researchers used a complex approach to operationalizing religiosity. This implies the simultaneous use of religious affiliation, participation and beliefs as indicators of religiosity, which may explain differences in people's inclination to participate in politics (Driskell et al. 2008; Guth et al. 2002). The simultaneous inclusion of these indicators into statistical models allows us to compare the effect that all these dimensions of religiosity have on political participation and even to identify the indicator that could best explain political participation.

***

"Religion matters. More specifically, religions matter," as put by Philpott (2007). But it is also the *context* that matters. Religions, as well as the individuals that affiliate with them, exist not in a vacuum but in a particular context. This context is formed by the type of religion that enjoys dominant position within the country and by the previous state–church relations. The same religious traditions may produce different local political theologies because of different relations with authorities or because they function in different environments, composed of different religions and with different predominant religious traditions. Even in today's secularized world, predominant religions influence our values and attitudes because religious values are already embedded into countries' *cultural* traditions. Religion is capable of shaping individual political behaviour through political theologies, community organizational structure and beliefs. But on the country level, all these mechanisms are supplemented and complicated by the context in which all the individuals operate. That is why conducting empirical analysis in order to grasp the religious roots of cross-country differences in political participation requires us to treat the local context very cautiously. It is important to control for predominant religion type and communist legacy as well as for other country specifics.

Empirical analysis

Hypotheses, data and methods

The main *hypothesis* of the paper is that European countries do differ in the way political participation is influenced by religiosity (H1). Generally, I expect to see the influence of religiosity on political participation of the Europeans. The paper suggests that we should study not only individual dimensions of religiosity, but also treat country specifics of religiosity and previous state–church relations experience as potential sources of variance. According to the theory, I expect that inclination to take part in politics will increase with the rise in religiosity (H2), while inter-confessional differences will be less pronounced and significant in particular countries only (H3). Finally, I expect the Orthodox religious tradition to exert negative influence on both individual behaviour and country-level results, and it will not be the effect of regime or communist legacy.

The *data* for the empirical analysis come from the ESS project for 2012 ("ESS Round 6: European Social Survey Round 6 Data," 2012). The dataset contains more than 48,000 individual level observations for 26 European countries and Israel.

The *dependent variable* is political participation, which is measured as an additive index. This is the sum of political actions performed by the respondent during the previous year, which includes signing petitions, attending demonstrations, working for political parties and non-governmental organisations (NGOs), joining boycotts, displaying political symbolics, contacting politicians and voting in the previous parliamentary elections. The index varies between 0 and 8, where 0 means that the respondent did not take part in any political action and 8 means that the respondent participated in every type of political action defined in the paper. Table 3.3 shows the descriptive statistics for the political participation index.

Though relatively few people performed six and more political actions, the overall quantity of activists allows us to examine the interaction between religiosity and political participation for this group. As it is an additive index, we should analyse the way it is composed of different political participation modes (presented in Table 3.4). Voting is the most popular mode of political participation, and other types of activities go far behind it. More than 76 per cent of Europeans voted in 2012, while only 19.5 per cent of the sample signed petitions and only 15.7 per cent joined boycotts. All other modes of political participation are even

46 Anna Kulkova

Table 3.3 Political participation index (descriptive statistics)

PP index	Freq.	%
0	8,677	18.06
1	21,871	45.53
2	7,986	16.63
3	4,647	9.67
4	2,567	5.34
5	1,277	2.66
6	650	1.35
7	275	0.57
8	85	0.18
Total	48,035	100

Table 3.4 Types of political actions performed by Europeans (descriptive statistics)

Political action performed	No (%)	Yes (%)
Voted	23.83	76.17
Signed petitions	80.53	19.47
Joined boycotts	84.31	15.69
Worked for NGO	86.67	13.33
Contacted politicians	87.52	12.48
Displayed political symbolics	92.54	7.46
Attended demonstrations	93.15	6.85
Worked for political parties	96.28	3.72

less popular among Europeans; details can be seen in Table 3.4. Nevertheless, it is still important to use the political participation index composed of as many components as possible, even if they add little to the index. People may engage in some modes of political activity while totally neglecting others.

According to the theory presented in the previous section, political participation may be influenced by several religious indicators: religious affiliation and practical religiosity (religious services attendance, praying frequency). The degree of religiosity indicator ("How religious are you?") available in the ESS dataset performed poorly in the analysis and was not used in recent specifications.

In order to control for other factors that can have an effect on political participation, I will use additional *control variables*: traditional socio-economic indicators (age, gender, income, education) as well as country-level specifics that include predominant religion, previous state–church relations, communist experience and country fixed effects.

Results

Empirical analysis results (presented in Table 3.8A) suggest that in today's Europe, religion does have an effect on the political participation of citizens.

Protestants and Jews turn out to be more active in politics than their non-affiliated fellow citizens, while Catholics and especially Orthodox Christians tend to be less active. Thus, our data support the theory that members of religious communities with strong discipline are more politically active than those from communities with weaker ties. On the other hand, the attendance of religious services proves to be positively connected with political participation as it was predicted by theory and, moreover, the chances to participate in politics increase steadily with the rise in religious activism. Individuals who reduce their religious activism to attending religious services on special holy days are only 13 per cent more likely to participate than those who never attend, while everyday attendees are 23 per cent more likely to participate compared to non-attendees.

The differences in political participation among confessions can be misleading: the vast majority of the Orthodox, for example, live in post-communist states where people gained the right to participate not so long ago and thus may simply lack the culture of participation. But several cases suggest that there may be something in the Orthodox doctrine or community structure themselves that leads to lower levels of political participation among the Orthodox. For example, in Poland and Germany, mean rates of political activism of the Orthodox are considerably low if compared to the whole population (0.6 versus 1.1 for Poland, and 1.0 versus 1.93 for Germany). On the other hand, in the Czech Republic, the Orthodox are even *more* active than the whole population: on average, Orthodox performed two political actions in a year, while the number for the population as a whole is 1.35. This finding suggests that even orthodoxy may exert a positive influence on political activism in a rather secular environment, but in countries with strong predominant religions, its effect may be negative.

Besides experiencing communist rule, countries differ in predominant religions that may affect overall rates of political participation. Thus, living in a predominantly Orthodox country (Bulgaria, Cyprus, Russia and Ukraine) will lead to 31 per cent fewer chances to participate if compared to citizens from the secular countries (Czech Republic, Estonia and Sweden). On the contrary, citizens of Protestant countries are typically 25 per cent more likely to participate than those from secular ones. Similarly, living in the predominantly Muslim-Orthodox and Catholic countries decreases chances to participate in politics, compared to living in secular countries.

Orthodox Christianity is associated with lower levels of political participation of both its followers (compared with the non-affiliated) and countries where it is a predominant religion. Additional tests are required in order to prove that it is religion that shapes political participation and not post-communist legacy or regime type that decrease overall participation rates in the Orthodox countries. To distinguish the effect of religion from the effect of regime and other country-level specifics, it may be helpful to compare Orthodox Christians from different countries: those where they form a majority and those where the Orthodox are only in a minority. If the Orthodox citizens in non-Orthodox countries are more active, then what we see is the effect of country specifics, while low levels of participation in all countries will speak for religious roots of the differences. Table 3.5 suggests that differences between Orthodox from these two categories are rather small and,

48 Anna Kulkova

Table 3.5 Average rates of political participation of the Orthodox living in predominantly Orthodox and non-Orthodox countries

The Orthodox are in majority?	PP index means
No	1.10
Yes	1.15

what is more important, the Orthodox from the non-Orthodox countries are even slightly less active. Statistical analysis results, presented in Table 3.10A, show that there is no statistical difference between these two categories of the Orthodox, if we take into account respondents' socio-demographic characteristics.

Finally, it is important to focus on the religious participation measures as predictors of political participation. Both attending religious services and praying are positively associated with political participation, but are the patterns similar among confessions? Theory predicts that more religious people will treat sexual minorities less positively because they are more conservative than their non-religious fellow-citizens (Olson et al. 2006). And this theory is supported by the data for all major confessions in Europe, except for the Orthodox (Kulkova 2015). Among the Orthodox, those who attend religious services once a month and more are statistically indistinguishable from non-attendees; unlike all other confessions, for them, homophobia is not connected with the degree of religiosity. On the contrary, differences in political participation between attendees and non-attendees, those who pray and those who don't, are rather similar among confessions and hold even for the Orthodox. This means that orthodoxy influences political participation in the same way as other religions, but it has something in its doctrine or community structure that doesn't promote political activism. Moreover, these findings prove that in today's world, the main cleavage lies not between confessions but between religious and non-religious individuals regardless of their religious tradition. While differences between confessions are unstable (differences do not hold for all countries, predominant religions and confessions), religious participation is a powerful and stable predictor of political participation that works for all confessions and for countries with different predominant religions. Table 3.12A suggests that in countries with all types of predominant religions, religious behaviour measures seem to affect political participation in a similar way: the rise in religiosity corresponds to the rise in political activism not only in Protestant and Catholic societies, but also in the Orthodox.

Discussion

Statistical analysis results suggest that in European countries, religiosity is linked to political participation. Generally, regular attendance of religious services and praying increase chances to participate in politics. This pattern holds for followers of all major European religious traditions and in countries with different predominant religions. On the other hand, inter-confessional differences in political participation appear weak and unstable: Protestants are slightly more active in politics, while Catholics are slightly less active in politics if compared to the non-religious, but in particular countries only. This means that the effect captured may not be a consequence of a religious doctrine but rather reflects some country-level specifics.

While almost all inter-confessional differences appear to be unstable, belonging to an Orthodox religious tradition and living in a predominantly Orthodox country both have a stable and negative effect on political participation. However, these results should be treated cautiously, as Orthodox Christianity enjoys predominant role mainly in post-communist countries. Thus, we can suggest an alternative hypothesis: it is not the Orthodox religious tradition that exerts negative influence on political participation, but the communist experience of political participation highly controlled by the state. Additional tests suggest a negative answer to this hypothesis: there is no difference in political participation between Orthodox Christians from predominantly Orthodox states and from those where they form only a minority. Consequently, it is something in a religious tradition itself that decreases political participation. The doctrine of "Ceasaro-Papism" that prescribes the integrationist approach towards the relations between church and state may be the first possible explanation of the trend. Orthodoxy and its clergy do not promote political activism because it is not a part of the religious tradition. On the other hand, as it was described in the theoretical section, members of religious communities with weaker ties are less likely to participate than those from cohesive communities. Orthodox religious communities are rather weak and unstable; there are no parishes with fixed membership. Thus, the second explanation may come from the social capital theory: weak interpersonal trust has no positive impact on political activism.

Despite achieving some interesting results, this paper has some methodological limitations, and the most crucial one is connected with the dependent variable. An additive index of political participation is a widely known measure that is used in several studies (Driskell et al. 2008; Guth et al. 2002), but it doesn't reflect the *degree of political activism*. It contains information on a *range* of political actions performed by the individual during 2012, but it doesn't define how many times each person attended a demonstration or signed petitions. Thus, the data is biased as we cannot differentiate between a person who once voted and a person who attended several demonstrations in a year. One possible solution to the dependent variable problem is to study its components (different types of political participation) separately. Unfortunately, it will lead us to the same problems: it would still be impossible to distinguish a regular attendee of demonstrations from one who performed it only once.

Nevertheless, the political participation index still can show whether a respondent's political life is diversified or if the respondent is conservative in terms of political participation. As religiosity proves to be connected with a range of political actions performed by the individual, it is important to mention that religiously active people tend to live a more diverse political life. Perhaps this happens because they are easier to mobilize by politicians when they are already mobilized by a religious community. Or, alternatively, perhaps involvement in a religious community promotes interpersonal trust and motivates attendees to take part in politics for the sake of the well-being of the community.

References

Alesina, A. and Giuliano, P., 2011. Preferences for redistribution, in: *Handbook of Social Economics*. Elsevier, pp. 93–131.
Arruñada, B., 2010. Protestants and Catholics: Similar work ethic, different social ethic. *The Economic Journal* 120, 890–918.
Beyerlein, K. and Chaves, M., 2003. The political activities of religious congregations in the United States. *Journal for the Scientific Study of Religion* 229–246.
Brady, H. E., Verba, S. and Schlozman, K. L., 1995. Beyond SES: A resource model of political participation. *American Political Science Review* 271–294.
Cho, W. K. T., Gimpel, J. G. and Wu, T., 2006. Clarifying the role of SES in political participation: Policy threat and Arab American mobilization. *Journal of Politics* 977–991.
Driskell, R., Embry, E. and Lyon, L., 2008. Faith and politics: The influence of religious beliefs on political participation. *Social Science Quarterly* (Wiley-Blackwell) 294–314. doi:10.1111/j.1540-6237.2008.00533.x.
Esmer, Y. and Pettersson, T., 2007. The effects of religion and religiosity on voting behavior, in: *The Oxford Handbook of Political Behavior*. Oxford University Press, New York, pp. 481–503.
Gershtenson, J., 2003. Mobilization strategies of the Democrats and Republicans, 1956–2000. *Political Research Quarterly* 293–308.
Grzymala-Busse, A., 2012. Why comparative politics should take religion (more) seriously. *Annual Review of Political Science* 15, 421–442.
Guth, J., Green, J. C., Kellstedt, L. A. and Smidt, C. E., 2002. Religion and political participation. Presented at the Annual Meeting of the American Political Science Association, American Political Science Association, pp. 1–31.
Harris, F. C., 1994. Something within: Religion as a mobilizer of African-American political activism. *The Journal of Politics* 56, 42–68.
Huntington, S. P., 1993. *The Third Wave: Democratization in the Late Twentieth Century*. University of Oklahoma Press.
Jones-Correa, M. A. and Leal, D. L., 2001. Political participation: Does religion matter? *Political Research Quarterly* 54, 751–770.
Knutsen, O., 2004. Religious denomination and party choice in Western Europe: A comparative longitudinal study from eight countries, 1970–97. *International Political Science Review* 25, 97–128.
Kulkova, A., 2015. The Interaction between religiosity and social conservatism: Russia and Europe. *Social Sciences and Modernity* 141–154.
Li, Y. and Marsh, D., 2008. New forms of political participation: Searching for expert citizens and everyday makers. *British Journal of Political Science* 247–272. doi:10.1017/S0007123408000136.
Macaluso, T. F. and Wanat, J., 1979. Voting turnout & religiosity. *Polity* 158–169.
McTague, J. M. and Layman, G. C., 2009. Religion, parties, and voting behavior: A political explanation of religious influence. In Guth, J., Lellstedt, L. A., and Smidt, C. E. *The Oxford Handbook of Religion and American Politics*. Oxford: Oxford University Press.
Norris, P. and Inglehart, R., 2011. *Sacred and Secular: Religion and Politics Worldwide*. Cambridge University Press, Cambridge.

Olson, L. R., Cadge, W. and Harrison, J. T., 2006. Religion and public opinion about same-sex marriage. *Social Science Quarterly* 87, 340–360.

Pepinsky, T. B. and Welborne, B. C., 2011. Piety and redistributive preferences in the Muslim world. *Political Research Quarterly* 491–505.

Philpott, D., 2007. Explaining the political ambivalence of religion. *American Political Science Review* 505–525.

Prutskova, E., 2012. The Concept of Religiosity: Operationalization in Empirical Research. *State, Religion and Church in Russia and Worldwide* 2(30), 268–293.

Putnam, R.D., 1995. Bowling alone: America's declining social capital. *Journal of Democracy* 65–78.

Roccas, S. and Schwartz, S. H., 1997. Church–state relations and the association of religiosity with values: A study of Catholics in six countries. *Cross-Cultural Research* 31, 356–375.

Van der Brug, W., Hobolt, S. B. and De Vreese, C. H., 2009. Religion and party choice in Europe. *West European Politics* 1266–1283.

Wald, K. D., Owen, D. E. and Hill, S. S., 1990. Political cohesion in churches. *The Journal of Politics* 197–215.

Wielhouwer, P. W., 2009. Religion and American political participation. *The Oxford Handbook of Religion and American Politics.* doi:10.1093/oxfordhb/9780195326529. 003.0014.

Appendices

Table 3.6A Predominant religions in European countries

Country	Predominant religion	Country	Predominant religion
Albania	Muslim	Kosovo	Muslim-Orthodox
Belgium	Catholic	Lithuania	Catholic
Bulgaria	Orthodox	Netherlands	Catholic-Protestant
Cyprus	Orthodox	Norway	Protestant
Czech Republic	Secular	Poland	Catholic
Denmark	Protestant	Portugal	Catholic
Estonia	Secular	Russia	Orthodox
Finland	Protestant	Slovak Republic	Catholic
France	Catholic	Slovenia	Catholic
Germany	Catholic-Protestant	Spain	Catholic
Hungary	Catholic-Protestant	Sweden	Secular
Iceland	Protestant	Switzerland	Catholic-Protestant
Ireland	Catholic	United Kingdom	Catholic-Protestant
Israel	Judaism	Ukraine	Orthodox
Italy	Catholic		

Notes: A country was considered to be secular if less than 25 per cent of all respondents were affiliated with some religious tradition(s). A country was considered to have two predominant religions if more than 15 per cent affiliated with the first religious tradition and more than 10 per cent with the second.

Table 3.7A Political participation rates among European countries in 2012 (ESS)

Country	PP index means	Country	PP index means
Lithuania	0.83	Ireland	1.59
Hungary	0.95	United Kingdom	1.6
Portugal	0.99	Holland	1.69
Bulgaria	1.02	Belgium	1.74
Slovenia	1.02	Italy	1.75
Russia	1.02	Swiss	1.88
Ukraine	1.03	France	1.91
Poland	1.11	East Germany	1.93
Estonia	1.14	Denmark	2.03
Kosovo	1.19	Spain	2.1
Slovakia	1.3	Finland	2.23
Cyprus	1.36	West Germany	2.33
Czech	1.37	Norway	2.5
Israel	1.47	Sweden	2.66
Albania	1.51	Iceland	3.21

Table 3.8A Political participation and religiosity: all countries

	(1)	(2)
Variables	Full model	Religious affiliation
Religious tradition s (compared to the non-affiliated)		
Catholic	**−0.058*****	0.004
	(0.014)	(0.013)
Protestant	0.011	**0.054*****
	(0.013)	(0.012)
Orthodox	**−0.133*****	**−0.085*****
	(0.022)	(0.021)
Jewish	**0.280*****	**0.319*****
	(0.057)	(0.057)
Muslim	**−0.070*****	−0.021
	(0.027)	(0.027)
Eastern religions	−0.002	0.048
	(0.074)	(0.073)
Attending religious services (compared to "Never")		
Less often than on holy days	0.017	
	(0.012)	
Only on special holy days	**0.081*****	
	(0.012)	
At least once a month	**0.119*****	

(countined)

Table 3.8A Continued

Variables	(1) Full model	(2) Religious affiliation
Once a week	(0.016) **0.160***	
More than once a week	(0.016) **0.172***	
Every day	(0.027) **0.207***	
	(0.045)	
SES	Yes	Yes
Country	Yes	Yes
Constant	−0.400***	−0.405***
	(0.031)	(0.031)
Observations	39,571	39,571

Notes: Robust standard errors in parentheses
***$p < 0.01$.

Table 3.9A Religiosity and political participation: controlling for country predominant religion

Variables	(6) Predominant religion
Religious traditions dummy	Yes
Attending religious services	Yes
Countries by predominant religion (compared to "Secular")	
Catholic	**−0.097***
	(0.017)
Protestant	**0.224***
	(0.017)
Catholic-Protestant	**−0.031**
	(0.016)
Orthodox	**−0.364***
	(0.020)
Muslim	0.046
	(0.032)
Orthodox-Muslim	**−0.188***
	(0.039)
SES	Yes
Constant	−0.345***
	(0.028)
Observations	39,571

Notes: Robust standard errors in parentheses
***$p < 0.01$, **$p < 0.05$.

Table 3.10A Religious services attendance and political participation among members of different religious traditions

	(1)	(2)	(3)	(4)	(5)	(6)
Variables	Non-affiliated	Catholic	Protestant	Orthodox	Jewish	Muslim
Attending religious services (compared to "Never")						
Less often than on holy days	0.021	0.012	0.027	**0.133****	**0.216****	0.017
	(0.016)	(0.030)	(0.027)	(0.065)	(0.074)	(0.058)
Only on special holy days	**0.080****	**0.078****	**0.106****	**0.231****	**0.135****	0.074
	(0.019)	(0.029)	(0.027)	(0.060)	(0.059)	(0.053)
At least once a month	0.011	**0.171****	**0.189****	**0.232****	0.032	0.095
	(0.050)	(0.030)	(0.033)	(0.064)	(0.091)	(0.091)
Once a week	0.013	**0.216****	**0.255****	**0.257****	0.012	0.043
	(0.080)	(0.030)	(0.036)	(0.070)	(0.070)	(0.075)
More than once a week	**−0.438****	**0.331****	**0.292****	**0.181***	−0.041	**0.277****
	(0.163)	(0.045)	(0.051)	(0.103)	(0.108)	(0.090)
Every day	**−0.418***	**0.438****	0.294	0.141	−0.048	**0.244****
	(0.229)	(0.082)	(0.187)	(0.136)	(0.085)	(0.085)
SES	Yes	Yes	Yes	Yes	Yes	Yes
Country	Yes	Yes	Yes	Yes	Yes	Yes
Constant	−0.505***	−0.312***	−0.086	−0.535***	−0.055	−0.449***
	(0.061)	(0.107)	(0.193)	(0.129)	(0.550)	(0.128)
Observations	15,330	10,317	5,165	4,643	1,251	2,159

Notes: Robust standard errors in parentheses
***p < 0.01, **p < 0.05, *p < 0.1.

Table 3.11A Praying frequency and political participation among members of different religious traditions

	(1)	(2)	(3)	(4)	(5)	(6)
Variables	Non-affiliated	Catholic	Protestant	Orthodox	Jewish	Muslim
Praying frequency (compared to "Never")						
Less often than on holy days	0.015	0.034	**0.051****	**0.110****	**0.252****	0.055
	(0.018)	(0.030)	(0.025)	(0.056)	(0.098)	(0.074)
Only on special holy days	0.012	0.050	0.030	**0.135****	−0.020	0.087
	(0.039)	(0.042)	(0.053)	(0.056)	(0.065)	(0.071)

(countined)

Table 3.11A Continued

Variables	(1) Non-affiliated	(2) Catholic	(3) Protestant	(4) Orthodox	(5) Jewish	(6) Muslim
At least once a month	0.125***	0.090**	0.144***	0.163***	0.053	0.101
	(0.037)	(0.036)	(0.037)	(0.062)	(0.121)	(0.102)
Once a week	0.068	0.118***	0.119***	0.251***	0.015	0.058
	(0.043)	(0.035)	(0.040)	(0.063)	(0.069)	(0.088)
More than once a week	0.065	0.159***	0.132***	0.222***	−0.163	0.122
	(0.041)	(0.0320)	(0.035)	(0.061)	(0.102)	(0.075)
Every day	0.079**	0.194***	0.146***	0.202***	−0.043	0.173***
	(0.031)	(0.029)	(0.027)	(0.054)	(0.060)	(0.056)
SES	Yes	Yes	Yes	Yes	Yes	Yes
Country	Yes	Yes	Yes	Yes	Yes	Yes
Constant	−0.510***	−0.329***	0.060	−0.508***	0.021	−0.479***
	(0.061)	(0.108)	(0.047)	(0.123)	(0.494)	(0.127)
Observations	15,330	10,317	5,165	4,643	1,251	2,159

Notes: Robust standard errors in parentheses
***p < 0.01, **p < 0.05, *p < 0.1.

Table 3.12A Religiosity and political participation among countries with different predominant religions

Variables	(1) Catholic	(2) Protestant	(3) Catholic-Protestant	(4) Orthodox
Religious traditions (compared to the non-affiliated)				
Catholic	−0.079***	−0.249	−0.013	0.142*
	(0.021)	(0.177)	(0.026)	(0.073)
Protestant	−0.048	−0.031	0.040*	0.373***
	(0.064)	(0.019)	(0.024)	(0.111)
Orthodox	−0.473***	−0.242	−0.192	0.021
	(0.097)	(0.215)	(0.144)	(0.034)
Jewish	−0.328*	−0.534**	−0.300	0.773
	(0.185)	(0.214)	(0.250)	(0.669)
Muslim	−0.386***	−0.213	−0.209**	0.090
	(0.075)	(0.158)	(0.099)	(0.061)
Eastern religions	−0.164	0.073	−0.007	0.143
	(0.187)	(0.159)	(0.107)	(0.308)
Attending religious services (compared to "Never")				
Less often than on holy days	−0.057**	0.004	0.047*	0.090**
	(0.025)	(0.022)	(0.025)	(0.043)

Table 3.12A Continued

Variables	(1) Catholic	(2) Protestant	(3) Catholic-Protestant	(4) Orthodox
Only on special holy days	−0.009	**0.094***	**0.091***	**0.193***
	(0.025)	(0.025)	(0.027)	(0.040)
At least once a month	**0.076***	**0.163***	**0.132***	**0.206***
	(0.029)	(0.037)	(0.033)	(0.048)
Once a week	**0.127***	**0.301***	**0.173***	**0.190***
	(0.028)	(0.047)	(0.036)	(0.055)
More than once a week	**0.230***	**0.199***	**0.145**	**0.145***
	(0.045)	(0.076)	(0.059)	(0.082)
Every day	**0.242***	**0.795***	**0.402**	0.135
	(0.085)	(0.256)	(0.175)	(0.118)
SES	Yes	Yes	Yes	Yes
Country	Yes	Yes	Yes	Yes
Constant	−0.570***	0.228***	−0.651***	−1.107***
	(0.052)	(0.053)	(0.054)	(0.083)
Observations	12,762	5,155	7,797	6,020

Notes: Robust standard errors in parentheses
***p < 0.01, **p < 0.05, *p < 0.1.

4 Religion and Values in the ESS
Individual and Societal Effects

Caillin Reynolds

Theoretical overview

That religion and values are fundamentally related and interdependent is an intuitively appealing idea. On one hand, religiosity can be conceived of as being one aspect of a whole system of values, mutually compatible with values that emphasize tradition and conformity and conflictual with an emphasis on self-indulgence and change. On the other, religion can be conceived of as a source of values, borne of personal reflection on beliefs about this world and the next, through adherence to the prescriptions and proscriptions of religious officials or through participation in a religious and moral community. Theorizing this linkage was at the forefront of the originative works of sociology and continues to be the subject of theoretical and empirical enquiry today.

The core thesis of this approach is that religion is a particularly important institution in determining and influencing values. By definition, the sociological concept of an institution is one that entails collective ways of doing things, informed by certain values, that confronts the individual as an objective reality (Berger and Berger, 1972). Consider the example of institution of the family and the differences in the values that inform the rights and responsibilities of its members in traditional and more modern societies. In more traditional societies, there is an emphasis on patriarchy, and the father has absolute rights over his spouse and children. In more modern societies, the family institution is informed by conceptions of equality and characterized by all spouses and children having certain fundamental rights.

One can therefore conceive of institutions as an objective embodiment of how to act, informed by certain values. Religion, the family and educational institutions are all theorised to be fundamental in socializing individuals in these values, where they become internalized in the individual. Consider how being part of a religious community would be key in socializing the members of its congregation, or the role of parents and teachers in socializing children in how to act and behave. As an assemblage of interlinked institutions, one would also expect that being members of the same society would produce a similar set of internalized values in individual members.

Religion, however, is theorised to occupy a distinctly important position in this system, in that it informs and legitimates values in other institutional spheres. Religion fulfils this function in societies where it occupies a dominant position. In some functionalist theories, religion occupies this role regardless of whether or not what one would intuitively recognise as religion is performing this function. Here theories of civil religion emerge to fill the gap left by the decline of traditional religions (Bellah 1970, pp. 168–186). In theories that adopt a more substantive definition of religion, religion ceases to fulfil this function in secularised societies (Dobbelaere, 2002).

The concept of a secularised *society* used here is an important one to demarcate. A secularised society is one in which the religious institutional sphere no longer exercises authority over the other institutional spheres of society. This means that other institutional spheres no longer look to the religious one for the legitimation described above. For example, educational institutions no longer necessarily need to legitimate the values they impart by reference to some religious precept or the directive of religious organizations. Rather, each institutional sphere either becomes independent or falls under the influence of other institutional spheres, such as the economic sphere. Educational institutions might, for example, shift their ethos from a religious one to one that concentrates on preparing individuals to be valuable entrants in the workforce. Importantly, this definition of a secular society does not exclude the possibility of its occupants being members of religious communities or holding strong religious beliefs. Nor does it exclude the possibility of religion still maintaining its influence over some institutional spheres.

Having briefly outlined the mechanism through which religion and values are interrelated, it is necessary to flesh out the concept of values itself. There is considerable theoretical and methodological dissonance in the theory and measurement of values, so the approach here will be to outline very generally the concept of values and then move to the specific theorisation and operationalisation in the European Social Survey (ESS).

Values are conceptions of social action that denote certain actions as desirable or good and certain actions as undesirable or bad. One can distinguish three relatively distinct types of values according to their level of generality, according to a schema developed by Haller (2002). At the most abstract and general, there are universal values that are present in every human civilisation – values such as justice, freedom or equality, that only differ across human societies in the relative emphasis that is placed on them. Secondly, there are more concrete values – what are referred to as societal value orientations – and these are more concrete applications by groups and societies of the more universal values described above. Examples here would be values such as gender equality or freedom of religion. Lastly, there are situational values, which entail concrete applications of values in specific social circumstances. The application of values of gender equality in relation to the family, or freedom of religion in relation to education, are some examples here. From here, there is a sliding transition to attitudes and behaviours, which are less general and more object specific. An example would be having a positive attitude towards same-sex marriage, informed by one's values on gender equality in the family and derived from a more general conception of the universal values of equality and freedom.

As guiding conceptions or images of what is desirable and undesirable, values are not directly observable. Only by examining a pattern among attitudes and behaviours can one discern the underlying values that guide these multiple actions and attitudes (Lesthaeghe and Moors, 2002). For example, one's attitude towards pre-marital sex, same-sex marriage or the necessity of having children are all relatively specific attitudes. But they can also be seen as expressing traditional/conservative or more modern/liberal family values.

The theoretical approach to values taken by the ESS follows the approach to values taken by Shalom Schwartz, and is one that is interested in basic values – ones that guide individuals in all domains of life. This contrasts with other approaches to values, like the approach taken in the European and World Values Surveys (Hagenaars et al. 2003). The concern of these studies are more domain specific values – those that are concretely related to politics, work, the family or religion, for example. With basic values, they are thought to guide attitudes and behaviour across all different domains of life. In a simple example, one would expect that one's attitude towards adopting new technologies in the workplace and one's attitudes towards same-sex marriage would both be influenced by the relative importance one attributes to values of conservatism versus openness to change. The contrary conception of values is that values are relatively domain specific – where one's work values and one's family values are relatively independent of each other.

Schwartz (1987) distinguishes 10 motivationally distinct basic human values, which are further theorised to form an integrated structure: attitudes and action are guided by the conflict and compatibilities between these values. So, as an example, negative attitudes towards divorce might be a reflection of tradition and

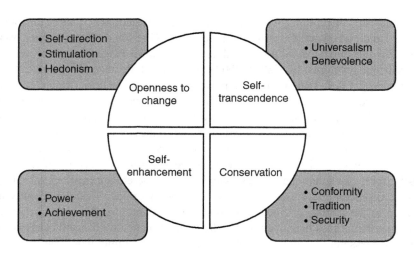

Figure 4.1 The integrated structure of values.

conformity values, but this might come at the expense of the values of hedonism and self-direction. The 10 distinct basic values are outlined in Figure 4.1. It shows how the conflicts and compatibilities between the 10 basic values also form two theoretically orthogonal dimensions – self direction versus self-transcendence, and conservation versus openness to change.

One of the more intriguing applications of Schwartz's theory is that these values can be mapped onto individuals or groups, visualising a profile of their integrated structure of values. Figure 4.2 (A) presents the value profile a single respondent picked out of the ESS dataset, a 77-year-old retired Norwegian man, who particularly emphasizes conformity and security, with very low levels of hedonism and stimulation. Comparing the Norwegian retiree with the value profile of a 19-year-old female Dutch student (B), the contrasts are quite clear (Figure 4.3). She measures very low on values of tradition and conformity and has much higher scores on hedonism. Both respondents, however, have similar scores on benevolence and achievement. Mapping the higher order dimensions on the two example individuals shows that they differ most on the openness conservation dimension and differ only slightly on the self-transcendence dimension (Figure 4.3).

Hypotheses

Having briefly outlined some of the relationships between religion and values, this section will deal with the linkages in more detail. Firstly, there are the individual level relationships between religion and values. Belonging to a religious denomination, participating in religious services and holding certain religious beliefs are all individual level religious variables. The focus here will be on the latter two variables, those that denote membership and participation in a religious community/organization/group. Religious beliefs are, however, an important source from which religion draws and legitimates values. Schwartz and Huismans (1995), for example, identify a number of resonances between certain values and theological beliefs, particularly submission to a higher authority and the denial of self-indulgence. It is assumed that integration into a religious community will

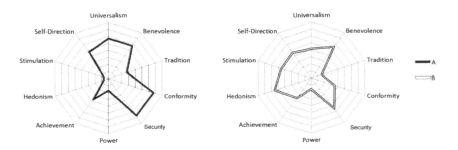

Figure 4.2 Value profile of individuals.

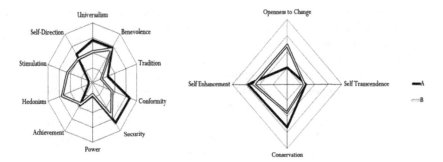

Figure 4.3 Value profiles compared.

entail a certain level of acceptance of these beliefs. Furthermore, Schwartz and Huismans (1995) also identify the social aspect of involvement in religious communities having an influence on their values. The social aspect of religiosity generally entails support for the prevailing social order and, with some exceptions, generally discourages innovation and dissent.

The focus in terms of individual values will therefore be on the dimension of openness to change versus that of conservation. It is hypothesised that individuals who are more religious will be more inclined to favour values on the conservation dimension, and less likely to favour values on the openness dimension. It is also expected that the relationship could operate in the opposite direction – where one's values influence whether one is religious or not. While it is expected that this mechanism would work both ways, the analysis will work on the assumption that one's religiousness influences one's values. It is hypothesised that individuals who are more religious (on each of these items) are more inclined to hold conservative values – conformity, security, tradition (conservation) – and less likely to hold other values such as hedonism and stimulation (openness to change). The mechanism of this linkage is one where religious belonging and participation are measures of how integrated and active an individual is within a particular religious community.

It is, however, very likely that both these religious variables and values are influenced by other socio-demographic variables, such as age or level of education. In order to establish the relevance of these differences in values between individuals with varying levels of religiosity, it is necessary to introduce controls to test whether these relationships hold net of the effects of these socio-demographic variables.

The preceding section delineated how it is expected that individual levels of religiosity and other sociodemographic variables have an effect on values. This approach, however, ignores the fact that these individuals are nested within particular groups, most importantly here, in specific societies or countries. Individuals within these societies share certain social experiences and history and interact with the same societal institutions. It is therefore probable that in addition to individual level differences in religiosity and other socio-demographic variables affecting differences in values (or within group effects), there will also be a societal effect, whereby the society to which one belongs will also contribute to differences in values (between group effects). For example, if one were trying to predict the value profile of two individuals, knowing their religious denomination, whether they attend religious services regularly, their age, gender and level of education, one could build a relatively good predictive model based on these individual level variables. It would be more appropriate, however, if one were to take account of whether the individuals in question live in Spain or Russia, Switzerland or Greece. Whether in fact it is necessary to take account of these between-group differences, and to what extent they matter, is something that can be tested and measured.

Having proposed that the society to which an individual belongs has a significant effect on one's values, it is further hypothesised that the characteristics of a society, specifically the religious characteristics of a society, will have an effect on one's values. There are numerous pertinent variables that could be used to distinguish societies in terms of its religious character – particularly aggregate levels of religious belief and participation or the degree to church-stage separation – but the analysis here will focus on a relatively simple parameter of the majority religious denomination of a country. It is hypothesised that this denominational make-up of a country will account for a large degree of the variance between countries in their effect on values.

Finally, it is hypothesised that in societies where a religious denomination is in the majority (over two-thirds) this will provide a supportive and insulating effect for its members, increasing the effect that individual religiosity has on values. The logic of this is that with more similarly religious peers and less outside influence, the effect of religiosity on values will be stronger.

Data and variables

The analysis uses the data from the sixth wave of the ESS (2014) and is weighted by the post-stratification weight, including design weight. Trends in denominational affiliation and religious attendance are taken from the cumulative ESS data file from wave one to six, and weighted by the post-stratification weight including design weight.

To measure values, the ESS uses the Portrait Value Questionnaire (PVQ) developed by Shalom Schwartz (2003) from his own work on the Schwartz Value Survey (SVS) (Schwartz and Bilsky 1987; Schwartz 1992; Schwartz 2007). Respondents are given a description of a person and are asked how much the person in the description is like themselves. So, in an example of the measurement of an aspect of the stimulation value, respondents are asked to rate on a scale of one to six if the person described thus, "He likes surprises and is always looking for new things to do. He thinks it is important to do lots of different things in life," is "very much like me" or "not like me at all." The conservation dimension is made up of values concerning conformity, security and tradition. The openness-to-change dimension is made up of values concerning self-direction, stimulation and hedonism.[1] Scores on each of the values are mean centred to correct for response tendencies in selections on each scale. This involves subtracting the mean score for all the items from each individual score on a certain value. This allows for the relative importance of each of the basic values to be measured.

Denominational belonging is measured according to two variables in the ESS – whether one belongs to a religious denomination at or not, and to which denomination one belongs at present. Catholic, Protestant, Eastern Orthodox and no denomination were chosen as four categories, with the remaining respondents coded as "other."

Attendance at religious services is measured according to the question of how often one attends religious services apart from special occasions and was recoded into three categories of attending monthly or more regularly, attending less than monthly and never attending.

Highest level of education is recoded into three categories of primary or lower secondary education, upper secondary education and post-secondary or tertiary education. Income is measured in three categories: low, medium and high income. And marital status is recoded into a dichotomous variable of never married and ever married (includes divorced, widowed, separated).

Multi-level analyses are carried out using the software *MLwiN*, with particular guidance from the excellent learning resources from the University of Bristol's *LEMMA* (Steele 2008) and the practical applications of multi-level analysis on ESS data from the *ESS EduNet* (Ringdal 2013).

An overview of religion and values in Europe

Before moving to testing the hypothesised relationships, a brief overview of the variation in religious variables and values across Europe is presented. Figure 4.4 presents the proportion of individuals within each country belonging to a religious denomination. In about a third of the countries surveyed, the majority belong to no religious denomination. At this end of the scale are countries like Estonia and the Czech Republic, where over two-thirds of the population do not belong to a denomination. At the other end of the scale are majority Catholic and Orthodox countries, with a mix of countries from both western (Portugal, Ireland, Italy) and eastern Europe (Poland, Lithuania, Bulgaria, Slovakia). In terms of change in a selection of countries over the six waves of the ESS, the pattern is one of slight declines in most countries but relative stability overall (Figure 4.5). Turning to trends in religious attendance across Europe, there is a similar but less pronounced pattern. Only in four of the countries surveyed (France, Belgium, Netherlands, the Czech Republic) does non-attendance outstrip attendance as the majority behaviour (Figure 4.6). Only in Poland and Ireland, however, does attending monthly or more exceed 50 per cent of the population. In some countries, there is a relatively even mix between regular and irregular attendance (e.g. Slovakia, Italy, Portugal) but the most common pattern is one where irregular attendance represents the majority behaviour. In terms of trends in regular attendance over the six waves,

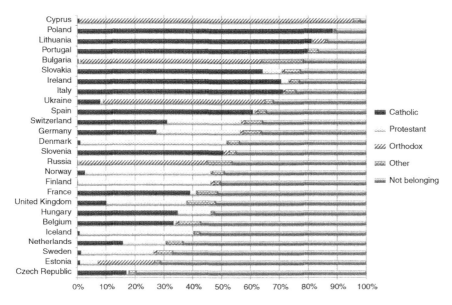

Figure 4.4 Denominations in ESS 6.

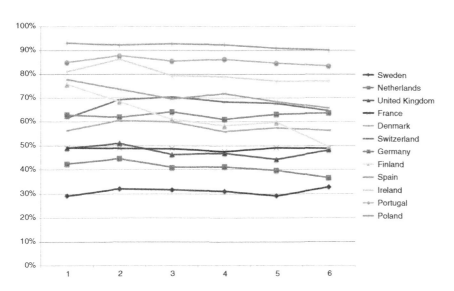

Figure 4.5 Denominational belonging ESS 1-6.

66 Caillin Reynolds

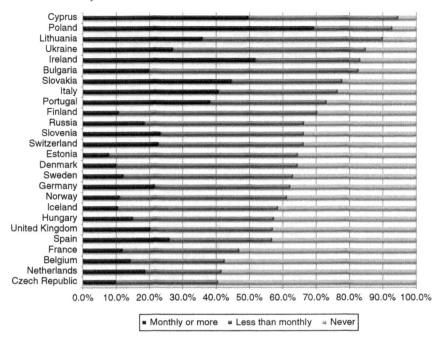

Figure 4.6 Religious attendance ESS 6.

the pattern is one of relative stability in most countries but of steeper decline in those countries that are characterised by having a larger proportions of regular attendance (Figure 4.7). Overall, the indicators depict a Europe where irregular attendance has become, or is becoming, the norm.

Analysis: Individual level

To test the individual level relationships, a linear regression was conducted of conservation as the dependent variable, and denomination and frequency of attendance as the main explanatory variables (Table 1). The initial model, with just religious explanatory variables, confirms that being Catholic, Protestant and other has a strong significant positive effect on conservation values. Being an Eastern Orthodox Christian, however, does not have a significant effect on conservation. Each of these effects treats no denomination as the reference category, meaning that, in comparison to having no religious denomination, being Catholic, Protestant or other makes one significantly different in terms of conservation values to someone who does not belong to a religious denomination.

Attendance is added as a second explanatory variable in the second model. Monthly or more regular attendance has a significant positive effect, as does attending less than monthly, but with a much smaller coefficient. For this variable,

Religion and Values in the ESS 67

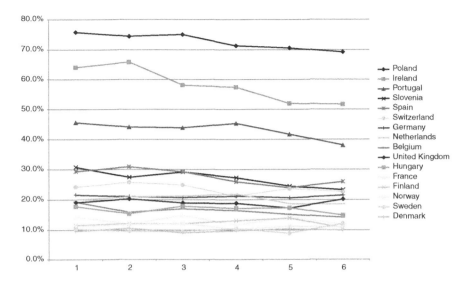

Figure 4.7 Religious attendance ESS 1-6.

never attending is used as the reference category, meaning that those who attend regularly and less regularly are significantly different in terms of conservation values to someone who never attends, with the effect of denomination held constant. It also indicates that, in comparison to never attending, regularly attending has a much larger effect than attending irregularly.

The r-square for these models with just the religious variables is, however, quite low at 0.076. This means that although the coefficients are large and significant, using only these two variables predicts only 7.6 per cent of a variation in conservation values. Adding socio-demographic variables in models three to six increases the r-square, particularly when age is added in Model 4. Also, when age is added, the coefficients for the religious variables decrease, particularly in relation to the effect of being Protestant. It suggests that a substantial amount of the effect of the religious variables is related to religious people generally being older, and less religious people younger. In contrast to being Protestant, Catholic or other, and attendance, retain their significant strong positive effects.

With the regression for openness to change, there is a fairly equivalent pattern of relationships as with conservation values (Table 4.2). As the two value dimensions are theoretically orthogonal dimensions, similar sized coefficients but in the opposite direction were expected. Essentially, religiosity and the other socio-demographic variables have a negative effect on openness values that is approximately equivalent in strength to the positive effect they have on conservation values. Being Orthodox now has a small but significant effect across the models, and the r-squared value is slightly lower, but overall it mirrors the conservation regression.

Table 4.1 Linear regression of conservation values

Dependent: Conservation	Model 1 β	Model 2 β	Model 3 β	Model 4 β	Model 5 β	Model 6 β
(Constant)	−.060	−.092	−.231	−.146	−.190	−.294
Catholic	.366**	.279**	.259**	.173**	.168**	.170**
Protestant	.211**	.163**	.170**	.027*	.020	.023*
Other	.320**	.237**	.217**	.241**	.240**	.228**
Orthodox (*Ref. No denom.*)	.007	.015*	.029	−.002	−.005	−.001
Monthly or more attend		.205**	.209**	.177**	.166**	.162**
Less than monthly attend (*Ref. Never attend*)		.051**	.065**	.073**	.067**	.066**
Primary education			.273**	.211**	.208**	.206**
Secondary education (*Ref. Tertiary*)			.141**	.146**	.150**	.144**
Age				.012**	.012**	.010**
Female					.103**	.096**
Low income						.072**
Medium income (*Ref. High income*)						.039**
Ever married (*Ref. Never married*)						.114**
R-square	.065	.076	.105	.234	.240	.246

Notes: **p < 0.05, *p < 0.1.

Table 4.2 Linear regression of openness-to-change values

Dependent: Openness to change	Model 1 β	Model 2 β	Model 3 β	Model 4 β	Model 5 β	Model 6 β
(Constant)	−.024	.002	.080	.003	.047	.158
Catholic	−.353**	−.278**	−.265**	−.188**	−.183**	−.183**
Protestant	−.169**	−.129**	−.133**	−.004	.004	.001
Other	−.345**	−.271**	−.258**	−.279**	−.279**	−.266**
Orthodox	−.027**	−.035**	−.044**	−.016**	−.013*	−.015*
Monthly or more attend		−.181**	−.183**	−.154**	−.142**	−.136**
Less than monthly attend		−.036**	−.045**	−.052**	−.047**	−.044**
Primary education			−.170**	−.114**	−.111**	−.121**
Secondary education			−.064**	−.069**	−.073**	−.073**
Age				−.011**	−.011**	−.009**
Female					−.102**	−.097**
Low household income						−.035**
Medium household income						−.018*
Ever married						−.141**
R-square	.065	.073	.085	.188	.194	.201

Notes: **p < 0.05, *p < 0.1.

Analysis: Multi-level

To examine the amount of variance in conservation and openness that is at the individual level and how much is at the country level, it is necessary to fit a variance components model and to calculate the variance component coefficient (ρ).

There are no explanatory variables in this model – just the dependent and the amount of variance that occurs at the group level (between countries) and at the individual level (within countries). Around seven percent of the variance in the conservation value is at the country level ($\rho = 0.0701$), and around nine percent for the openness value variance is at the country level ($\rho = 0.09002$). That is, 7 percent of the variance in conservation values is due to differences between countries, and 9 percent of the variance in openness values is due to difference between countries. A likelihood ratio test is carried out to test the significance of these effects. Very basically, this tests whether it is worth taking into account country effects or whether an individual-level model would be more appropriate.

To do this, the model takes into account the data having two levels and compares it with a model that treats the data as being only at the individual level – comparing the null multi-level model with the null single-level model to see if they are significantly different from each other. The test statistic proves highly significant for both value dimensions[2] – demonstrating that country effects are significant and signifying that a multi-level model that takes into account these country effects is needed.

Examining the ranked country level residuals of the model demonstrates how the country level affects the dependent values (Figure 4.8). Countries such as Slovakia, Bulgaria and Poland have the largest positive country effect on conservation, and countries such as Iceland, Denmark and Sweden have the largest negative effect on conservation. Countries like Ireland and Britain appear to have little effect.

With the ranked residuals of the openness model (Figure 4.9), there is a fairly similar reflection of this pattern, but with countries such as Bulgaria, Slovakia and Poland having a negative effect this time and countries like Iceland and Denmark having the largest positive country effect on openness. The same countries, roughly, occupy the middle of the scale, having little or no effect on openness.

For the multi-level analysis, first explanatory variables at the individual level are added, and again the amount of variance that remained at the country level is estimated (Table 4.3). As might be expected, the addition of individual level explanatory variables reduced the variance at the country level by a half per cent. It was hypothesized, however, that the effect of religiosity – measured by denomination and attendance – on values would vary from country to country. To test this, another likelihood ratio test is conducted between the model that treats denomination and attendance as fixed, and one that allows them to vary by country. In other words, the likelihood ratio test compares the model with denomination and attendance having the same effect in all countries and the model with attendance having a differential effect in different countries. In relation to denomination[3] and attendance,[4] there is strong evidence that their effects differ across countries.

To restate the hypotheses for the multi-level model, the majority denomination in a country will account for a significant amount of the country variance in values. And the effect of belonging to a denomination and attending religious services regularly will be stronger in countries that have a majority denomination as opposed to mixed denominational countries.

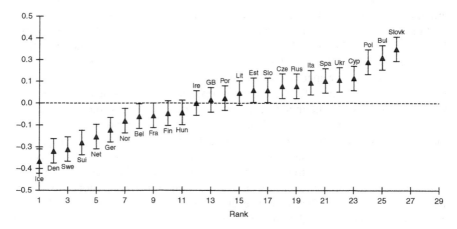

Figure 4.8 Ranked country level residuals (u_0j) of conservation values.

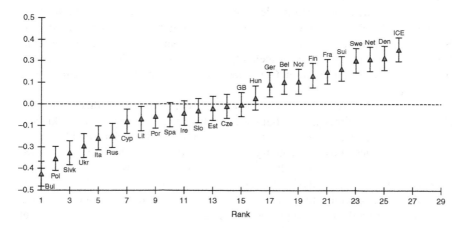

Figure 4.9 Ranked country level residuals (u_0j) of openness values.

First a model was fitted that included just the individual level variables from the earlier regression (the religious variables) as well the significant demographic variables. Now that the model is accounting for the variance at the country level, the coefficients are slightly smaller but still significant. Approximately 6.5 per cent of the variance is at the country level. The first hypothesis is that the majority denomination of a country will account for a large amount of the variance at the country level. When this variable is added to the model and the variance partition coefficient is calculated, the country-level variance is reduced from 6.5 per cent to 2.6 per cent. So, a large amount of the difference between countries on conservation is captured by the majority denomination of a country. The coefficient for being a Protestant majority country, however, is insignificant,

Table 4.3 Multi-level model of conservation values

Dependent: Conservation values	Base Model	Model with country level	Cross-level Interaction Model
Constant	−.265	−.402	−.393
Belong to a denomination	.137**	.137**	.131**
Attend monthly or More	.137**	.137**	.138**
Attend less than monthly	.053**	.053**	.02
(All demographic vars. included not shown)			
Catholic majority		.203**	.173**
Protestant majority		−.006	−.005
Orthodox majority		.260**	.307**
(Ref. Mixed)			
Belong* Catholic majority			.042*
Belong* Protestant majority			−.01
Belong* Orthodox majority			−.02
Attend monthly* Catholic majority			−.01
Attend monthly* Protestant majority			.087*
Attend monthly* Orthodox majority			−.073**
Variance at country level	6.5%	2.60%	2.60%

Notes: **p < 0.05, *p < 0.1.

possibly indicating that a majority denomination only matters if the majority is either Catholic or Orthodox.

The second hypothesis is that the individual effect of denomination and attendance on conservation will vary according to whether a denomination is in the majority, as opposed to being a mixed country. To do this, cross-level interactions between each society type and each individual religious variable are calculated. The results turn out to be mixed. Belonging to a denomination in a Catholic country appears to have a significant positive effect on conservation. Regularly attending in an Orthodox country, however, appears to have a negative effect. Generally, the coefficients for each interaction are insignificant, so the overall hypothesis cannot be confirmed.

The results for the openness model are broadly the same (Table 4.4). In terms of the majority denomination accounting for a large amount of the variance at the country level, the results are again positive, with variance at the country level reduced from 8.5 per cent to 3.8 per cent with the addition of a majority denomination. Again it appears that majority denomination is only significant in relation to Catholic and Orthodox countries.

In relation to cross-level interactions, belonging to a denomination in Catholic and Orthodox countries has a significant negative effect on openness, as does attending regularly in Orthodox countries. Overall, the hypothesis cannot be confirmed, but the significant cross-level interactions for Orthodox and Catholic

Table 4.4 Multi-level model of openness-to-change values

Dependent: Openness-to-change values	Base Model with level 1 variables	Model with country level	Cross-Level Interaction Model
Constant	−.127	−.127	−.125
Belong to a denomination	−.121**	−.121**	−.078**
Attend monthly or More	−.085**	−.086**	−.078**
Attend less than monthly	−.018**	−.018*	−.013
(All demographic vars. included not shown)			
Catholic majority		−.189**	−.140*
Protestant majority		.02	.069
Orthodox majority		−.319**	−.329**
Belong* Catholic majority			−.071**
Belong* Protestant majority			−.0001
Belong* Orthodox majority			−.084**
Attend monthly* Catholic majority			−.021
Attend monthly* Protestant majority			−.091**
Attend monthly* Orthodox majority			−.085**
Variance at country level	8.50%	3.80%	3.80%

Notes: **p < 0.05, *p < 0.1.

belonging suggest that more complex cross-level interactions might prove worthwhile.

Conclusion

The analysis produced several key findings. First, that being integrated and active in a religious group has a significant effect on one's values, and this relationship holds net of differences caused by socio-demographic variables; second, that age is the strongest socio-demographic predictor of one's values, but the effects of religiosity still hold when it is controlled for; and third, that the society to which an individual belongs has a significant effect on differences in values, net of differences between individuals within societies.

The proposal that it is the religious make-up of a society that accounts for these differences between societies was not firmly demonstrated. There is some evidence to suggest that the denominational make-up of a society has some influence on the effect that societies have on values. Introducing controls for other societal-level characteristics, such as levels of socio-economic development, might prove a productive means of testing this hypothesis further. Using different societal level religious characteristics as variables, such as church–state relations or aggregate levels of religiosity, might also prove very worthwhile.

With regard to the changing place of religion in shaping the values of members of society, this study has provided evidence that belonging to and participating in religious groups and communities continues to be an important predictor of one's values throughout Europe. This relationship appears to be quite strong, particularly for those who attend regularly. Attending irregularly also had a significant effect on values, but this is a rather weak relationship. The effect of irregular attendance on values is only slightly different from never attending. With the overall trends depicting a Europe where irregular attendance has become, or is becoming, the norm, this weak relationship may also become the defining relationship between individual religiosity and values.

Whether the place of religion as an influential and legitimating force over the other institutions of society is changing is a question that requires further research. Analyses of all six waves of the ESS, as well as other repeated cross-national surveys of values such as the EVS, would be an ideal resource to begin investigating such questions empirically.

Notes

1 For a more detailed description of the construction of these values measures and their summary into the higher order orthogonal dimensions, see Schwartz (2003).
2 Conservation likelihood ratio: 94393–91388 = 3005 with 1d.f. ($p < .0001$); Openness-to-change likelihood ratio: 95921–91636 = 4285 with 1 d.f. ($p < .0001$).
3 Conservation likelihood ratio: 88511–88340 with 3df = 171 ($p < .001$); Openness-to-change likelihood ratio: 89429–89221 with 3df = 208 ($p < .001$).
4 Conservation likelihood ratio: 88603–86563 with 1df = 2040 ($p < .001$). Openness-to-change likelihood ratio: 87736–87684 with 1df = 52 ($p < .001$).

References

Bellah, R. N. (1970) *Beyond Belief: Essays on Religion in a Post-Traditional World*, Berkeley: University of California Press.

Berger, P. L. and Berger, B. (1972) *Sociology: A Biographical Approach*, New York: Basic Books.

Dobbelaere, K. (2002) *Secularization: An Analysis at Three Levels*, Brussels: Peter-Lang.

European-Social-Survey (2014) *ESS1-6, European Social Survey Cumulative File Rounds 1-6*, Bergen: Norwegian Social Science Data Services.

Hagenaars, J. A., Halman, L. and Moors, G. (2003) Exploring Europe's basic values map. In Arts, W., Hagenaars, J. A. and Halman, L., eds., *The Cultural Diversity of European Unity: Findings, Explanations and Reflections from the European Values Study*, Leiden: Brill, 23–58.

Haller, M. (2002) Theory and method in the comparative study of values: Critique and alternative to Inglehart. *European Sociological Review*, 18(2), 139–158.

Lesthaeghe, R. and Moors, G. (2002) Life course transitions and value orientations: Selection and adaptation. In Lesthaeghe, R., ed. *Meaning and Choice: Value Orientations and Life Course Decisions*, Brussels: NIDI/CBGS Publications, 1–44.

Ringdal, K. (2013) *Learning Multilevel Analysis*. ESS EduNet, Norwegian Social Science Data Services.

Schwartz, S. H. (1992) Universals in the content and structure of values: Theoretical advances and empirical tests in 20 countries. *Advances in Experimental Social Psychology*, 25(1), 1–65.

Schwartz, S. H. (2003) A proposal for measuring values orientations across nations. *Questionnaire Development Report of the European Social Survey*, Chapter 7, pp. 259–319.

Schwartz, S. H. (2007) A theory of cultural value orientations: Explication and applications. In Esmer, Y. and Pettersson, T., eds., *Measuring and Mapping Cultures: 25 Years of Values Surveys*, Leiden; Boston: Brill, 33–78.

Schwartz, S. H. and Bilsky, W. (1987) Toward a universal psychological structure of human values. *Journal of Personality and Social Psychology*, 53(3), 550–562.

Schwartz, S. H. and Huismans, S. (1995) Value priorities and religiosity in four Western religions. *Social Psychology Quarterly*, 58(2), 88–107.

Steele, F. (2008) *Module 5: Introduction to Multilevel Modelling Concepts*, LEMMA VLE, University of Bristol, Centre for Multilevel Modelling [online], available at www.cmm.bris.ac.uk/lemma/course/view.php?id=13#m05 [accessed 08/11/2014].

Section II
Social Identity

5 Work–Life Conflict of Working Couples Before and During the Crisis in 18 European Countries

Michael Ochsner and Ivett Szalma

Introduction

During most of the twentieth century, families were organized according to the so-called male breadwinner family: the father worked full-time and the mother stayed at home to care for the children. In the past few decades, this model has been in the process of being replaced all over Europe by a new form of familial organisation: the dual-earner family. In this model, childcare responsibilities and domestic work have to be addressed after work as well as shared between the partners or outsourced altogether. The fact that both parents work leads to organisational challenges that can lead to work–life conflicts, that is, "a form of inter-role conflict in which the role pressures from the work and family domains are mutually incompatible in some respect" (Greenhaus and Beuttel 1985, p. 77). This change of the family model is linked to changes in the economic situation in European countries. While western European countries saw multiple economic crises since the late 1970s and rising unemployment rates as well as rising international competition, eastern European countries faced the transformation from socialist systems to market economies, thus giving up full employment and changing not only their economic but also their social system. This led to the integration of the female work force into the economic system in western countries and the need for many couples to earn two incomes in order to live comfortably on, or even cope with, the household income both in the west and in the east. In this article, we examine the factors that influence the work–life conflict of working couples. We furthermore investigate whether there are differences in these factors before and during the financial crises that most European countries have been facing since the second half of 2008.

Despite the fact that there are a lot of studies on work–life conflict, the concept is not clearly defined. On the one hand, it is unclear what "work" actually means in this context. In most research, work is defined as paid work (van der Lippe et al. 2006; Gallie and Russell 2009; Steiber 2009), whereas in other studies housework is also involved (Aliaga 2006). On the other hand, it is not clear either what belongs to the private sphere: only leisure time spent on entertainment and relaxation or anything else that falls outside of paid work, including, for example, housework and childcare? Hence, researchers use the term *work–life conflict* widely in different ways (Pichler 2009).

Furthermore, work–life conflict can be subdivided into *time-*, *strain-* and *behaviour*-based work–life conflicts (Greenhaus and Beutell 1985; Steiber 2009). Time-based conflict refers to the conflict that arises when the time devoted to one role makes it difficult for the individual to participate in the other role. *Strain*-based conflict occurs when strain experienced in one role crosses over and interferes with participation in another role. Finally, the *behavioural*-based work–life conflict refers to incompatibility in expectations regarding behaviour in different roles (e.g. in the work domain, the expected proper behaviour is objectivity and secretiveness, while in the family domain, subjectivity and openness are expected; see Greenhaus and Beutell 1985). Only a few studies on the last type of work–life conflict exist probably because, up to now, questions capturing this domain are rarely available in the large cross-national surveys. However, questions to measure the other two domains of work–life conflict are frequently available in cross-national surveys.

Finally, work–life conflict can be studied in two directions: role pressures can emerge from the work sphere and interfere with the family or life sphere, that is, the work-related work–life conflict; or it can emerge from the life or family sphere and transfer into the work sphere, that is, the life-related work–life conflict.

In this study, we are particularly interested in the effect of the financial crisis on work–life conflict. Such effects can be of a different nature. Firstly, workers might feel that their jobs are more insecure (Kalleberg 2009). Simultaneously, they might also become more vulnerable because it is more difficult for unemployed people to find a new job in an economic environment characterized by high unemployment rates (Oesch and Lipps 2012; Kalleberg 2009). Secondly, the job situation might have become more precarious; work intensity as well as the number of working hours increase, and unconventional work schedules become more frequent (Gash and Inanc 2013). Thirdly, the crisis can lead to reduction in pay or to the necessity of doing a less interesting job (Bettio et al. 2013). Consequently, we focus only on the work-related side of the work–life conflict. Most researchers are convinced that examples in this direction of the conflict are more frequent (Kinnunen and Mauno 1998; Pichler 2009; Steiber 2009; McGinnity and Russell 2013) than conflicts deriving from the family sphere and having negative effects on the work sphere. We furthermore focus on working couples because they report the highest level of work–life conflict (Crompton and Lyonette 2006; Forsberg 2009; Voydanoff 2005; van der Lippe et al. 2006). We furthermore restrict our definition of work–life conflict to time- and strain-based work–life conflict because, first, we think that the crisis is likely to have an impact on these two domains. And while the behavioural domain will be less affected by the crisis, it is more related to personal dispositions, the family organisation, the type of work and the type of organisation at work, all of which are not so much subject to change because of the crisis. Furthermore, our data source does not provide items to measure this domain.

To summarize, we define *work–life conflict* as a conflict that emerges from pressures arising in the work sphere and that impact the life sphere, that is, the work-related work–life conflict. We focus on dual-earner households (or working couples) and regard work as paid work exclusively and life as everything outside of paid work. Finally, we are exploring time-based and strain-based sources of work–life conflict.

The questions we address here are politically relevant: If working couples' work–life conflicts have worsened due to the crisis, then states should introduce (more) measures in order to reconcile work and family life. Only if the work–life conflicts of working couples have remained unchanged should states focus only on the well-being of unemployed people in order to mitigate the effects of the current crisis.

In order to analyse these questions, we use the second and fifth rounds of the European Social Survey (ESS), which were carried out in 2004 and 2010, respectively. The ESS is a large-scale and highly standardized academically conducted survey and enables us to analyse data on work–life conflicts in 18 European countries before and during the financial crisis that started in 2008.

Our article is structured as follows. The next section will review the results of previous research about how labour market structures influence the work–life conflict and then briefly considers the possible crisis's effects on work–life conflict. In section three, we will present our hypotheses. In section four, we will describe the surveys, the measurement of the key indicators and the methods applied. It will be followed by the empirical results in section five. Section six will conclude with a summary of the findings, a description of the limitations and a short reflection on paths for future research.

Determinants of work–life conflicts before and during the crisis

Most research examining work–life conflict during the crisis (Hofacker and König 2013; Russell and McGinnity 2013; Bettio et al. 2013) reports similar variables influencing work–life conflict as research on work–life conflict before the crisis (Crompton et al. 1996; Gallie and Russell 2009; van der Lippe et al. 2006): long working hours, working overtime, unpredictable working hours and working on weekends or evenings all increase work–life conflict. Since the working schedule is a very important factor of work–life conflict, we differentiate between two basic types of working schedules: quantity and quality of the working schedule. Quantity of the working schedule refers to the amount of hours a person has to work usually as well as to overwork. A higher amount of working hours and overwork increase work–life conflict (Crompton and Lyonett 2006; Grönlund and Öun 2010; van der Lippe et al. 2006; Hofacker and König 2013; Russell and McGinnity 2013; Bettio et al. 2013). Besides the quantity dimension of the working schedule, the quality dimension also matters. The quality of the working schedule refers to when respondents spend their time at work. For example, some people have to work at unsocial times, such as working on weekends or evenings; some have to work at unpredictable times, for example, working overtime at short notice. Working under such conditions can increase work–life conflict for several reasons; for example, it can make it difficult to organise a common family programme (Tausig and Fenwick 2001; Pichler 2009; Steiber 2009).

The unpredictable working hours such as working overtime at short notice, working evenings or nights and working weekends can cause not just *time*-based but also *strain*-based problems that can create work–life conflict. Steiber (2009) found that women tend to experience more *strain*-based work–life conflict, while men tend to experience *time*-based work–life conflict. According to the theory of Hochschild (1989), this might be due to the fact that in all European countries, men spend more time in paid work than women, and it is a widely accepted norm that men work full-time. Thus, men have a higher risk for *time*-based work–life conflict, while women's higher risk of *strain*-based work–life conflict arises often from the dual burden of doing the lion's share of housework and working for pay.

Russell and McGinnity (2013) examined different kinds of relationships between the current crisis and work intensity in Ireland, one of the countries most affected by the crisis. They distinguished between direct and indirect effects of the crisis. They categorized two effects as direct: subjective insecurity and reduction in wages; and three effects as indirect: responsibility, autonomy and supervision. They found that both the direct and indirect effects of the crisis played a role in the increasing work–life conflict (Russell and McGinnity 2013). Hofacker and König (2013) investigated the effect of flexible working conditions on work–life conflict during the crisis in 25 countries, based on ESS data. They found that the irregularity and unpredictability of working hours increased work–life conflict. Not only one's own but also a partners' amount of working hours and an unsocial unpredictable work schedule can increase work–life conflict (Russell and McGinnity 2013). However, Hofacker and König (2013) found that this relation is gender specific: only women's work–life conflicts increase due to their partners' non-standard working hours. Supposing that unpredictable working hours have been increased during the crisis, Hofacker and König (2013) state that the workers' work–life conflict has been worsened due to the crisis.

So far, there is little research attempting to explain the work–life conflicts by country differences. The majority of research focuses only on one country. Previous studies examining more countries found that family policy has no alleviating effect on work–life conflict (van der Lippe et al. 2006; Scherer and Steiber 2007; Steiber 2009). As an explanation, Scherer and Steiber (2007) argue that work–family conflict is greater in those countries where most women are employed and not just those who find it particularly easy to combine work and family responsibilities. However, Hofacker and König (2013) found a contradicting result. They showed that work–life conflict among working couples is lower in the Scandinavian and the liberal states, where either the state or the market promotes support for couples, than in the conservative regimes and post-socialist countries. However, they examined the relationship between the type of welfare regime and work–life conflict during the crisis.

Previous studies differ from ours: Russell and McGinnity (2013) do not control for any country level variables, while Hofacker and König (2013) focus on welfare regimes. The other difference is that both studies use only the fifth wave of ESS without concentrating on the change between the waves before and during the crisis.

Research questions

The aim of this paper is to examine the determinants of work–life conflict among working couples before and during the current financial crisis, with a special focus on changes in these determinants during the current crisis. The research is guided by the following research questions:

1   How does the crisis affect the effects of the quantity and quality of a working schedule on work–life conflict (e.g. amount of working hours, unsocial and unpredictable working hours)? There are the following possibilities: 1a) There is no change at all; 1b) There is a change in the scale of work–life conflict: while the effects of the working hours stay the same, the amount of work–life conflict increases; 1c) the effects of the working hours *increase* during the crisis because the situation is more difficult and the crisis increases the stress-level of individuals, which leads to a stronger effect of the working hours on work–life conflict; 1d) the effects of the working hours *decrease* during the crisis because the work–life conflicts of the worse-off are already full-fledged and cannot be increased. However, the former better-offs become more anxious to stay in a decent position. Hence, the effects of the working hours on work–life conflict get less strong because of the increasing work–life conflicts of those in better situations.
2   Do the crisis's direct effects on the household situation influence the work–life conflict?
3   Do the crisis's direct effects on the job situation influence the work–life conflict?
4   Are there significant differences between countries in work–life conflict and does the economic situation of the country influence work–life conflict?

Data and sample

We used data from 18 European countries gathered in the second and fifth round of the European Social Survey (ESS) in the years 2004 and 2010. The ESS is a large-scale, cross-national longitudinal survey initiated by the European Science Foundation in order to study changing social attitudes and values in Europe. The ESS is a cross-sectional survey carried out every two years, consisting of a core module fielded every round and two rotating modules. We used the module "Family, Work and Well-Being" as it contains a wealth of information on the important topics to analyse work–life conflicts. This module was first implemented in 2004 and was repeated in 2010. This repetition can be considered as a natural experiment because the worst economic crisis since the Second World War broke out between the two rounds and affected all European countries, but to different degrees. The countries examined in this study are Belgium, the Czech Republic, Denmark, Estonia, Finland, Ireland, Germany, Greece, Hungary, the Netherlands, Norway, Poland, Portugal, Slovenia, Spain, Sweden, Switzerland and United Kingdom. They were selected according to data availability in both waves. However, while Slovakia, France and Ukraine participated in both rounds, we could not include them in the analysis because of filter errors or different operationalisations of our key variables in these countries.[1]

Since the focus of this research is on the work–life conflict of working couples, we included only those respondents who work and whose partner also works in a paid job. Since the ESS interviews only one member per household, the data used contains information from one member of a couple about his or her own and his or her partner's employment situation. In order to get a homogeneous sample, we limited our analysis to those workers who are aged between 18 and 60.[2] Furthermore, we included only employed persons in our analysis because, on the one hand, the effects of working conditions on work–life conflicts are likely to be different for employed than for self-employed or employed in family businesses; and on the other hand, some variables we use derive from questions that were only asked of employed respondents. The total working sample size was 7563 in 2004 and 7151 in 2010. The 18 nations contributed between 251 (Greece, 2004) and 683 respondents (Germany, 2010) to the pooled data set. In most countries, the number of respondents by gender was quite but not perfectly equal (46–64 per cent women).

Like any data set, the ESS is affected by item non-response. Because some of the main variables we used are part of the demographic background variables, the amount of missing values is a little bit higher than usual in the ESS. If we look at all variables that were included in the model, the rate of item non-response for one or more variables amounts to 16 per cent in 2004 and 13 per cent in 2010. Thus, if we had used complete case analysis, we would have lost about 15 per cent of the respondents overall. This is well above the 5 per cent threshold that Little and Rubin (2003) advocate as a rule of thumb for using complete case analysis. If we look at individual countries, the amount of missingness varies between 3 per cent (Norway, 2010) and 45 per cent (Slovenia, 2004).[3] In seven out of 18 countries, more than 20 per cent of the respondents had a missing value in the variables of our model; thus, we would have lost a lot of respondents using complete case analysis at the expense of power and at the risk of biased estimates. Therefore, we applied multiple imputation (MI) in order to account for the uncertainty introduced in our analysis by item non-response. MI is, along with full information maximum likelihood (FIML), a well-established procedure for the treatment of missing values (see Schafer and Graham 2002). While complete case analysis or pair-wise deletion – the most often used procedures to treat item non-response – assume missingness completely at random (MCAR), MI only assumes missing at random (MAR).[4] In social science research, the latter is an assumption that is very likely met, at least as sufficiently as MI can be used (cause for missingness is an unobserved variable with a correlation with missingness of lower than $r = 0.4$. See Collins et al. 2001, p. 347; Graham et al. 1997; Schafer and Graham 2002, p. 173), while MCAR is rarely met and causes biased and inefficient estimates when missingness exceeds 5 per cent (Little and Rubin, 2003).

Because most of the variables in our model are ordinal variables, we imputed the missing values using multiple imputation by chained equations. We used the "ice" framework in Stata 13 that allows for handling perfect prediction by the augmented regression algorithm (White et al. 2010, p. 2271) as well as collinearity of predictor variables. We use ordinal logistic regression to impute ordinal variables and multinomial logistic regression to impute categorical variables. Variables with a seven-point scale or more were imputed using linear regression with predictive mean matching in order to preserve the observed values. We calculated m = 10 imputations. For the analysis, we used the in-built procedure for analysing multiply imputed data in Stata 13 that implements the Rubin's Rules to reflect the uncertainty introduced by the missingness of the data (Rubin 1987, p. 21). We used all variables in the model, including the dependent variable following the suggestions of Collins et al. (2001, p. 348), Meng (1994, p. 553), and White et al. (2011, p. 384–385).[5] Since we are studying the change between 2004 and 2010 and we suppose that there may be gender and country differences, we imputed the missing data separately for each year by gender and country, thus preserving the data structure (or in other words modelling possible interactions of year, gender and country with the variables in the models; Graham 2009, p. 562; von Hippel 2009, pp. 286–287).

Measurement

Our measure of work–life conflict is based on four single indicators of work–life conflict; all four were involved in both rounds. Respondents were asked:

How often do you…
1 …keep worrying about work problems when not working?
2 …feel too tired after work to enjoy things one would like to do at home?
3 …find that your job prevents you from giving the time to partner or family?
4 …find that your partner or family gets fed up with the pressure of your job?

Each item is measured on a five-point scale, where 1 means never and 5 means always.

The measures are concerned with the spill-over of stress from work into life. The first two items refer to the extent to which work intrudes into life in general, while the other two items measure how work intrudes into family life (Gallie and Russell 2009). For our analyses, we built an additive index of all four items ranging from 0 to 16,[6] where 0 indicates an absolute lack of work–life conflict and 16 represents the highest possible level of work–life conflict.

We measure the respondent's and the partner's working schedule, differentiating between the quantity and quality of the working time. First, we operationalize the quality of the working schedule by the amount of average working hours using the self-reported information on how many hours the respondent and his or her partner, respectively, normally work a week. These questions include any paid or non-paid overtime, so it is different from weekly contracted hours. Second, we operationalize the quality of the working schedule as the level of unsocial working time of the respondents and their partners using three questions on the frequency of (a) weekend work, (b) evening work and (c) overtime at short notice. The answer categories are situated between 1 (never) and 5 (every week) for variable (a) and between 1 (never) and 7 (every day) for variables (b) and (c). Because of the different scale of the variables, we formed an additive index of the variables' z-standardised values. A higher value of the index represents a higher level of the unsocial time commitment.

In order to measure the work intensity, we included three variables in the analysis, one of which concentrates on time-based work intensity. It is measured by the agreement on a five-point Likert scale with the following statement: "I never seem to have enough time to get everything done in my job." The other focuses on the strain-based side of the work intensity – "My job requires that I work very hard" – and is based on the same scale. Due to small numbers in the extreme categories, we recoded the two variables into three categories and reversed the scale in order to ease interpretation: 1 stands for "disagree," 2 for "neither agree nor disagree," and 3 for "agree." The third variable measures the freedom in organizing working time, which can compensate for work–life conflict caused by work intensity. The respondents have to tell on a four-point scale how true the following statement is: "I can decide the time I start and finish work." Of course, these measures are only available for the respondents and not for their partners.

In order to have a measure for the impact of the crisis on work on the individual level, we use two variables, one on changes in the job situation, the other on changes in the household situation.[7] Both variables are only available for the 2010 data. To measure how the respondent's job situation changed during the three years before the survey (2010), we created a dummy variable indicating whether a change occurred in the job situation measured by four dummy variables pointing to the occurrence of the following four situations: the respondent (1) had less security in their job, (2) had to take a reduction in pay, (3) had to work shorter hours and (4) had to do less interesting work. If the respondent experienced one of the four changes, the dummy variable takes the value of 1; if the respondent experienced no changes at all, it takes the value of 0.[8] We measured changes in the household situation using three items asking the respondents whether they (1) had to draw savings or get into debt to cover ordinary living expenses, (2) had to cut back expenses for holidays or household equipment or (3) had to manage lower household income. All of the three items are measured on a seven-point scale, where 0 indicates that the respondents have not experienced it at all and 6 means that the respondents have experienced it a great deal. We added these items and treated the new index as continuous variable.

Furthermore, we included basic demographic and other sociological features as control variables, such as the respondents' gender and age, their highest level of education, their occupational situation, the presence of a child in the household and the subjective level of income.[9] Age is measured as a categorical variable:

18–29, 30–9, 40–49 and above 50 because we do not expect a linear effect. The educational level is measured by three categories: low, medium and high. These categorizations are based on International Standard Classification of Education (ISCED) codes, low meaning lower secondary level, high meaning tertiary level and medium meaning everything in between. The occupational situation is measured by two variables. First, we created a simplified variable reducing the International Standard Classification of Occupations (ISCO) codes available in the ESS to three categories: elementary occupations (ISCO codes between 1000 and 4999); service workers, craft, skilled agriculture (ISCO codes 5000–8999); and managers, highly qualified professionals, and clerks (ISCO codes above 9000). Second, we use a dummy variable for respondents with a work contract that is limited in time. The presence of (at least) a child in the household has three values: 0 if the couple does not have a child younger than 18 living with them, 1 if the couple has a child between 7 and 18 years old and 3 if the couple has a child younger than 7 years old. Subjective income is measured by an item asking which description comes closest to how the respondents feel about their household income nowadays: 1 means "living comfortably on present income" 2 means "coping on present income," 3 means "finding it difficult on present income" and 4 means "finding it very difficult on present income." We had to combine levels 3 and 4 because of too few cases in the 4th level. We also inverted the scale for ease of interpretation.

In order to measure the effect of the state of the economy at the country level, we used the annual percentage growth rate of the gross domestic product per capita (GDP) in Euro. The annual growth rate of the GDP varied between –3.6 (Switzerland) and 8.6 per cent (Hungary) in 2004 and –7.19 per cent (Ireland) and 10.79 per cent (Norway) in 2010. We chose this measure because the financial crisis had and is having a dramatic impact on GDP (Papell and Prodan 2012) and because GDP growth is a standard measure of the economic situation in a country. As a second measure for the state of the economy of a country, we included the unemployment rate. As a measure of (long-term) crisis, we included the difference in long-term GDP growth (5 years average) between 2004 and 2010 in the model for 2010 (see Table 5.1). We took all the country-level data from the multilevel data set of the ESS; thus, the GDP per capita and the unemployment rates are taken from Eurostat.

Analytical procedure

To analyse our data, multiple methods were applied. First, we interpreted descriptive statistics by comparing mean values. At the next stage, an explanatory model was constructed by applying multi-level fixed-effects linear regression. We used the software Stata 13 to calculate the multilevel regressions. We applied multilevel – or hierarchical linear – regression models to account for the data's complex variance structure, as individuals are nested in countries and, hence, the independence of observations assumption of ordinary least squares (OLS) regression models is violated and the OLS estimates would be biased (Hox 2010; Snijders and

Table 5.1 Descriptive statistics on work–life conflict and GDP growth per capita, differences between 2004 and 2010

Country	WLC 2004	WLC 2010	WLC Difference	Difference between Gender	Difference in Growth percentages	Growth 2004	Growth 2010	Difference Long-Term Growth (5 years)
BE	6.44	6.76	0.32	0.63	−1.52	0.8	−0.7	0.05
CH	5.70	6.04	0.34	−0.23	12.56	−3.6	9	0.29
CZ	6.08	7.25	1.17	−0.22	−5.00	5	0	−0.09
DE	6.54	6.92	0.38	−0.66	3.19	−2.4	0.8	0.11
DK	6.25	6.29	0.05	0.55	1.16	0	1.2	0.04
EE	6.51	7.18	0.67	0.10	−6.45	6.5	0	−0.33
ES	5.81	6.20	0.39	−0.17	−5.23	1.1	−4.1	−0.13
FI	6.88	7.06	0.18	0.09	−0.72	0	−0.7	0.03
GB	6.66	6.67	0.01	0.06	1.41	2.2	3.6	−0.13
GR	5.52	7.05	1.53	−0.11	−9.53	2.6	−6.9	−0.14
HU	5.99	6.11	0.11	−0.04	−8.57	8.6	0	−0.44
IE	4.83	4.94	0.11	−0.52	−7.19	0	−7.2	−0.36
NL	5.77	5.78	0.01	0.29	−0.62	−1.4	−2	0.02
NO	5.85	5.93	0.08	−0.27	10.79	0	10.8	0.10
PL	6.99	6.54	−0.45	1.40	4.40	4.2	8.6	0.31
PT	4.66	5.41	0.75	0.81	0.02	−1.5	−1.5	0.05
SE	6.16	6.78	0.62	0.40	14.84	−0.7	14.2	0.09
SI	5.90	6.32	0.42	−0.11	−4.05	0	−4.1	−0.03

Bosker 1999). Applying multilevel models has the advantage of recognizing the partial interdependence of individuals within the same group – or citizens within the same country in our case. Formulated in a less formal way and adapted to our research question, citizens of a given country would not necessarily form views about work–life conflicts independent from each other. For example, if the state helps to reconcile work and family life, it is possible that a citizen of this country will manifest a lower level of work–life conflict than the same citizen would manifest in another country where the state does not provide any help.

We estimate four models following the bottom-up procedure, starting with the least complex model (Hox 2010, pp. 56–59). Consequently, we start with an intercept-only model in order to decompose the variance of the dependent variable into individual and country-level variance. The second model includes socio-demographic, job-characteristic and job-intensity variables. In the third model, we added the variables indicating the changes in the job and the household situation on the individual level. These questions were only asked in 2010. Consequently, this model is only applied to the 2010 data. Finally, we included the country-level variables in the models. We do not report log-likelihoods and its derivatives (Deviance, BIC, AIC) because they are not interpretable after multiple imputation. However, our goal is not to compare the model fit of different models; thus we can do without log-likelihoods.

Results

Descriptive analysis

Analysing the data of 18 European countries for 2004 and 2010 using the ESS, we find that work–life conflict varies on the country level from 4.66 (Portugal) to 6.99 (Poland) in 2004 and from 4.94 (Ireland) to 7.25 (the Czech Republic) in 2010. Generally, the lowest levels of work–life conflict in 2004 appear in Portugal and Ireland, with Greece also scoring quite low. The highest levels appear in Poland, Finland, the United Kingdom, Germany and Estonia. In 2010, the lowest levels of work–life conflict are still present in Ireland and Portugal, while the highest levels are experienced in the Czech Republic, Estonia, Finland and Greece (see Table 5.1). This points to changes in work–life conflict between 2004 and 2010 in some countries. In fact, the work–life conflict increased between the two periods in all of the countries except Poland. However, the changes are generally small, ranging from –0.45 in Poland to 1.53 in Greece on a scale from 0 to 16. The biggest increase of work–life conflict occurred in Greece, the Czech Republic, Portugal, Estonia and Sweden.

Combining the level and change in work–life conflict, we find that those countries in which respondents experienced the highest increase in work–life conflict were also among those countries that showed the highest level of work–life conflict in 2010, that is, the Czech Republic and Greece. This corresponds with the findings of Kentikelenis et al. (2011) and Haugh et al. (2010).

In some countries, there are some differences between the changes in work–life conflict experienced by men and by women. While the differences in change are sometimes several times as big as the overall change (e.g. in Poland, the change in men's work–life conflict was 1.4 higher than women's, while the change between 2004 and 2010 overall was –0.45), the difference is still small considering the country mean of work–life conflict (6.54 for Poland in 2010). There was a stronger increase among men than among women in Poland, Portugal, Belgium and Denmark, while in Germany and Ireland, women experienced a stronger increase in work–life conflict (see Figure 5.1 and Table 5.1).[10]

Multivariate analysis

In order to address our research questions, we conducted multilevel fixed-effect regression models using Rubin's Rules (Rubin 1987) to combine the estimates of the 10 imputations of the missing values. This leads to standard errors that account for the uncertainty due to the missing data. We used the bottom-up multi-level modelling approach advocated by Hox (2010, pp. 56–59) starting with a base model for both years (2004 and 2010) that only decomposes the variance of the dependent variable, work–life conflict, into individual and country-level variances. Thus, we will get a first indication of whether there are country differences in work–life conflict. We already see in Table 1 that the differences between countries are not that big. However, it is not clear yet how this relates to the differences at the individual level. Table 5.2 shows that the

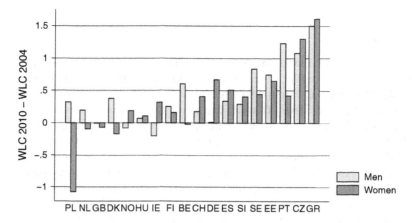

Figure 5.1 The difference in work–life conflict levels between 2004 and 2010 in 18 European countries by sex and country, sorted by level of increase (work–life conflict index varies between 0 and 16).

Source: ESS Multilevel Data.

Table 5.2 Base model: multi-level fixed-effects model for work–life conflict in 2004 and 2010 respectively, no explanatory variables

	Base Model 2004	Base Model 2010
Intercept	6.00***(0.15)	6.39***(0.15)
Country level variance ($\sigma^2 u$)	0.36	0.36
Individual level variance ($\sigma 2\varepsilon$)	8.75	8.49
Intra-class correlation (ρ)	0.04	0.04
N (respondents)	7563	7151
G (countries)	18	18

Notes: ***$p < 0.001$.

first impression of the descriptive analysis is correct: the intra-class correlation (ICC) amounts to $\rho = 0.04$ in both years. This can be considered as small (Hox, 2010, p. 244).

In the next step, we model the individual level variables that are available in both years, that is, not using the variables measuring the impact of the crisis that are only available for 2010 (see Table 5.3, Model 1).

We find that women experience a slightly higher work–life conflict than men. Respondents with a higher education report a slightly higher level of work–life conflict. There are differences between 2004 and 2010: while in 2004, only respondents with a tertiary education report a significantly higher work–life conflict than the others, in 2010, the respondents with a low education report a significantly smaller work–life conflict than the others. However, the effect goes into a consistent direction in both years (the difference between low education and high

Table 5.3 Multi-level linear regression estimates of the determinants of work–life conflict in 2004 and 2010

Work–life conflict	M1: Individual-level variables		M2: Individual-level crisis variables	M3: Individual and country-level variables	
	2004	2010	2010	2004	2010
Fixed Effects					
Intercept	4.16***	3.51***	2.72***	3.69***	2.66***
Gender					
Female	0.39***	0.32***	0.33***	0.39***	0.33***
Education (Base: middle)					
Low	−0.14	−0.32*	−0.30*	−0.13	−0.30*
High	0.43***	0.20	0.19	0.43***	0.19
Age (Base: 18–29)					
30–39	0.22*	0.16	0.20	0.22*	0.20
40–49	0.20	0.30**	0.39***	0.20	0.39***
50+	0.02	0.24*	0.36***	0.02	0.36***
Income (Base: coping)					
Difficult	0.68***	0.80***	0.54***	0.67***	0.55***
Comfortable	−0.43***	−0.45***	−0.23**	−0.42***	−0.24**
Child in household (Base: no child)					
Child 7–18	0.02	0.18***	0.19***	0.02	0.18***
Child 0–6	0.15	0.30***	0.30***	0.15	0.30***
Working contract (Base: unlimited)					
Limited	−0.03	0.37**	0.26	−0.03	0.26
Occupation (Base: elementary)					
Service workers	0.05	0.35***	0.35***	0.06	0.35***
Highly qualified	0.48**	0.67***	0.68***	0.48**	0.68***
Strain at work (Base: neither nor)					
Disagree	−0.56***	−0.30*	−0.27*	−0.56***	−0.28*
Agree	0.49***	0.52***	0.52***	0.49***	0.52***
Time pressure at work (Base: neither nor)					
Disagree	−0.68***	−0.84***	−0.81***	−0.68***	−0.81***
Agree	0.74***	0.70***	0.68***	0.75***	0.68***
Flexibility of schedule (Base: not at all true)					
A little true	−0.02	0.09	0.10	−0.02	0.10
Quite true	0.03	0.15	0.15	0.03	0.15
Very true	0.01	−0.14	−0.12	0.02	−0.12

(*continued*)

Table 5.3 Continued

Work–life conflict	M1: Individual-level variables		M2: Individual-level crisis variables	M3: Individual and country-level variables	
	2004	2010	2010	2004	2010
Quantity of working schedule					
Working hours	0.03***	0.04***	0.04***	0.03***	0.04***
Partners' working hours	–0.01*	–0.00	–0.00	–0.01*	–0.00
Quality of working schedule					
Unsocial time	0.36***	0.32***	0.31***	0.36***	0.31***
Partners' unsocial time	0.06***	0.05**	0.04*	0.06***	0.04*
Crisis					
Household			0.05***		0.05***
Job			0.53***		0.53***
Country level					
GDP growth				2.52	1.27
Unemployment				0.06**	0.01
Difference in 5-year growth					0.82
Variance components					
Country-level variance (σ_u^2)	0.26	0.31	0.34	0.19	0.30
Individual-level variance (σ_ε^2)	6.44	6.23	6.09	6.44	6.09
Explained variance					
R2 individual	0.26	0.27	0.28	0.26	0.28
R2 country	0.30	0.14	0.14	0.47	0.18
R2 total	0.27	0.26	0.27	0.27	0.28

Notes: *p < 0.05; **p < 0.01; ***p < 0.001. N = 7563 in 2004 and N = 7151 in 2010, G = 18 in both years. Log-likelihoods and their derivatives are not reported because they are not interpretable after multiple imputation.

education is always significant). Note, however, that the effect is quite small. The relation between age and work–life conflict also varies between the years. While in 2004, the group of 30–39-year-olds had a higher work–life conflict than the 18–29-year-olds, in 2010, the respondents older than 40 reported a higher work–life conflict. The subjective income has a significant effect on work–life conflict: People who are coping on present income or find it difficult on present income have a higher level of work–life conflict than those who report that they can live comfortably on present income. The effect of subjective income is quite stronger than that of age and education and it is stronger in 2010 than in 2004. While having at least one child did not significantly affect work–life conflict in 2004, we find that having at least one child increases work–life conflict in 2010, although to a moderate degree. Having a child aged 0–6 years increases work–life conflict more than having a child aged 7–17.

The job-related variables have mostly the expected significant effects. While having a limited working contract has no effect on work–life conflict in 2004, it has an effect in 2010. There are also differences in effects between 2004 and 2010 when it comes to the kind of work respondents do: while only highly qualified workers report a higher work–life conflict than the others in 2004, the service workers also report a higher work–life conflict than elementary workers in 2010. The effects also increase considerably from 2004 to 2010. Thus, it seems that the crisis also hit the service workers who report higher work–life conflicts in 2010. Both strain at work (the need to work hard) and time pressure at work have a strong effect on work–life conflict; time pressure even has the strongest effect of the categorical variables in the model. Surprisingly, the flexibility of the working schedule, that is, whether the respondent can decide the starting and ending time of his or her working schedule, cannot alleviate work–life conflict. Looking at the quantity dimension of the working schedule reveals a surprising result: while the amount of working hours has the expected significant positive effect on work–life conflict, the working hours of the partner do have a (very small) negative effect, which is even significant in 2004. Hence, if partners work a lot, this does not increase work–life conflict. Rather, it had an alleviating effect in 2004. The quality dimension of the working schedule significantly affects work–life conflict: both the respondents' own as well as their partners' amount of working at unsocial times influence the work–life conflict of the respondents significantly. As expected, the effect of the respondents' own working at unsocial times has a much stronger effect than their partners'. There is no remarkable change in the effects between 2004 and 2010.

Model 2 shows the results including the variables measuring the crisis on the individual level. These variables are only available in 2010. Changes in the household, like cutting household budget or holidays, increase the work–life conflict. However, the effect is quite small. Changes in the job, like doing a less interesting job, has a significant effect, which shows that those people who reported that they were affected directly by the crisis in some way experienced a higher level of work–life conflict. Including these variables in the model does not change much compared to the individual level Model 1: the explained variance on the individual level and in total increases by 1 per cent, while the explained variance on the country level does not change. All coefficients stay roughly the same with one exception: having a limited working contract does not influence work–life conflict significantly any more.

The country-level variables are introduced in Model 3. Not surprisingly, the variables do not have a strong effect. In fact, only the unemployment rate has an effect on work–life conflict, even only in 2004. In countries with a higher unemployment rate, people reported a higher work–life conflict in 2004. In 2010, however, this effect does not hold any more. The country-level variables explain an additional 17 per cent of the variance at the country level in 2004, but only an additional 4 per cent in 2010. This is no surprise as the variance at the country level is quite small, as both the descriptive analysis reported in Table 5.1 suggests and the low intra-class correlation coefficient reported in Table 5.2 confirms.[11]

After this first look at the results of the multilevel models, we return to our research questions. The results suggest that both the quality and quantity of the working schedule have an effect on work–life conflict. However, this does not change much between 2004 and 2010. The overall increase in work–life conflict (see the intercepts of the multilevel regressions in Table 5.2) is also quite small. Thus, we conclude that there is not a big change due to the crisis when it comes to the working schedule, thus favouring the possibility 1a) from research question 1. Thus, the quantity (of the respondents' working schedule) as well as the quality (of both partners' working schedule) of the working schedule seem to be a predictor of work–life conflict, irrespective of the economic situation. Addressing research question 2, that is, whether the direct effects of the crisis on the household affect work–life conflict, we find in Model 2 that indeed respondents who experienced more constraints to the household in the three years before 2010 – such as the need to manage on a lower household budget, to draw on savings or to cut back on holidays or household equipment – do report a higher work–life conflict. The same holds true for the direct effects of the crisis on the job situation (research question 3): people who report a change to their job situation in the three years before 2010 – like having to do less interesting work, to take a reduction in pay, to work shorter hours or having less job security – also report a higher work–life conflict. Concerning research question 4, there is little evidence for differences in work–life conflict across countries. The country means of work–life conflict range between 4.66 and 6.99 in 2004 as well as between 4.94 and 7.25 in 2010, which amounts to a range of 2.3 in both years. This is a small difference considering that the work–life conflict index ranges from 0 to 16 on the individual level. The low intra-class correlations of $\rho = 0.04$ suggest that, indeed, the clustering of individuals in countries is not that strong – or, in other words, not much of the variance is due to variance between countries. Furthermore, our measures for the economic crisis on the country level proved to be not significant with the exception of the unemployment rate in 2004, which just seems to confirm the rule that there is not much influence from the country level. The significant effect of the unemployment rate as well as the (small) rise in work–life conflict in 2010 and the expected direction of the other country-level variables point towards the fact that in countries in more difficult economic situations, work–life conflict might increase. However, the results clearly show that work–life conflict is very dependent on the individual level. This is also supported by the fact that we do not find big differences in the predictors' effects between 2004 and 2010.[12] The crisis has a clear impact on a personal level, but the crisis does not hit all people from the same country in the same way.

While the models explain about 30 per cent of the variance, the single effects are quite small (for example, being a woman increases work–life conflict, ranging from 0 to 16 by 0.39 in 2004). This points to the fact that an accumulation of negative situations creates tensions between duties at work and in private life. We test this by defining groups at different levels of predictor variables and contrasting them with the rest of the sample using a regression of the group dummies on work–life conflict. Firstly, we take a selection of predictors resulting in very small groups at low- and high stress-level (Extremes 1): the high stress-level is defined by (a) having difficulties with current income, (b) being a highly qualified worker, (c) having both time- and strain-based stress at the job, (d) working more than 35 hours a week and (e) both the respondent and his or her partner not belonging to the lowest quartile of working at unsocial times. The low-level stress group is defined by (a) at least coping with income, (b) not having either strain- or time-based stress at the job and (c) both partners belonging to the lower half of working at unsocial times. Of course, this leads to quite small extreme groups; the high stress-level group amounts to 30,[13] and the low stress–level group amounts to 108 persons. The difference is quite large (6.86 in 2004 and 7.00 in 2010) and significant (see the "Extremes 1" columns in Table 5.4). Because of the small number of respondents in the extremes, we also defined less extreme high and low stress-level groups amounting roughly to 5 per cent of the sample (Extremes 2).[14] The differences become only slightly smaller (see the "Extremes 2" columns in Table 5.4). The results nicely illustrate some of the findings the multilevel regression models hinted at: The overall level of work–life conflict of all respondents not selected for the extremes at low or high stress-level increased from 2004 to 2010, although only slightly (from 6.1 to 6.5 for the "Extremes 1" selection, and from 6.1 to 6.4 for the "Extremes 2" selection; see the "all others" category in Table 5.4). However, what changed considerably is the low stress–level group: first, the number of respondents in this group is cut almost by half from 2004 to 2010 for both operationalisations of extremes. At the same time, the work–life conflict in this

Table 5.4 Comparing the effect of different stress-levels at home and at work on working couples' work–life conflict

	Extremes 1				Extremes 2			
	2004		2010		2004		2010	
	N	Mean	N	Mean	N	Mean	N	Mean
Descriptive								
High stress	30	9.56 (0.39)	33	10.81 (0.45)	270	8.66 (0.16)	254	9.11 (0.14)
All others	7408	6.10 (0.03)	7052	6.45 (0.04)	6966	6.09 (0.04)	6703	6.41 (0.04)
Low stress	108	2.70 (0.27)	55	3.81 (0.36)	310	3.17 (0.15)	187	3.98 (0.19)
Regression								
High stress		3.46*** (0.53)		4.36*** (0.51)		2.57*** (0.18)		2.70*** (0.18)
Low stress		3.40*** (0.28)		−2.64*** (0.39)		−2.92*** (0.17)		−2.44*** (0.22)

Notes: ***p < 0.001. N = 7563 in 2004 and N = 7151 in 2010. Standard errors in brackets. Note that the absolute numbers of the groups do not sum up to the total N because of variance between imputations.

group increased from 2.7 in 2004 to 3.8 in 2010 for the "Extremes 1" selection, and from 3.2 to 4.0 for the "Extremes 2" selection. The high stress-level groups stayed more or less constant in size from 2004 to 2010, but the work–life conflict of these groups increased quite considerably.

Conclusions

In this chapter, we analysed work–life conflict in 18 countries before and during the financial crisis that hit all European countries to at least some extent from 2008 on. Four research questions guided our analysis: (1) How does the crisis affect the relationship between the quality and quantity of the working schedule and work–life conflict? (2) Do the crisis's direct effects on the household situation influence work–life conflict? (3) Do the crisis's direct effects on the job situation affect the work–life conflict? (4) Are there differences between countries in work–life conflict and does the economic situation of the country influence work–life conflict?

We used hierarchical linear multi-level regression to analyse the predictors of work–life conflict in 18 countries in 2004 and 2010. Concerning our first research question, our results confirmed previous research (Gallie and Russell 2009; Tausig and Fenwick 2001; White et al. 2003): the amount of working hours and working at unsocial times are important predictors of work–life conflict. However, the amount of the partner's working hours did not show significant effects on the work–life conflict of the respondents, which contradicts the findings from Gallie and Russell (2009) and Tausig and Fenrick (2001). Yet, the partner's working at unsocial times significantly increases the work–life conflicts of the respondents. Additionally, those respondents who report any type of work intensity report a higher level of work–life conflict (Gallie and Russell 2009). Work pressure, both time- and strain-based, increase work–life conflict. We furthermore found evidence of a strong impact of the direct effects of the crisis on the individual level (see research questions 2 and 3): Both the crisis' impact on the household situation as well as on the job situation significantly increases work–life conflict. When it comes to the country level (research question 4), our results suggest that work–life conflict is determined almost exclusively by the personal situation. Only 4 per cent of the total variance is due to country level variance (the intra-class correlation amounts to $\rho = 0.04$). Hence, the country level predictors did not explain much variance and only the unemployment rate was a significant predictor, but only in 2004: In countries with a higher unemployment rate, there was a slightly higher average level of work–life conflict.

Additionally, we got a surprising result regarding children present in the household: most previous studies (Gallie and Russell, 2009; Tausig and Fenwick, 2001) show that having children increases work–life conflict. However, we found that this was not true in 2004, when having children is not significant. Yet, our findings confirm the results of the previous studies for 2010. As expected, the presence of a child aged 0–6 years in the household increases work–life conflict even more than a child aged 7–18.

Women experience a slightly higher work–life conflict than men, all else held constant. Furthermore, education and the type of occupation are also significantly related to work–life conflict: having a higher education and a job with a higher qualification increases work–life conflict. As expected, the subjective income is also a strong predictor for work–life conflict: respondents who have difficulties living on current income report a higher work–life conflict than those who cope on current income, while respondents who live comfortably on their current income experience a lower work–life conflict.

Overall, the effects of the single predictors appear to be relatively low. However, they explain almost 30 per cent of the variance of the individual level, pointing to the fact that an accumulation of different stressors can lead to a strong increase in work–life conflict. Indeed, by combining strong predictors and defining groups at both ends of the stress-level – that is, a group with a high level of stress as well as a group with a low level of stress – we find that there are quite big differences between those groups from the rest, and of course between the two extremes.

This last finding, combined with the small difference in work–life conflict between countries, has policy relevance. We can conclude that the crisis hit not only those who lost their jobs during the crisis but also those workers who work a lot, work hard, have children, have difficulties living on their income and have experienced changes in their household and job situation. Thus, policy makers should pay close attention not only to those people who are out of the labour market but also to the very vulnerable who work and experience stress on different dimensions such as high pressures in the job (responsibilities, time schedules, work intensity, flexibility) as well as at home (i.e. having children, having to cut back on household budgets or having a lack of equipment). Summing up, we can extend the conventional vulnerable groups, the unemployed and working poor, by a third vulnerable group: high stress-level working couples.

This not only holds true for the states that were hit harder by the crisis but for all countries. It seems that businesses in countries on which the crisis had less impact in terms of macro-economic measures are taking measures to increase productivity as well, leading to higher levels of work–life conflict among medium to highly qualified workers.

Our results are also of interest to the research community. So far, most research on work–life conflict has focused on single countries, and not much is known as to whether there are differences between countries. We investigated the country differences of work–life conflict in two periods: before and during the financial crisis starting in 2008. We found that work–life conflict is determined largely by individual predictors and that there are not many differences between countries. We also found that there are not many changes in the predictors' effects on work–life conflict between the two points in time, 2004 and 2010. The change seems more to be a change of scale (more people experience work–life conflict and also the respondents in the low stressor group experience a higher work–life conflict in 2010 than in 2004). However, we used two cross-sectional data sets and therefore did not observe respondents at the two points in time. Thus, future research should use panel data. For us, this was not an option since there are no panels including variables on work–life conflict that are comparable between countries. Since we found that country differences in work–life conflict are negligible, researchers can use panel data for single countries. Furthermore, the survey we used did not interview both partners. While our research showed some interesting results about couples, that is, that the amount of partners' working hours is not increasing respondents' work–life conflict, this finding could be investigated in more detail if data for both partners of a couple was available. Finally, our next step would be to analyse gender differences in the predictors of work–life conflict.

Notes

1 France's variable for employment status in 2004 differs in the number of categories from those of the other countries and cannot be recoded. Many variables we used are filtered on this variable. Slovakia and Ukraine are not used because of filter errors or irregularities affecting some variables we use.
2 We chose this upper limit because there are different retirement ages in the countries we examine. The inclusion of those people who already reached the retirement age but are still on the labour market would bias our sample because they represent that portion of retired people who choose to work and, hence, their work–life conflicts are likely to be lower than those of the other workers.
3 Almost 50% of missing values seems to be quite high. However, in simulation studies, often missing rates of 80% are used, and multiple imputation proved to be stable even with as small samples as $n = 50$ (Schafer and Graham, 2002). Multiple imputation has been developed for situations with a high ratio of missing values. It is often applied in cases where more than 50% missing values occur.
4 Because of space restrictions, we do not present an in-depth description of the theoretical and statistical details. Please see Schafer and Graham (2002, 150–155) for a detailed description of the typology of missingness. The concept and terminology go back to Rubin (1976).
5 We remind the reader that the goal of MI is not to predict the "true" values of the missing values for the respondents but to find efficient and valid estimators for the relationships between the variables at interest in the population. Thus, the important goal is the optimal use of the joint distribution of the variables in the model (Schafer and Graham, 2002, p. 149).
6 We added all variables and subtracted 4 from the total in order to have a scale that is easier to interpret.
7 These questions were elaborated by Gallie et al. in order to measure the perceived effects of the recession in the person's job and household situation.
8 We also checked whether an additive index ranging from 0 to 4 would give different results. However, the same results were obtained. The main effect was between those respondents who did experience a change and those who did not. Thus, we opted for the more parsimonious model.
9 We decided to apply the subjective income instead of the absolute income because subjective income can have a higher effect on work–life conflict than the absolute income. People feeling rich (or feeling that they earn enough) are less likely to experience stress and, hence, probably work–life conflict. The absolute income doesn"t tell us whether and how much people actually worry about their income. Furthermore, there are more missing values for the absolute than the subjective income.
10 Note, we do not have longitudinal data. The reported differences are differences in country means, not differences in experienced work–life conflict of one and the same person.

11 Because of the low intra-class correlation and the low number of countries, we also checked whether the insignificant effects of the country-level variables are due to over-modelling. Thus, we ran models with each country-level variable as the only country-level predictor. The results were roughly the same; only the unemployment rate in 2004 proved to influence work–life conflict significantly (and the coefficient was exactly the same in 2004). The coefficient for GDP growth in both years almost doubled when introduced alone, but the standard error also increased heavily.
12 While one could argue that this is because in 2004 economies in Europe had just recovered from the IT-bubble crisis of 2001, we do think that the situation in 2004 was much better than in 2010; in particular, the prospects were quite positive.
13 Note that the number of respondents in the groups differ between imputations because there were missing values among these variables.
14 The "Extremes 2" groups are defined as follows: members of the "Extremes 2" group at high stress-level have at least a child aged 18 or younger, are highly qualified workers, have both time- and strain-based stress at the job, work more than 35 hours a week and both respondent and his or her partner do not belong to the lowest quartile of working at unsocial times. The "Extreme 2"-group at low stress-level is characterized by not reporting any time- or strain-based stress at the job and both partners belong to the lowest quartile of working at unsocial times.

References

Aliaga, C. (2006). How is the time of women and men distributed in Europe? EUROSTAT, Statistics in focus, Population and Social Conditions, 4/2006, European Communities. Retrieved from: http://ec.europa.eu/eurostat/en/web/products-statistics-in-focus/-/KS-NK-06-004.

Bettio, F., Corsi, M., D'Ippoliti. C., Lyberaki, A., Samek, M., Verashchagina, L. and Verashchagina, A. (2013). *The Impact of the Economic Crisis on the Situation of Women and Men and on Gender Equality Policies*. Synthesis Report. Luxembourg: Publications Office of the European Union.

Collins, L. M., Schafer, J. L., and Kam, C.-M. (2001). A comparison of inclusive and restrictive strategies in modern missing data procedures. *Psychological Methods*, 6(4), 330–351. doi:10.1037/1082-989X.6.4.330.

Crompton, R., Gallie, D. and Purcell, K. (1996). Work, economic restructuring and social regulation. In R. Crompton, D. Gallie and K. Purcell (eds.) *Changing Forms of Employment: Organisations, Skills And Gender* (pp. 1–20). London: Routledge.

Crompton, R. and Lyonette, C. (2006). Work–life balance in Europe. *Acta Sociologica*, 49(4), 379–393.

Forsberg, L. (2009) Managing Time and Childcare in Dual-Earner Families: Unforeseen Consequences of Household Strategies. *Acta Sociologica*, 52(2), pp. 162–175

Gallie, D. and Russell, H. (2009). Work-family conflict and working conditions in Western Europe. *Social Indicators*, 93, 445–467.

Gash, V. and Inanc, H. (2013). Insecurity and the peripheral workforce. In D. Gallie (ed.) *Economic Crisis, Quality of Work, and Social Integration* (pp. 142–168). Oxford: Oxford University Press.

Graham, J. W. (2009). Missing data analysis: Making it work in the real world. Annual Review of Psychology, 60, 549–576. doi:10.1146/annurev.psych.58.110405.085530.

Graham, J. W., Hofer, S. M., Donaldson, S. I., MacKinnon, D. P. and Schafer, J. L. (1997). Analysis with missing data in prevention research. In K. Bryant, M. Windle & S. West (eds.), *The Science of Prevention: Methodological Advances from Alcohol and Substance Abuse Research* (pp. 325–366). Washington, DC: American Psychological Association.

Greenhaus, J. H. and Beutell, N. J. (1985). Sources of conflict between work and family roles. *Academy of Management Review*, 10, 76–88.
Grönlund, A. and Öun, I. (2010). Rethinking work-family conflicts: Dual earner policies, role conflict and role expansion in Western Europe. *Journal of European Social Policy*, 20(3), 179–195.
Haugh, D., Mourougane, A. and Chatal, O. (2010). *The Automobile Industry In and Beyond the Crisis*. Economics Department Working Paper No. 745. Retrieved from http://search.oecd.org/officialdocuments/displaydocumentpdf/?doclanguage=en&cote=eco/wkp(2010)1.
Hochschild, A. R. (1989). *The Second Shift: Working Parents and the Revolution At Home*. New York, NY: Viking.
Hofacker, D. and König, S. (2013). Flexibility and work–life conflict in times of crisis: A gender perspective. *International Journal of Sociology and Social Policy*, 33(9–10), 613–635.
Hox, J. J. (2010). *Multilevel Analysis: Techniques and Applications* (2nd ed.). New York, NY: Routledge.
Kalleberg, A. (2009). Precarious work, insecure workers: Employment relations in transition. *American Sociological Review*, 74, 1–22.
Kentikelenis, A., Karanikolos, M., Papanicolas, I., Basu, S., McKee, M. and Stuckler, D. (2011). Health effects of financial crisis: Omens of a Greek tragedy. *The Lancet*, 378, 1457–1458.
Kinnunen, U. and Mauno, S. (1998). Antecedents and outcomes of work–family conflict among employed women and men in Finland. *Human Relations*, 51 (2), 157–177.
Little, R. J. A. and Rubin, D. B. (2003). *Statistical Analysis with Missing Data* (2nd ed.). New Jersey, NJ: Wiley InterScience.
McGinnity, F. and Russell, H. (2013). Work–family conflict and economic change. In D. Gallie (ed.) *Economic Crisis, Quality of Work, and Social Integration* (169–194). Oxford: Oxford University Press.
Meng, X.-L. (1994). Multiple-imputation inferences with uncongenial sources of input. *Statistical Science*, 9, 538–73.
Oesch, D. and Lipps, O. (2012). Does unemploymnt hurt less if there is more of it around? A panel analysis of life satisfaction in Germany and Switzerland. *European Sociological Review*, 27(2), 288–290.
Papell, D. H. and Prodan, R. (2012). The statistical behavior of GDP after financial crises and severe recession. *The B.E. Journal of Macroeconomics*, 12(3), 1–29.
Pichler F. (2009). Determinants of work–life balance: Shortcomings in the contemporary measurement of WLB in large-scale surveys. *Social Indicator Research*, 92(3), 449–469.
Rubin, D. B. (1976). Inference and missing data. *Biometrika*, 63(3), 581–592. doi:10.1093/biomet/63.3.581.
Rubin, D. B. (1987). *Multiple Imputation for Nonresponse in Surveys*. New York, NY: Wiley.
Russell, H. and McGinnity, F. (2013). Under pressure: The impact of recession on employees in Ireland. *British Journal of Industrial Relations*, 52(2), 286–307. doi:10.1111/bjir.12018.
Schafer, J. L. and Graham, J. W. (2002). Missing data: Our view of the state of the art. *Psychological Methods*, 7(2), 147–177. doi:10.1037/1082-989X.7.2.147.
Scherer, S. and Steiber, N. (2007). Work and family in conflict? The impact of work demands on family life in six European countries. In D. Gallie (ed.), *Employment*

Systems and the Quality of Working Life (pp. 137–178). Oxford: Oxford University Press.

Snijders, T. A. B. and Bosker, R. J. (1999). Multilevel Analysis: An Introduction to Basic and Advanced Multilevel Modeling. London: Sage.

Steiber, N. (2009). Reported levels of time-based and strain-based conflict between work and family roles in Europe: A multilevel approach. Social Indicators Research, 93, 469–488.

Tausig, M. and Fenwick, R. (2001). Unbinding time: Alternate work schedules and work–life balance. *Journal of Family and Economic Issues*, 22(2), 101–119.

Van der Lippe, T., Jager, A. and Kops, Y. (2006). Combination pressure: The paid work–family balance of men and women in European countries. *Acta Sociologica*, 49(3), 303–319.

Von Hippel, P. T. (2009). How to impute squares, interactions, and other transformed variables. *Sociological Methodology*, 39(1), 265–291. doi:10.1111/j.1467-9531.2009.01215.x.

Voydanoff, P. (2005). Toward a conceptualization of perceived work–family fit and balance: A demands and resources approach. *Journal of Marriage and Family*, 67, 822–836.

White, I. R., Daniel, R. and Royston, P. (2010). Avoiding bias due to perfect prediction in multiple imputation of incomplete categorical variables. *Computational Statistics and Data Analysis*, 54, 2267–2275.

White, I. R., Royston, P. and Wood, A. M. (2011). Multiple imputation using chained equations: Issues and guidance for practice. *Statistics in Medicine*, 30(4), 377–399. doi:10.1002/sim.4067.

White, M., Hill, S., McGovern, P., Mills, C. and Smeaton, D. (2003). 'High-performance' management practices, working hours and work–life balance. *British Journal of Industrial Relations*, 41(2), 175–195.

6 A Tale of Two Surveys

Using the European Social Survey and the European Working Conditions Survey to Predict Welfare Attitudes by Work Regime

Amy Erbe Healy and Seán Ó Riain

Introduction

How can the strengths of different surveys be combined to better answer social science questions? This research examines the possibility of using the European Working Conditions Survey (EWCS) in tandem with the European Social Survey (ESS) to assess how work regimes shape attitudes towards welfare in the EU-15. The paper makes two major contributions. First, it assesses the value of the ESS 2004 and 2010 modules on work through a comparison of the "workplace regimes" constructed from the data in these special questionnaire modules with those constructed from the more extensive data available in the EWCS of 2005 and 2010. Second, the paper takes advantage of the more extensive attitudinal variables in the ESS to examine the effect of working under a particular workplace regime on attitudes to government redistribution of income and provision of social insurance, protection and/or investment. It also suggests that further thought be given to the modules with which future ESS rounds of the work organisation module are combined.

Understanding work organisation and welfare attitudes

Esping-Andersen's seminal work *Three Worlds of Welfare Capitalism* (1990) clearly demonstrated how welfare-state regimes across Europe were linked to national histories of class politics. Different constellations of welfare policies and institutions were explained by the efforts of social classes to protect themselves from "commodification" in the labour market. Ironically, however, Esping-Andersen and others in this approach had little to say about production and workplace politics itself.

The worlds-of-welfare approach was replaced as the dominant framework in comparative political economy by the *varieties of capitalism* approach in the 2000s. This approach re-focused the comparative study of capitalism on production, with the potential to incorporate analyses of workplace politics. However, it also moved the study of capitalism away from the politics of class to the question of risk in the labour market, distinguishing between two main groups: those with general skills who face little risk in the labour market and those with specific skills who rely more on social protections as they are more vulnerable in the labour market (Hall and Soskice 2001). Each approach therefore poses a different logic of welfare politics – each incomplete for our purposes.

More recent research has sought to tie sector, workers' experiences of precarity and skill level to attitudes towards welfare. Rueda (2005, 2006) and Emmenegger (2009) have both researched the link between precarity and welfare. Rueda argues that certain types of welfare that offer security and job protection are advantageous only to "insiders," those who have permanent jobs. As such, a symbiotic relationship has developed between "insiders" and those with political power (unions and political parties): "insiders" vote for social democrats who, in turn, support welfare policies that serve "insiders" through protection.

In a similar vein, Wren and Rehm (2014) have argued that employees' skill level and sector is correlated with welfare attitudes; specifically, highly skilled workers (those with tertiary education) who are employed in internationally exposed sectors (such as producer services and manufacturing) have more negative views towards welfare than both highly skilled workers in non-exposed sectors (public and personal services sector) and low-skilled workers (those without tertiary education) in any sector. They warn that since the producer service sector is expanding with growth in jobs for those with tertiary education, support for welfare will wane. Both authors implicitly link workplace regime to welfare attitudes, with support for welfare grounded in those institutionally protected at work and in the labour market – those in exposed sectors outside social protections are least favourable towards welfare.

Emmenegger (2009), however, disputes this link. He has found no link between "insider" and "outsider" status, as such. Most crucially, he argues that just because "outsiders" do not have security in their present position, there is no reason to believe that they do not aspire to have job security in future work. Furthermore, "insider–outsider" status is not fixed over time. Instead, more in keeping with Wren's and Rehm's view, he suggests that the self-employed and those he calls "upscales" – higher-level professionals, managers and administrators – are less likely to support job security in that they do not have the same need of it. However, research by Schwander et al. (2015) has come to almost the exact opposite conclusion, suggesting that many high skilled workers are precarious workers who may also have a stake in welfare protections. They suggest that there is the possibility of a future "cross-class alliance" between high-skill and low-skill precarious workers.

Therefore, while there seems to be consensus that parts of the work relationship may be significant in determining welfare attitudes, there is no agreement as to what is important or why. Moreover, existing literature uses a highly simplified concept of the organisation and politics of work. There are various different forms of work organisation in contemporary capitalism. Lorenz and Valeyre (2005) defined four basic types of work regime: "Simple," "Lean production," "Learning" and "Taylorist." "Simple" jobs are monotonous jobs at the low-end of the intensity/autonomy spectrum with low learning opportunities, low autonomy and also few control mechanisms bar direct supervision. "Taylorist" jobs also have relatively low learning and autonomy but are coupled with higher control mechanisms such as machine speed and team rotation of tasks and, thus, higher intensity of work. "Learning" jobs, on the other hand, allow employees more opportunities to learn with higher autonomy and more responsibility for quality management (see also Appelbaum and Batt 1994). At the upper end of the intensity spectrum, "Lean production" jobs also allow for more learning opportunities and relatively high autonomy in comparison with "Taylorist" and "Simple" jobs, but with multiple control mechanisms. These four workplace regimes are spread unevenly across the "worlds of capitalism," suggesting that different political and economic accommodations between work, the labour market and welfare are possible (see also Amable 2003).

The analysis in this paper extends this concept of workplace regimes to incorporate additional aspects of both the employment relationship and of working time, given that these systematically vary across these regimes. For example, while not explicitly part of their definitions of work regimes, Lorenz and Valeyre show that "Learning" jobs had higher levels of training, higher proportions of unlimited work contracts and more employees receiving compensation for the performance of the organisation than other types of work regimes. Employees in "Lean production" jobs received relatively less training than those in "Learning" jobs but still much higher than those in "Simple" or "Taylorist" jobs. Ciccia and Ó Riain (2013) document the complexities of new forms of working time with high autonomy work (such as "Learning" jobs) associated with flexible work schedules, which may improve work–life balance but are also more likely to "bleed" into overtime and non-traditional work hours.

With these various forms of workplace organisation, there are also different forms of welfare provision, which offer a number of potential logics for support for governmental welfare policies. These include the redistribution of income in the interests of equality; a social insurance and social protection role, whether for the poorest or through the full range of income; and social investments such as training, education, research and so on. Numerous categories overlap across these redistributive, protection and investment roles, for example, the case of childcare. The post-Fordist workplace regimes, whether "Lean" or "Learning" focused, are often more demanding, not only of the employees but also of the systems that produce and reproduce them and of the organisations that operate them. These complex institutional demands of the fastest growing workplace regimes are a potential basis for a new "welfare coalition" based more around investment and protection than around redistribution and protection.

Each approach within comparative political economy has implications for the well-documented link between the type of welfare regime and public attitudes towards welfare. Indeed, they also suggest that more attention should be paid to the impact of workplace and employment regimes on attitudes to welfare; these regimes can generate different interests in various forms of social protection as well as a range of workplace deals whose own legitimating principles may or may not be supportive of expansive social welfare, in whatever form.

Methods

To assess the relationship between work regime and welfare attitudes, we first define typologies of work regimes in terms of work organisation, employment relationship and work schedule using latent class analysis. Then, with that information, we analyse the relationship between work regime and welfare attitudes.

While the analysis is straightforward, data limitations create complexity in answering our research question. There is no one existing data set that allows for an in-depth study of both workplace regime and welfare attitudes. Therefore, this research examines the possibility of using two different surveys, the EWCS and the ESS, to assess attitudes towards welfare across work regimes in the EU-15. Both surveys have used random sampling methods to gather representative samples from across Europe at the country level. The EWCS contains extensive information on the employment relationship, time organisation and work organisation over five waves, with the last two waves taking place in 2005 and 2010. However, it does not gather attitudinal data. Rounds 2 and 5 of the ESS (2004 and 2010, respectively) contain a module on work and well-being (with more limited data than the EWCS on work organisation and employment relations) and extensive data on attitudes.

Initially, EWCS data was analysed with work organisation, time organisation and employment relation variables to determine the types of work regimes that exist within manufacturing (see Table 6.11A for a list of all variables and relevant coding). Then, analyses were done again on a reduced set of variables in ESS 2004/2010 and also EWCS 2005/2010 with the variables that exist in both data sets. The ESS and EWCS solutions were compared to assess whether or not the two different sources of data were producing the same types of work regime solutions. The initial solution from the full analysis of EWCS data was then used as a template for defining the types of work regimes that were produced from the subsequent analyses on the ESS and EWCS with fewer variables. Using the two variables related to welfare attitudes that are available in Rounds 2 and 5 of the ESS and the work regimes, chi-square and logistic regression analyses assessed whether or not attitudes varied significantly based on work regime.

To define regimes, we use latent class analysis (LCA) to predict typologies of work regimes within manufacturing. LCA is a type of clustering, data-reduction technique that works with discrete variables (nominal and ordinal). It predicts the probabilities that certain types of individuals will be in a particular latent class or underlying sociological category (see McCutcheon 1987 and Vermunt and Magidson 2005). It is analogous to factor analysis except that the variables included are not continuous. Given that all of the variables included in this analysis (and that were included in Lorenz's and Valeyre's analysis (2005)) are categorical, it is a more appropriate method of analysis than factor analysis. In finding a set of mutually exclusive latent classes (in this case, work regimes), it accounts for the distribution of cases within a cross-tabulation of the data. Also, if the same set of observed variables used to estimate the latent classes are present in multiple populations or with the same population at different points of time, then it is possible to determine if the latent variable is invariant ("equivalent") across populations and/or time. Multi-level LCA is one method for doing this. Multi-level LCA determines if there are dependencies between latent classes at a "higher" level, in this case across EU-15 countries and across time, and produces groupings of classes based on probabilities associated with each latent class.

We have used three types of variables in this analysis: indicators, inactive covariates and a grouping variable. Indicators are the observed (manifest) variables that are being used to define the classes of the latent variable, which in our research is work regime. As stated before, they include variables for work organisation, time organisation and employment relationship. Variables that were included as inactive covariates[1]/independent variables in the ESS analysis were gender, age, education, occupation, tenure, size of company and world of capitalism (Nordic, Continental, Southern and Liberal), as well as values that may impact attitudes towards welfare (helping others, desire to be rich, equality and strong government). In the EWCS analysis with reduced variables, all of the employment organisation variables that are not present in the ESS (and that had been used as indicators in the full analysis) were also used as inactive covariates to help further differentiate work regimes. The variable that was used for the multi-level LCA as a grouping variable is country-by-year. Given that work regime and welfare attitudes are correlated with welfare-state regime, this makes it possible to assess the influence of welfare-state regime on the probability of a worker being exposed to different types of work regimes.

For this analysis, we include only those employees who work in the manufacturing sector[2] within the EU-15 countries that had complete data sets for both the ESS and the EWCS. Luxembourg, France, Italy and Austria were not included because of missing data in 2004, 2005 and/or 2010. Agricultural employees and those in the armed forces have also been excluded. Final sample sizes were as follows: ESS 2004, $n=$ 1545; ESS 2010, $n=$ 1274; EWCS 2005, $n=$ 1315; and EWCS 2010, $n=$ 1705.

Similarly to Gallie's (2013) weighting strategy, the weighting was done in a two-step process. First, we have used the post-stratification weights provided with each data set. Then, to make sure that the results were not dominated/distorted either by big countries or by countries with larger samples, each country per year was weighted to be the same size as the smallest n across all data sets (see also Kankaraš et al. 2011 and Siegers 2011).

Europe's workplace regimes: The basic picture

Initially, we analysed a merged EWCS data set from 2005 and 2010 with variables for work organisation, working time and employment relations. Table 6.1 presents the goodness-of-fit indices from that analysis. Within LCA, goodness-of-fit indices are produced with the latent class solution to help the researcher pick the best solution in terms of the number of classes (and number of groups from the grouping variable, if a multi-level LCA is being used). For this analysis, we have presented the L^2 (the likelihood ratio chi-square) and Bayesian information criterion (BIC) to

Table 6.1 Goodness of fit indices, full EWCS analysis

1 group	1 cl	2 cl	3 cl	4 cl	5 cl	6 cl	7 cl
Log–likelihood (LL)	−15,944.6	−15,429.2	−15,123.8	−14,977.8	−14,869.4	−14,789.6	−14,741.3
BIC (based on LL)	32,061.2	31,180.98	30,720.67	30,579.28	30,512.96	30,503.75	30,557.84
Npar	24	45	66	87	108	129	150

2 group	1 cl	2 cl	3 cl	4 cl	5 cl	6 cl	7 cl
Log–likelihood (LL)	−15,944.6	−15,374.4	−15,078.7	−14,922.9	−14,817.6	−14,717.8	−14,661.2
BIC (based on LL)	32,068.36	31,085.72	30,652.02	30,498.16	30,445.09	**30,403.27**	30,447.67
Npar	25	47	69	91	113	135	157

3 group	1 cl	2 cl	3 cl	4 cl	5 cl	6 cl	7 cl
Log–likelihood (LL)	−15,944.6	−15,360.7	−15,066.5	−14,905.3	−14,798.9	−14,700.6	−14,630.4
BIC (based on LL)	32,075.53	31,072.63	30,649.1	30,491.6	30,443.67	**30,411.88**	30,436.41
Npar	26	49	72	95	118	141	148

Source: Authors' analysis of Eurofound data (2005, 2010).

assess goodness of fit. The lowest BIC is considered to be the best fitting solution; it uses the likelihood chi-square statistic and adjusts for degrees of freedom and also sample size. However, as discussed by Siegers (2011), goodness-of-fit indicators should not be the only consideration when choosing a final model: "Models that are clearly interpretable and correspond to theoretical expectations might be preferred, although other models show a better fit of the data" (2011, p. 398). Goodness-of-fit indices can also indicate whether or not multi-level LCA is warranted. We have chosen the model with six-classes and three-country/year groupings as our "template" for the remainder of the analysis.

While a model of six-classes and three-country/year groupings does not provide the lowest BIC, it is very close in fit to the best-fitting six-class, two-country/year solution. The work regimes (and associated probabilities) were also very similar for both the two-country/year and the three-country/year grouping solutions. The three-country/year grouping model was chosen because it is more interesting in terms of the way that countries from the same worlds of welfare capitalism tend to cluster together, as shown in Table 6.2. Consistently, Belgium, Germany, Ireland and the United Kingdom cluster together (Continental/Liberal grouping); the Netherlands, Sweden and Finland cluster together (Nordic and the Netherlands grouping) and Greece and Portugal cluster together (the Southern grouping). Two countries – Spain and Denmark – appear once in their expected groupings (Southern and Nordic, respectively) but also appear once with the Continental/Liberal group, indicating that the probabilities associated with work regimes for those countries have changed over the course of the survey.

Table 6.2 Country groupings from full EWCS analysis

	Continental & Liberal	*Nordic & Netherlands*	*Southern*
Group size	0.44	0.32	0.23
Clusters			
Learn	0.22	0.38	0.09
Lean extend	0.28	0.14	0.19
Taylor	0.20	0.06	0.37
Simple	0.13	0.04	0.29
Learn extend	0.11	0.18	0.05
Lean shift	0.06	0.19	0.00
	Belgium05	**Denmark10**	Greece05
	Belgium10	Finland05	Greece10
	Denmark05	Finland10	Portugal05
	Germany05	Netherlands05	Portugal10
	Germany10	Netherlands10	**Spain05**
	Ireland05	Sweden05	
	Ireland10	Sweden10	
	Spain10		
	United Kingdom05		
	United Kingdom10		

Source: Authors' analysis of Eurofound data (2005, 2010).

As can be seen from Table 6.2, each country/year grouping has different probabilities of being in specific work regimes. The six work regimes are presented in Table 6.3. Three of the work regimes that emerged from the LCA analysis of manufacturing data – "Learn," "Simple" and "Taylorist" – are very similar to the work regimes produced from Lorenz's and Valeyre's analysis (2005). The "Learn" regime typifies jobs that have high learning opportunities and high autonomy with quality standards.

The "Simple" regime is the opposite, with few learning opportunities and low autonomy. It also has the highest prevalence of jobs that are precarious, meaning limited contracts or no contracts at all. "Taylorist" regimes also have low learning and little autonomy. However, they have high control mechanisms such as deadlines, productions norms, machine speed, boss oversight, colleague pace and quality standards, making them higher intensity jobs.

The three other regimes produced from our analysis are: "Lean extend," "Lean shift" and "Learn extend." In some ways, they are extensions of the typologies produced by Lorenz and Valeyre. The addition of time organisation variables in terms of fixed time, actual hours, weekends and evening and/or night work has produced some new regime typologies. While also high in learning and autonomy, the original work regime "Learn" is differentiated to "Learn extend" for those who put in well over 48 hours a week, including weekends, evenings and/or nights, with no fixed time schedule (similar to the group found by Ciccia and Ó Riain [2013]). While Lorenz and Valeyre had a regime simply for lean work organisation, there is no basic lean work regime in our solution. Instead, "Lean" is either "Lean extend" for those who may be more likely to work overtime and "Lean shifts" for those who work weekends and/or evening–night shifts. Both of the lean regimes are typified not only by relatively high learning with some autonomy (though not as much as the learn regimes) but also more control mechanisms. "Lean extend" jobs are typified by deadlines, customers, production norms, boss oversight, quality standards, colleague pace and task rotation. "Lean shift" jobs are typified by production norms, machine speed, task rotation and quality standards. They are high intensity jobs that "bleed" into the time outside of the standard work week.

The results of this analysis on both work organisation and employment relation variables in the EWCS gives us a "template," as such, of work regimes. These are the work regimes that exist within manufacturing in Europe.

Comparing datasets in the analysis of workplace regimes

Since the ESS does not have many of the work organisation variables that are needed to define our typologies, this full solution gives us a point of comparison to see how accurate the results are of an analysis on a reduced set of variables that are present in both the EWCS and the ESS.

Equivalence within LCA refers to the level of comparability of solutions derived from analyses of the same observed variables with different populations or with the same population at different points in time (see Eid et al. 2003, Kankaraš et al. 2011 and McCutcheon 2002 for a more thorough discussion). While both surveys

Table 6.3 Work regimes from full EWCS analysis (6 regimes, 3 groups)

	Learn	Lean extend	Taylorist	Simple	Learn extend	Lean shift
	Cluster 1	Cluster 2	Cluster 3	Cluster 4	Cluster 5	Cluster 6
Cluster size	0.24	0.21	0.19	0.14	0.12	0.09
Indicators						
Contract						
Permanent	0.88	0.82	0.74	0.64	0.93	0.85
Fixed term	0.07	0.10	**0.14**	**0.15**	0.03	0.14
Other	0.04	0.08	**0.12**	**0.21**	0.04	0.01
Hours						
Under 20 hours	0.06	0.01	0.01	0.04	0.00	0.05
20–34 hours	0.12	0.04	0.06	0.10	0.01	0.11
35–47 hours	0.78	0.82	0.84	0.80	0.62	0.80
48 hours plus	0.04	0.14	0.09	0.05	**0.37**	0.04
Evening/night						
Yes	0.08	0.49	0.43	0.29	**0.95**	**0.95**
No	0.92	0.51	0.57	0.71	0.05	0.05
Weekends						
Yes	0.09	0.42	0.29	0.33	**0.71**	**0.57**
No	0.91	0.58	0.71	0.67	0.29	0.43
Fixed time						
Yes	0.73	0.71	0.93	0.85	0.22	0.84
No	0.27	0.29	0.07	0.15	**0.78**	0.16
Work-related train						
Yes	0.38	0.44	0.17	0.06	0.66	0.55
No	0.62	0.56	0.83	0.94	0.34	0.45
Autonomy						
Yes (order and speed)	**0.81**	0.53	0.08	0.29	**0.83**	0.48
Some (order or speed)	0.15	0.27	0.20	0.29	0.14	0.28
None	0.04	0.20	**0.72**	**0.42**	0.03	0.23
Unforeseen problems						
Yes	0.93	0.96	0.54	0.53	0.98	0.86
No	0.07	0.04	**0.46**	**0.47**	0.02	0.14
Complex tasks						
Yes	0.77	0.90	0.33	0.20	0.89	0.58
No	0.23	0.10	**0.67**	**0.80**	0.11	0.42
Deadlines						
Most or all of the time	0.26	**0.74**	**0.58**	0.10	**0.59**	0.28
Sometimes	0.29	0.19	0.26	0.22	0.26	0.30
Almost never or never	**0.44**	0.07	0.15	**0.68**	0.15	**0.42**
Customers						
Yes	**0.52**	**0.78**	0.49	0.41	**0.79**	0.33
No	0.48	0.22	0.51	0.59	0.21	0.67

Table 6.3 Continued

	Learn	Lean extend	Taylorist	Simple	Learn extend	Lean shift
	Cluster 1	Cluster 2	Cluster 3	Cluster 4	Cluster 5	Cluster 6
Production norms						
Yes	0.36	**0.88**	**0.83**	0.19	0.48	**0.72**
No	0.64	0.12	0.17	0.81	0.52	0.28
Machine speed						
Yes	0.12	**0.59**	**0.76**	0.18	0.06	**0.69**
No	0.88	0.41	0.24	0.82	0.94	0.31
Boss						
Yes	0.21	**0.67**	**0.75**	0.45	0.18	0.20
No	0.79	0.33	0.25	0.55	0.82	0.80
Colleague pace/ task rotation						
Colleague pace and task rotation	0.21	**0.56**	0.35	0.15	0.29	0.36
Task rotation, no colleague pace	0.30	0.11	0.06	0.20	0.16	**0.48**
Colleague pace, no task rotation	0.14	0.27	**0.42**	0.19	0.19	0.03
Neither	**0.34**	0.06	0.17	**0.46**	**0.36**	0.13
Quality standards						
Yes	0.78	0.99	0.90	0.59	0.67	0.94
No	0.22	0.01	0.10	**0.41**	0.33	0.06
Learn new things						
Yes	0.89	0.96	0.40	0.40	0.96	0.81
No	0.11	0.04	**0.60**	**0.60**	0.04	0.19

Source: Authors' analysis of Eurofound data (2005, 2010).

have been recoded to have the same observed variables (see Table 6.11A), some of the questions were worded slightly differently and coded differently. While the variables have been rationalised to the fullest extent possible, the results are not completely equivalent. As such, we chose to analyse the ESS data and the EWCS data separately in terms of generating work regimes.[3]

Goodness-of-fit indices are presented in Tables 6.4 and 6.5. The best fit (lowest BIC) for the merged ESS data set is a five-class, three-group model. For the merged EWCS data set, the best fit is a five-class, two-group model. However, for the EWCS, the fit is very similar for either the two-group or three-group model. For comparison's sake, we will use the five-class, three-group solution from both surveys. Ultimately, we are trying to determine if the results are "equivalent" enough for us to use our typologies of work regimes to predict welfare attitudes.

Table 6.6 presents the work regimes from both data sets. Given that there are fewer variables in this analysis than the initial EWCS analysis with a full set

Table 6.4 Goodness of fit indices, ESS variables

1 group	1 cl	2 cl	3 cl	4 cl	5 cl	6 cl
Log-likelihood (LL)	−8,216.9	−7,969.13	−7,850.4	−7,810.21	−7,778.11	−7,758.33
BIC (based on LL)	16,534.36	16,110.66	15,945.04	15,936.49	15,944.12	15,976.41
Npar	14	24	34	44	54	64

2 group	1 cl	2 cl	3 cl	4 cl	5 cl	6 cl
Log-likelihood (LL)	−8,216.9	−7,889.65	−7,773.93	−7,726.76	−7,675.68	−7,642.05
BIC (based on LL)	16,541.55	15,966.08	15,813.64	15,798.33	15,775.19	15,786.95
NPar	15	26	37	48	59	70

3 group	1 cl	2 cl	3 cl	4 cl	5 cl	6 cl
Log-likelihood (LL)	−8,216.9	−7,869	−7,752.54	−7,701.01	−7,644.69	−7,616.72
BIC (based on LL)	16,548.73	15,939.14	15,792.42	15,775.56	**15,749.12**	15,779.38
Npar	16	28	40	52	64	76

4 group	1 cl	2 cl	3 cl	4 cl	5 cl	6 cl
Log-likelihood (LL)	−8,216.9	−7,866.69	−7,750.38	−7,693.92	−7,639.06	−7,605.89
BIC (based on LL)	16,555.91	15,948.89	15,809.66	15,790.11	15,773.78	15,800.83
Npar	17	30	43	56	69	82

Source: Authors' analysis of ESS data (2004, 2010).

Table 6.5 Goodness of fit indices, EWCS reduced analysis

1 group	1 cl	2 cl	3 cl	4 cl	5 cl	6 cl
Log-likelihood (LL)	−7,504.55	−7,283.58	−7,151.9	−7,110.22	−7,058.64	−7,038.27
BIC (based on LL)	15,095.68	14,725.91	14,534.7	14,523.5	14,492.51	14,523.92
Npar	12	22	32	42	52	62

2 group	1 cl	2 cl	3 cl	4 cl	5 cl	6 cl
Log-likelihood (LL)	−7,504.55	−7,235.08	−7,084.62	−7,029.37	−6,972.56	−6,950.06
BIC (based on LL)	15,102.9	14,643.34	14,421.79	14,390.68	**14,356.42**	14,390.79
NPar	13	24	35	46	57	68

3 group	1 cl	2 cl	3 cl	4 cl	5 cl	6 cl
Log-likelihood (LL)	−7,504.55	−7,225.69	−7,072.6	−7,015.11	−6,956.42	−6,926.75
BIC (based on LL)	15,110.12	14,639	14,419.41	14,391.01	**14,360.22**	14,387.48
NPar	14	26	38	50	62	74

Source: Authors' analysis of Eurofound data (2005, 2010).

Table 6.6 Work regimes from reduced EWCS and ESS analysis

ESS	Learn	Simple/ Taylor	Lean shift	Lean/learn extend	Simple/ Taylor Sh	EWCS	Learn	Simple/ Taylor	Lean shift	Lean/learn extend	Simple/ Taylor Sh
Cluster size Indicators	0.34	0.27	0.15	0.13	0.11	Cluster size Indicators	0.31	0.29	0.18	0.15	0.07
Contract						Contract					
Permanent	0.87	0.72	0.86	0.96	0.72	Unlimited	0.87	0.75	0.83	0.92	0.53
Fixed term	0.10	**0.13**	0.12	0.04	**0.08**	Limited	0.08	**0.11**	0.13	0.04	**0.21**
other	0.03	**0.15**	0.02	0.00	**0.21**	No contract	0.05	**0.14**	0.04	0.04	**0.25**
Hours						Hours					
under 20 hours	0.02	0.02	0.03	0.00	0.00	under 20 hours	0.04	0.01	0.06	0.00	0.00
20–34 hours	0.09	0.09	0.10	0.00	0.00	20–34 hours	0.11	0.07	0.14	0.00	0.00
35–47 hours	0.83	0.83	0.82	0.53	0.38	35–47 hours	0.84	0.91	0.80	0.57	0.43
48 hours plus	0.06	0.05	0.05	**0.46**	**0.62**	48 hours plus	0.01	0.01	0.00	**0.43**	**0.57**
Eve/night						Eve/night					
Yes	0.05	0.22	**0.98**	**0.71**	**0.70**	Yes	0.13	0.30	**0.83**	**0.86**	**0.66**
No	0.95	0.78	0.02	0.29	0.30	No	0.87	0.70	0.17	0.14	0.34
Weekends						Weekends					
Yes	0.08	0.19	**0.58**	**0.49**	**0.73**	yes	0.09	0.16	**0.63**	**0.68**	**0.96**
No	0.92	0.81	0.42	0.51	0.27	no	0.91	0.84	0.37	0.32	0.04
Fixed time						Fixed time					
Yes	0.64	0.98	0.94	0.30	0.86	yes	0.72	0.96	0.78	0.29	0.63
No	0.36	0.02	0.06	**0.70**	0.14	no	0.28	0.04	0.22	**0.71**	0.37

(*continued*)

Table 6.6 Continued

ESS	Learn	Simple/ Taylor	Lean shift	Lean/learn extend	Simple/ Taylor Sh	EWCS	Learn	Simple/ Taylor	Lean shift	Lean/learn extend	Simple/ Taylor Sh
Work related train						Work related train					
Yes	0.46	0.07	**0.54**	**0.79**	0.24	Yes	0.38	0.12	**0.50**	**0.70**	0.16
No	0.54	0.93	0.46	0.21	0.76	No	0.62	0.88	0.50	0.30	0.84
Autonomy						Autonomy					
Yes (order and speed)	**0.76**	0.12	**0.57**	**0.98**	0.31	Yes (order and speed)	**0.81**	0.15	**0.42**	**0.81**	0.19
Some (order and/or speed)	0.18	0.23	0.26	0.02	0.29	Some (order and / or speed)	0.15	0.26	0.30	0.15	0.27
None	0.07	**0.65**	0.18	0.00	**0.40**	None	0.04	**0.59**	0.28	0.04	**0.54**
Learn new things ESS						Learn new things EWCS					
A little true	**0.31**	**0.39**	**0.32**	0.14	0.27	No	0.10	**0.52**	0.22	0.02	0.47
Quite true	**0.32**	0.21	**0.31**	**0.31**	0.33						
Very true	0.24	0.08	0.23	**0.53**	0.30						

Source: Authors' analysis of ESS & Eurofound.

of variables, it is perhaps unsurprising that the best-fitting models have fewer numbers of classes. While the probabilities associated with the solutions from the ESS and the EWCS analyses are not identical, they are broadly similar. The work regimes produced from the two separate analyses are also broadly similar. It is noteworthy that, without the variables for work organisation, it becomes difficult to differentiate between "Lean" and "Learn" regimes and "Taylorist" and "Simple" regimes. As such, a few of the regimes have combined from the first analysis (Table 6.3), producing a slightly less differentiated set of work regimes. There is still a "Learn" regime that has high autonomy and high learning, and "Lean shift," which has high learning, moderately high autonomy and evening/night work and weekends. "Simple" and "Taylorist" have combined into one regime typified by little learning and low autonomy. This regime also has a slightly higher probability of precarious work, though not nearly as high as the new regime, "Simple/Taylorist shifts", which has low learning (in the EWCS regime), low autonomy, high levels of fixed-term and no-contract jobs coupled with high levels of overtime, evening and/or night work and weekend work. Surprisingly, there is a much higher probability of learning within the ESS data, possibly associated with the fact that there is also a higher prevalence of overtime and evening/night work in that solution. Finally, given that there are no control mechanism variables in the analysis, "Lean extend" and "Learn extend" from the full analysis have combined into one regime that contains both. It is typified by high learning, high autonomy and an intense work schedule that includes overtime, evenings/nights and weekends.

To assess whether the definitions of typologies are correct, the work organisation variables from the full EWCS were included as inactive covariates in the reduced analysis as presented in Table 6.7. Given that they were "inactive," they do not impact the solution of the work regimes. Instead, they are simply listed in cross-tabulation form with the solution. As such, it is possible to see how these variables vary across regimes. However, given that they were not used to define regimes, they are not as highly differentiated as they would be if they were used as indicators in the analysis.

As with the full analysis from Table 6.3, the "Learn" regime seems to be related to quality standards in terms of control mechanisms but nothing else. The "Lean/Learn extend" regime is also related to quality standards but also somewhat to deadlines, customers and production norms. Both the "Simple/Taylorist" regime and the "Simple/Taylorist shift" regime seem to have a relatively high association with boss oversight, as would be expected given that those regimes have low autonomy. As such, the regime labels still seem appropriate with each regime typology.

As a means of assessing "equivalence" of solution between the data sets, country/year groupings between solutions were compared, as presented in Table 6.8. Both analyses could be said to have produced a "Continental/Liberal" group, a "Nordic and the Netherlands" group and a "Southern" group. However, the configuration of the countries is slightly different, which explains why the probabilities of groups being in different regimes are also slightly different.[4]

Table 6.7 Inactive covariates from analysis on EWCS: work organisation

EWCS	Learn	Simple/ Taylorist	Lean shift	Lean/learn extend	Simple/ Taylorist shifts
Unforeseen problems					
Yes	**0.88**	0.66	**0.84**	**0.95**	0.65
No	0.12	0.34	0.15	0.05	0.35
Missing	0.00	0.01	0.00	0.00	0.00
Complex tasks					
Yes	**0.72**	0.46	**0.61**	**0.87**	0.48
No	0.28	0.53	0.38	0.13	0.52
Missing	0.00	0.00	0.01	0.00	0.00
Deadlines					
Most or all of the time	0.36	0.43	0.46	**0.56**	**0.54**
Sometimes	0.30	0.24	0.23	0.26	0.15
Almost never or never	0.34	0.33	0.31	0.17	0.30
Missing	0.00	0.00	0.00	0.00	0.00
Customers					
Yes	0.57	0.47	0.55	**0.73**	**0.66**
No	0.43	0.53	0.44	0.27	0.33
Missing	0.00	0.01	0.01	0.00	0.01
Production norms					
Yes	0.50	**0.61**	**0.64**	**0.64**	**0.60**
No	0.49	0.38	0.35	0.36	0.40
Missing	0.01	0.01	0.01	0.00	0.00
Machine speed					
Yes	0.27	**0.49**	**0.50**	0.29	**0.55**
No	0.72	0.50	0.49	0.71	0.44
Missing	0.01	0.01	0.01	0.00	0.01
Boss					
Yes	0.33	**0.61**	0.38	0.34	**0.57**
No	0.66	0.38	0.60	0.65	0.43
Missing	0.01	0.01	0.02	0.01	0.01
Colleague pace/task rotation					
Both	0.31	0.29	**0.38**	**0.40**	**0.34**
Task rotation	0.25	0.14	0.24	0.17	0.14
Colleague pace	0.18	0.31	0.19	0.19	0.25
Neither	0.26	0.26	0.18	0.24	0.27
Quality standards					
Yes	**0.81**	**0.82**	**0.86**	**0.80**	**0.74**
No	0.18	0.17	0.13	0.20	0.25
Missing	0.01	0.01	0.01	0.00	0.01

Source: Authors' analysis of Eurofound data (2005, 2010).

Across both data sets, the probabilities of being in "Simple/Taylorist" and "Simple/Taylorist shift" regimes is much higher in the Southern country grouping than in any other, especially the Nordic and the Netherlands group, where those types of jobs are almost non-existent. The Continental/Liberal group also has a relatively high probability of "Simple/Taylorist" jobs within manufacturing, but

Table 6.8 Country groupings from reduced EWCS and ESS analysis

ESS	Group 1	Group 2	Group 3	EWCS	Group 1	Group 2	Group 3
Size	0.40	0.37	0.23	Size	0.49	0.28	0.24
Clusters				Clusters			
Learn	0.32	0.53	0.06	Learn	0.32	0.14	0.50
Sim./Tay.*	0.31	0.05	0.60	Sim./Tay.*	0.25	0.60	0.03
Lean shift	0.13	0.22	0.03	Lean shift	0.21	0.03	0.28
Lean/learn ext.	0.13	0.20	0.004	Lean/learn ext.	0.18	0.07	0.19
Sim./Tay.* shifts	0.11	0.001	0.30	Sim./Tay.* shifts	0.04	0.17	0.001

Continent/Liberal	Nordic/Netherlands	South	Continent/Liberal	South	Nordic/Netherlands
Belgium04	Denmark04	Greece04	Belgium05	Germany05	Denmark10
Belgium10ESS	Denmark10ESS	Greece10ESS	Belgium10	Greece05	Finland05
Germany04	Finland04	Ireland04	Denmark05	Greece10	Finland10
Germany10ESS	Finland10ESS	Portugal04	Germany10	Portugal05	Netherlands10
Ireland10ESS	Netherlands04	Portugal10ESS	Ireland05	Portugal10	Sweden05
Spain04	Netherlands10ESS		Ireland10	Spain05	
Spain10ESS	Sweden04		Netherlands05		
United Kingdom04	Sweden10ESS		Spain10		
United Kingdom10 ESS			Sweden10		
			United Kingdom2005		
			United Kingdom2010		

Source: Authors' analysis of ESS & Eurofound data.
Note: *Sim./Tay. is an abbreviation for Simple/Taylor.

it is surpassed by the "Learn" regime, which has higher autonomy and learning opportunities. And, finally, the Nordic and the Netherlands group is predominated by jobs in the "Learn" regime, followed by "Lean shift" jobs. It also has the highest level of "Lean/Learn extend" jobs of any country grouping.

Work regimes and welfare attitudes

In terms of attitudinal data towards welfare, there are two variables that were included in the ESS in Rounds 2 and 5: "Government should reduce income inequality" (in both surveys) and "Government should reduce poverty" (only in 2010).[5] The first relates to the role of the government in directly reducing inequalities, primarily (presumably, based on the question) based on cash. While this could involve, in principle, a number of government roles, it relates most directly to redistribution between income groups. The second relates to the role of government in providing a safety net – while still having a strong cash focus, the mechanisms could relate to services as well as finances, and this variable generally implies a role ensuring social protection from risk in the labour market rather than the redistribution of income across income groups. While not ideal, the differences in the questions are nonetheless distinct enough to be instructive. Arguably, the income differences question is fundamentally about the income politics of classes, while the poverty question taps a concern with protection and/ or insurance against extreme risk in the labour market.

To determine whether or not work regime is related to attitudes towards welfare, inactive covariates for the two welfare variables were added to the ESS analysis. As shown in Table 6.9, the cross-tabulations indicate that there is a relationship between the two. It is especially apparent for the variable "gincdif" (the government should take measures to reduce income difference). Those in "Simple/Taylorist" regimes (regular hours or shifts) seem much more likely to agree and strongly agree that the government should reduce income difference and prevent poverty. Those in the "Lean/Learn extend" regime, on the other hand, seem to have the highest probability of disagreeing or disagreeing strongly. While the differences are not as extreme in 2010 for the variable "gvprppv" (the government should do much more to prevent people falling into poverty), in that a much higher percentage of people across all workplace regimes agree generally, the same pattern still exists.

Chi-square analysis on both sets of variables ("gincdif" and work regime, and "gvprppv" and work regime) indicates that there is a significant relationship between work regime and welfare attitudes for both. Chi-square for "gincdif" and work regime is 113.7 with 16 d. f. (p = .000); chi-square for "gvprppv" and work regime is 39.6 with 16 d.f. (p = .001).

Obviously, there are many other variables related to attitudes towards welfare that may be impacting these results. As such, logistic regression was done on both of the welfare attitude variables separately (now coded to "yes" for those who strongly agree and agree and "no" for all others) with probabilities associated with work regimes as independent variables. We have also controlled for gender,

Table 6.9 Inactive covariates from analysis on ESS: attitudes towards welfare

	Learn	Simple/ Taylorist	Lean shift	Lean/learn extend	Simple/ Taylorist shifts
gincdif: The government should take measures to reduce income difference					
Agree strongly	0.19	**0.37**	0.20	0.10	**0.30**
Agree	**0.40**	**0.41**	**0.40**	0.33	**0.41**
Neither agree nor disagree	0.17	0.10	0.18	**0.24**	0.12
Disagree	0.19	0.07	0.18	**0.25**	0.10
Disagree strongly	0.04	0.02	0.04	**0.07**	0.04
Missing	0.03	0.04	0.01	0.01	0.02
gvprppv*: The government should do much more to prevent people falling into poverty					
Agree strongly	0.36	**0.52**	0.38	0.26	**0.59**
Agree	0.44	**0.37**	0.46	0.47	**0.34**
Neither agree nor disagree	**0.13**	0.07	0.08	**0.16**	0.04
Disagree	**0.06**	0.03	0.05	**0.10**	0.02
Disagree strongly	0.01	0.01	0.03	0.01	0.00

Source: Authors' analysis of ESS data (2004, 2010).
Note: * Of those in Round 5 who answered the question.

occupation, education, age, tenure within job, company size, union membership, region (world of capitalism) and values: richness, helping others, equality and strong government.[6] Table 6.10 presents the results of this analysis of ESS data. All work regime odds ratios are in reference to someone being in the "Simple/Taylorist" regime.

As can be seen in Table 6.10, there are significant work regime differences in welfare attitudes, and these are most clearly differentiated in the variable "gincdif" (the government should take measures to reduce income difference). In reference to those within the "Simple/Taylorist" regime, all other regimes are less supportive of a reduction in income inequality. The most negative group is the "Lean/Learn extend" regime. Given that we cannot differentiate based on work intensity (having had no work control variables in the definition of the regimes), all that we can conclude is that those who work for extended hours and who have higher learning opportunities and autonomy in their jobs are the least likely to support redistributive welfare policies. Significantly, this effect persists even after controlling for occupation and education, suggesting that the politics of work has an independent effect on welfare politics. In terms of degree, those who work shifts ("Simple/Taylorist shifts" and "Lean shifts") are also less supportive than those who do not. Those who do not have the capacity to earn more through extra and/or unsociable work hours ("Simple/Taylorist" and "Learn" work regimes) are the most supportive of increased income equality through government intervention.

Table 6.10 Logistic regression predicting welfare attitudes, ESS data R2 and R5

Income difference	Odds ratio	Std. Err.		Prevent poverty	Odds ratio	Std. Err.	
(relative to Simple/Taylorist)				(relative to Simple/Taylorist)			
Learn	0.68	0.16	*	Learn	1.26	0.59	
Lean shift	0.62	0.15	**	Lean shift	1.84	0.71	
Lean/learn extend	0.39	0.09	**	Lean/learn extend	1.03	0.46	
Simple/Taylorist shift	0.49	0.18	*	Simple/Taylorist shift	6.47	3.76	**
(Gender relative to male)							
Female	1.29	0.14	**				
(Occupation relative to ISCO1)				(occupation relative to ISCO1)			
ISCO2	1.57	0.33	**	ISCO5	1.96	0.50	**
ISCO3	1.86	0.31	**				
ISCO4	1.80	0.44	**				
ISCO5	2.40	0.72	**				
ISCO7	2.54	0.58	**				
ISCO8	3.04	0.67	**				
ISCO9	2.30	0.60	**				
(Education relative to less than lower secondary)				(Education relative to less than lower secondary)			
Upper secondary	0.72	0.14	*	Lower secondary	0.25	0.12	**
Tertiary	0.66	0.33	**	Upper secondary	0.29	0.14	**
				Post-secondary	0.35	0.15	**
(Relative to union member)				Tertiary	0.16	0.04	**
Not a union member	0.75	0.12	*				
(Relative to Continental)				(Relative to Continental)			
Nordic	0.72	0.18		Nordic	0.92	0.44	
Southern	4.34	1.18	**	Southern	6.42	3.76	**
Liberal	1.60	0.45	*	Liberal	1.50	0.46	
Equality important	1.36	0.20	**	Equality important	1.87	0.38	**
Strong government important	1.37	0.17	**	Strong government important	1.66	0.23	**
_cons	0.62	0.35		_cons	7.05	5.59	**

Notes: Controlling for gender, occupation, education, age, tenure, company size, union, values: Richness, helping, equality, strong government and region (world of capitalism) – *only significant independent variables have been displayed*; clustered standard errors.
**p < 0.05, *p < 0.1.

In terms of the variable "gvprppv" (the government should do much more to prevent people falling into poverty), the differences between most of the regimes are not significant. The regime that is statistically significantly different from the rest with the highest level of support for poverty prevention is the

"Simple/Taylorist shift" regime. Therefore, those who work the most unsociable hours with the least amount of autonomy and learning opportunities are also the people who are most in favour of the government doing more to prevent poverty. However, if we use "Simple/Taylorist shift" as our reference regime, then the "Lean shift" also becomes statistically significantly different from all other regimes – except the reference category – and second in the level of support for poverty prevention. Thus, those who do shift work, whether with high autonomy and learning or low, are more supportive of government protection provisions than those who do not.

Quite obviously, the regime a person is exposed to at work is related to their attitudes towards welfare in terms of income differences and poverty prevention. Looking at the results, we find evidence that income redistribution politics tracks the logic of Esping-Andersen's analysis, while the politics of risk and protection tracks the logic of *varieties of capitalism*. In terms of attitudes towards income redistribution, the results indicate that workers in jobs with the lowest autonomy and lowest levels of skill development strongly believe that the government should address income equality, even when variables such as occupation and education are taken into consideration. At the other end of the spectrum, those in "Lean/Learn extend" are the most negative; this is linked to a workplace deal where total commitment is often traded for sizeable income, undermining any potential support for redistribution of income. Looking at country groupings, the Nordic countries are the least supportive. Negativity towards income redistribution may be linked to an already active government but more fundamentally may be linked to a focus in Nordic welfare on collectively provided social services rather than on income redistribution. The southern Europeans are the most supportive; they also have much higher levels of income inequality than the Nordic or Continental countries and may feel that the government needs to increase measures for income redistribution.[7]

In estimating attitudes towards income equality through government intervention, the background variables that are significant are the classic class variables such as occupation and union membership. Esping-Andersen's approach focused on class politics and how they take the form of historically different institutionalised bargains (in this case, the degree and form of de-commodification through the welfare state). These outcomes are influenced by class interests, power resources in the union movement, dominant political party and related forces. These are significant independent variables in our analysis of this dimension of welfare politics – suggesting the continuing importance of a class politics of income redistribution.

However, the politics of preventing poverty is somewhat different. Groups that are highly exposed to labour market risk are more likely to support the government role, reflecting the emphasis on "outsiders" in the varieties-of-capitalism perspective. Those in "Simple/Taylorist shift" regimes are the most supportive. This is the group with the highest level of precarious workers, including the highest level without any type of contract at all. Similarly, those with little or no education are more supportive than all other education levels. Again, they have fewer resources for finding work than other workers, should they lose their present job. In looking at country groupings, southern Europe is by far the most supportive.

Given that the economic crisis hit this part of Europe the hardest, arguably they are also facing the highest level of risk as a region and would be more likely to seek active government protections.

This suggests that the class politics of income may operate in ways that are not only different and overlapping but also potentially in tension with the politics of risk in the labour market. There are no straightforward politics of an enhanced governmental role.

Conclusion

This analysis has used two different surveys, the ESS and the EWCS, to define work regimes within manufacturing across Europe. The initial analysis of the EWCS, with both work organisation and employment relationship variables, showed that there are six typologies of work regime clearly differentiating "Learn," "Simple" and "Taylorist" regimes plus "Learn extend," "Lean extend" and "Lean shifts." Clearly, there are jobs that are at the upper end of the intensity spectrum ("Lean extend" and "Lean shifts") and some at the bottom ("Simple").

However, in trying to relate work regimes to welfare attitudes, it was necessary to use the ESS, which has fewer of the variables needed to build work regimes. Therefore, while it was possible to form regimes based on autonomy, learning and time organisation, it was difficult to assess work intensity without information on control mechanisms used in work organisation. Given that intensity based on time (i.e. shift work) had a significant impact on welfare attitudes, it seems plausible that intensity caused by control mechanisms used on the job may also lead to significant differences. However, to do this, the ESS would need to add additional variables to its work and welfare module regarding control mechanisms used on the job.

While this research has focused only on manufacturing jobs (an exposed sector, per Wren and Rehm [2014]), it has found diverse attitudes across the sector dependent on work regime – as well as a variety of other factors. The next step in assessing the relationship between work regime and welfare attitudes would be to analyse non-exposed sectors, such as personal services and public administration, to determine if there is diversity of attitudes within those sectors as well. At the very least, from our analysis of manufacturing, it seems safe to conclude that attitudes are complex and cannot be attributed to only one or two attributes associated with work, such as sector and precarity. Instead, the complexity of the work regime needs to be taken into consideration. We also need to expand our analysis to include macro-level variables such as GDP and unemployment rate, which may help to explain differences in attitudes towards welfare. Critically, our analysis suggests that different "socio-political logics" may well affect different dimensions of welfare politics.

We hope that for future rounds of the ESS, consideration could be given to including more questions regarding control mechanisms on the job with its work and welfare module; in that way, it will be possible to estimate work regimes with ESS data. Then, if the work and well-being module could be run with the welfare module, it would be possible to fully assess the impact of work regime on support for government welfare initiatives.

Notes

1 Inactive covariates do not define latent classes; their distribution is shown with the latent class solution as a cross-tabulation.
2 For future research, we will do a similar analysis on other sectors (exposed vs. non-exposed) to test the hypothesis put forward by Wren and Rehm (2014).
3 Initially, we analysed each wave of the ESS and the EWCS data separately and then merged 2004 and 2010 for the ESS and 2005 and 2010 for the EWCS; we assessed "equivalence" by comparing the number of latent classes and general structure of the latent classes. Results of these analyses can be requested from the authors. Finally, as a further check to ensure that typologies were clustering based on the observed variables rather than on the source of the data, we merged the ESS data with the EWCS data (further rationalising variables where necessary), as shown in Table 6.12A.
4 Table 6.12A provides the country/year groupings from an analysis of all of the data sets (EWCS 2005, EWCS 2010, ESS 2004 and ESS 2010) merged together as a final check as to whether the solutions were "equivalent" across data sets or if they were clustering differently based on survey. The results indicate that the country/year groupings stay much the same whether the data sets are analysed together or separately with the exception of Netherlands EWCS 2005, which moves to the Nordic and the Netherlands group from the Continental group when all data sets are merged together.
5 It is only within ESS Round 4 that there is extensive data on welfare attitudes. However, the data in ESS Round 4 on employment relations and work organisation is too limited to use this data set for this analysis.
6 Income was not included in this analysis because of the high number of missing values.
7 Further analysis of the relationship between welfare attitudes and work regimes will be done using multi-level modelling, which includes relevant macro-level variables such as GDP and unemployment rates to help explain obvious country and country–group differences.

References

Appelbaum, E. and Batt, R. (1994). *The New American Workplace: Transforming Work Systems in the United States.* Ithaca, NY: Cornell ILR Press.
Amable, B. (2003). *The Diversity of Modern Capitalism.* Oxford: Oxford University Press.
Berg, M. C., and Veenhoven, R., (2010). Income inequality and happiness in 119 nations. In Greve, B. (Ed.) *Social Policy and Happiness in Europe.* Edgar Elgar: Cheltenham UK.
Ciccia, R. and Ó Riain, S. (2013). Beyond the standard work model? Varieties of flexible working time organization in Europe. NIRSA Working Paper No. 71, National Institute for Regional and Spatial Analysis, Maynooth University.
Eid, M., Langeheine, R. and Diener, E. (2003). Comparing typological structures across cultures by multigroup latent class analysis: A primer. *Journal of Cross-Cultural Psychology*, 34, 195–210.
Emmenegger, P. (2009). Barriers to entry: Insider/outside politics and the political determinants of job security regulations. *Journal of European Social Policy*, 19(2), 131–146.
Esping-Andersen, G. (1990). *The Three Worlds of Welfare Capitalism.* Princeton: Princeton University Press.
European Social Survey (2004). European Social Survey Round 2. available: www.europeansocialsurvey.org/ [accessed 27 April 2015].

European Social Survey (2010). *European Social Survey Round 5*. available: www.europeansocialsurvey.org/ [accessed 27 April 2015].

Eurofound (2005). *European Working Conditions Survey Wave 4*. Dublin: Eurofound.

Eurofound (2010). *European Working Conditions Survey Wave 5*. Dublin: Eurofound.

Gallie, D. (2013). Economic crisis, the quality of work, and social integration: Issues and context. In Gallie, D. (ed) *Economic Crisis, Quality of Work & Social Integration: The European Experience*. Oxford: Oxford University Press, 1–29.

Hall, P. A. and Soskice, D. (eds) (2001). *Varieties of Capitalism: The Institutional Foundations of Comparative Advantage*. Oxford: Oxford University Press.

Kankaraš, M., Moors, G. and Vermunt, J. (2011). Testing for measurement invariance with latent class analysis. In Davidov, E., Schmidt, P. and Billiet, J. (eds), *Cross-Cultural Analysis: Methods and Applications*. London: Routledge, 359–384.

Lorenz, E. and Valeyre, A. (2005). Organisational innovation, human resource management and labour market structure: A comparison of the EU-15. *The Journal of Industrial Relations*, 47(4), 424–442.

McCutcheon, A. (1987). *Latent Class Analysis*. Newbury Park: Sage Publications.

McCutcheon, A. (2002). Basic concepts and procedures in single- and multiple group latent class analysis. In Hagenaars, J. and McCutcheon, A. (eds), *Applied Latent Class Analysis*. Cambridge: Cambridge University Press, 56–85.

Rueda, D. (2005). Insider-outsider politics in industrialized democracies: The challenge to social democratic parties. *American Political Science Review*, 99(1), 61–74.

Rueda, D. (2006). Social democracy and active labour-market policies: Insiders, outsiders and the politics of employment promotion. *British Journal of Political Science*, 36(3), 385–406.

Schwander, H., Häuserman, S. and Kurer, T. (2015). High-skilled outsiders? Labor market vulnerability, education and welfare state preferences. *Socio-Economic Review*, 13(2), 235–258.

Siegers, P. (2011). A multigroup latent class analysis of religious orientation in Europe. In Davidov, E., Schmidt, P. and Billiet, J. (eds) *Cross-Cultural Analysis: Methods and Applications*. London: Routledge, 385–412.

Vermunt, J. and Magidson, J. (2005). *Latent Gold 4.0 User Guide*. Belmont, Massachusetts: Statistical Innovations Inc.

Wren, A. and Rehm, P. (2014). The end of consensus? Labour market developments and the politics of retrenchment. *Socio-Economic Review*, 12(2), 409–435.

Appendices

Table 6.11A EWCS and ESS variables

	Final coding	ESS Original variable	EWCS 2005 Original variable	EWCS 2010 Original variable
Contract	Permanent Fixed term Other	wrkctra	q3b	q7
Hours	Under 20 hours 20–34 hours 35–47 hours 48 hours plus	wkhtot	q8a	q18
Eve/night	Yes No	wrkengt	q14b & q14a	q33 & q32
Weekends	Yes No	wrkwe	q14c & q14d	q34 & q35
Fixed time	Yes No	dcsfwrk	q16a_c	q37d
Work related train	Yes No	atncrse	q28a_1 & q28b_1	q61a & q61b
Autonomy	Yes (order and speed) Speed or order None	wkdcorga & wkdcpce	q24a & q24c	q50a & q50c
Education	Less than lower secondary education (ISCED 0–1) Lower secondary education completed (ISCED 2) Upper secondary education completed (ISCED 3) Post-secondary non-tertiary education completed (ISCED 4)	edulvla	ISCED	efl_isce

(continued)

	Final coding	ESS	EWCS 2005	EWCS 2010
		Original variable	Original variable	Original variable
Company size	Tertiary education completed (ISCED 5-6) under 10 10 to 99 100–499 500 and over	estsz	q6	q11
Tenure	1 year or less 2–3 years 4–5 years 6–9 years 10 years or over	yrcremp	q2d	q12
Occupation	ISCO1 – Legislators, senior officials and managers ISCO2 – Professionals ISCO3 – Technicians and associate professionals ISCO4 – Clerks ISCO5 – Service workers and shop and market sales workers ISCO7 – Craft and related trades workers ISCO8 – Plant and machine operators and assemblers ISCO9 – Elementary occupations	ISCOCO	ISCO	ISCO_8_1
Learn new things EWCS	Yes No		q23f	q49f
Learn new things ESS	Not at all true A little true Quite true Very true	jbrqlrn		
The government should take measures to reduce income difference	Agree strongly Agree Neither agree nor disagree Disagree Disagree strongly	gincdif		

	Final coding	ESS	EWCS 2005	EWCS 2010
		Original variable	Original variable	Original variable
The government should do much more to prevent people falling into poverty	Agree strongly	gvprppv		
	Agree			
	Neither agree nor disagree			
	Disagree			
	Disagree strongly			
Unforeseen problems	Yes		q23c	q49c
	No			
Complex tasks	Yes		q23e	q49e
	No			
Deadlines	Most or all of the time		q20b_b	q45b
	Sometimes			
	Almost never or never			
Customers	Yes		q21b	q46b
	No			
Production norms	Yes		q21c	q46c
	No			
Machine speed	Yes		q21d	q46d
	No			
(continued)				
Boss	Yes		q21e	q46e
	No			
Colleague pace and task rotation	Colleague pace and task rotation		q21a & q26a	q46a & q53
	Task rotation, no colleague pace			
	Colleague pace, no task rotation			
	Neither			
Quality standards	Yes		q23a	q49a
	No			
Rich	Yes	imprich		
	No			
Equal	Yes	ipeqopt		
	No			
Help	Yes	iphlppl		
	No			
Strong government	Yes	ipstrgv		
	No			

Table 6.12A Country groupings from reduced EWCS/ESS merged analysis

Merged ESS/EWCS	Group 1	Group 2	Group 3
Group size	0.42	0.31	0.26
Clusters			
Learn	0.31	0.51	0.09
Simple/Taylor	0.31	0.04	0.61
Lean shift	0.17	0.27	0.03
Lean/learn extend	0.14	0.18	0.04
Simple/Taylor shifts	0.07	0.01	0.24
Country and year	Belgium2004	Denmark2004	Germany2005
	Belgium2005	Denmark2010	Greece2004
	Belgium2010	Denmark2010ESS	Greece2005
	Belgium2010ESS	Finland2004	Greece2010
	Denmark2005	Finland2005	Greece2010ESS
	Germany2004	Finland2010	Ireland2004
	Germany2010	Finland2010ESS	Portugal2004
	Germany2010ESS	Netherlands2004	Portugal2005
	Ireland2005	Netherlands2005	Portugal2010
	Ireland2010	Netherlands2010	Portugal2010ESS
	Ireland2010ESS	Netherlands2010ESS	Spain2005
	Spain2004	Sweden2004	
	Spain2010	Sweden2005	
	Spain2010ESS	Sweden2010ESS	
	Sweden2010		
	United Kingdom2004		
	United Kingdom2005		
	United Kingdom2010		
	United Kingdom2010ESS		

Source: Authors' analysis of ESS data (2004 and 2010) and Eurofound data (2005, 2010).
Notes: 2004 data are ESS data; 2005 data are EWCS data; and 2010 data are from both data sets and are labelled *ESS* to differentiate from the EWCS data.

7 Societal-Level Equality and Well-Being

Marguerite Beattie

The Nordic countries have developed among the most equal modern societies, both in terms of income[1] and gender.[2] Sweden has even effectively changed its language to be more egalitarian with its "Du-reformen," attenuating the use of titles and formal versus informal pronouns, and with its invention of a gender-neutral, third-person, singular pronoun: "hen." They are also the societies that regularly survey as having the highest subjective well-being,[3] perhaps best illustrated by their Zen-like habit of taking it slow, enjoying nature and relaxing in their mid-forest cabins. Is there a connection between their equality and well-being? If so, how does it work? The current chapter will investigate the relationship between societal-level equality and well-being and some mechanisms that underlie it.

Equality as presented in intergroup relations research

There exists some theoretical and empirical background explaining the benefits of equality in the field of intergroup relations. Intergroup relations is also at the macro level of analysis, so it is fitting that the field involves theory and research on equality. To begin, it would behove us to define what we mean by equality. Simon sees equality as "an active ingredient of respect" (2007, p. 312). In accordance with the Kantian idea of respect for all persons, Simon's research explicates that respect is predicated on the idea that a person should be shown dignity and is an equal; equality, here, is "at the level of shared humanity or dignity as a human being" (p. 319). Simon also adds Simmel's idea of self-determination, which he writes is a "corollary of universal equality" (p. 312), and Feinberg's idea of '"the recognizable capacity to assert claims"' (p. 322) to the understanding of equality. Similarly, groups can be viewed as equal in dignity, respect and rights. *Equality*, for our purposes, can be defined as the conceptualization of people and groups as having the same dignity and therefore deserving the same respect, rights, status and amount of power.

Equality, along with a few intertwined concomitants, can be found prevalently in prejudice and conflict reduction research. Allport's (1954) seminal theory on the effect of contact attests:

> Prejudice (unless deeply rooted in the character structure of the individual) may be reduced by equal status contact between the majority and minority

groups in the pursuit of common goals. The effect is greatly enhanced if this contact is sanctioned by institutional supports (i.e., by law, custom or local atmosphere), and provided it is of a sort that leads to the perception of common interests and common humanity between members of the two groups. (p. 281)

Four factors have been extrapolated from Allport's work: "(1) equal status of the groups in the situation, (2) common goals, (3) intergroup cooperation, and (4) the support of authorities, law or custom" (Pettigrew et al. 2011, p. 273). Furthermore, a meta-analysis has shown these optimal conditions to be an "interrelated bundle rather than independent factors" (Pettigrew and Tropp 2006, p. 751). It makes sense that equality would be accompanied by cooperation and common goals, while inequality would be accompanied by competition and ego- or ingroup-centric goals. Competition is inherently a zero- or negative sum game that creates inequality and opponents; cooperation is a positive sum game that is conducive to equality and common goals.

Subsequent research has validated Allport's Intergroup Contact Theory (Pettigrew and Tropp 2006; Pettigrew et al. 2011). Pettigrew and Tropp's meta-analysis of 696 samples revealed that "greater intergroup contact is generally associated with lower levels of prejudice (mean $r = -.215$)," and 94 per cent of the samples showed an inverse relationship (Pettigrew and Tropp 2006, p. 766). Although they are not the only factors that have been shown to reduce prejudice, Allport's optimal conditions resulted in a noticeably higher mean effect size. Moreover, the reduction of prejudice has generalized to other outgroup members (and even to other outgroups, a process called deprovincialisation) rather than to just familiarized individual outgroup members. Prejudice reduction has been effected with other types of outgroups in addition to ethnic groups, such as gay, disabled and mentally ill minorities. "They [the contact effects] appear to be universal – across nations, genders, and age groups" (Pettigrew et al. 2011, p. 271). The direction of causality has been shown to be bidirectional; reduced prejudice can lead to increased contact, but increased contact also leads to reduced prejudice. Finally, while knowledge is a minor mediator, empathy and anxiety reduction are major mediators between prejudice reduction and intergroup contact.

More classic research has theorized about similar connections between cooperation and common goals and conflict and prejudice reduction. Sherif et al. (1961) designed the famous Robbers Cave experiment to test their theories on intergroup conflict and cooperation. At a summer camp, boys from similar backgrounds were divided into two groups. The organisers separated the groups enough to build group identities in the first stage, and in the second they introduced competition. Gradually, the groups became antagonized and started to verbally and physically assault each other. A third stage then introduced superordinate goals that produced "reciprocally cooperative and helpful intergroup actions" (p. 144). Little by little, the cumulative effects of activities in the third stage ameliorated the participants' attitudes and behaviour. (Interestingly, research has shown the shift from competitive to cooperative reward structures to be more difficult than the shift from cooperative to competitive reward structures [Johnson et al. 2006]). It should be noted that Sherif et al. (1961) point out that equality alone did not change behaviour and attitudes, but cooperation and common goals were necessary as well.

In a review of prejudice reduction, Paluck and Green (2009) reveal even more evidence for the benefits of equality, cooperation and common goals. One study reviewed incorporated elements of "Allport's (1954) conditions for ideal intergroup contact: equal status, a common (survival) goal, authority sanction, and intimate contact" while also incorporating the "intensity and naturalistic quality" of Sherif et al.'s (1961) experiment. "[W]hite teens from the heterogeneous groups reported significantly less aversion to blacks and gays and described themselves as less 'prejudiced' compared to the homogeneous group teens" (p. 355). Besides contact theory, which is greatly supported in this review, social identity and categorisation theories suggest that expanding the ingroup through recategorization (making a superordinate group salient) or integrative models (making a superordinate group salient while maintaining distinct subgroups, which has the added benefit of preserving multiculturalism) can increase cooperation with the outgroup under equal status conditions. Integrative models in particular have achieved empirical and normative support. Likewise, Wenzel et al. (2007) discuss the advantages and dangers of superordinate identities. While superordinate identities can be valuable by "the inclusion of the sub-level outgroup in one's extended self, implying that positive sentiments, cooperation, empathy, altruism, and so on will likely be extended to those outgroup members" (p. 363), it is important to ensure that one group does not claim to be more prototypical of the superordinate identity as that can preserve or increase prejudice. Allport (1954) also discusses the possibilities and benefits of superordinate identities with his section on humanity as an ingroup (pp. 43–46). Identifying with members of outgroups or, even more preferably, with humanity as the ingroup, should allow one to better understand others. Consequently, it comes as no surprise that empathy and perspective-taking have also been shown as effective interventions in prejudice reduction (Paluck and Green, 2009).

Cooperative learning interventions are efficacious in reducing prejudice and have the interrelated outcomes of increased perspective-taking and social support (Paluck and Green, 2009). Cooperative learning was theorized in Morton Deutsch's theory of social interdependence and was popularized through Eliot Aronson's "Jigsaw classroom" technique, in which participants learn from and teach one another. Accordingly, the theory of social interdependence posits similar hypotheses about the outcomes of cooperation and competition (Johnson and Johnson 2005). The main premise of social interdependence theory is that "the structure of the goals of the people in the situation determines how participants interact and the interaction patterns determine the outcomes of the situation" (p. 292). In other words, cooperation and competition are two structures that influence interaction and consequently outcomes. Johnson and Johnson (2005) provide a table (Table 7.1) demonstrating evidence of the immense advantages of cooperation regarding various dependent variables from research spanning 110 years.

Table 7.1 Mean effect sizes for impact of social interdependence on dependent variables

Characteristic	Cooperative vs. competitive	Cooperative vs. individualistic	Competitive vs. individualistic
Dependent variable			
Achievement	0.67	0.64	0.30
Interpersonal attraction	0.67	0.60	0.08
Social support	0.62	0.70	−0.13
Self-esteem	0.58	0.44	−0.23
Time on task	0.76	1.17	0.64
Attitudes toward task	0.57	0.42	0.15
Quality of reasoning	0.93	0.97	0.13
Perspective-taking	0.61	0.44	−0.13
High quality studies			
Achievement	0.88	0.61	0.07
Interpersonal attraction	0.82	0.62	0.27
Social support	0.83	0.72	−0.13
Self-esteem	0.67	0.45	−0.25
Condition			
Mixed operationalisations achievement	0.45	0.13	–
Pure operationalisations achievement	0.74	0.61	–

While the benefits of cooperation, common/superordinate goals/identity and equality are our main focus, it is interesting to consider the contrasting factors: competition, ego- and/or ingroup-centric goals/identities and inequality. As Karmela Liebkind (1984) explains, "as long as people do not share equal rewards and/or honour irrespective of their contribution to society, the rivalry for values of various kinds can lead to ethnic discrimination as a conscious or subconscious means of blocking whole groups of competitors" (pp. 27–28). Here, the connection between competition and discrimination is made clear in a similar vein to Sherif et al.'s (1961) competition stage. Jasinskaja-Lahti et al. (2009) provide evidence for the inverse effect of attenuating superordinate identities. In their study, "perceived discrimination resulted in national disidentification, which, in turn, increased hostile attitudes towards the national out-group" (p. 105). Disidentifying with a superordinate identity, in other words, has the opposite, negative effect, in contrast to identifying with a superordinate identity.

One group divisor seems to underlie and reinforce a majority of group divisions. Divisions based on ethnicity, gender, mental health and physical ability usually coincide with socioeconomic divisions. Ethnic minorities are usually poorer (although sometimes wealthier as is the case with the Swedish-speaking Finns), women are paid less than men and those with mental illness and physical disability are mired in poverty. As Allport (1954) points out, even African Americans are better described as belonging to a "caste" than a race as they are "more Caucasian in their racial descent than African" and suffer from "socially imposed handicaps peculiar to lower caste – not natural handicaps engendered by racial inheritance. Discrimination in employment, segregation in housing, and all other stigmata are marks of caste alone" (p. 320). He describes how "[c]aste and class do […] offer culturally provided opportunities for building prejudices" and even "children are inclined to ascribe all sorts of virtues to upper-class individuals and all sorts of defects to members of the lower classes" (p. 323). Allport also describes how in a system with vertical mobility (and for our purposes, competition and inequality of outcome), those who are threatened by losing their status or those who have lost their status are more prejudiced (pp. 222–224). So not only do socioeconomic divisions have the identical consequences in comparison to other divisions, but they can also be seen to reinforce group divisions.

In conclusion, equality, cooperation, common and superordinate goals and identities, empathy and perspective-taking can all be seen as interconnected factors that mitigate intergroup prejudice and conflict. Equality is a demonstration of respect for all persons. Cooperation and common goals and identities can buttress equality. Equality and superordinate identity allow for greater empathy, understanding and the ability to perspective-take, as others are seen as similar or at least worth the effort to try to understand. With these concomitants and their positive outcomes, subjective well-being would understandably correspond. Equality and its concomitants lay the foundations for a more harmonious social environment in which neither conflict nor prejudice are evoked.

Societal health

Besides intergroup relations' argument for equality, there is further evidence that equality leads to psychologically and physically healthier societies in many other respects. Wilkinson and Pickett (2006, 2009, 2011) found income equality to be associated with lower homicide rates, lower obesity, lower health and social problems in general, less global warming contribution, less drug abuse, less imprisonment, less mental illness and fewer teenage births. In addition, they found income equality to be linked with increased foreign aid, increased social mobility, longer life expectancy and higher child well-being. While these findings provoked some debate, Hiilamo and Kangas (2012) compared Wilkinson's and Pickett's claims to counterclaims presented by Saunders (2011), finding greater support for Wilkinson and Pickett than Saunders.

Accordingly, an egalitarian system may be the most psychologically healthy environment for us. Without the perceived or objective barriers of differences, we can better understand and empathize with others. This facilitates less outgroup differentiation and more universalistic thinking. Theoretically, social support, which has been found to be the greatest predictor of well-being (Oishi 2012, p. 161), should be increased through the universalistic thinking of solidarity and cooperation. Rather than competing with others for ingroup- or self-interest, we can cooperate to achieve collective interests. Competition has also been linked to high levels of stress; Vitaliano et al. (1984) found that anxiety and stress were higher for medical students, who identified peer competition as a significant stressor, than for psychiatric patients. If we believe that others cooperate, then we cooperate more

(Kelley and Stahelksi 1970), and prosocial behaviour will be increased. People with a prosocial orientation are more likely to cooperate and work toward joint outcomes and equality of outcomes (Van Lange 1999). Once "personal fairness" is met (e.g. we have been treated equitably), then we exhibit altruistic behaviour above self-interested behaviour (Miller 1977). All these factors appear to be highly interdependent; equality is associated with innumerable positive outcomes.

Economic growth

The positive outcomes mentioned heretofore focus on social cohesion and health, but there is yet another arena that holds an argument for reducing inequality: economics. In the field of economics and among lay people, there has been a debate between the incentives hypothesis and the opportunities hypothesis. The former posited that the inequality is economically beneficial in that it incites a desire to get ahead; thus, individuals work harder to become materially successful and show that they are among the meritorious, deserving individuals in a society. The latter posited that with resources more evenly distributed, a greater number of people will have the means to provide a greater contribution to society. The most recent analysis of the evidence has supported the opportunities hypothesis and has indicated that income inequality in fact reduces economic growth (Ostry et al. 2014; OECD 2015). As Martin Luther King, Jr. (1968, p. 1) metaphorically illustrated this finding in a speech: It's all right to tell a man to lift himself by his own bootstraps, but it is a cruel jest to say to a bootless man that he ought to lift himself by his own bootstraps.

Subjective well-being

Heretofore, the outcomes discussed have been objective measures of well-being. They are the factors that theoretically contribute to human prosperity. What is yet to be discussed is how well-off people actually say they are under different levels of equality. Gender equality has been found to increase subjective well-being for both women and men (Bjørnskov et al. 2007). The research on income equality and subjective measures of well-being, however, has been ambivalent so far. Oishi (2012) expounds on the history of research done on income equality and subjective well-being. Income inequality and subjective well-being have been shown to be significantly negatively correlated, and income equality predicts subjective well-being. However, when wealth is controlled, this relationship has usually disappeared (Diener et al. 1995). Other studies have not shown a significant relationship either (Stevenson and Wolfers 2008; Berg and Veenhoven 2010). Berg and Veenhoven (2010, p. 12) explain that perhaps inequality increases activity, which in turn increases happiness. One critique of Wilkinson and Pickett (2011) is precisely these findings that subjective well-being is not always predicted by income equality; Wilkinson and Pickett (2012) respond that perhaps the subjective nature itself is unreliable since subjective measures of physical health have been found to be unreliable. However, measures of subjective well-being have been validated, for example by friends and stability over time (Oishi 2012, p. 19).

With the preponderance of evidence against inequality provided by Wilkinson and Pickett and the interrelatedness of equality with so many other positive outcomes, it would theoretically follow that subjective measures of well-being would also benefit from income equality.

A new study presented here aims to contribute to this question. As opposed to previous studies, the current study has the advantage of using a more accurate measure of income inequality that accounts for redistributive effects: the post-tax-and-transfer Gini Coefficient. Comparisons of rankings of countries before and after taxes-and-transfers show significant changes, emphasizing the importance of using the latter measure for a more accurate representation. Using an affective measure (happiness) and a cognitive measure (life satisfaction) of subjective well-being, the current study asks three research questions. First, does income equality predict happiness and life satisfaction? Second, if so, is it only because those nations are wealthier? That is, if national income is controlled, does income equality still predict happiness and life satisfaction? Third, what are the psychological mechanisms behind the relationships found? Both fairness and trust have been found to mediate the relationship between happiness and equality (Oishi et al. 2011). Moreover, trust has been found to be associated both with economic prowess and income equality (Helkama 2004; Wilkinson and Pickett 2011). Therefore, both trust and fairness will be tested as mediators.

Method and data

The data used in the current study were gathered from two sources: the European Social Survey (ESS) from the years 2002–2012 and the Organization for Economic Co-operation and Development (OECD) from the matching years. Although these data are unfortunately primarily limited to one geographic area, that is, Europe, they were chosen because of their high validity: The OECD calculates a post-tax-and-transfer Gini Index, which takes into account the greater equality achieved by redistribution through taxation and public cash transfer. Other studies have not used post-tax-and-transfer Gini. One advantage of this data size limitation is that the cultures and languages are more similar and thus these potential confounding variables are somewhat controlled naturally. The number of matching country and year data across the six variables that are used in the current study is 82. At most, a country is represented six times in different years, while some countries only have available matching data for one year.

Measures

There are six measures in the current study: net national income in USD per capita, the post-tax-and-transfer Gini Index, trust, fairness, happiness and life satisfaction. Net national income in USD per capita (M = 26281.64, SD = 8413.18) was obtained from the OECD, which defines it as "gross domestic product plus net receipts of wages, salaries and property income from abroad, minus the depreciation of fixed capital assets (dwellings, buildings, machinery, transport equipment and physical infrastructure) through wear and tear and obsolescence" (OECD 2015). Post-tax-and-transfer Gini Index also calculated by the OECD (M = 0.30, SD = 0.04) measures income equality throughout a society, with 0 representing perfect equality and 1 representing perfect inequality. Trust (M = 5.05, SD = 0.60) was measured by the ESS on an 11-point Likert scale with the item, "Generally speaking, would you say that most people can be trusted, or that you can't be too careful in dealing with people? Please tell me on a score of 0 to 10, where 0 means you can't be too careful and 10 means that most people can be trusted." Fairness (M = 5.63, SD = 0.85) was measured in the ESS on an 11-point Likert scale with the item, "Do you think that most people would try to take advantage of you if they got the chance, or would they try to be fair? Please tell me on a score of 0 to 10, where 0 means most people try to take advantage of me and 10 means that most people try to be fair." Happiness (M = 7.28, SD = 0.60) was also measured by the ESS on an 11-point Likert scale with the item, "Taking all things together, how happy would you say you are? Please answer using this card, where 0 means extremely unhappy and 10 means extremely happy." Satisfaction with life (M = 6.97, SD = 0.80) was also measured by the ESS on an 11-point Likert scale with the item, "All things considered, how satisfied are you with your life as a whole nowadays? Please answer using this card, where 0 means extremely dissatisfied and 10 means extremely satisfied." While the OECD data were already on a country level, the ESS data were averaged for each country in order to obtain the country level for that data.

Results

Post-tax–and-transfer Gini predicting happiness and life satisfaction

Two regression analyses were computed with the Post-tax-and-transfer Gini coefficient predicting happiness and life satisfaction. All tolerance values exceeded .10 (and VIFs < 10), indicating no problems with multicollinearity (Meyers et al. 2006). Also, the largest correlation between predictors was -0.52, which is less than .8, the heuristic figure suggesting possible multicollinearity (Meyers et al. 2006). In the analysis using happiness as the dependent variable, happiness scores were regressed on post-tax-and-transfer Gini coefficients. The R^2 of 0.24 was significant; $F(1, 81) = 26.15, p < .001$. Gini's standardized coefficient was significant, $\beta = -.494, t = -5.114, p < .001$. In the analysis using life satisfaction as the dependent variable, life satisfaction scores were regressed on post-tax-and-transfer Gini coefficients. The R^2 of 0.27 was significant; $F(1, 81) = 30.55, p < .001$. Again, Gini's standardized coefficient was significant, $\beta = -.523, t = -5.528, p < .001$. This indicates that a low post-tax-and-transfer Gini coefficient makes a significant contribution to both happiness and life satisfaction but even more so to life satisfaction.

Controlling for national income

Second, two hierarchical multiple regression analyses were computed to answer the question of whether income accounts for the subjective well-being in nations or whether income equality still plays a role. All tolerance values exceeded .10 (and VIFs < 10), indicating no problems with multicollinearity (Meyers et al., 2006). Also, the largest correlation between predictors was 0.69, which is less than .8, the heuristic figure suggesting possible multicollinearity (Meyers et al. 2006). In block one of the analysis, using happiness as the dependent variable, happiness scores were regressed on post-tax-and-transfer Gini coefficients. The R^2 of 0.48 was significant; $F(1, 80) = 74.54$, $p < .001$. In block two of the same analysis, net national income per capita was added to the regression. The change in R^2 was .07; $F(1, 79) = 12.63$, $p = .001$. In block one of the analysis, using life satisfaction as the dependent variable, life satisfaction scores were regressed on post-tax-and-transfer Gini coefficients. The R^2 of 0.45 was significant; $F(1, 80) = 65.14$, $p < .001$. In block two of the same analysis, post-tax-and-transfer-Gini was added to the regression. The change in R^2 was .10; $F(1, 79) = 17.85$, $p < .001$. This indicates that post-tax-and-transfer Gini makes a significant, unique contribution to both happiness and life satisfaction, even after controlling for national income per capita.

Trust and fairness as mediators

There is precedent for trust and fairness being found as mediators between subjective well-being and income equality as in Oishi et al.'s 2011 study on the United States. Therefore, the current study analyses trust and fairness, firstly as mediators between Gini and happiness and secondly as mediators between Gini and life satisfaction. Trust and fairness were found to be so highly correlated, $r(83)= 0.93$, $p < .001$, that they were analysed separately. With trust as a mediator between Gini and happiness, the test statistic for the Sobel test is –4.03, with an associated p-value of less than .001. With fairness as a mediator between Gini and happiness, the test statistic for the Sobel test is –4.36, with an associated p-value of less than .001. Secondly, with trust as a mediator between Gini and life satisfaction, the test statistic for the Sobel test is –4.09, with an associated p-value of less than .001. With fairness as a mediator between Gini and life satisfaction, the test statistic for the Sobel test is –4.27, with an associated p-value of less than .001. In other words, trust and fairness can be said to be psychological mechanisms underlying the relationship between income equality and happiness/life satisfaction. For illustrations of the mediation paths with raw (unstandardised) regression coefficients and standard errors, see Figures 7.1–7.4.

Discussion

The current study asked three research questions. In answer to the first, post-tax-and-transfer Gini significantly predicted both happiness and life satisfaction. In answer to the second, post-tax-and-transfer Gini significantly predicted both happiness and life satisfaction even when national income was controlled. Finally, in answer to the third, trust and fairness both mediated the relationships between income equality and happiness and life satisfaction.

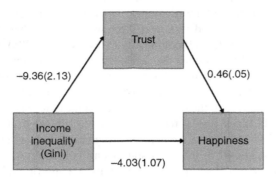

Figure 7.1 Mediation of Gini and happiness by trust.

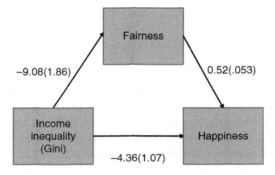

Figure 7.2 Mediation of Gini and happiness by fairness.

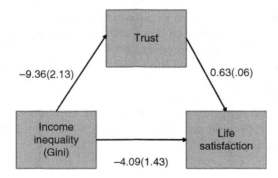

Figure 7.3 Mediation of Gini and life satisfaction by trust.

The present study uses a more robust measure, the post-tax-and-transfer Gini Index, than previous studies, which use the pre-tax-and-transfer Gini Index. The post-tax-and-transfer Gini Index is less available and has been calculated for fewer countries over fewer years than some other measures of income inequality. However, while the number is smaller, the validity of the measure is greater;

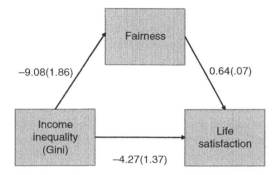

Figure 7.4 Mediation of Gini and life satisfaction by fairness.

the post-tax-and-transfer Gini Index takes into account the equalizing effects of governmental redistribution. In addition, similarities in cultures and languages in the analysed countries serve as a natural control, as large differences in culture and language could affect happiness and life satisfaction scores.

It is a limitation of the present study that some of the same countries are used repetitively, and it is assumed that each a country in each year is unrelated to the same country in another year. Consequently, some countries are given more weight than others. However, as the available data for post-tax-and-transfer Gini is limited, it is necessary to use the countries repetitively for now. There is precedent for using the same country or states in separate years, but one has not been given more weight than others (Oishi et al. 2011; Valdmanis 2014). In addition, at this time only current national income information is available from the OECD; the second set of analyses should be recalculated when details of constant national income are available.

Further research will be able to utilise the increasing availability of data as well as investigate other measures of the same or similar concepts. More time points will become available and measures will almost certainly become increasingly accurate. One additional measure of interest in this subject area is Hofstede's Power Distance (Taras et al. 2012), a subjective measure of inequality. In preliminary analyses, it seems to be an even greater predictor of subjective well-being than objective measures of socioeconomic inequality.

Economic growth both nationally and individually is a widespread goal. However, evidence as to when and at what levels it makes us happy is mixed (Oishi 2012). It seems to be more important to live in a rich country than be rich as an individual, perhaps because of the public goods available (Diener et al. 2010). Many other variables affect well-being. Social support, for example, has been found to be the greatest predictor of subjective well-being (Oishi 2012; Helliwell et al. 2015). Income equality is a sociocultural factor that minimizes feelings of superiority and inferiority and creates a harmonious, trusting environment conducive to well-being. Interest in researching these variables that impact happiness has been growing.

As people start to look to happiness rather than GDP as ultimate goals, research on subjective well-being will be increasingly sought after. Bhutan has already directed its attention to Gross National Happiness, and David Cameron has started a happiness index in the United Kingdom. Research findings on happiness and income equality have important public policy implications. From progressive taxation to welfare benefits, public policy can increase or decrease equality. Progressive taxation on its own has even been associated with subjective well-being (Oishi et al. 2011). As it is now, inequality is increasing almost everywhere in the world (OECD 2011). We have the ability to change the world through politics, but there are many competing ideas as to how the world should be changed. Social research is indispensable in that regard; it discovers how the world can be made a physically and mentally healthier place to live.

Notes

1 According to measures of income equality calculated by the Organisation for Economic Co-operation and Development, the World Bank, the United Nations Development Programme and the CIA World Factbook.
2 According to measures of gender equality calculated by the United Nations Development Programme, the World Economic Forum and Social Watch.
3 According to measures of subjective well-being calculated by the European Social Survey, the World Values Survey, and the Gallup World Poll.

References

Allport, G. W., 1954. *The Nature of Prejudice*. Reading, MA: Addison-Wesley.
Berg, M. C., and Veenhoven, R., 2010. Income inequality and happiness in 119 nations.
Bjørnskov, C., Dreher, A. and Fischer, J. A.V., 2007. On gender inequality and life satisfaction: Does discrimination matter? *SSE/EFI Working Paper Series in Economics and Finance No. 657*.
Diener, E., Diener, M. and Diener, C., 1995. Factors predicting the subjective well-being of nations. *Journal of Personality and Social Psychology*, 69(5), 851.
Diener, E., Ng, W., Harter, J. and Arora, R., 2010. Wealth and happiness across the world: Material prosperity predicts life evaluation, whereas psychosocial prosperity predicts positive feeling. *Journal of Personality and Social Psychology*, 99(1), 52.
European Social Survey, 2015. *ESS Rounds 1–6*. [Data Files]. Retrieved from www.europeansocialsurvey.org/data/.
Helkama, K. (2004) Arvot, luottamus ja kilpailukyky OECD-maissa (Values, trust and competitiveness in the OECD countries). In Risto Alapuro & Ilkka Arminen (eds.), *Vertailevan tutkimuksen ulottuvuuksia (Dimensions of comparative research)* (p. 145–152). Helsinki: WSOY.
Helliwell, J. F., Layard, R. and Sachs, J. eds., 2015. *World Happiness Report 2015*. New York: Sustainable Development Solutions Network.
Hiilamo, H. and Kangas, O., 2012. Following false prophets? Eight rounds on the dangers of income inequality (Väärien profeettojen jäljillä? Kahdeksen erää tuloerojen vaarallisuudesta). *Yhteiskuntapolitiikka-YP* 77 (2012): 2.
Jasinskaja-Lahti, I., Liebkind, K., and Solheim, E., 2009. To identify or not to identify? National disidentification as an alternative reaction to perceived ethnic discrimination. *Appl. Psychol.* 58, 105–128. doi:10.1111/j.1464-0597.2008.00384.x.

Johnson, M. D., Hollenbeck, J. R., Humphrey, S. E., Ilgen, D. R., Jundt, D. and Meyer, C. J., 2006. Cutthroat cooperation: Asymmetrical adaptation to changes in team reward structures. *Acad. Manage. J.* 49, 103–119.

Johnson, D. W. and Johnson, R. T., 2005. New developments in social interdependence theory. *Genet. Soc. Gen. Psychol. Monogr.* 131, 285–358.

Kelley, H. H. and Stahelski, A. J., 1970. Social interaction basis of cooperators' and competitors' beliefs about others. *Journal of Personality and Social Psychology*, 16(1), 66.

King, Jr., M. L., 1968. Remaining awake through a great revolution. Available at http://kingencyclopedia.stanford.edu/encyclopedia/documentsentry/doc_remaining_awake_through_a_great_revolution/ (accessed 7.21.15).

Liebkind, K., 1984. Minority identity and identification processes: A social psychological study. Maintenance and reconstruction of ethnolinguistic identity in multiple group allegiance. *Commentationes Scientiarum Socialium* 22. Helsinki: The Finnish Society of Sciences and Letters.

Meyers, L. S., Gamst, G. and Guarino, A., 2006. *Applied Multivariate Research*. Thousand Oaks, CA: Sage.

Miller, D. T., 1977. Altruism and threat to a belief in a just world. *Journal of Experimental Social Psychology*, 13(2), 113–124.

OECD. Divided we stand – Why inequality keeps rising. In: An overview of growing income inequalities in OECD countries: Main findings. (Ed OECD): OECD 2011; www.oecd.org/els/social/inequality.

OECD, 2015. Net national income (indicator). doi:10.1787/af9be38a-en (Accessed May 20, 2015).

OECD, 2015. *Gini (at disposable post tax and transfer)* [Data file]. Retrieved from http://stats.oecd.org/.

OECD, 2015. *In It Together: Why Less Inequality Benefits All*, OECD Publishing, Paris. http://dx.doi.org/10.1787/9789264235120-en.

Oishi, S., 2012. *The Psychological Wealth of Nations: Do Happy People Make a Happy Society?* West Sussex, UK: Wiley-Blackwell.

Oishi, S., Kesebir, S. and Diener, E., 2011. Income inequality and happiness. *Psychological Science*, 22(9), 1095–1100.

Oishi, S., Schimmack, U. and Diener, E., 2011. Progressive taxation and the subjective well-being of nations. *Psychological Science*, 0956797611420882.

Ostry, J., Berg, A. and Tsangarides, C., 2014. Redistribution, inequality, and growth. *IMF Staff Discussion Note*, February.

Paluck, E. L. and Green, D. P., 2009. Prejudice reduction: What works? A review and assessment of research and practice. *Annu. Rev. Psychol.* 60, 339–367.

Pettigrew, T. F., and Tropp, L. R., 2006. A meta-analytic test of intergroup contact theory. *J. Pers. Soc. Psychol.* 90, 751.

Pettigrew, T. F., Tropp, L. R., Wagner, U. and Christ, O., 2011. Recent advances in intergroup contact theory. *Int. J. Intercult. Relat.* 35, 271–280.

Saunders, P. (2011). *Beware False Prophets: Equality, the Good Society and the Spirit Level*. Policy Exchange: London.

Sherif, M., Harvey, O.mJ., White, B.mJ., Hood, W.mR., Sherif, C. W. and others, 1961. *Intergroup Conflict and Cooperation: The Robbers Cave Experiment*. University Book Exchange, Norman, OK.

Simon, B., 2007. Respect, equality, and power: A social psychological perspective. *Gr. Organ.* 38, 309–326.

Stevenson, B. and Wolfers, J., 2008. Happiness inequality in the United States (No. w14220). National Bureau of Economic Research.

Taras, V., Steel, P. and Kirkman, B. L., 2012. Improving national cultural indices using a longitudinal meta-analysis of Hofstede's dimensions. *Journal of World Business*, 47(3), 329–341.

Valdmanis, V. G. Factors affecting well-being at the state level in the United States. *Journal of Happiness Studies*, 16, 985. doi:10.1007/s10902-014-9545-0.

Van Lange, P. A., 1999. The pursuit of joint outcomes and equality in outcomes: An integrative model of social value orientation. *Journal of Personality and Social Psychology*, 77(2), 337.

Vitaliano, P. P., Russo, J., Carr, J. E. and Heerwagen, J. H., 1984. Medical school pressures and their relationship to anxiety. *Journal of Nervous and Mental Disease*, 172(12), 730–736.

Wenzel, M., Mummendey, A. and Waldzus, S., 2007. Superordinate identities and intergroup conflict: The ingroup projection model. *Eur. Rev. Soc. Psychol.* 18, 331–372.

Wilkinson, R. G. and Pickett, K. E., 2006. Income inequality and population health: A review and explanation of the evidence. *Social Science & Medicine*, 62(7), 1768–1784.

Wilkinson, R. G. and Pickett, K. E., 2009. Income inequality and social dysfunction. *Annual Review of Sociology*, 35, 493–511.

Wilkinson, R. G. and Pickett, K., 2011. *The Spirit Level: Why greater Equality Makes Societies Stronger*. Bloomsbury Press.

Wilkinson, R. G. and Pickett, K., 2012. The authors respond to questions about *The Spirit Level*'s analysis. Retrieved from https://www.equalitytrust.org.uk/authors-respond-questions-about-spirit-levels-analysis.

Section III
Political Identity and Security

Part IV

Political identity and security

8 Corruption in European Countries
A Cross-National Comparison[1]

Kristyna Chabova

Introduction

Corruption is perceived as one of the most serious threats to society and to good governance. Corruption decreases the quality of the public sector in many areas and can trigger civic unrest (Brown et al. 2011; Pellegata 2012). Corruption distorts the formal system of rules and governance (Scott 1972, p. 2). Moreover, as Karklins adds (2005, p. 4), corruption involves the loss of equal access to public power and position, which leads to a loss of public trust and belief in the political system. Corruption is also dangerous from an economic point of view. It can be a barrier to economic growth (World Bank [WB] 1997b); it also negatively impacts the ratio of investment to gross domestic product (GDP) (Mauro 1995; WB 1997a) and the level of foreign investment (Wei and Wu 2001). Corruption can also contribute to an uncertain business climate, can hold back state reform and can nourish organized crime (Rose-Ackerman 1999, p. 17).

For these reasons, many social scientists have tried to discover and describe the root causes of corruption. This task is complicated by the fact that corruption is a clandestine activity, which makes it very difficult to measure and to detect its true effects as well as its underlying causes. Authors discussed in this paper agreed on four variables, which are connected to the level of corruption in a country. According to their research, higher GDP per capita, lower income inequality, higher share of Protestants in a country and higher trust among people all decrease the level of corruption. These four hypotheses will be tested in this paper. However, all of these authors conducted their research on a global level and none took into account different cultural backgrounds of the countries. Corruption is a very complicated phenomenon and probably behaves differently in different cultural contexts. I believe that a cross-country analysis including only European countries, which share a common culture, could show the validity of previous research. This article therefore looks at whether the four variables that influence the level of corruption on a global level behave similarly when tested only on a European level. In accordance with previous research, I will be using data from the World Bank (WB) for the economic variables and the dependent variable control of corruption, and all waves (2002–2012) of the European Social Survey (ESS) for the cultural variables. Taking into account only European countries also allows for a more specific focus on the special case of post-communist countries, which were the last countries to have undergone the transition to democracy in Europe. Model analysing these four hypotheses will be therefore tested on a dataset divided by the country's history. The results will show if post-communist countries today, more than a quarter of a century after the collapse of communism, behave as European countries that never experienced the rule of communism, or if there is a different pattern concerning corruption in these countries.

Corruption in Europe

Corruption in European countries is on a much lower level compared to most of the world, particularly in Scandinavian and western European countries, which consistently hold the top places as countries with the lowest levels of corruption. On the other hand, countries with a communist history generally have higher levels of corruption (Shleifer 1997), and political corruption there is certainly a serious problem (Karklins 2005). It is suggested (Rose 2001, p. 105; Rose-Ackerman 1999) that corruption is the greatest obstacle to progress and to democratization in post-communist societies.

There are several hypotheses explaining higher levels of corruption in post-communist countries. Research and data show that in authoritarian regimes, the level of corruption is higher than in democratic regimes, and yet, surprisingly, there are mixed results regarding the effect of democracy on the level of corruption concerning the transition to democracy (Blake and Martin 2006; Pellegata 2012; Triesman 2000). Brown (2011) presents a hypothesis that the effect of democracy on corruption is non-linear and that for this reason the results describing the effect of democratization on corruption are mixed. According to Pellegata's analysis, countries that are moving from non-democracy to democracy (hybrid mode) have a higher level of corruption in the beginning of the transformation than they had under the non-democratic regime. However, over time, the level of corruption slowly begins to decline (Pellegata 2012). This theory is supported by Triesman's findings, in which his regression model shows that the current level of democracy does not have any effect on the level of corruption but that long exposure to democracy lowers corruption (Triesman 2000). Graph 1 shows the situation in post-communist countries as measured by the WB. Their composite indicator is entitled "control of corruption" and it is based on 22 underlying data sources, which are rescaled and combined to create a composite indicator that "captures perceptions of the extent to which public power is exercised for private gain, including both petty and grand forms of corruption, as well as the 'capture' of the state by elites and private interests (WB, n.d.)." This indicator goes from 3 to –3, where 3 means that the country is able to control the level of corruption quite well, and –3 means that there is almost no control of corruption in the country. Figure 8.1 shows the average control of corruption in 10 post-communist countries[2] in a 10-year period. The graph shows that in the case of post-communist countries, it seems that the level of corruption does not decrease over time; on the contrary, there is a slight decrease in the control of corruption. This suggests that in post-communist countries, the exposure to democracy does not result in lower levels of corruption. Also, according to Johnson (2005, p. 31), democratization in central Europe has not reduced corruption.

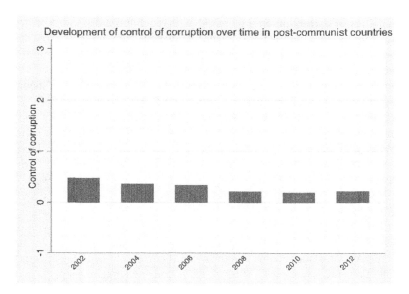

Figure 8.1 Control of corruption in post-communist countries.

However, one must bear in mind that there is a huge difference between corruption resulting from a long-term cultural tradition and corruption resulting from the chaos of transition (Miller et al. 2001, p. 21). In communist regimes, corruption was normal and widespread (Rose et al. 1998); corruption was not abnormal but was the norm itself. The WB distinguishes corruption as either systemic or isolated (1997a). When corruption is isolated, it is rare; the norm is not to be corrupt, and cases of corruption can easily be tracked down and punished. On the other hand, where corruption is systemic, formal rules still exist, but they are superseded by informal rules. As the WB adds: "It may be a crime to bribe a public official, but in practice the law is not enforced or is applied in a partisan way, and informal rules prevail" (1997a, p. 13). Many people in post-communist countries believe that corruption in their countries is or was systemic; however, even after transition to democracy, the post-communist countries preserve their specific system of informal rules (Karklins 2005) and, as Rose et al. add: "changing regimes does not dispose of the problem but creates new opportunities for corruption" (Rose et al. 1998, p. 219). Therefore, it seems that corruption in post-communist countries is perceived differently, which suggests that the theories explaining corruption on a global level might not hold.

Causes of corruption

There is a vast amount of research trying to ascertain the reasons for corruption and why the level of corruption is higher in some countries than in others.

Many authors examined particular countries, but cross-national research measuring the causes of corruption on a global level is much more difficult to carry out and therefore the literature is not immense. However, there are still some studies concluding that there are several variables influencing the level of corruption (or the perception of corruption in most cases) on a global level.

First, corruption is likely to be the cause and also the consequence of inequality (Husted 1999; Rose-Ackerman and Soreide 2006, p. 23). For example, Gupta et al. (2002) found a significant correlation between income inequality and corruption in a selection of 37 countries. The authors argue that corruption increases inequality; in fact, an increase of one standard deviation in corruption increases the Gini coefficient of income inequality by 11 points. On the other hand, You and Khagram (2005, p. 70) argue that inequality increases corruption as well. They say: "Income inequality increases the level of corruption through material and normative mechanisms. The wealthy have both greater motivation and more opportunity to engage in corruption, whereas the poor are more vulnerable to extortion and less able to monitor and hold the rich and powerful accountable as inequality increases." Also, Uslaner claims that the roots of corruption lie in the unequal distribution of resources in society (2009, p. 127). You and Khagram suggest that this effect might be larger in democratic countries where the powerful are forced to hide their dishonest corrupt activities, whereas in autocratic regimes, the powerful can oppress the poor without having to hide it (2005). This implies that the effect of income inequality might be less strong in post-communist countries in comparison to European countries, which have never experienced communist rule.

Next, GDP per capita is certainly connected to the level of corruption, as suggested by many authors. For example, Kaufmann et al. (1999, p. 15) found that countries with higher GDP per capita have lower levels of corruption; a similar effect was also observed by other authors (Gupta et al. 2002; Lambsdorff 2003; Triesman 2000). However, as in the case of inequality, it is not clear in which direction this influence goes. Poor countries could be lacking resources for fighting corruption, and, consequently, high levels of corruption could inhibit the growth of GDP, so the countries remain poor (Husted 1999; Paldam 2002). Moreover, high corruption can deter foreign investment in a country, causing the GDP per capita to decline (Mauro 1995).

In addition to economic factors, such as GDP per capita or inequality, there are cultural factors that could be important in trying to ascertain the reasons for corruption. Due to the low variance of cultural factors over time, it is perceived that cultural factors influence corruption and not the other way around (Rose-Ackerman and Soreide 2006, p. 17). La Porta et al. (1999) showed that countries with a predominant Protestant population have lower corruption levels than countries that are predominantly Muslim, Orthodox or Catholic. This hypothesis was accepted also by Triesman (2000) in his paper. The reason for this might be in accordance with Max Weber's theory on the relationship between Protestantism and capitalism described in his book *The Protestant Ethic and the Spirit of Capitalism* (1904). Protestants are more individualistic compared to Catholics, Orthodox Christians or Muslims, who have stronger family relations and therefore operate more on a level of connections and ties, which can serve as a ground for corrupt activities. La Porta et al. (1999) provide evidence that Catholicism, Orthodox Christianity and Islam are more "hierarchical" and exhibit inferior government performance, which might explain higher levels of perceived corruption.

Finally, high interpersonal trust is believed to be connected with lower levels of corruption (Adsera et al. 2003; Uslaner 2005). La Porta et al. (1999) argue that higher levels of interpersonal trust might ease the communication between officials and the public and thus lower corruption. Bjornskov and Paldam (2005, pp. 59–75) constructed a time series study examining the relationship between trust and corruption, concluding that changes in trust (measured as social capital) are a cause for changes in corruption.

Several other variables were observed to have an influence on corruption, such as common law legal system (La Porta et al. 1999), Britain's former colonies (Triesman 2000) or oil (Arezki and Bruckner 2009). However, none of these variables are relevant in the case of European countries, because there is very low variability; it is often only one or two countries that differ from the others.

I derive four hypotheses from the arguments above:

- H1: Control of corruption will be higher in countries with lower income inequalities.
- H2: Control of corruption will be higher in countries with higher GDP per capita.
- H3: Control of corruption will be higher in countries with a higher share of Protestants.
- H4: Control of corruption will be higher in countries with higher generalized trust.

How to measure corruption?

There is an ongoing academic debate on how to measure corruption and whether it is even possible to measure it. Corruption is a clandestine activity and there are no official statistics on the number of corruption cases. Unlike most other criminal activities, in the case of corruption, there is no motivation to report the cases to the police. The parties involved in corruption have an incentive to hide this activity (unlike theft, etc.). And the third party who loses money or power due to corruption usually does not even know that the crime has occurred. Therefore, it is due to the good work of the police or to the moral qualities and integrity of the people concerned who refuse to get involved in corrupt activities that corruption does not stay concealed.

Due to the hidden nature of corruption, there are no direct ways to measure it; nevertheless, there are several indirect ways of getting information on the level of corruption in a country (Tanzi 1998). One possibility is to use the cases of convictions of corruption, even though there is a threat that those cases actually measure the skills and effectiveness of the police and justice system rather than the true level of corruption (Charron et al. 2013, p. 5). When the number of such convictions is high, it may mean that the actual level of corruption is very high. However, it could also mean that due to the efficient work of the police, which is successful in bringing charges against corrupt individuals, the level of corruption may only seem to be higher, while in reality it could be much lower than in countries where the police and legal system are incompetent.

The second option for measuring corruption is by conducting experiments. There have not been many experiments studying corruption, because it is quite difficult to simulate an environment where people are willing to take or offer a bribe. However, there is one experiment specifically looking at differences between countries with a history of communist rule and countries without this burden. Ariely et al. (2015) compared the tendency to cheat between Germans from former East and West Germany. The authors found that respondents whose parents come from East Germany and those who had spent a long time under communist rule cheated significantly more. Surprisingly, it did not matter in which part of Germany the respondents currently live, as the past and the family background were the determining factors. This shows that the tendency to cheat persists a long time after the environment has changed, suggesting that there might be the same effect concerning corruption. Experiments are probably one of the most valid methods for research on corruption; however, this method does not allow for cross-national comparison as easily as surveys.

The third option for measuring corruption is expert assessment. Expert assessment data are based on the opinions of experts from several areas who are presumed to have deep knowledge of the situation in a particular country (Charron et al. 2013, p. 44). This type of data is published by Freedom House, for example, or by the PRS group as the International Country Risk Guide (ICRG). Expert assessment might seem like a valid method for measuring the level of corruption; however, there are potential problems. For example, the method is less transparent, because the exact methodology for assessing the level of corruption is not publicly available. Moreover, experts usually have an idea of what the level of corruption in a particular country is, based on various other indicators, and therefore they can base their assessments on this knowledge and thus create the problem of "free-riding" (Charron et al. 2013, p. 43).

The fourth method of measuring the level of corruption is to use public opinion surveys, which measure either people's perceptions of corruption or their direct or indirect experience with corruption. Measuring the respondent's direct experience with corruption could be a plausible method of measuring corruption; however, most of the time it only measures corruption on the lowest level – petty corruption. One of the few surveys measuring direct experience with corruption conducted on the European level is a survey done by the ESS in 2004. The question most relevant for this paper was worded: "How often, if ever, has each of these things happened to you in the last five years? Public official asked favour/bribe for service." The possible answers were "never," "only once," "twice," "three or four times" and "five times or more." Figure 8.2 shows the average answers for this question for each country recoded to a binary answer based on whether the respondent experienced corruption at least once in the past 5 years. One can observe that most of the countries have very low direct experience with corruption. In 18 of the 24 countries, less than 5 per cent of the respondents had experienced a request for bribery. However,

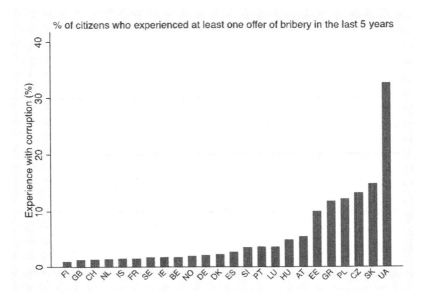

Figure 8.2 Direct experience with corruption, ESS, 2004.

Estonia, Greece, Poland, the Czech Republic and Slovakia have poorer results, with the number of respondents who experienced corruption between 10 and 15 per cent. Ukraine has the worst results by far with almost 33 per cent of respondents claiming that a public official has asked at least once for a favour or bribe for a service in the past 5 years. Unfortunately, the questions on corruption were included in the ESS only once; it is therefore impossible to observe development in time.

Perceptions of corruption could be measured by public opinion surveys or by composite indicators measuring perceptions by citizens and by experts or businessmen as well. The results of people's perceptions of corruption are questionable for the same reasons as the measure of convictions. People's opinions on this subject could be influenced, for example, by the media. Free press is able to report about corruption, whereas in autocratic regimes, due to censorship of the press, the public can rarely learn about corruption cases. And as Karklins adds, this can lead people into falsely believing that authoritarian regimes are less corrupt than democratic societies and thus can build support for authoritarians or nostalgia for previous dictatorships, as is often the case in some segments of post-communist society (2005, p. 7). However, even though there are obvious drawbacks in measuring the perception of corruption, there are certain advantages as well. Unlike the method of expert assessments, citizens usually have no idea of the scores in corruption their country had obtained in previous years, so there is very little danger of the so-called "free-riding" (Charron et al. 2013, p. 44; Triesman 2000). Also, opinion polls are highly correlated across time cross-nationally, which reflects a certain degree of reliability (Triesman 2000); and finally, the subjective evaluation of corruption seems to influence government decisions and the political behaviour of citizens as well (Mauro 1995).

Some institutions use the perception of corruption as part of a composite index of corruption. This composite index consists of multiple sources, which evaluate the level of corruption. It could be a public opinion survey, expert assessment, firm surveys and so on. Composite indicators are the most widely used among researchers whose papers I present and, moreover, this method is growing rapidly as a means of evaluating countries in various areas (Bandura 2008). The most well-known composite indicators are the Corruption Perception Index (CPI) from Transparency International; and the control of corruption, which is part of the Governance Indicators published by the WB. CPI by Transparency International is older, dating back to 1995, while the WB indicator was launched in 1996.

I believe that even though none of the mentioned methods of measuring corruption is ideal, I will use composite index as being the best and most widely used tool for measuring corruption in a cross-country research.

Methodology

For my analysis, I focus on 29 countries, all in Europe; I do not use the complete dataset of the ESS consisting of 36 countries, as four of them (Kosovo, Albania, Latvia and Romania) do not have data for the variables used in this paper. I dropped Israel and Turkey because they are not European countries (or only partly as in the case of Turkey), and finally I dropped Russia, because it is the only country in the dataset which is non-democratic.[3] Of the countries included, 10 do have a communist past and the rest (19) do not. I use the ESS and WB data as the sources for my dataset. I use all six waves of the ESS, dating from 2002 to 2012. Not all the countries were surveyed in all the waves for all the questions concerned, so the dataset is not balanced.

I pool the data so I have 142 country waves, and then I perform ordinary least squares (OLS) regression analysis to determine the effects of various variables on corruption.

Dependent variable

As discussed above, most of the authors use composite indicators for measuring corruption; the most widely used is the CPI by Transparency International and control of corruption by the WB. Due to the fact that Transparency International changed its methodology several times since the beginning of its research and discourages people from comparing their data over time (TI 2012), I will use the control of corruption by the WB.

The data are collected every year and the WB data are comparable over time; therefore it is possible to pool the data across multiple years.

Figure 8.3 shows the level of corruption as measured by the control of corruption indicator. One can see that post-communist countries have a very low level of control of corruption compared to countries that never experienced communist rule. The best performers among post-communist countries are Estonia, Slovenia and Hungary.

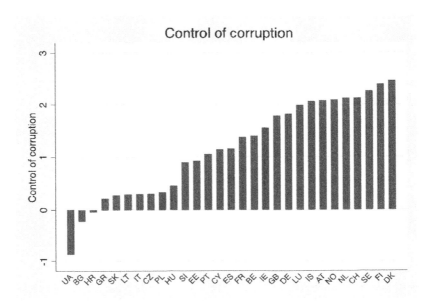

Figure 8.3 Control of corruption, pooled data.

Independent variables

I tested two economic variables that have been found as being important for the level of corruption, GDP and income inequality measured by the Gini coefficient; and then cultural variables as measured by trust in people and the share of practicing Protestants in a country.

For the GDP per capita, I use the WB data, and for the measure of inequality I use the Gini coefficient by UNU Wider. For the cultural indicators I use the data from the ESS. For the question on trust, the respondents were asked whether they believe that most people could be trusted or whether they think that a person should be more careful in trusting others. The authors quoted in this paper used the same question to analyse the effect of trust on corruption. To discover the share of Protestants in a country, respondents were asked which religion or denomination they belong to at present. I recoded the variable into a binary variable (Protestant/others), showing how high the number of Protestant respondents was in a country.

Results

I fitted three regression models. First, I tested whether the theories explaining the level of corruption on the global scale also work on a European level. I expected that the results should be similar to those on the global scale, that is, that a higher GDP per capita, lower income inequality, higher generalized trust and a higher share of Protestants should be connected with higher levels of the

152 Kristyna Chabova

Table 8.1 Determinants of control of corruption (OLS regression)

	1.1. Full Model	1.2. Democracies with no experience of communism	1.3. Democracies with communist past
Gini coefficient	0.008	−0.03**	0.062***
	(0.008)	(0.009)	(0.008)
GDP per capita	0.00003***	7.42e–06*	0.0001***
	(0.000003)	(3.96e–06)	(7.01e–06)
Share of	0.007**	0.009**	0.022**
Protestants	(0.003)	(0.003)	(0.006)
Generalized trust	0.221**	0.2214**	0.093
	(0.076)	(0.083)	(0.061)
Intercept	−1.09	1.016	−3.13
Adjusted R^2	0.78	0.69	0.87
Number of cases	132	89	43

Notes: *$P < 0.10$; **$P < 0.05$; ***$P < 0.01$.

control of corruption. The results can be seen in Table 1 as Model 1.1. The share of people claiming to be Protestant, generalized trust and GDP per capita support the hypothesis, but surprisingly, the Gini coefficient is not significant, meaning that income inequality is not connected to the control of corruption in Europe. Splitting the countries according to their experience with the communist rule and testing them separately might explain this surprising result.

As discussed above, communism has a strong influence on the level of corruption in a country. It is therefore possible that the effect of variables could be very different in countries that have a history of communist rule as opposed to countries that did not experience communist rule.

Countries with no experience of communism

Next, I divide my dataset according to the history of countries: whether the country experienced communist rule or not. Firstly, I tested the same model on countries that do not have a communist history, and then on countries with a communist history. As we can see in Model 1.2, countries without a history of communist rule show different results than in the previous model. In fact, this model fully supports the theories discussed in the first section from the research on the global level – trust among people, the share of Protestants in a country and the Gini coefficient have all significant effect on the control of corruption. GDP per capita is significant only on alpha=0.1 level. One possible explanation might be that having a successful economy only lowers corruption to a certain level; however, when the economy exceeds this level, the effect loses its strength. This hypothesis is supported by Figure 8.4.

This suggests that countries with a democratic history behave as expected and they support all four hypotheses on the global scale.

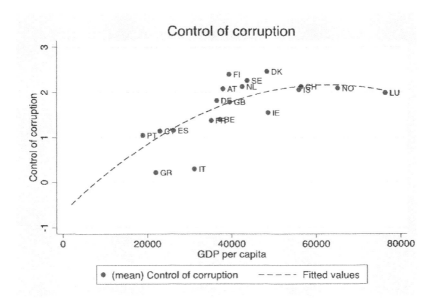

Figure 8.4 Scatter plot: countries with no communist past.

Countries with communist past

However, the last model, Model 1.3, which only includes countries with a history of communist rule, shows a very different situation and unexpected results. GDP per capita and the share of Protestants in a country still play a significant role in the control of corruption. On the other hand, trust in people is not significant, and even though the Gini coefficient is significant, it is so in the opposite direction than expected. This is very different from the results of the full model and of the model of traditionally democratic countries, suggesting that the history of communist rule has a strong influence on the level of corruption.

The model including only countries with a communist history shows that, in contrast to theories concerning this issue, trust in other people does not seem to have any effect on the control of corruption in postcommunist countries. According to several authors, the proportion of people who trust others is systematically lower in post-communist countries when compared to western European democracies (Norris 2001, p. 11; Putnam 1993), as can also be seen in Figure 8.5.

It might possibly be the case that citizens do not trust anybody even though others might be honest and not corrupted. Low trust might not be connected to the level of corruption, because citizens generally in post-communist countries believe that they cannot trust the government and public officials, which could explain the non-significance of the result.

However, there may be an alternative explanation of how trust can influence the level of corruption in post-communist countries. Trust in others can be

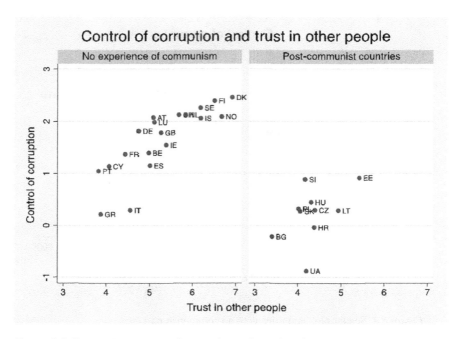

Figure 8.5 Scatter plot: control of corruption and trust in other people.

distinguished into "generalized trust" and "particularized trust." Uslaner observed a clear distinction between these two types of trust; generalized trust is labelled as trust in most people (as in the case of a question posed in the ESS survey), and particularized trust, on the other hand, is labelled as "faith in people we know or we think we know" (Uslaner 2002). In post-communist countries, there might be higher particularized trust combined with very low generalized trust, which would explain the non-significant effect in the model.

This hypothesis is supported by Bădescu, who studied particularized trust in Bulgaria (2003). The combination of low generalized trust and high particularized trust may create a strong base for corrupt activities. Citizens might prefer to operate on informal levels using the ties of family friends whom they trust, rather than relying on strangers. This could increase the level of corruption in a country significantly. Unfortunately, the ESS does not pose any question on particularized trust, so this hypothesis is open for future research.

Income inequality

The second variable, which does not behave as expected, is the Gini coefficient. Theories suggest that more equality should be connected to less corruption. However, as we see in the case of post-communist countries, the relationship is the reverse; that is, in countries with more equality, there is more corruption.

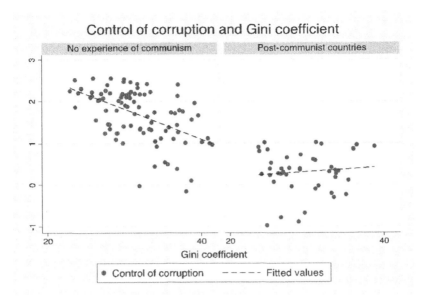

Figure 8.6 Scatter plot, pooled data: control of corruption and Gini coefficient.

As Uslaner writes: "The connection between inequality and the quality of government is not necessarily so simple: As the former Communist nations of Central and Eastern Europe show, you can have plenty of corruption without economic inequality" (Uslaner 2009). The scatter plot in Figure 8.6 shows a very small positive effect between the control of corruption and the Gini coefficient, which, however, is bigger in a model with all variables. This means that the relationship is more complicated and that other variables seem to have a bigger influence than income inequality in post-communist countries.

There are at least two possible explanations for this phenomenon. One explanation could be that there was a development of income inequality in time, while corruption remained static. This could, in pooled data, create a negative effect between income inequality and control of corruption. A similar explanation is suggested by Uslaner (2009), who argues that even though post-communist countries have low income inequality and high levels of corruption – which undermines the theory of income inequality increasing corruption – this state is only temporary. According to him, after transition to democracy, income inequality should boost and catch up with the rest of Europe. However, as Figure 8.7 shows, this point is not valid yet. Income inequality on average is not rising; on the contrary, it is slightly decreasing. This hypothesis is therefore not valid.

An alternative explanation for this can be found in the ideology of communism. The communist ideal was that everybody should be made equal; therefore, countries that experienced more severe communist rule should theoretically be more equal, and at the same time they might have lower control of corruption.

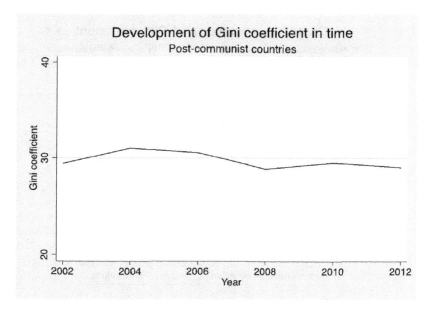

Figure 8.7 Gini coefficient in post-communist countries.

A comparative study of post-communist countries would be needed to test this hypothesis.

Finally, accepting that corruption is widespread in post-communist countries (Karklins 2005) might lead us to a different explanation. When income inequality is low, everybody has a more or less equal economic opportunity to bribe. On the other hand, when income inequality is very high, there are more poor people (connected to the fact that GDP per capita is lower in post-communist countries) who are not financially able to bribe, so corruption activities remain only for those who are wealthy.

These are just preliminary hypotheses, which could eventually explain the reversed effect of income inequality on the level of corruption in post-communist countries. However, more research is needed to state what the real reason behind this phenomenon is.

Conclusion

Corruption is very difficult to study; it is a hidden activity and it is impossible to observe it directly. Fortunately, there is an increasing amount of research and data using indirect ways of observing corruption such as Transparency International or the WB. There is also a rising number of cross-national studies discovering and testing the possible causes and consequences of corruption. Research on a global level agrees that Gini coefficient, GDP per capita, share of Protestants in a country and trust among people are connected to the level of corruption.

This paper tested these claims on a European level. Results showed that except for the Gini coefficient, which was insignificant, all the theories hold. However, the model showed very surprising results when the countries were split according to their history (countries with communist past and the rest). Countries that never experienced a communist rule fully supported findings on the global level. On the other hand, post-communist countries had very different and surprising results. Only GDP per capita and the share of Protestants in a country seem to have an influence on the level of corruption. However, contrary to popular belief, trust among people and low economic inequality are not connected to low levels of corruption in countries with a communist history. In the case of economic inequality, the very opposite is the case. I present several hypotheses why this might be the case; however, the exact reasons are open for further research.

It is clear that post-communist countries are different in many areas from the rest of Europe; corruption is no exception. The effective control of corruption is vital for good governance. More research is needed to discover the specific influences of various variables on the level of corruption in post-communist countries, and consequently, what should be done in order to decrease the level of corruption and to improve the quality of governance in those countries.

Notes

1 This paper was supported by the grant of the Ministry of Education, Youth, and Sports nb. LM2010012. I would like to thank the foundation of Josef Hlavka for their support.
2 Countries included are Bulgaria, Croatia, the Czech Republic, Estonia, Hungary, Lithuania, Poland, Slovakia, Slovenia and Ukraine.
3 According to institutions measuring democracy in Russia such as Freedom House or Polity IV. My analysis distinguishes "Democracies with no experience of communism" and "Democracies with communist past"; Russia does not fit into any of these categories.

References

Adsera, A., Boix, C. and Payne, M. (2003). Are you being served? Political accountability and quality of government. *Journal of Law, Economics, & Organization, 19*(2), 445–490. doi:10.1093/jleo/ewg017.

Arezki, R. and Bruckner, M. (2009). *Oil Rents, Corruption, and State Stability: Evidence from Panel Data Regressions* (No. WP/09/267) (pp. 1–29). IMF.

Ariely, D., Garcia-Rada, X., Hornuf, L. and Mann, H. (2015). *The (True) Legacy of Two Really Existing Economic Systems* (No. 2014-26) (pp. 1–26). University of Munich.

Bandura, R. (2008). *A Survey of Composite Indices Measuring Country Performance* (pp. 1–96). United Nations Development Programme – Office of Development Studies.

Bădescu, G. (2003). Social trust and democratization in the post-communist societies. In *Social Capital and the Transition to Democracy* (pp. 120–140). London and New York: Routledge.

Bjornskov, C. and Paldam, M. (2005). Corruption trends. In J. G. Lambsdorff, M. Taube, and M. Schramm, *The New Institutional Economics of Corruption*. Abingdon: Routledge.

Blake, C. H. and Martin, C. G. (2006). The dynamics of political corruption: Re-examining the influence of democracy. *Democratization, 13*(1), 1–14. doi:10.1080/13510340500378191.

Brown, D. S., Touchton, M. and Whitford, A. (2011). Political polarization as a constraint on corruption: A cross-national comparison. *World Development*, *39*(9), 1516–1529. doi:10.1016/j.worlddev.2011.02.006.

Charron, N., Lapuente, V. and Rothstein, B. (2013). *Quality of Government and Corruption from a European Perspective: A Comparative Study of Good Government in EU Regions*. Northampton: Edward Elgar Publishing.

Gupta, S., Davoodi, H. and Alonso-Terme, R. (2002). Does corruption affect income inequality and poverty? *Economics of Governance*, *3*, 23–45.

Husted, B. W. (1999). Wealth, culture, and corruption. *Journal of International Business Studies*, *30*(2), 339–359.

Johnson, M. (2005). *Syndromes of Corruption: Wealth, Power, and Democracy*. Cambridge: Cambridge University Press.

Karklins, R. (2005). *The System Made Me Do It: Corruption in Post-Communist Societies*. Armonk, NY ; London: M.E. Sharpe.

Kaufmann, D., Kraay, A. and Zoido-Lobatón, P. (1999). *Governance Matters* (No. 2196). WB.

La Porta, R., Lopez-de-Silanes, F., Shleifer, A. and Vishny, R. (1999). The quality of government. *The Journal of Law, Economics and Organization*, *15*(1), 1–58.

Lambsdorff, J. G. (2003). How corruption affects productivity. *Kyklos*, *56*(4), 457–474.

Mauro, P. (1995). Corruption and growth. *The Quarterly Journal of Economics*, *110*(3), 681–712.

Miller, W. L., Grodeland, A. B. and Koshechkina, T. Y. (2001). *A Culture of Corruption?: Coping with Government in Post-Communist Europe*. Budapest, NY: CEU Press.

Norris, P. (2001). Making democracies work: Social capital and civic engagement in 47 societies. Presented at the European Science Foundation EURESCO Conference on Social Capital: Interdisciplinary Perspectives at the University of Exeter.

Paldam, M. (2002). The cross-country pattern of corruption: Economics, culture and the seesaw dynamics. *European Journal of Political Economy*, *18*, 215–240.

Pellegata, A. (2012). Constraining political corruption: An empirical analysis of the impact of democracy. *Democratization*, *20*(7), 1195–1218. doi:10.1080/13510347.2012.688031.

Putnam, R. (1993). *Making Democracy Work: Civic Traditions in Modern Italy*. Princeton: Princeton University Press.

Rose, R. (2001). A diverging Europe. *Journal of Democracy*, *12*(1), 93–106. doi:10.1353/jod.2001.0014.

Rose, R., Mishler, W. and Haerpfer, C. (1998). *Democracy and its Alternatives: Understanding Post-Communist Societies*. Baltimore, Maryland: The John Hopkins University Press.

Rose-Ackerman, S. (1999). *Corruption and Government: Causes, Consequences, and Reform*. Cambridge: Cambridge University Press.

Rose-Ackerman, S. and Soreide, T. (2006). *International Handbook on the Economics of Corruption*. Cheltenham: Edward Elgar Publishing.

Scott, J. C. (1972). *Comparative Political Corruption*. Englewood Cliffs, N.J: Prentice-Hall.

Shleifer, A. (1997). Government in transition. *European Economic Review*, 355–410.

Tanzi, V. (1998). *Corruption Around the World* (Vol. 45, pp. 1–36). International Monetary Fund.

TI. (2012). *Corruption Perceptions Index 2012: Technical Methodology Note* (pp. 1–3). Transparency International.

Triesman, D. (2000). The causes of corruption: A cross-national study. *Journal of Public Economics*, *76*, 399–457.

Uslaner, E. M. (2002). *The Moral Foundations of Trust*. Cambridge: Cambridge University Press.

Uslaner, E. M. (2005). Trust and corruption. In J. G. Lambsdorff, M. Taube and M. Schramm, *The New Institutional Economics of Corruption*. Abingdon: Routledge.

Uslaner, E. M. (2009). Corruption. In G. T. Svendsen and G. L. H. Svendsen, *The Handbook of Social Capital: The Troika of Sociology, Political Science and Economics* (pp. 127–142). Northampton: Edward Elgar Publishing.

WB. (1997a). *Helping Countries Combat Corruption* (pp. 1–73). The World Bank.

WB. (1997b). *World Development Report: The State in a Changing World*. New York: Oxford University Press.

WB. (n.d.). *Control of Corruption* (pp. 1–2). The World Bank. Retrieved from http://info.worldbank.org/governance/wgi/pdf/cc.pdf.

Wei, S. J. and Wu, Y. (2001). *Negative Alchemy? Corruption, Composition of Capital Flows, and Currency Crises*. NBER Working Paper Series 8187.

You, J.-S. and Khagram, S. (2005). A comparative study of inequality and corruption. *American Sociological Review*, 70(1), 136–157.

9 Changing Tendencies of Youth Political Participation in Europe
Evidence from Four Different Cases

Dàniel Oross and Andrea Szabó

Introduction

The argument is put forth that citizens today, especially younger generations, seem to prefer participating in the extra-parliamentary realm, in non-hierarchical and informal networks. Though some researchers have interpreted these trends as reflecting growing scepticism and apathy (Henn et al. 2002), many others have called attention to the danger inherent in formulating oversimplified claims such as "the youth have become disillusioned with politics" (Zukin et al. 2005, pp. 118–189), and sometimes young people are heralded as innovators of politics, as creators of new forms of participation (O'Toole et al. 2003), it being claimed that young people engage in other forms of political participation in ways that orthodox research does not explore. Stolle and Hooghe (2011) found that contrary to some pessimistic assumptions, the shift of citizens from traditional forms of participation to emerging forms of participation has not led to an increase in political inequality on major socio-demographic dimensions.

While in the past decades there has been a clear decrease in traditional forms of political participation (voting, participation in political organizations, connection to political institutions) in western Europe, other indicators show an increase in issue-driven civic participation (Dalton 2008; Inglehart 1997; Norris 2002; Klingemann and Fuchs 1995; Pattie et al. 2004; Kriesi 2008). In other words, voting, campaigning and participation in political parties may have become unpopular, but participation in protests and citizen lobby groups has clearly gained popularity. The different attempts at conceptualization have engendered an emerging methodological consensus according to which research focusing on explaining political participation should seek to identify different forms of participation and group them into clusters. Our paper differentiates two categories: electoral participation, which means participation at parliamentary elections; and non-electoral participation, meaning participation in political organizations as well as forms of participation related to these organizations (such as campaigning, participation in meetings, wearing the symbols of these organizations and direct forms of political participation, i.e. sit-ins, blockades and expressive and symbolic acts).[1]

In order to investigate the reasons behind the changing forms of citizens' political participation, this paper contributes to a better understanding of regional differences in Europe. The aim of the paper is to gain a deeper understanding of the context dependency and conceptual meaning of youth participation by studying four dissimilar cases (Austria, Belgium, Switzerland and Hungary) among the European countries surveyed by the European Social Survey. The paper also aims to contribute to citizenship studies by measuring the distance between the level of participation of young people and adults within the European societies. To explore the sources of active participation among young people,[2] it is important to see more clearly how big the gap is between young people and adults and what the most striking aspects of the difference are. How do contextual factors (political structures, processes and debates) influence young people's political participation and how did it change recently? How do electoral laws influence the level of participation in the four selected countries?

This paper explores the political participation gap between younger and older people since little is written about how different electoral contexts affect this difference. After presenting different perspectives on youth participation in the selected four cases, we will give a quick overview of the difference between adults and young people concerning political interest and turnout at elections in Europe. After formulating two hypotheses, we will present our results, which enable readers to have a closer insight into those specific contextual causes that might stand behind the interrelations among different forms of political participation.

Aim of the study

The political opportunity structure paradigm in social movement research states that political opportunities shaped by access to the political system or alliance and conflict structures influence the choice of protest strategies and the impact of social movements on their environment (Kitschelt 1986, p. 58). Drawing from this paradigm, and regarding findings of Stolle and Hooghe (2005, p. 44) on young people's participation, this paper supposes that if young people participate less intensively than adults, this is not just a matter of less interest but might also be a result of differences in their political opportunity structures. While no switch exists to activate political participation on the part of young people, changes in electoral systems (compulsory voting, lowering the age of voting) can have an important impact.

This paper compares European countries with similar political systems that differ in one institutional variable (compulsory electoral system and electoral system with lowered voting age) and countries with different political systems that differ in one critical institutional variable (post-communist political system, representative versus direct democracy).

Since the aim of the paper is to compare youth participation in different political and cultural contexts, it uses a universal base model that identifies relevant factors, places them on different levels and allows for systematic comparison level by level (Esser and De Vreese 2007, p. 1198). Therefore, the hypotheses of the paper are formulated on both systemic and institutional levels.

Different perspectives on youth participation

The effect of compulsory voting on participation
(the Belgian perspective)

A system of compulsory voting legally requires citizens to participate in elections (Birch 2008; Jackman 2001). Currently, five countries in western Europe retain compulsory voting laws (Belgium, Cyprus, Greece, Liechtenstein and Luxembourg). Belgium was the first country in the world to introduce compulsory voting in 1892; therefore, it has the longest tradition, and compulsory voting has a great impact on citizens' participation since it holds for all elections, national and municipal, as well as elections for the European Parliament (Quintelier et al. 2011, p. 12).

The literature suggests that younger people refrain from taking part in elections and it is hoped that compulsory voting might induce young citizens to participate (Wattenberg 2007). According to Quintelier (2008, p. 25), because of the compulsory voting in Belgium, there is no regular "political participation"-panic among Belgian youth and for this reason the government has also less interest in political participation. However, a recent analysis (Quintelier et al. 2011) found that compulsory voting tends to boost the participation of all groups within society, not just of one specific group. Other authors (Quintelier et al. 2011) have demonstrated exactly the opposite of the above mentioned expectation: older age groups are more strongly affected by compulsory voting than younger age groups, thus rendering the age gap in voter turnout even larger than it would be in other voting systems.

The effect of lowering the voting age on participation
(the Austrian perspective)

Lowering the voting age to 16 years has not only been an issue debated among policy makers and interest groups but also in recent scientific research (Chan and Clayton, 2006; Franklin 2004; Wattenberg 2007). Supporters of such a reform argue that lowering the voting age would have a positive impact on electoral participation. Critics of giving citizens under 18 the right to vote argue that such teenagers lack the ability and motivation to participate effectively in elections. Some authors add that rather than focusing on whether to give them the right to vote at 16 or 18, it would seem more appropriate to concentrate on giving young people better preparation for exercising their civil rights (Hudon and Fournier 2003). There are only a few but a growing number of states in Europe where the voting age at national elections is below 18 years. Austria[3] was the first country where the voting age was lowered from 18 to 16 in 2007;[4] then Norway introduced it in 2011 and then Scotland in 2014. Being the first country in Europe to lower voting age makes Austria one of the very few countries with a general voting age that low and provides us with a particularly interesting group of young voters.

By testing whether the level of political interest is merely the result of a maturation process or if it is also connected to being enfranchised, Zeglovits and

Zandonella (2011) found that enfranchising makes a difference when it comes to the development of political interest: both indicators of political interest, subjective political interest and frequency of following the news showed higher interest among the enfranchised 16- and 17-year-old in 2008 than among the non-enfranchised 16- and 17-year-old in 2004. More recent results confirmed that adolescents at this age have increased their level of political maturity to the point that they are as mature as older voters (Zeglovits and Schwarzer 2009; Wagner et al. 2012).

The effect of direct democracy on participation (the Swiss perspective)

Citizens in direct democracies are regularly called upon to co-determine policy decisions. Citizens can launch referendums against a broad range of governmental decisions, and they can initiate new constitutional articles any time (Kunz et al. 2014).[5] Switzerland is an interesting case, since although numerous instruments of direct democracy are available in Switzerland, because most of these instruments are a Swiss peculiarity, they are not included in the international comparisons.

In order to influence the political process, young Swiss men and women use a variety of different forms of participation. Instruments of direct democracy not only promote related forms of participation but apparently also cause a snowball effect. When young people learn that they can make a difference through their political commitment, on the basis of this experience, they may be more willing to make a greater effort, be it through a time-demanding commitment or by studying more about political issues. Young Swiss respondents are less likely to go to the polls, and the voter turnout in this age group is lower than in other western European countries. There is a significant difference in voting turnout, since that is less important for young Swiss people compared to other forms of participation (Rothenbühler et al. 2012, p. 43).

The effect of the post-communist heritage on participation (the Hungarian perspective)

For post-communist countries, disenchantment from politics and low self-perceived political efficacy are still very serious problems. Considering the similarities in political attitudes and behaviour among the citizens of post-communist countries, the category of "post-communism" still has not lost its relevance (Howard 2003). The changes in post-communist countries are happening slowly and sporadically (Mierina and Rungule 2012). In Hungary, civic participation is low even as compared to other post-communist countries. Therefore, we claim that the post-communist heritage of the country seems to have an enduring negative impact on political participation. Compared to electoral participation, among the whole population the level of participation in non-electoral forms of political participation is still low; electoral participation is 2.5–3 times higher than the most preferred other form of participation (Kern and Szabó 2011, p. 22). Although for young people, dealing with the mechanisms of institutional politics is not popular, out of the different forms of political participation, direct democratic participation (demonstrations, flashmobs and petitions) and issue politics are the most preferred activities (Oross 2013). This might indicate changes in electoral behaviour, but we should not overestimate the impact of this change, since all previous Hungarian and international comparative research findings substantiate the thesis that the political interest of young Hungarians is very low and decreasing (Kern and Szabó 2011).

A view on the European landscape

Concerning political participation, most discussions revolve around declining political interest, dropping participation and low turnout at elections in Europe.[6] This section of our paper highlights the gap among adults' and young citizens' participation and presents a brief overview of these topics before elaborating our hypotheses. In order to have a general overview of political participation in Europe, we have chosen the European Social Survey (ESS) 4 dataset (2008), since that was the round when the most countries (31) participated in the research.

Concerning the second question, electoral participation, Figure 9.2 shows the percentage of people living in different European countries who reported that they had participated in the last elections in 2008 (ESS 4). Danish people come in first with 88.1 per cent, whereas Swiss people are the least willing to vote in elections with 52.9 per cent. Although in most cases, results indicate how much interest in politics and electoral participation is closely related, there are cases (as for example the Swiss case) where it is only the social and electoral context that can explain these results. As for the selected four countries, these results show that we included countries from the first (Belgium), second (Hungary and Austria) and last third (Switzerland) as well.

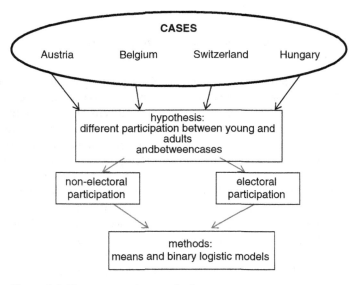

Figure 9.1 The process of our analysis.

Youth Political Participation in Europe 165

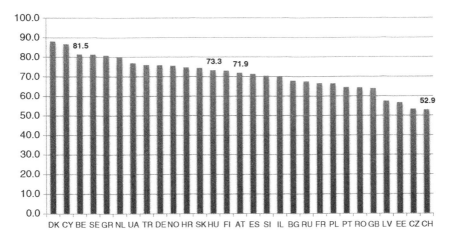

Figure 9.2 Voted in last national election? (Whole population, percentage).
Source: ESS_4, 2008. Own calculation.

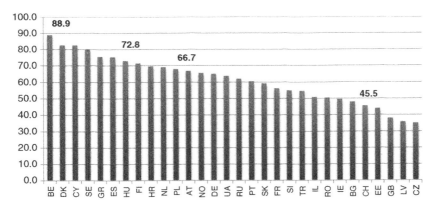

Figure 9.3 Voted in last national election? (Young people/only respondents/percentage).
Source: ESS_4, 2008. Own calculation.

Figure 9.3 shows that the order of the selected countries is similar among young citizens. However, in Belgium, young people have a higher level of participation than adults and the difference is very small between Hungarian young people and adults, while young people have a lower level of participation than adults in Austria and Switzerland, and there is quite a big difference.

Finally, Figure 9.4 shows that lowering the voting age has quite an important impact when we consider those citizens who are not eligible to vote. In this case,

166 *Dàniel Oross and Andrea Szabó*

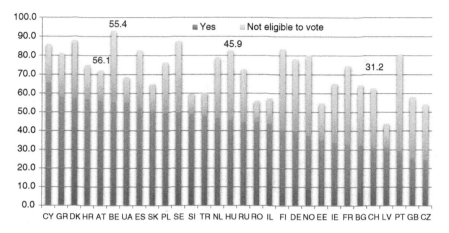

Figure 9.4 Voted in last national election? "Yes" and "Not eligible to vote" answers (whole population, percentage).
Source: ESS_4, 2008. Own calculation.

the order of the countries changes: due to the fact that lowering the voting age in Austria results in a lower percentage of citizens who are not eligible to vote, Austria comes first among the selected four cases.

Hypotheses

Systemic level

On the systemic level, we are first concerned with historical and cultural traditions in different European regions. By comparing four different cases, we assume that it is the different social context of socialization that matters. It is the different role of institutions and agents of socialization within the process of the mobilization of young people that determines different participatory patterns within the four selected countries.

Scholars who write about the decline in political participation expect that the young generation has tuned out of conventional forms of political participation, ranging from voting to party membership, joining other groups, contacting politicians and attending group meetings (Putnam 2000; Macedo et al. 2005). However, older generations are also expected to adopt emerging repertoires over time as these forms of participation become more mainstream and are easily available political tools for everyone.

Since interest in politics is a key indicator of traditional political participation, we expect to find the trends (as presented by Figures 9.2 and 9.3) concerning political interest to also be decisive for non-electoral participation. The difference between young people and adults is the smallest in Belgium, indicating that compulsory voting has an impact irrespective of age. Based on the differences and on the differences in opportunity structures (access to the political system and the available mobilization channels), we assume that compulsory vote has a spillover effect on non-electoral participation. Austria comes second; contrary to the general European trend, the interest in politics of young people in Austria increased between 2002 and 2008. As argued above, lowering the voting age might also have had an impact on this trend. Interest is relatively high in Switzerland, but the difference among young people and adults is bigger. Hungary fits into the decreasing trend, and young people's interest in politics is low. We also expect that since Swiss citizens take part in non-conventional forms of participation, the age gap will be smaller than in the case of electoral participation.

Hypothesis 1: The difference between adults' and young people's non-electoral participation in Belgium will always be smaller than in the Austrian, Swiss and Hungarian cases.

Institutional level

On the institutional level, we look at the structural context of a political institution, namely the influence of electoral laws on electoral participation.

Since interest in politics is a key indicator of traditional political participation, we expect to find the trends (as presented by Figures 9.2 and 9.3) decisive also for electoral participation with slight differences. As we have presented earlier (Figures 9.4, 9.5 and 9.6), in Belgium, citizens are not particularly interested in politics; however, based on their participation at general elections, they are among the three most participative countries in Europe, which can be probably explained as the impact of compulsory voting (Quintelier 2008, p. 25). Austrian citizens are in the middle group concerning both their level of political interest and their electoral participation, but lowering the voting age causes in Austria a lower percentage of citizens who are not eligible to vote. Hungarian citizens are characterized by a post-communist heritage of participation (Kern and Szabó 2011, p. 22); although they are among the group least interested in politics, as for their electoral participation, they are in the middle. Although Swiss citizens are among the most interested Europeans, concerning their political participation at general elections, the level is very low, which might be the result of the fact that being asked to go to polls is required by direct democracy (Freitag et al. 2010). These trends lead us to the hypothesis that compulsory voting has a positive effect on electoral participation and thus tends to boost the participation of all groups within society. Therefore, we suppose that the difference between adults and young people in electoral participation will be the smallest in Belgium among the selected countries. We suppose that lowering the voting age has a positive effect on young people's participation in Austria. We also expect that in Hungary and Switzerland, the level of electoral participation will be lower, not because those young people do not want to vote but because they cannot vote.

Hypothesis 2: The difference between adults and young people in electoral participation will always be smaller in Belgium than in Austria, Hungary and Switzerland.

Data and methods

The empirical investigation demands particular type of data. For the aims of the research, the ideal type of data is longitudinal, where the same people are contacted first when they are younger and then when they are older. Such data are rare. However, to some degree, they can be substituted if the same questions in the same form are repeated in succeeding empirical data collections and if they cover a sufficiently long time horizons over which the examination of the changes over time can be accomplished (Robert and Valuch 2013, p. 126).[7] The comparison is made by examining the responses of young adults in a general population survey, the ESS, which offers a reliable measurement of civic attitudes and behaviours for various European societies.

The paper analyses the six datasets (2002–2012) of the ESS.[8] When selecting the dependent and independent variables, the main criteria was that they were all investigated during the ESS surveys between 2002 and 2012. This way, some kind of longitudinal effect can be examined, so the date of the "investigation" has also been included within the analysis.

Dependent variables[9]

These variables indicate the relationship of the respondents to their social context in both countries and show the fundamental differences concerning their relationship to the political system. The first dependent variable is "voted in last national election."

The second dependent variable is a participation index. The index was created in two steps. First, we created a base index that could have a value between 0 and 7, which is used to include those seven forms[10] of participation that are in the ESS (0 when respondents are not involved in any forms and 7 if they participated in every form in the last 12 months).

All elements of the index fitted well, as shown by the high value of Cronbach's Alpha: 0.638. Then, to take a binary logistic model, the 0–7 base index was transformed into a value between 0 and 1. The value was 0 if the respondent did not participate in any activity; 1 means that the respondent had some involvement.

As any index, our index has limitations, primarily that all forms of participation get the same weight in the model even though different forms need different levels of individual involvement and different tools.

Control variables

The explanatory variables were distinguished at two levels: variables at systemic level and variables at individual level. We have used 15 variables (indexes) during the analysis in our binary logistic models (see Appendix).

Methodology

For the empirical analysis, we used different statistical methods. First, we compared changes in the differences in non-electoral participation at each round, country by country. Then during the analysis, binary logistic regression was used parallel for Hungarian, Belgian, Austrian and Swiss respondents in order to see the characteristics of each selected country separately. The binary logistic regression was run for the non-electoral participation indexes and also for the electoral participation.

Results

Hypothesis 1: The difference between adults' and young people's non-electoral participation in Belgium will always be smaller than in the Austrian, Swiss and Hungarian cases.

In Belgium, values of the index indicating the difference between young people and adults concerning non-electoral participation (see Table 9.1) have a small variance (0.01–0.04), and the six datasets indicate no big differences concerning the participation index of young people and adults. The value of the index is around 0.48 both for young people and for adults. It has the highest value in the third dataset and the lowest in the fifth. Although the difference is statistically not relevant, it is worth mentioning that young people's non-electoral participation index was higher than that of adults in four datasets out of six – this contradicts the "political participation-panic" that young people and certain other groups have a lower level of participation than adults. The Austrian case shows many similarities to the Belgian values of the difference index between young people and adults concerning non-electoral participation: they are small to the point of being statistically not relevant (0.01–0.04). Just as in Belgium, young people's non-electoral participation index was higher than that of adults in two datasets out of four (although the difference is statistically not relevant).

In Switzerland, values of the difference index between young people and adults concerning non-electoral participation have higher variance (0.03–0.14). The value of the index is around 0.47 for young people and 0.57 for adults. It has the highest value in the fourth dataset (–0.14) and the lowest in the second (-0.03). However, in all datasets, adults proved to be more active than young people.

As for non-electoral participation, Hungary differs completely from the other countries. The main difference is that the value of the non-electoral participation index is very low both for adults (0.19) and for young people (0.13). Concerning the six datasets, non-electoral participation is four times higher in Austria and in Belgium. Values of the index indicating the difference between young people and adults concerning non-electoral participation have a high variance (0.07–0.21). Adults are more active than young people in all datasets (just as in the case of Switzerland), but it is more precise to note that while adults have a low level of non-electoral participation, young people hardly have any.

Table 9.1 Difference in non-electoral participation (young and adult people, index, 0–1 means, standard deviation)

Dataset	Statistics	Belgium			Switzerland			Austria			Hungary		
		<30	29+	diff.	<30	29+	diff.	<30	29+	diff.	<30	29+	diff.
Dataset 1	Mean	0.57	0.53	**0.04**	0.53	0.63***	-0.1	0.52	0.51	**0.01**	0.18	0.21	*-0.03*
	Std. Dev.	0.5	0.5	0	0.5	0.48	**0.02**	0.5	0.5	0	0.39	0.41	*-0.02*
Dataset 2	Mean	0.44	0.41	**0.03**	0.52	0.55	-0.03	0.47	0.52	**-0.05**	0.1	0.18***	*-0.08*
	Std. Dev.	0.5	0.49	**0.01**	0.5	0.5	0	0.5	0.5	0	0.3	0.39	*-0.09*
Dataset 3	Mean	0.57	0.55	**0.02**	0.46	0.56***	-0.1	0.47	0.51	**-0.04**	0.14	0.19	*-0.05*
	Std. Dev.	0.5	0.5	0	0.5	0.5	0	0.5	0.5	0	0.35	0.39	*-0.04*
Dataset 4	Mean	0.49	0.48	**0.01**	0.45	0.56***	-0.11	0.49	0.45	**0.04**	0.15	0.21**	*-0.06*
	Std. Dev.	0.5	0.5	0	0.5	0.5	0	0.5	0.5	0	0.35	0.41	*-0.06*
Dataset 5	Mean	0.38	0.42	**-0.04**	0.43	0.53***	-0.1				0.15	0.2*	*-0.05*
	Std. Dev.	0.49	0.49	0	0.5	0.5	0				0.35	0.4	*-0.05*
Dataset 6	Mean	0.44	0.45	**-0.01**	0.44	0.58***	-0.14				0.07	0.13***	*-0.06*
	Std. Dev.	0.5	0.5	0	0.5	0.49	0.01				0.26	0.34	*-0.08*
All data	**Mean**	**0.48**	**0.48**	0	**0.47**	**0.57**	-0.1	**0.49**	**0.49**	0	**0.13**	**0.19**	*-0.06*
	Std. Dev.	**0.49**	**0.49**	0	**0.49**	**0.49**	0	**0.49**	**0.5**	-0.01	**0.34**	**0.39**	-0.05

Source: ESS 1–6. Own calculation.

Notes: ***F-test significant at level 0.001. **F-test significant at level 0.01. *F-test significant at level 0.05.

Youth Political Participation in Europe 171

Our results partly verified the first hypothesis. In Belgium the difference between young people's and adults' participation is very low; there is almost no difference between them. The difference is slightly higher in Austria, but the mean values of the non-electoral participation indexes are similar in both countries (0.48/49). However, the Swiss and Hungarian (even though Hungary is the most dissimilar case) data show similarities from several aspects of non-electoral participation that might be a surprising result. The main reason for the similarities is the fact that the difference between young people's and adults' non-electoral participation is higher (although the difference is statistically not high) in these countries. What makes these countries similar is the fact that in both cases, adults are more active than young people.

But what motivates individuals to participate? In order to better understand those factors that might explain the above mentioned features of non-electoral participation, as a second step of the analysis we ran binary logistic regression for the four selected countries.[11]

Out of 15 selected variables, only six are significant in all selected countries: two of them are individual level variables (age and having a diploma), while four are systemic variables (social tendency, political interest, political attitude factor and feeling close to a political party).

According to our hypotheses, the difference between adults and young people's non-electoral participation in Belgium will be always smaller than in the Austrian, Swiss and Hungarian cases. As Table 9.2 clearly indicates, in the Hungarian and the Swiss case, age is a significant variable. It increases the likelihood of one's non-electoral participation (Exp B 0.74 in Hungary and 0.82 in Switzerland) negatively, meaning that adults are more likely to take part in non-electoral forms of political participation than young people. We found a positive sign of the models – although not significant – only in Austria, so participation by young people is higher than older people only in that case.

Out of these six variables, having a diploma is the variable that significantly increases the chance that a given citizen has non-electoral participation in all selected cases (Exp B is 1.52 in Belgium, 1.82 in Switzerland, 1.88 in Austria and 1.92 in Hungary). This means that there is a socio-cultural effect that has influence on non-electoral participation in all selected countries.

Respondents' interest in politics and their closeness to a given party has influence (even though to a different extent) on non-electoral participation in all selected cases. In all four cases, political interest has utmost importance in the development of non-electoral participation. Increase in participation is most likely in the Hungarian case (Exp B is 2.47) and in Belgium (Exp B is 1.79). A fundamental political tendency is indicated by political attitudes; it is important to note that in all four cases, non-electoral participation was higher if there was a party that the given citizen felt close to. This variable increased the likelihood of participation the most in Austria (Exp B is 2.64), but it also doubled the likelihood of participation in Hungary.

Hypothesis 2: The difference between adults and young people in electoral participation will always be smaller in Belgium than in Austria, Hungary and Switzerland.

Table 9.2 Non-electric participation logistic binary model

Dependent: Participation index (0–1)	Belgium B	Exp (B)	Sig.	Switzerland B	Exp (B)	Sig.	Austria B	Exp (B)	Sig.	Hungary B	Exp (B)	Sig.
Age (dummy 1=young)	**−0.05**	**0.95**	**0.41**	**−0.2**	**0.82**	**0.01**	**0.05**	**1.05**	**0.53**	**−0.3**	**0.74**	**0.00**
Clsprty (dummy, 1 = yes)	0.57	1.77	0.00	0.58	1.79	0.00	0.90	2.64	0	0.71	2.04	0.00
Collection_year_BE/ SW_CH_HU	−0.34	0.71	0.00	0.02	1.02	0.71	−0.15	0.86	0.02	−0.09	0.91	0.22
Diploma (dummy 1 = ISCED 5–6)	0.42	1.52	0.00	0.6	1.82	0.00	0.63	1.88	0	0.65	1.92	0.00
Elementary (dummy, 1 = ISCED 0–1) (1)	0.42	1.52	0.00	0.68	1.97	0.00	−0.3	0.74	0	0.34	1.41	0.00
FAC_happy	−0.04	0.96	0.21	−0.02	0.98	0.63	0.15	1.16	0	−0.07	0.94	0.09
FAC_political_attitudes	−0.14	0.87	0.00	−0.19	0.83	0.63	−0.16	0.85	0	−0.2	0.82	0.00
FAC_social_tendency	0.45	1.57	0.00	0.29	1.34	0.00	0.24	1.28	0	0.28	1.32	0.00
FAC_social_trust	0.10	1.11	0.00	0.13	1.14	0.00	0.16	1.17	0	0	1	0.92
FAC_trust	0.06	1.07	0.09	−0.08	0.92	0.05	−0.16	0.85	0	−0.07	0.93	0.14
Gender (dummy, 1 = male)	0.13	1.14	0.01	−0.02	0.98	0.66	−0.83	0.92	0.18	0.1	1.11	0.16
Pol_intr (dummy, 1 = 1–2)	0.58	1.79	0.00	0.62	1.86	0.00	0.64	1.89	0	0.91	2.47	0.00
Subinat_g (dummy, 1 = good) (1)	0.05	1.05	0.34	0.08	1.08	0.17	0.25	1.28	0.17	0.08	1.08	0.59
Subinat_w (dummy, 1 = wrong)	0.22	125	0.07	0.35	1.42	0.06	0.3	1.03	0.61	0.06	1.06	0.61
Zrlgdgr (Z-sore, religion)	−0.04	0.96	0.08	0.02	1.02	0.48	0.006	1.006	0.855	0.2	1.23	0.00
Constant	0.65	1.91	0.00	−1	0.37	0.00	−0.76	0.47	0	−2.78	0.06	0.00

Statistics

	−2 Log likelihood	Cox & Snell R Square	Nagelkerke R Square
Belgium	10049,335	,135	,181
Switzerland	8162,067	,110	,149
Austria	6332,017	,126	,168
Hungary	4875,693	,103	,167

Source: ESS 1–6. Own calculation.

As a starting point of our analysis, we have formulated the second hypothesis according to the characteristics of compulsory vote, which is supposed to influence electoral participation in Belgium in a special manner, thus making Belgium a different case from the others.

Table 9.3 shows the percentage of respondents answering "yes" retrospectively to the question whether they voted or not during the last parliamentary elections. Data shows that in all rounds (except for the sixth Belgian dataset) adults are more active (in some cases much more active) in electoral participation than young people are. Table 9.3 also indicates that, out of the selected cases, electoral participation is the highest in Belgium both among young people and adults. Electoral participation is the second highest in Austria, followed by Hungary, while Switzerland comes last.

According to what respondents reported, participation levels of adults in Belgium were around 90 per cent in all datasets, while among young citizens there is an increasing trend (from 70 per cent to 91 per cent). Although adults' electoral participation was higher in almost all rounds, the difference between young people and adults is not high, in some rounds being almost insignificant.

The level of electoral participation is the second highest in Austria both among young people and adults, although there is a higher variance between the values of the different datasets. The high amplitude of the reported values might be the result of inaccuracy of respondents' memories. There is a clear difference concerning the activity of the two groups: young people take part in elections in a much (to a statistically relevant extent) lower lever than adults. The fourth dataset (collected in 2008, one year after the change in the electoral law) does not mirror any effect on youth participation.

Out of the four cases, Hungary comes third both among young people and adults. Table 9.3 shows a decreasing trend among adults (from 84 per cent to 75/76 per cent) while young people's participation changes hectically (between 73 per cent and 59 per cent) from one round to the other – these high levels of participation are in sharp contrast to the low levels of non-electoral participation. There is a high level of difference (to a statistically relevant extent) between young people and adults, showing that adults are more active in electoral participation.

Electoral participation is the lowest for both groups in Switzerland. Instead of showing similarities to adult groups in other selected countries, adults' electoral participation resembles more the level of participation among young Austrians. The level of young people's participation is different from any other group (it is between 33 per cent and 48 per cent). The difference between young people and adults is the highest in Switzerland.[12]

Our results verified the second hypothesis. We found the smallest difference between young people's and adults' electoral participation in Belgium. The difference is slightly higher in Austria. In sharp contrast to the low levels of non-electoral participation, we found a higher level of electoral participation both among adults and young people in Hungary, while electoral participation is the lowest for both groups in Switzerland.

Table 9.3 Voted in last national election? "Yes" answer, %

	Belgium			Switzerland			Austria			Hungary		
	<30	29+	diff.	<30	29+	diff.	<30	29+	diff.	<30	29+	diff.
Dataset 1	70	90***	−20	33	75***	−42	78	91***	−13	69	84***	−15
Dataset 2	86	93***	−7	46	71***	−25	62	86***	−24	59	83***	−24
Dataset 3	92	93	−1	36	70***	−34	75	91***	−16	68	79***	−11
Dataset 4	89	93*	−4	46	68***	−22	67	81***	−14	73	82***	−9
Dataset 5	88	89	−1	37	67***	−30				63	75***	−12
Dataset 6	91	89	2	48	70***	−22				59	76***	−17
All data mean	86	91.2	−5.2	41	70.2	−29.2	70.5	87.3	−16.8	65.2	79.8	−14.7

Source: ESS 1–6. Own calculation.
Notes: ***Pearson Chi-Square significant at level 0.001. **Pearson Chi-Square significant at level 0.01. *Pearson Chi-Square significant at level 0.05. Cramer's–V, see Appendix.

Table 9.4 Voted in last national election Logistic Regression Model

Dependent: Voted (0–1)

	Belgium			Switzerland			Austria			Hungary		
	B	Exp (B)	Sig.	B	Exp (B)	Sig.	B	Exp (B)	Sig.	B	Exp (B)	Sig.
Age (dummy 1 = young)	**−0.38**	**0.69**	**0.00**	**−0.93**	**0.40**	**0.00**	**−0.89**	**0.41**	**0.00**	**−0.51**	**0.60**	**0.00**
Clsprty (dummy, 1 = yes)	0.39	1.48	0.00	1.04	2.83	0.00	1.56	4.74	0.00	1.60	4.93	0.00
Collection_year_BE/_SW_CH_HU	−0.01	0.99	0.93	0.10	1.11	0.14	0.19	1.21	0.04	0.41	1.50	0.00
Diploma (dummy 1 = ISCED 5–6)	0.13	1.13	0.28	0.30	1.35	0.00	−0.01	1.00	0.97	0.55	1.72	0.00
Elementary (dummy, 1 = ISCED 0–1) (1)	0.42	1.52	0.00	0.13	1.14	0.13	−0.23	0.79	0.04	0.34	1.40	0.00
FAC_happy	0.16	1.17	0.00	0.26	1.29	0.00	0.06	1.06	0.23	0.08	1.08	0.04
FAC_political_attitudes	−0.21	0.81	0.00	−0.11	0.90	0.04	0.18	1.20	0.00	−0.06	0.94	0.19
FAC_social_tendency	0.04	1.05	0.35	0.05	1.05	0.22	0.16	1.17	0.00	0.03	1.03	0.42
FAC_social_trust	0.08	1.08	0.13	0.15	1.16	0.00	0.08	1.08	0.10	0.01	1.01	0.89
FAC_trust	0.16	1.18	0.01	0.08	1.09	0.09	0.03	1.03	0.60	0.11	1.11	0.02
Gender (dummy, 1 = male)	−0.05	0.95	0.58	0.12	1.12	0.08	−0.08	0.93	0.39	−0.14	0.87	0.06
Pol_intr (dummy, 1 = 1–2)	0.26	1.30	0.01	1.21	3.34	0.00	0.91	2.49	0.00	0.75	2.11	0.00
Subinat_g (dummy, 1 = good) (1)	0.11	1.12	0.24	−0.22	0.80	0.00	−0.11	0.90	0.25	0.46	1.59	0.00
Subinat_w (dummy, 1 = wrong)	−0.33	0.72	0.06	−0.44	0.64	0.04	−0.11	0.90	0.62	−0.21	0.81	0.04
Zrlgdgr (Z-sore, religion)	−0.12	0.89	0.01	0.12	1.12	0.00	0.12	1.12	0.02	0.15	1.17	0.00
Constant	1.77	5.85	0.00	−0.73	0.48	0.00	0.73	2.08	0.00	−0.25	0.78	0.18

(1) Categorical variables Statistics

	−2 Log likelihood	Cox & Snell R Square	Nagelkerke R Square
Belgium	4167,097[a]	,020	,045
Switzerland	5766,193[a]	,203	,285
Austria	3549,254a a	,152	,252
Hungary	4934,581[a]	,156	,237

Source: ESS 1–6. Own calculation.

Just as in the case of the first hypothesis, we ran binary logistic regression for the four selected countries in order to better understand those factors that might explain the above mentioned features of electoral participation (Table 9.4).[13]

To sum up the most important results, we found that out of variables at individual level, age has a significant negative impact on electoral participation in all selected cases, meaning that the older the respondent, the more likely he or she is to have taken part in the last elections. Age is thus working the same way for non-electoral and for electoral participation.

Unlike in cases of non-electoral participation, having a diploma does not increase the likelihood of electoral participation in all selected countries – this variable did not prove to be significant in Belgium and in Austria, although it was true for the other three countries (Exp B 1.35 in Switzerland, 1.72 in Hungary).

The argument that electoral participation is considered to be a much more political activity than non-electoral participation is underlined by the fact that interest in politics and closeness to a party show significant correlation. Closeness to a given party is significantly increasing one's electoral participation in all four cases: Exp B = 4.93 in Hungary and 4.74 in Austria (which is the most significant variable in these two countries), 2.83 in Switzerland and 1.48 in Belgium. In each of the other three countries, political interest is significant and positive. So, as in the case of non-electoral participation, without any general political affinity or without a minimum of political awareness, there is no electoral participation either among young citizens or among adults.

Conclusions

Although evidence tells us about a general trend in European societies about young citizens' declining political interest, dropping participation and low turnout at elections, the different opportunity structures and different institutional backgrounds do have an influence on this trend. Our results from the four selected cases have shown that differences in political opportunity structures matter, and we found rather surprising correlations among factors that determine citizens' participation. We found that social integration has the strongest link to both electoral and non-electoral participation.

Our results indicate that compulsory voting is the most effective in reducing the gap between adults' and young people's participation, both for non-electoral participation and for electoral participation.

As for non-electoral participation, compulsory voting in Belgium reduces the gap between adults and young people the most – young people being more active than adults – while lowering the voting age has a smaller effect on it in Austria (young Austrians are as active as adults). Though the difference is slightly higher in Austria, the mean values of the non-electoral participation indexes are similar in both countries (0.48/49).

Swiss and Hungarian data show similarities concerning non-electoral participation, since in both cases adults are more active than young people. Even though we found the highest levels of non-electoral participation in Switzerland, the gap between adults and young people is bigger than in the Belgian and the Austrian cases. The level of non-electoral participation is the lowest in the Hungarian case, and comparing the results of the six datasets, differences between young people and adults are highest in Hungary because young Hungarians have hardly any non-electoral participation.

When analysing those factors that might explain the above mentioned features of non-electoral participation, we found similarities in all selected cases, meaning that although levels of non-electoral participation are different, the same significant variables motivate individuals to participate. Therefore, we found that beyond the level of political interest, opportunity structures do have relevant effects on non-electoral participation.

Adults are more active (in some cases much more active) in electoral participation than young people. Conforming to our hypotheses, the characteristics of compulsory vote in Belgium reduced the gap between adults and young people the most, while lowering the voting age reduced the percentage of non-eligible voters but had a smaller effect on it in Austria (since the level of electoral participation among young people did not increase and we could not detect a diminished gap between adults' and young people's electoral participation either). However, since Austria has participated only in four out of the six ESS datasets, we had limited data. Therefore, this is definitely an issue where further research is needed. Being the most dissimilar, the Hungarian case mirrors that the category of "post-communism" still has not lost its relevance. Electoral participation is a distinguished form of participation and, in sharp contrast to the low levels of non-electoral participation, we found a higher level of electoral participation both among adults and young people.

The differences are quite high between adults and young people, and electoral participation is the lowest for both groups in Switzerland.

As for factors that might explain the aforementioned features of electoral participation, we found that age has an important role in all selected cases, showing that at an individual level, socialization has a cohort effect on the acceptance of electoral rules. It is also worth noting that electoral participation seems to be much more influenced by systemic level variables than individual, socio-demographic or socio-cultural variables. The more a citizen trusts political institutions, the higher the likelihood of electoral participation and, parallel to this, individual satisfaction seems to have the same effect in all selected cases. According to our results, non-electoral participation is influenced more by individual variables, while electoral participation depends more on social and political factors.

Notes

1 The literature differentiates a third form of political participation: "new" or "virtual" forms of political participation typically require low levels of commitment and few resources. With the help of the internet, it has become possible to take part in both traditional and collective forms of political participation, for example, through blogging, posting and other forms of social media use – but this third one is not analysed in this paper due to lack of data within the ESS questionnaire.
2 Following the categorization of Eurostat, the paper defines young people as persons aged between 15 and 29 years.

3 It is also interesting to note that in Austria, compulsory voting was introduced in 1924. Although at national level it was abolished after the presidential elections in 1925, in the region of Tyrol it has been practiced until 2004.
4 The federal law on the Change of the Rights to Vote (32/BNR (XXIII GP)) provides the right for young people who have reached the 16th year of age to vote on a local, regional, national and European level.
5 Kunz et al. (2014, p. 1) argue that there are four reasons that we expect to find higher levels of political participation in a direct democracy. 1. All citizens are asked to campaign for and vote about these referendums and initiatives, therefore direct democratic institutions allow for experiencing direct personal influence. 2. The repeated exposure to referenda and initiatives leads to a repeated actualization of knowledge about the issue placement of political actors and one's personal issue stance. Thinking about the issue at stake and the probable position of the parties involved before taking a voting decision makes citizens feel more and more competent about what is going on and raises their internal political efficacy further. 3. Referenda and initiatives trigger political discussions of policy issues and stimulate citizens to seek for additional political information (Kriesi, 2005). 4. Referenda and initiatives are preceded by policy-centred information campaigns in which the issues at stake are explained and debated in the media (Bowler and Donovan 2002; Freitag et al. 2010; Kriesi 2005, p. 8).
6 One of the main reasons for concerns about unequal participation is that electoral abstention might have negative impact on other forms of political engagement and involvement. It is assumed that the habit of voting has positive spillover effects on political knowledge, on reading of newspapers and on other forms of engagement and involvement (Lijphart 1997). Empirical evidence for this claim, however, is scarce.
7 The paper writes about the impact of the explanatory variables on the dependent variables and it aims to uncover connections and relations between them. This entails terminological causal explanations, but being based on a cross-sectional investigation, the paper cannot reveal causal relationships.
8 The ESS is a major comparative survey conducted in 20 countries with approximately 42,000 respondents. The ESS is supported by the European Science Foundation and adheres to rigorous methodological norms. As such, it can be considered the most reliable measurement of political attitudes available for European young people and adults (For more detailed information, see www.europeansocialsurvey.org/).
9 For a full list of variables, see Appendix.
10 These forms are: 1. Worked in political party or action group last 12 months; 2. Worked in another organization or association last 12 months; 3. Worn or displayed campaign badge/sticker last 12 months; 4. Contacted politician or government official last 12 months; 5. Signed petition last 12 months; 6. Taken part in lawful public demonstration last 12 months; 7. Boycotted certain products last 12 months.
11 Models can be analyzed for each country, since the value Nagelkerke R is between 0.149 and 0.181 and the models are significant.
12 In one dataset, adults' level of participation is twice as high as that of young people.
13 Statistics of the binary regression models do not have the same level of consistency: while in Hungary and in Switzerland and Austria Nagelkerke R^2 is above 0.2, this value is very low (around 0.04) in the case of Belgium. So in the cases of the latter countries, independent variables have insignificant influence on our dependent variables – we could claim that those control variables that we used are not the ones that determine the characteristics of electoral participation.

References

Birch, S. (2008).: *Full Participation: A Comparative Study of Compulsory Voting*. United Nations University Press, Tokyo, New York, Paris.

Bowler, S. and Donovan, T. (2002). Democracy, Institutions and Attitudes about Citizen Influence on Government. *British Journal of Political Science*, 32(2), pp. 371–390

Chan, T. W. and Clayton, M. (2006). Should the voting age be lowered to sixteen? Normative and empirical considerations. *Political Studies*, 54, 533–558.

Dalton, R. J. (2008). Citizenship norms and the expansion of political participation. *Political Studies*, 56, 76–98.

Esser, F. and De Vreese, C. H. (2007). Comparing young voters' political engagement in the United States and Europe. *American Behavioral Scientist*, Volume 50, Number 9. doi:10.1177/0002764207299364.

Franklin, Mark N. (2004). *Voter Turnout and the Dynamics of Electoral Competition in Established Democracies since 1945*. Cambridge University Press, Cambridge.

Freitag, M. and Stadelmann-Steffen, I. (2010). Stumbling block or stepping stone? The influence of direct democracy on individual participation in parliamentary elections. *In Electoral Studies*, 29, 472–483.

Henn, M., Weinstein, M. and Wring, D. (2002). A generation apart? Youth and political participation in Britain. *The British Journal of Politics & International Relations*, 4 (2), 167–192.

Howard, M. (2003). *The Weakness of Civil Society in Post-Communist Europe*. Cambridge: Cambridge University Press.

Hudon, R. and Fournier, B. (2003). How Old Is Old Enough to Vote. Youth Participation in Society. *Perspectives électorales/Electoral Insight*, vol. 5, n° 2, juillet 2003, pp. 36–41.

Inglehart, R. (1997). *Modernization and Postmodernization*. Princeton, Princeton University Press.

Jackman, S. (2001). Compulsory voting. *International Encyclopedia of the Social and Behavioral Sciences*. Elsevier: Oxford, UK.

Kern, T. and Szabó, A. (2011). *A politikai közéleti részvétel alakulása Magyarországon, 2006-2010*. In Tardos, R., Enyedi, Z., and Szabó, A. (eds.): *Részvétel, képviselet, politikai változás*. Budapest, DKMKA.

Kitschelt, H. (1986). Political opportunity structures and political protest: Anti-nuclear movements in four democracies. *British Journal of Political Science* (1986): 57–85, 58.

Klingemann, H. and Fuchs, D. (1995). *Citizens and the State*. Oxford: Oxford University Press.

Kunz, R., Moeller, J., Esser, F. and De Vreese, C. (2014). Comparing political participation in different institutional environments: The mobilizing effect of direct democracy on young people. In M. J. Canel and K. Voltmer (eds.), *Comparing Political Communication across Time and Space: New Studies in an Emerging Field* (pp. 117–134). Houndmills, Basingstoke, Hampshire: Palgrave Macmillan.

Kriesi, H. (2008). Political mobilization, political participation and the power of the vote. *West European Politics*, 31(1), 147–168. http://dx.doi.org/10.1080/01402380701834762.

Lijphart, A. (1997). Unequal participation. Democracy's unresolved dilemma. *American Political Science Review*, 91, 1–14.

Macedo, S., (Ed.). (2005). *Democracy at risk: How political choices undermine citizen participation, and what we can do about it*. Washington DC: Brookings Institution.

Mierina, I. and Rungule, R. (2012). Youth and political alienation in post-communist countries. *The Second ISA Forum of Sociology Abstract Book*, International Sociological Association, Buenos Aires: Sage, p. 517.

Norris, P. (2002). *Democratic Phoenix. Reinventing Political Activism*. Cambridge, Cambridge University Press.

Oross, D. (2013). Promoting active citizenship at the local level in Hungary: The role of youth organizations. In *Questions of Civil Society: Category-Position-Functionality* (R. Schattkowsky and A. Jarosz, eds.) Cambridge Scholars Publishing, Newcastle upon Tyne. 289–303.

O'Toole, T., Lister, M., Marsh, D., Jones, S., and McDonagh, A. (2003). Tuning out or left out? Participation and nonparticipation among young people. *Contemporary Politics*, Vol. 9, No. 1, 2003, pp. 45–61.

Pattie, C., Seyd, P., and Whiteley, P. (2004): *Citizenship in Britain: values, participation and democracy*, Cambridge: Cambridge University Press.

Putnam, R. (2000). *Bowling Alone: The Collapse and Revival of American Community*. New York, NY: Simon and Schuster.

Quintelier, E. (2008). Why study youth political participation in Belgium? (paper delivered at the Centre for Political Research) https://soc.kuleuven.be/web/files/2/6/Reseach%20Day%20Quintelier.pdf.

Quintelier, E., Hooghe, M. and Marien, S. (2011). The effect of compulsory voting on turnout stratification patterns: A cross-national analysis. *International Political Science Review*, 1–21. doi:10.1177/0192512110382016.

Robert, P. and Valuch, T. (2013). Generaciok a tortenelemben es a tarsadalomban. *Politikatudomanyi Szemle*, XXII. evf., 4. szam. 116–139.

Rothenbühler, M., Ehrler, F. and Kissau, K. (2012). CH@YOUPART Politische Partizipation junger Erwachsener in der Schweiz. *Schweizer Kompetenzzentrum Sozialwissenschaften* FORS, Bern.

Stolle, D. and Hooghe, M. (2005). Youth organisations within political parties: Political recruitment and the transformation of party systems. In Forbrig, J. (2005), *Revisiting Youth Political Participation, Challenges for Research and Democratic Practice in Europe*. Council of Europe Publishing.

Stolle, D. and Hooghe, M. (2011). Shifting inequalities. *European Societies*, 13(1), 119–142. doi:10.1080/14616696.2010.523476.

Wagner, M., Johann, D. and Kritzinger, S. (2012): Age group differences in issue voting: The case of Austria. *Electoral Studies*, 31(2), 372–383.

Wattenberg, M. P. (2007). *Is Voting For Young People?* Pearson Longman, New York.

Zeglovits, E. and Schwarzer, S. (2009). Lowering voting age in Austria – evaluation of accompanying campaigns for 16–18-year-olds. Paper presented at the ECPR 5th General Conference, Potsdam, September 10–12.

Zeglovits, E. and Zandonella, M. (2011). Political interest among young Austrians before and after lowering voting age. Paper presented at the 6th ECPR General Conference, Reykjavik, August 25–27, 2011.

Zukin, C., Keeter, S., Molly, A. Jenkins, K. and Delli Carpini, M. X. (2005). *A New Engagement? Political Participation, Civic Life, and the Changing American Citizen*. New York, Oxford University Press.

Appendices

Table 9.5A List of variables in the analysis

Variable	Contents	Comments	Availability
Voted	If respondent "voted" in last national election	(0 = if "not", 1181 = if "yes")	Individual level
Participation index	It consists of the following variables: 1. Worked in political party or action group last 12 months; 2. Worked in another organization or association last 12 months; 3. Worn or displayed campaign badge/sticker last 12 months, 4. Voted in last election; 4. Contacted politician or government official last 12 months; 5. Signed petition last 12 months; 6. Taken part in lawful public demonstration last 12 months; 7 Boycotted certain products last 12 months.	(values: 0–7, recoded 0–1) Index parameter: Cronbach's Alpha .638. Cronbach's Alpha based on standardized items .649	Individual level
Age (Age: name of variable in the table)	If respondent is young or not	1= if young <30 year	Individual level
Education (diploma: name of variable in the table) (elementary: name of variable in the table)	If the respondent has university diploma or not; If the respondent has higher level of education than elementary level or not.	diploma 1=has, 0=not; elementary1= has, 0=not	Individual level
Gender (Gender: name of variable in the table)		(1 = male, 0 = female)	Individual level
Religion (Zrlgdgr: name of variable in the table)	How religious are you?	(0–10 scale, Zscore)	Individual level

Table 9.5A (Continued)

Variable	Contents	Comments	Availability
Subjective income attitude (Subinat_g: name of variable in the table) (Subinat_w: name of variable in the table)	Feeling about household's income	(good 0–1, wrong 0–1)	Individual level
Individual trust factor (FAC_social_trust: name of variable in the table)	Principal components: Most people can be trusted or you can't be too careful, Most people try to take advantage of you, or try to be fair).	Reliability statistics: Cronbach's Alpha: 0.711; Initial Eigenvalues: 1.48; Cumulative %: 74.14	Systemic level
Individual satisfaction factor (FAC_happy: name of variable in the table)	Principal components: How happy are you? How satisfied with life as a whole?	Reliability Statistics: Cronbach's Alpha: 0.829; Initial Eigenvalues: 1.71; Cumulative %: 85.66	Systemic level
Social tendency factor (FAC_social_ tendency: name of variable in the table)	Principal components: How often socially meet with friends, relatives or colleagues? Taking part in social activities compared to others of same age.	Reliability statistics: Cronbach's Alpha: 0.534; Initial Eigenvalues: 1.41; Cumulative %: 70.63)	Systemic level
Factor of trust (FAC_trust: name of variable in the table)	Principal components: trust in country's parliament; trust in politicians, trust in political parties; trust in the European Parliament; trust in the United Nations, trust in the legal system; trust in the police.	Reliability statistics: Cronbach's Alpha: 0.898; Initial Eigenvalues: 4.367; Cumulative %: 62.38	Systemic level
Political attitude factor (FAC_political_ attitudes: name of variable in the table)	Principal components: Satisfaction with the government? How satisfied with the way democracy works in country? How satisfied with the national government?	Reliability statistics: Cronbach's Alpha: 0.821; Initial Eigenvalues: 2,208; Cumulative %: 73,596	Systemic level
Political interest (Pol_intr: name of variable in the table)	How interested in politics?	1 = interested, 0 = not interested	Systemic level
wave (Collection_ year_BE/_SW_ CH_HU: name of variable in the table)	Year of election		Systemic level
Close party (Clsprty: name of variable in the table)	Feel closer to a particular party than all other parties	(1 = yes, 0 = no)	Systemic level

Table 9.6A Statistics voted in last national election? "Yes" answer, % (Cramer's–V in all dataset and in all countries)

	Belgium	Switzerland	Austria	Hungary
	Cramer-V	Cramer-V	Cramer-V	Cramer-V
Dataset 1	0.228	0.247	0.146	0.151
Dataset 2	0.095	0.139	0.211	0.208
Dataset 3	0.020	0.173	0.162	0.077
Dataset 4	0.051	0.160	0.147	0.088
Dataset 5	0.013	0.221	–	0.100
Dataset 6	0.027	0.184	–	0.133

10 Untangling our Attitudes Towards Irish Citizen Involvement and Democracy

Perspectives from the European Social Survey and Implications for Higher Education

Aoife Prendergast

Is there such a concept as the "democratic mind-set"? Clearly, there is a need to understand both the practical and the political nature of democracy for citizens in democratic countries internationally. If one is to assume that we are the creators of our own destiny, we have a collective responsibility. Does a democratic mind-set motivate us to address the gap of inclusion, social justice and equality? Similarly, this chapter will explore how one can identify the commencement of a democratic mind-set and discuss the complexities in encouraging this in the ever-evolving nature of higher education against the backdrop of managerialism and neoliberalism. Given that the concept of democracy can take many forms, one such method used to establish the relationship between social sciences education and democracy is inquiry-based learning.

First, it is vital to define and untangle our understanding of democracy.

> Democracy is a way of personal life controlled not merely by faith in human nature in general but by faith in the capacity of human beings for intelligent judgment and action if proper conditions are furnished… I am willing to leave to upholders of totalitarian states of the right and the left the view that faith in the capacities of intelligence is utopian
> John Dewey, *Creating Democracy – The Task before Us*, 1939, p. 229

Reflecting on this definition by John Dewey now in 2015, some 76 years later, one considers that democracy is a complex concept that takes into account a variety of personal and political factors. Now, more than ever, the role of the individual is significant. In social sciences education, it has traditionally been seen as an important socializing arena for preparing students to become active citizens. Conceptions of active critical citizenship and the role of education in citizenship, however, have varied. On one hand, the economic and instrumental needs of society drive towards technically oriented citizens who will fill necessary workforce roles (Giroux 2002). Universities and colleges serve as a pipeline, socializing and training prospective workers to fulfil economic interests. On the other hand, higher education institutions are also an arena for preparing citizens for a public democracy, civic leadership and public service. To participate in a public democracy, students need to be educated to bring a range of competencies and world views to understand and respond to human and social dilemmas.

Cook and Westheimer (2006) state that "if people are not born democrats, then education surely has a significant role to play in ensuring that democrats are made" (p. 348). Therefore, there is a convincing argument for the development of a democratic "mind-set" in any undergraduate academic module or assessment in social sciences education. Education is a fundamental human right. As such, it is clearly the responsibility of the state and a core element of any development policy committed to social justice. According to Archer (2006, p. 7), "Securing the right to education is key to enabling people to secure other human rights, yet the right to education is violated by governments around the world. The location and the specific commencement of developing the "mind-set" of democracy are difficult to conceptualise and establish for both the learner and the academic. Focusing on attempting to explore this democratic mind-set in undergraduate social sciences education, it can be seen that with any pedagogic approach, it is important to align learning outcomes, teaching and learning activities and assessment tasks, particularly where the intention is to encourage deep, rather than surface, approaches to learning (Biggs 2003).

Biggs outlines

"The essential feature of a teaching system designed to emulate professional practice is that the crucial assessments should be performance-based, holistic, allowing plenty of scope for students to input their own decisions and solutions" (Biggs 2003, p. 237).

Surely, this relates directly to creating and developing a democratic mind-set in social sciences education through an inquiry-based approach. This approach would allow individuals to reflect on their own role as citizens, identify their democratic values and principles and analyse their own decisions that would encourage them to become critically educated democratic citizens. This, Biggs argues, requires criterion- rather than norm-referenced assessment and adopting a much more holistic and divergent approach involving significant peer and self-assessment, all features that inquiry-based curricula increasingly reflect. This is the first step in developing a democratic "mind-set." One would argue that significant self-assessment and self-awareness is crucial to the commencement of a democratic mind-set.

Moreover, the commencement of the democratic "mind-set" is dependent on the classroom organisational structure. Academics and students need to challenge and prepare themselves – for example, by analysing group-based activities to aid implementation and identifying using hands-on investigation and research activities. The academic or facilitator needs to establish how they will guide students to reflect on their own learning process. One has to acknowledge and appreciate that this is a difficult process. It has been widely accepted by academic staff and the quality assurance system. However, many difficulties still occur. For example, accusations of "managerialism" have been documented (Hussey and Smith 2003), and while it is seen as emblematic of a "new" learner-focused higher education by some, it can be viewed by others as reductionist – more suited to training than education.

Biggs's notion of constructive alignment (1999, 2003) has been one of the most influential in reforming the curriculum in higher education. It has been successfully utilised by quality assurance systems globally. In summary, Biggs describes constructive alignment occurring when three key curriculum elements – the intended learning outcomes, the teaching and learning activities and the assessment tasks – are balanced. A constructivist understanding of learning starts with the notion that the learner constructs their learning through relevant activities. Fundamentally, this underpins their approach. Effective alignment ensures consistency throughout. Intentions are made transparent and communicated to the learner; the lecturer selects and uses teaching and learning methods likely to achieve these intentions, and assessment tasks reflect those intentions. The entire system is designed to enable the students to learn rather than leave them wondering and questioning what is involved in the course of study or on what they will be assessed.

This reverts us back to the original definition of inquiry-based learning (IBL), which, to use the words of O'Rourke and Kahn, should be understood as "a broad umbrella term used to describe approaches to learning that are driven by a process of enquiry" (O'Rourke and Kahn (2005, p. 1). Therefore, we can now see IBL as a comprehensive strategy for promoting a democratic mind-set in social sciences education. It is evident that the trend is moving towards more constructivist pedagogies, with the students being active within their own learning and development, significantly changing the type of learning that academic libraries need to support (Levy 2005). This shift in pedagogy requires new kinds of learning spaces to support activities that promote democracy, such as group work and autonomous study (Milewicz 2009; Scottish Funding Council 2006).

Commitment to a democratic mind-set utilizing an IBL approach reflects the widespread move in higher education in recent years from a teacher-centred conception of the learning process towards an increasingly student-centred model. Pedagogic research has demonstrated that students are more likely to adopt "deep" learning strategies when they are both challenged and supported to engage actively with the questions and problems of their discipline (Marton et al. 1993; Prosser and Trigwell 1999; Ramsden 2003). This illustrates the importance of promoting a democratic mind-set. Seeing learning as a process of knowledge construction means that teaching moves away from the transmission of information towards the design of learning tasks and environments that will support students' active engagement with their subject (Biggs 1999). Learning through inquiry in its many forms is, increasingly, recognised as a powerful pedagogical strategy in this respect and one that can be applied successfully to lower as well as to higher levels of study in higher education (Elton 2001; Jenkins et al. 2003). Its further benefits include the development of a wide range of metacognitive and other learning skills and the enhancement of student motivation and commitment in relation to both the process of studying and the discipline itself (Brew 2001; Jenkins et al. 2003; Khan and O'Rourke 2003). At the same time, learning through inquiry is a strategy that, in making the links between research and learning more explicit, has the potential to strengthen the "teaching–research nexus" within universities (Elton 2001; Marsh and Hattie 2002; Neumann 1994). This chapter outlines the adoption of IBL to encourage a democratic mind-set. It also discusses the current Irish educational context and provides recommendations for future practice.

Is it worth the trouble and hassle?

Considering the possibility of delivering an IBL approach will aid in the development of a democratic "mind-set." However, given its complex nature, locating, commencing and motivating this approach may prove difficult and may be fraught with negativity. From my own personal experience, once anyone is involved in facilitating an inquiry-based approach to promote a democratic mind-set in social sciences education and has the opportunity to see what exactly students can do when given the permission to think and learn independently, he or she usually becomes an advocate for an IBL approach to social sciences education. I would argue that some academics can see how students think, what they know and how they are learning by engaging in IBL. This allows academics to intervene early with students having difficulty before it develops into a more complicated issue.

To encourage a democratic mind-set, on a practical level, the IBL approach could be effective if the following is adhered to. First, learners must be *alert*, *clear* and *motivated*. This represents a change in approach from the standard passive lecture where the student has little or no input. Therefore assessment will have to differ – an active approach will have to occur. Perhaps this is why IBL is feared by academics and students alike. In my personal opinion, it is a natural way for students to develop their own democratic mind-set, given the evidence suggested to date.

Characteristics of a democratic mind-set in social sciences education

An inquiry-based approach is characterized by the tendency to address general themes over a long period with less specific content objectives; it may involve questions for which there are no known answers, and it is less dependent on the research of others (McMaster University 2007). This would allow for a true and authentic experience of the democratic mind-set.

The main characteristics of IBL in social studies education are discussed by Kahn and O'Rourke (2005) as follows:

- Engagement with a complex problem or scenario (for example, a societal problem or issue) that is sufficiently open-ended to allow a variety of responses or solutions.

- Students direct the lines of enquiry and the methods employed.
- The enquiry requires students to draw on existing knowledge and identify their required learning needs.
- Tasks stimulate curiosity in the students, encouraging them to actively explore and seek out new evidence.
- Responsibility falls to the students for analysing and presenting evidence in appropriate ways and in support of their own responses to the problem.

IBL offers flexibility to develop a range of skills, including those required for lifelong learning which, in turn, address some of the major contemporary issues in society and in higher education.

- The modern economy places a premium on the ability to create and synthesise knowledge; open enquiries allow the development of this skill and other key transferable skills.
- Strong leadership skills in managing complex enquiries and projects are particularly important in every workplace.
- The focus on enquiry helps in synthesising learning, which can be an issue in modular and inter-disciplinary programmes; enquiries typically cross "boundaries" and encourage deeper thought.

However, a key consideration in pedagogical design for promoting democracy is that learning activities need to be open-ended enough to allow for students to engage in genuine exploration. Students need to investigate authentic questions and issues – questions and issues to which there might well be alternative responses and solutions. Traditionally, inquiry projects have tended to be seen as activities that students will be ready to engage in only when they have already acquired a certain body of knowledge in their discipline through other means.

IBL is an appropriate method of learning because it has a significant role to play in professional practice development (Price and Price 2000; Price 2001). It empowers students to take control of their learning (Dahlgreen and Dahlgreen 2002) and enhances the development of skills that are transferable to the practice areas in social studies.

Commitment to IBL reflects the widespread move in higher education in recent years from a teacher-centred conception of the learning process towards an increasingly student-centred model.

How educators in the social sciences conceptualise and facilitate democracy

I propose that, in an ideal world, student inquiry should be central to the undergraduate and postgraduate learning experience for promoting a democratic mindset in social sciences education. However, designing a new curriculum, new assessment and new teaching tools and resources is a challenge in contemporary higher education. Encouraging and motivating students through a fundamental change in learning is a time-consuming and costly effort.

IBL in social sciences is student-centred; individuals must take responsibility for their own learning, identifying what they need to know to better understand and manage problems and determining where they will find that information.

In IBL, academic staff are facilitators and guide the students through the process. Roles remain different. The practical adoption and implementation of IBL approaches, in terms of the desired impact on the student learning experience in Irish higher education, should incorporate the following:

- It should occur in small student groups – approximately 4–6 students.
- Academic staff/educators as facilitators.
- The problem must form the organising focus and the stimulus for learning.
- The learning is student-centred.
- New information and knowledge is acquired through self-directed learning.

One of the most widely accepted goals of social studies education is to produce knowledgeable and caring citizens. It is, therefore, imperative that students have the opportunity to participate in public issues and have a meaningful voice within their community. Students must learn how to gather information, solve problems and make civic decisions (Saxe 1997). Thus, educators and staff in higher education institutions should encourage their students to create their own questions, cultivate investigative strategies, formulate theories and apply new concepts to their own lives in a variety of methods (Fitzsimmons and Goldhaber 1997).

The current Irish context – higher education

Ireland's higher education system has played a major role in the development of Irish society and the economy. It will have an even more critical role to play in the coming decades as we seek to rebuild an innovative knowledge-based economy that will provide sustainable employment opportunities and good standards of living for all our citizens. Its role in enabling every citizen to realise their full potential and in generating new ideas through research are and will be the foundation for wider developments in society.

The development of the higher education system in the years to 2030 will take place initially in an environment of severe constraints on public finances. There is increasing demand to invest in education to support job creation and innovation and to help people back into employment following the impact of the recent recession and its profound impact on society as a whole and indeed its footprint on higher education and pedagogical design for future employment needs. In the wider world, globalisation, technological advancement and innovation are defining economic development, making people more mobile internationally as they seek out career opportunities (Department of Education and Skills 2011).

Currently, the higher education sector in Ireland is comprised of seven universities, Dublin Institute of Technology, 13 Institutes of Technology, seven specialist colleges and a small number of private colleges. Ireland has one of the highest educational participation rates in the world, with over 81 per cent of Irish students completing second-level education and over 60 per cent entering higher education (OECD 2010). Public expenditure on higher education is slightly less than the European Union (EU) average. Graduates from Irish higher education institutions are considered the most employable in Europe, and Ireland produces more graduates per 1,000 inhabitants than any other European country (Aubyn et al. 2009).

In recent years, higher education in Ireland has been the subject of negative attention that has emphasised the substantial financial cost, rather than the value and contribution it provides to wider Irish society and to the overall economy. This criticism sometimes seems to imply that higher education policy operates on the basis of autopilot, continuing on a pre-set course with little or no human intervention for much of the time (Magennies 2012).

A variety of external pressures impact on the way third-level academic institutions provide their services, and these have driven changes in the way learning and teaching take place.

First, there is the increased financial burden of higher education on the national treasury due to universal participation rates and the funding of education for the knowledge economy. This has led to increasing demands from government for greater efficiency, improved service with quality enhancement and consequential reduced per capita funding. Secondly, changing academic roles for staff combined with increased pressure to produce research, the use of information technology in student learning and the availability of world-class learning and resources to students through the internet has meant that the traditional methods of teaching and learning are now rapidly evolving and changing.

One of the most significant changes in higher education in Ireland in the past decade is the manner in which the digital world and the educational space have become intertwined. For a generation who remembers tape recorders and photocopiers as tools of contemporary innovation and genius and clouds as meteorological phenomena, the dramatic and ever evolving world of acronyms such as Moodle and VLE echoes fundamental shifts in change patterns that have revolutionised the educational spaces in which students engage in learning. The movement is rapid, and virtual learning spaces are now the traditional methods of educational engagement, learning and assessment. A reflection on the impact and value of the digital world for IBL has to occur as these valuable tools must been seen as enablers for creative engagement if they are to move beyond the earlier understanding of their role as an effective way of sharing content.

The third pressure involves academic change due to the changing demands of society for fairer access to the benefits of a tax-subsidized resource with a focus on lifelong learning that is student-centred. This leads to a widened diversity of student intake and changing demands on the part of students. Demographic shifts in Ireland as numbers of school leavers decrease could facilitate increased opportunities for mature students, those who suffer from economic disadvantage and disabled students.

Facilitating change

Developing and fostering a positive democratic mind-set utilising the core characteristics in IBL is vital. This change is transformative; it is a challenge that requires us to reflect on what exactly we are seeking to achieve, as well as reflecting on strategies that can lead to the accomplishment of these goals.

One crucial difficulty in facilitating this change in a department, or indeed in an institution at large, lies in the fact that we cannot see clearly what is to come. We spend the majority of our time reversing into the future, judging and choosing on the basis of the present experience and the past as we have lived or observed it. Indeed, urgent standard tasks such as marking and setting examinations and assessments often have significant importance in the everyday operational tasks of an academic. Little time is focused on reflecting on methodologies such as IBL. Hence, very often there is a negative reaction to changes that "appear to come out of nowhere."

Renfro and Morrison (1983) reflect:

> Although changes may seem to come upon us without warning, experience shows this is rarely the case. Unfortunately we often disregard or misinterpret the signals of change. We tend to spend our time on issues we perceive to be the most important right now; we fail to scan our surroundings for changes that are in the early stages of development. The flood of problems that forces us into crisis management makes concern for emerging issues to appear to be a luxury. It is not. It is a necessity. (p. 1)

Promoting democracy through an IBL approach is best achieved through a successful structuring of the year through the delivery of modules in a traditional lecturing/delivery based around a central IBL question. This particular scenario can achieve strong results across a wide range of student aptitudes.

Challenges in current higher education – flipping and stripping the status quo

So how can we even attempt to address this "decent" democratic mind-set? In current times, the context of higher education is shifting rapidly. Higher education institutions are under increasing pressure to be more accountable and the resultant managerialism that is supposed to deliver such accountability is "characterised by a distrust of academics" and an ever-increasing "battery of mechanisms of audit and control generated by the state and instituted by senior and middle academic-managers" (Kolsaker 2008, p. 515, cited in O'Connor 2013, p. 66). This has seen the introduction of "cycles of institutional reviews," which largely "ignored the fact that measures to monitor quality related to teaching have long existed" in Irish universities (O'Connor 2013, p. 67). Is it possible to encourage a democratic mind-set in this process? Indeed, academics are now required to be evaluated by external examiners, have their teaching quality and research output evaluated, adhere to individual workload models and academic activity profiles and undergo annual performance and development reviews, all processes that have been described by "those who are not opposed to accountability" as being "wasteful of resources that could be more effectively used in front-line activity" (Morley 2003, cited in O'Connor 2013, p. 68; see also Garvin 2012).

Much restrictions are inevitable in a neoliberal system that, by and large, envisions higher education only in terms of its contribution to the creation of the famed "knowledge economy" (Allen 2007). As such, social engagement, for example, is merely defined in terms of "the commercialisation of research" and not in "terms of equity or social justice" (Lynch 1999, cited in O'Connor 2013, p. 68). Such views have had significant implications in that the Irish state, the EU and "various corporate interests... have stressed that the allocation of state monies to research in science and technology is essential for economic growth" (O'Connor 2013, p. 74). However, this has resulted in the overwhelming majority of research funding going to limited areas in science, engineering and technology in recent years (Lynch et al. 2012). Focus on concepts and topics such as democracy are virtually non-existent. As primary agents of change in contemporary higher education, academic staff and educators should enable students and colleagues to not only participate in transforming a world of democratic difference, but to act, to initiate change; they should be action-centred rather than student-centred (Biesta 2007).

Decency as a core value must start with educational leaders. It is crucial to provide opportunities for leaders to practice saying exactly they think, hear others' ideas, share values and beliefs and work together to act on the plurality of ideas and beliefs. Decency, caring for others, guides this interaction. The compliance and group think at all levels of academic standing needs to be targeted. Education is not a compliance profession – educators have a duty of care to encourage interaction and interface with clauses of democracy and encouragement of expression. With compliant and group thinking, how do educational leaders influence change, let alone creativity and democratic principles? How can they encourage action to locate one's place in the world and to change it to accommodate the complexity of difference? Decency in this instance requires risk-taking that advocates for valuing difference and plurality. Decency in educational leadership assumes commitment to learning. That indicates the dedication to thinking and the time needed to process concepts and ideas. We face a decisive junction in the exploration of democratic education in higher education on a national and a global level. The need to perform has exceeded the mind-set – we are now in the depths of a consumerist culture that does not remotely motivate students to engage and perform in democracy. In addition, this consumerist culture does not necessarily improve the quality of teaching in academic institutions. Despite these obvious weaknesses of the consumerist culture in higher education, it is infiltrating every aspect of university life. Educators and academics are slow to advocate for resistance to these fast-moving changes in our culture and workplaces. Education is now seen as a product, not a process.

Plans for the future: Modifying our mind-set

The challenges of adopting an IBL approach in the social sciences are not only complex but in many cases are also institution specific. The difficulties associated with creating student-driven, inquiry-based collaborative activities are various. One must consider resource and time commitments for both academics and students alike. Encouraging open dialogue, ensuring participation throughout the process and the consideration of previous experiences are all complicated factors that must be greatly appreciated. It is both important and urgent to prioritise and push the promotion of the democratic mind-set on the educational agenda. However, capacity for change needs to be analysed also.

IBL is, by necessity, resource intensive, and as such it requires strong support, especially at the departmental level. Murray and Savin-Baden (2000) argue that organisational support is a crucial element in ensuring the successful introduction of such a curriculum, and this also includes opportunities for staff development. The approach, particularly in its purer forms, challenges the traditional transmission mode of teaching and is resource intensive in terms of staff. This inevitably means increased staffing levels for IBL courses. If the inquiry involves fieldwork, then this is a further cost. From funding to technology to approval, institutional support can make or break a strategy for learning. In a perfect setting, students should challenge the tutor in the same way the tutor should challenge the student. Monetary support for resources and technology are not equally available to various institutions, their faculty or students. Based on budgetary priorities, some social science departments fall below the curve on institutional support. Faculty training in various methodologies should take place at all levels but is hindered by the same problems. At a crucial time of budget crunching, the faculty-to-student ratio is often much greater than it should be.

Conclusion

There is a substantial need to recognise that learning in and from social sciences education requires resources, comprehensive support and prioritising. Government and policy makers in education need to lead the way in directing this democratic mind-set, developing new ways of learning. The core recommendation of the delivery of an IBL approach is vital. In addition, this cannot be achieved without developing productive relationships between education providers, citizens and representatives in the democratic government system in programme design and implementation. The overall aim is to ensure that we have meaningful critically engaged students in social sciences education. In turn, education should inform the democratic mind-set highlighted in this chapter. If one poses the question of democracy and decency in the same sentence, we should be in a position to confirm the definition of decency in the context of democracy and education. Clearly, students must become engaged in "decency" and apply the core value or even principle of decency to become democratic citizens. In conclusion, an IBL approach to social sciences education, developing the core values and principles of democratic citizens, will provide the catalyst for democracy.

Guerin and Hennessey (2010) argue that an IBL approach helps students to overcome the difficulties in linking theory to practice. Dodd (2007) suggests that an important facet of this is in information literacy, which is the ability to identify, find, evaluate and use information in an ethical way. In the current digital age, it makes sense to incorporate an IBL approach, particularly in the social sciences, as the emphasis on application of social theory in the "real world" is relevant. Additionally, the ability to question material, resources and theories is an essential component of the IBL process. This should be a fundamental part of every module in social science undergraduate degree programmes.

There is tremendous pressure to radically change academic practices and, in particular, assessments. Unfortunately, as many academic changes have demonstrated, on occasion, change fails to achieve the results promised by specific approaches because their members resist change.

Organisational readiness needs to be valued in any change process. For IBL to be successful in the social sciences context, change commitment and goal commitment is necessary to implement organisational change. A shared resolve to pursue the courses of action involves engagement of higher education with wider society, and this will take many forms. It includes engagement with business and industry; with the civic life of the community; with public policy and practice; with artistic, cultural and sporting life; and with other educational providers in the community and region, and it includes an increasing emphasis on international engagement (Department of Education and Skills 2011, p. 79).

The following issues have surfaced repeatedly:

- The resistance of both academics and students to include IBL in their curriculum.
- The fear, loss of control and of the unknown, unfamiliarity of both academics and students with the principles and practices of IBL.
- The intense scrutiny that IBL is subjected to in order to "prove" that it works at least as well as traditional methods is substantial.

For IBL to be successful in social sciences, these barriers are overcome through insightful leadership, department "buy-in" and ownership, with the recognition of the need for academics and students to have sufficient time to learn from their own experiences by trial and error and make modifications that promote reflective adaptation to new learning/teaching methods.

I believe that an IBL approach to teaching and learning appropriately reflects the aim of social sciences education of producing critically reflective practitioners who actively inquire into the knowledge, skills and value base required to address the social issues they will face in their professional careers.

It inevitably depends on the will and the action of the individuals, systemic institutional structures, cultures and forces involved. We must embrace change wholeheartedly if we are to fulfil our destiny of ensuring that democracy equals decency. Decency in democracy encourages activism. An activist in the social sciences is an educated and politically astute individual. The will to achieve this is lying dormant in many of us, and now is the time to work towards its development and realization in systematic and collective ways. Educators and academics in individual institutions can work at the local level, regionally or at the national level to achieve socially responsible goals. Celebrating the current achievements of the social sciences is also important. There is a need for appropriate strategies to inform those in positions of power and influence of the importance and necessity of a strong social sciences presence. It is this kind of discipline that can educate our children to be socially active, democratic, decent and responsible citizens. There is no time to lose. We can frame the future agendas for social sciences and education; we just need to harness the various intellectual, social and political resources available to us in order to achieve it.

So where does democracy fit in the "marketplace" of higher education? If we continue on the path we have created in higher education institutions internationally, we are attacking the remaining traces of social democracy under the pretence of limited funding, resources and austerity. The duty and onus is on us as educators not to remain silent and complicit with this – we should not be afraid to challenge these "ideas" of education. Educational leaders need to engage constructively with political structures and civic communities. Negotiation, talking and dialogue is not sufficient to enact any change in our thinking regarding democracy in our educational system. A comprehensive understanding of the explicit connections between and among civic and political entities needs to be identified and analysed. Biesta (2007, p. 14) argues that "it is living the precepts of democracy, acting so that everyone has the opportunity to be a subject, [so that] everyone has the opportunity to act and, through their actions bring their beginnings and initiatives into the world of difference and plurality."

Educational leaders have a responsibility and a duty to engage and involve themselves in human interactions, not simply abiding by a list of characteristics or attributes associated with democracy. Doing that, according to Arendt (1958), requires living and being in the social and political world of difference and plurality. It is asking community members what they want and what they need, listening to their values, and, as a consequence, learning to think differently. It is also educating community members by asking the questions to help them think about solutions that will improve their quality of life and encouraging them "to dream about a better world" (Tippett 2010). "Democratic habits and values must be taught and communicated through life of our society, our legal institutions, our press, our religious life, our private associations, and the many other agencies that allow citizens to interact with each other and to have a sense of efficiency. The best protection for a democratic society is well-educated citizens" (Ravitch and Viteritti 2001, p. 28).

Democracy is important, it should be studied, and, for it to be meaningful and tangible, it must be fully cultivated throughout the educational experience (Kurth-Schai and Green 2006; Westheimer and Kahne 2002, 2003, 2004).

References

Allen, K. (2007) *The Corporate Takeover of Ireland*, Dublin: Irish Academic Press.

Arendt, H. (1958) *The Human Condition*. University of Chicago Press: Chicago.

Aubyn, M. (2009). European economy: Study on the efficiency and effectiveness of public spending on tertiary education. European Commission Directorate – General for Economic and Financial Affairs Publications.

Biesta, G. J. J. (2007). Why 'what works' won't work. Evidence-based practice and the democratic deficit of educational research. *Educational Theory*, 57(1), 1–22.

Biggs, J. (1999). *Teaching for Quality Learning at University* (pp. 165–203). Buckingham: SRHE.

Biggs, J. (2003). *Aligning Teaching and Assessment to Curriculum Objectives*. Imaginative Curriculum Project, LTSN Generic Centre.

Brew, A. (2001). *The Nature of Research: Inquiry in Academic Contexts*. London: Routledge Falmer.

Cook, S. and Westheimer, J. (2006). Introduction: Democracy and education. Canadian Journal of Education, 29(2), 347–358.

Dahlgreen, M. and Dahlgreen, L. (2002) *Portraits of PBL: Students' Experiences of the Demonstration Phase*. Santa Monica, CA: RAND.

Department of Education and Skills (2011) National Strategy for Higher Education to 2030. Dublin: Department of Education and Skills.

Dewey, J. (1916) *Democracy and Education: An Introduction to the Philosophy of Education*. New York: Macmillan.

Dewey, J. (1939). Education and American culture. In J. Ratner (Ed.), *Intelligence in the Modern World*. New York: New Library.

Dodd, L. (2007) 'The impact of problem-based learning on the information seeking behaviour and information literacy of veterinary medicine students at University College Dublin', *Journal of Academic Librarianship*, 33(2), pp. 206–216.

Durkheim, E. *(1897/1951). Suicide, A Study in Sociology*. New York: Free Press.

Elton, L. (2001) Research and teaching: Conditions for a positive link. Teaching in Higher Experience Questionnaire. *Studies in Higher Education*, 16, 129–150.

Fitzsimmons, P. F. and Goldhaber, J. (1997). Siphons, pumps, and missile launchers: Inquiry at the further and higher education [Online]. Edinburgh: Scottish Funding Council.

Garvin, T. (2012) A confederacy of dunces: The assault on higher education in Ireland. In Walsh, B. (Ed.), *Degrees of Nonsense: The Demise of the University in Ireland*, Glasnevin Publishing.

Giroux, H. (1992) *Border Crossings. Cultural Workers and the Politics of Education*. New York: Routledge.

Giroux, H. (2002) Neoliberalism, Corporate Culture and the Promise of Higher Education: the university as a democratic public sphere. *Harvard Educational Review*, 72(4), 1–31.

Greene, D. (2007) Gatekeepers: The role of adult education practitioners and programs in social control, *Journal for Critical Education Policy Studies*, 5(2), www.jceps.com/?pageID=article&articleID=107.

Guerin, S. and Hennessy, E. (2010) Linking theory to practice in applied developmental psychology using enquiry-based learning. [Online]. Available at: www.ucd.ie/t4cms/ucdtli0041.pdf.

Hussey, T. and Smith, P. (2003) The uses of learning outcomes. *Teaching in Higher Education*, Vol. 8, No. 3, 2003, pp. 357–368.

Jenkins, A., Breen, R., Lindsay, R. and Brew, A. (2003). *Re-shaping Higher Education: Linking Teaching and Research*. London: Routledge-Falmer.

Kahn, P. and O'Rourke, K. (2005) "Understanding enquiry-based learning", in Handbook of Enquiry and Problem-based Learning: Irish Case Studies and International Perspectives, eds T. Barrett, I. Mac Labhrainn and H. Fallon. Galway: All Ireland Society for Higher Education (AISHE) and Centre for Excellence in Learning and Teaching (CELT), NUI Galway. pp. 1–12.

Kurth-Schai, R. and Green, C. (2006). *Re-envisioning Education and Democracy*. Greenwich, CT: Information Age.

Levy, P. and Roberts, S. (Eds) (2005) *Developing the New Learning Environment: The Changing Role of the Academic Librarian*. London: Facet.

Lynch, K., Grummell, B. and Devine, D. (2012) *New Managerialism in Education: Commercialisation, Carelessness and Gender*. London: Palgrave Macmillan.

Marton, F., Dall'Alba, G., and Beaty, E. (1993). Conceptions of learning. *International Journal of Educational Research*, 19, 277–300.

Marsh, H. W. and Hattie, J. (2002). The relation between research productivity and teaching effectiveness – Complementary, antagonistic, or independent constructs? *Journal of Higher Education*, 73(5), 603–641.

McMaster University (2007). What is Unique About Inquiry Courses? www.mcmaster.ca/cll/inquiry/whats.unique.about.inquiry.htm (Accessed Jan 04 2014).

Milewicz, E. J. (2009). Origin and development of the information commons in academic libraries. In Forrest, C. and Halbert, M. (eds), *A Field Guide to the Information Commons*, pp. 3–17. Lanhan, Maryland: Scarecrow Press Amsterdam: Swets and Zeitlinger.

Murray, I and Savin-Baden, M. (2000). Staff development in problem-based learning. *Teaching in Higher Education*, 5(1), 107–126.

Neumann, R. (1994). The teaching–research link: Applying a framework to university students' learning experiences. *European Journal of Education*, 29, pp. 323–338.

O'Connor, P. (2013). *Higher Education and the Gendered World of Senior Management*. Manchester: Manchester University Press.

OECD (2010) *Education at a Glance 2010*, Organisation for Economic Co-Operation.

Price, A. and Price, B. (2000) Problem-based learning in clinical practice: Facilitating critical thinking. *Journal for Nurses in Staff Development*, 16, 6, 257–266.

O'Rourke, K. and Kahn, P. (2005) Understanding enquiry-based learning. In T. Barrett, I. Mac Labhrainn, and H. Fallon (Eds.) *Handbook of Enquiry and Problem-based Learning*. Irish Case Studies and International Perspectives, Galway: AISHE and NUI Galway.

Price, B. (2001) Enquiry-based learning: An introductory guide. *Nursing Standard*, 15(2), 45–52.

Prosser, M. and Trigwell, K. (1997). *Relations between Perceptions of the Teaching Environment Public Spending on Tertiary Education*. European Commission Directorate-General for Purposes, Problems, and Possibilities (pp. 39–55). Albany, NY: State University of New York.

Prosser, M. and Trigwell, K. (1999) *Understanding Learning and Teaching: The experience of higher education*. Buckingham: SRHE and Open University Press.

Ramsden, P. (1991). A performance indicator of teaching quality in higher education: The Course Experience Questionnaire. *Studies in Higher Education*, 16, 129–150.

Ramsden, P. (2003). *Learning to Teach in Higher Education*. London: Routledge/Falmer.

Ravitch, D. and Viteritti, J. P. (2001). *Making Good Citizens: Education and Civil Society*. New Haven, CT: Yale University Press.

Renfro, W. L. and Morrison, J. L. (1983). Scanning the external environment. In J. L. Morrison, W. L. Renfro, and W. I. Boucher, eds., *Applying Methods and Techniques of Futures Research*. New Directions for Institutional Research Number 39. San Francisco: Jossey-Bass.

Saxe, D. W. (1997). The distinctive mission of social studies education. In E. W. Ross, (Ed.), *The Social Studies Curriculum: Purposes, Problems and Possibilities*. Albany: State University of New York Press. (39–55).

Scottish Funding Council. (2006). Spaces for learning: A review of learning spaces in setting. *CD Practice*, 4, 1–7.

Tippett, C. D. (2010). Refutation text in science education: A review of two decades of research. *International Journal of Science and Mathematics Education*, 8(6), 951–970.

Tippett, K. (Producer). (2015, June 6). Speaking of faith. [Audio podcast]. Retrieved from http://speakingoffaith.publicradio.org.

Westheimer, J. and Kahne, J. (2003). Teaching justice: Indoctrination, neutrality, and the need for alternatives. Paper presented at the annual meeting of the American Educational Research Association, Chicago, IL.

Westheimer, J. and Kahne, J. (2002). Educating for democracy. In Hayduk, R. and Mattson, K. (Eds.) *Democracy's Moment: Reforming the American Political System for the 21st Century*. Lanham, MD: Rowman and Littlefield.

Westheimer, J. and Kahne, J. (2004). What kind of citizen? The politics of educating for democracy. *American Educational Research Journal*, 41(2), 237–269.

Section IV
Familial Identity

11 Fatherhood in Russia
Fertility Decisions and Ideational Factors

Alexandra Lipasova

Introduction: Fatherhood crisis in Russia

Gender studies take a prominent place in the field of modern social research. However, the discussion of gender problems is mainly focused on the understanding of a new role and place for women in society and on the topic of work–life balance for women. The topic of fathers/fatherhood and fathering practices is less popular among researchers, which deepens traditional gender inequality in family relations and makes the role of the father seem secondary compared to that of the mother.

We know far less about fathers than we know about mothers. We tend to count fathers less, notice them less and understand less about the correlations between fatherhood and childcare and between fatherhood and paid work. We do know, however, that most fathers function differently from mothers. Traditionally, we expected that to be the case: we presumed that fathers worked for money and that mothers cared for children and the household. This traditional ideal is now a minority family form. Less than 10 per cent of families with children under age 18 conform to the pattern of a single male breadwinner and female stay-at-home spouse (Dowd 2000). Nevertheless, we retain the traditional model, wrapped in egalitarian, gender-neutral ideology.

The gendered differential of mothers' and fathers' parenting persists, although in somewhat modified form. In Russia, the presence of children rarely changes men's paid work patterns. Men continue to do paid work with little or no break, temporary or otherwise, because of children. Women are far more likely to accommodate work to family, and therefore make changes to their paid work patterns by their choice of job, by their choice of hours or by working part-time. In Russia, in a majority of two-parent families with young children, although both parents often work in the paid workforce, one parent takes a break in their career to care for children under three (a minimal age at which a child can be accepted to a state day-care institution) and less often to care for children under six or seven (when they start school). The parent that stays at home is nearly always the mother.

Caretaking patterns of mothers and fathers are similarly distinctive. Fathers generally do not perform an equal share of caretaking or housework, regardless of the employment status of the mother. Fathers take on some domestic tasks. Mothers, however, commonly do a "second shift" of household work in addition to their paid work (Hochschild 1997). To the extent that men provide greater domestic help, therefore, it doesn't double the nurturing and attention available to children. Men's actions usually conform to an unequal rather than a coequal caretaking role. In this model, secondary caretakers have the power and the money in the relationships and their caretaking is overwhelmingly economic.

In the past in Soviet Russia, according to many authors, fatherhood was a set of practices and concepts that pushed fathers into the providing and bread-winning sphere but underestimated them as fathers (Tartakovskaya 2008). According to some Russian data, financial support of the family is still considered as one of the most important functions of a father. That is why many researchers connect the diminishing significance of the father in the family with the falling social status of an economically successful man.

This fatherhood crisis in Russia can be considered in three autonomous contexts (Kon 2009).

First, it is an aspect of family crisis. In this context, the researcher's attention is focused on the following trends: instability of marriage, the changing criteria of the marriage success, the problems of equally shared partnership obligations in the situation where both partners work, the evolving non-traditional forms of family and partnership and so on.

Second, it is an aspect of masculinity crisis: the weakening of traditional male hegemony accompanied by changes in traditional notions about manhood, the conflict between labour and family obligations, the transition from compulsory to optional fatherhood, newly evolving fathering practices and psychological problems connected with them.

All these factors influence men's self and gender identity, which correspond with their self-respect and private attitudes: what one needs to become a father, what the criteria of an effective father are, what the advantages and disadvantages of fatherhood are as seen by modern fathers and how important fatherhood is for their subjective well-being.

Third, it is an aspect of power crisis. The power used to be that of a male, a father, a patriarch. The diminishing power of a particular father in a particular family begins from a diminishing power of a country leader, but there is an inverse relation between these two processes. Here we can talk about macro-social problems.

Fertility decisions and their possible explanations

But whether to become a father is also a choice to make. This paper focuses on the fertility decisions of Russian men. The falling number of children being born is a concern in many European countries, including Russia. The level of fertility under the replacement rate (it is currently 1.7, according to 2013 data) has been a trend for several years. An improved demographic situation is set as one of the main goals of Russian state family policy, as well as maintaining traditional family values. These can be achieved only in an officially registered marriage with the aim of having three or more children (Koncepcija 2014). However, in modern Russia, two out of three mothers have only one child, and the share of mothers with three children and more does not exceed 7 per cent (ibid: 5).

Demographic analyses argue that the low fertility rate is not due to less desire to have children but rather to the postponement of having them from early to later adulthood, which results in lower overall fertility (Rostgaard and Moberg 2015). This tendency is a main trait of the so-called "second demographic transition." The main literature on this topic has focused mainly on women and their reproductive decisions; however, it is equally important to investigate this from the male perspective. The question then is whether the male postponement in fertility has the same effect.

The postponement theory, however, may not be the only factor leading to overall low fertility. Despite the tendency in Eastern European countries and Russia to have children at a relatively younger age, this has not led to changes in the low fertility rates in these countries (Billari and Kohler 2004). This suggests that other, less instrumental factors may also be important, including structural, situational and cultural explanations.

As far as structural explanations are concerned, the changes in childbearing have long been believed to be caused by the increasing involvement of women in the labour market. From the micro-economic theory perspective, the opportunity cost of giving birth to a child and simultaneously losing income has been held to explain why increases in women's employment outside the household have been accompanied by falling fertility rates (Becker 1991).

Generally, there is a substantial gap between fertility intentions and fertility behaviour at the individual level. Obviously, certain couples cannot implement their fertility plans for biological reasons (sub-fertility), but this group doesn't exceed 4–5 per cent of the population (Rossier and Bernardi, 2009). Other important factors are changes in the conjugal relation, a low quality partnership and changes in the partner's fertility intentions. All these obstacles may lead to a delay in the transition to adulthood and a consequent postponement of fertility plans.

Other explanations based on the structural approach have argued that fertility behaviour is also a response to actual and expected unemployment opportunities as well as general economic conditions, encouraging or discouraging an individual to take breaks from the labour market. This is especially true for Russia. Highly qualified women are afraid to lose professional skills in the rapidly changing business environment (Gapova 2006). When a woman takes maternity leave, her employer has to artificially keep her place, and thus companies have less interest in hiring women. That pushes women to employment in the state sector where the salaries are comparatively lower, while men continue working in the private sector. This deepens the inequality and women's social dependency on the state and on their partners, who are obliged to earn more.

Some studies consider the situational constraints caused by shifting family forms to be influential, such as the tendency to cohabitate rather than marry or living in less committed "living-apart-together" (LAT) relationships (Vovk 2005). Nowadays, 25 per cent of children in Russia are born to couples who are not officially married. Another situational factor of perhaps greater importance is whether unions between men and women are in fact formed. For instance, in Moscow, the amount of single women exceeds the amount of single men by

1 million (Shadrina 2014). The significance of educational homogeny seems especially important, as men and women seem to choose partners based on educational backgrounds. Certain studies indicate that women are more likely to marry men of the same educational level (Blossfeld and Timm 2004), which becomes all the more important as a consequence of women's increasing educational attainment. However, men with lower education stand in a poorer competitive situation, a tendency that can be observed in Russia (Shadrina 2014).

A cultural approach to fertility decisions emphasizes the importance of individual attitudes and societal norms present in a certain society. These so-called ideational factors affect the decision on occurrence (whether or not to have children), timing of childbirth (when to have children) and male fertility rate (number of children). Ajzen's "theory of planned behaviour" (Ajzen, 1991) gained credit among demographers as an economical means of framing the relationship between individual characteristics and beliefs and the way the latter are linked to intentions and their realization. This theory is one of socio-psychological models seeking to explain behaviour through the mediation of behavioural intentions and addressing the open issue of the gap between intentions and realized behaviour. Given that the data available through the European Social Survey (ESS) concerning the association between ideational factors and actual fertility behaviour is not longitudinal panel data, it is difficult to trace the footprints of lifestyle preferences on actual fertility. Still, ESS data allow us to reveal the association between individual behaviour, attitudes and societal norms. According to Settersten (2003), for example, one of the explanations for the discrepancy between potential and achieved childbearing after age 40 is believed to be the so-called social age deadline, that is, the individual attitudes and social norms prescribing the oldest acceptable age for giving birth (Settersten 2003). Billari et al. (2011) argue that there is a considerable variation across Europe in terms of whether people feel that such a deadline exists and if so, which age they indicate as the oldest acceptable. This difference is supposed to indicate that the social age is intimately conditioned by the social context and generally accepted norms. It suggests that it is crucial to take into account variation in national as well as individual perceptions about the appropriate childbearing age. Billari also finds that the societal norms concerning the oldest age of childbearing are positively and significantly correlated with the existing rate of late fertility (Billari and Goisis, 2011). This not only proves that a social age deadline is one of many factors determining childbearing but also that attitudes regarding social age should also be central in any analysis of male fertility, including attitudes to the ideal age of becoming a father.

Sobotka and Testa argue that although general trends indicate an increasing societal acceptance of the choice to remain "child-free," parenthood still constitutes a highly valued and normatively supported part of most individuals' biographies (Sobotka and Testa 2008). They also suggest that men's influence on couples' fertility decision-making may equal the influence of women. Indeed, several studies found that in case of disagreement between partners, men's intentions have a very similar influence on subsequent childbearing and that their resistance against having another child usually prevails. This effect may be, however, much weaker when a woman is childless. The authors also note that there is an increasing tendency among men to withdraw from binding commitments and from parenthood in particular (Sobotka and Testa 2008). Many young Europeans do not perceive parenthood as an inevitable part of their life course. As far as negative intentions and uncertainty about parenthood are concerned, until around the age of 30, intended childlessness among men surpasses the levels found among women; around 20 per cent of childless women and 30 per cent of childless men do not intend to have a child or are uncertain. Uncertainty is more common than the negative intention until the mid-30s, and it increases most markedly after the age of 30, when many people probably realize that their partnership situation or socio-economic position might not become sufficiently favourable for parenthood in the foreseeable future. Close to half of childless men and women aged 30–34 express negative intentions or uncertainty. The intention not to have a child increases most sharply among women after the age of 35 and surpasses intended childlessness among men. This is partly a selection effect – most of the women who plan to have children realize their intention before reaching this age, and the share of people who are voluntarily childless increases as a result. But it appears to be also an effect of a "reality check"; many women, facing a "deadline" posed by approaching biological infertility, realize they will never become mothers. At the age of 35–39, only one-quarter of childless women and one-third of childless men express an unambiguous intention to become parents (Sobotka and Testa 2008).

Intentions to remain childless are usually related to a combination of several reasons, which often consist of a mixture of lifestyle choices and different constraints or adverse personal circumstances. Although there is a vast cross-country heterogeneity in the proportion of respondents choosing different reasons and the number of reasons per respondent, respondents in most countries have typically chosen several reasons in justification of their intentions. Even the reason that ranks as the least important, namely the desire on the part of the respondent's partner not to have a child, has been cited as important on average by one-fifth of respondents. Many respondents selected concern about the future of their children as an important reason. It was the most frequently chosen reason among women and the second most frequent reason among men. This reason is fairly difficult to interpret, as it may have different meanings for diverse groups of respondents. Among many young people, it probably reflects general feelings of uncertainty about the future. Interestingly, there were no differences between men and women and between the respondents from the former communist countries and from the other regions of Europe. In all these cases, more than 40 per cent of respondents listed concern about the future as an important reason for their intention. Among men, intentions are strongly influenced by their partnership situation. Having no steady partner was the most frequent reason, mentioned as important by half of childless men who intended to remain childless or were uncertain. For women, a lack of a steady partner is relatively important as well. However, it ranked lower than concern about the possible consequences of parenthood for material well-being and fear that life would not be enjoyable with a child. Health reasons were relatively important for women as well, especially in Central and Eastern Europe (Sobotka and Testa 2008).

Attitudes towards children and childlessness are generally comparable between men and women, but they differ by partnership status, have a considerable age gradient and depict wide cross-country differences. Respondents in Belgium and the Netherlands, generally, show the most positive attitudes towards childlessness, whereas relatively traditional attitudes prevail in the post-communist societies of Central and Eastern Europe as well as in Austria and "familistic" Italy (Sobotka and Testa 2008). Childbearing is often seen in these countries as a duty towards society; childless people are commonly considered as unhappy, and respondents strongly accentuate the value of happy family life with children. Thus, the low childlessness levels recorded until recently in all Central and Eastern European societies will continue to shape people's generally negative attitudes towards voluntary childlessness. The very positive evaluation of family life, expressed also by the majority of younger childless respondents, may also be, in part, a consequence of the family patterns of the previous era.

This paper continues the line of cross-country analysis of people's reproduction choices and is aimed at estimating the importance of men's individual attitudes as well as social norms of entering into and timing of fatherhood in relation to the fertility decisions of individual fathers, contrasting Russia with other European countries.

Data and methods

The analysis is built on the data from the third round of the ESS (2006). The sample for Russia consisted of 545 men aged 40 and over (40+). This age group was chosen as the most representative for the analysis, since men over 40 are more likely to have made their reproduction decisions. The ESS includes individual attitudinal questions concerning the ideal age of becoming a father ("In your opinion, what is the ideal age for a man to have become a father?"), the age that is regarded as the "deadline" for fathering ("At what age would you say a man is too old to father?") and the importance of fatherhood for being considered an adult ("To be considered an adult, how important is it to have become a father?"), as well as the individual's and societal attitudes towards childless men ("Do you approve/disapprove if a man chooses not to have children?" and "Do you agree with the statement, 'Most people would react if a man chooses not to have children'?"). The indicators are weighted according to ESS standards.

The results of the research have shown that in Russia, ideational factors are strongly associated with actual fertility behaviour. Fatherhood is a practice that most men over 40 have experienced: 92.4 per cent of men 40+ are fathers. Russian men are younger (about 26.6 years old) compared to Europeans when having their first child but generally have fewer children (2.0 on average, while the number of children for most European countries is about 2.4) (Table 11.1). The ideal age of becoming a father and the social age deadline for fathering are generally lower (24 and 45 years respectively for Russia) (Table 11.2). Russian men have a much higher disapproval rate for voluntary childlessness (83 per cent in Russia compared to 6 per cent in Denmark, for instance) (Table 11.3). This difference in the

Table 11.1 Occurrence, timing and male fertility rate: percentage of men who have a child (men 40+), average age of becoming a father and number of children (fathers 40+)*

Countries/Regions**	Child	No child	Age when fathering	Number of children
Russia	92.4%	7.6% (545)	26.6 (479)	2.0 (486)
Scandinavian countries	84.6%	15.5% (1.082)	27.9 (912)	2.4 (915)
Continental Europe	82.1%	17.9% (1.838)	27.9 (1.449)	2.3 (1.453)
Southern Europe	84.2%	15.8% (638)	28.4 (548)	2.4 (555)
Western Europe	85.4%	14.6% (564)	28.6 (432)	2.4 (437)
Eastern Europe	90.5%	9.5% (1.180)	26.2 (1.073)	2.3 (1.070)

Notes: * Average number of children is based only on men 40+ who have fathered, not to be compared with total fertility rate calculated for all men of fertility age. The figure in brackets stands for the unweighted quantity of respondents.

** The countries are grouped according to EUROSTAT classification: Scandinavian countries are Denmark, Finland, Norway and Sweden; Continental Europe consists of Belgium, the Czech Republic, France, Netherlands, Germany and Austria; Southern Europe includes Spain, Portugal and Cyprus; Western Europe is Ireland and the United Kingdom; Eastern Europe consists of Bulgaria, Hungary, Poland, Ukraine, Slovakia, Slovenia and Estonia.

Table 11.2 Attitudes towards ideal age, social age deadline of fatherhood, all men (40+)*

Countries/Regions	Ideal age	Social age deadline
Russia	24.3 (457)	45.0 (380)
Scandinavian countries	25.8 (985)	47.4 (980)
Continental Europe	26.8 (1.582)	47.1 (1.636)
Southern Europe	27.0 (560)	45.8 (516)
Western Europe	25.5 (472)	47.3 (451)
Eastern Europe	24.9 (1.045)	44.8 (905)

Notes: *Not including "No ideal age" and "Never too old" responses. The figure in brackets stands for the unweighted quantity of respondents.

attitudes may serve as a proof that postponement of fatherhood is more likely if one does not think that fatherhood is important for being considered an adult and also if one has a high ideal age and social age deadline for fathering (see Figure 11.1). If a man disapproves of childlessness, he is more likely to have fathered a child (odds ratio of childlessness of 0.7 compared to men who don't disapprove). The odds of being childless for men who find fatherhood important for being considered an adult is 0.34 compared to those men who are neutral or find it unimportant.

Unfortunately, regression analysis of the Russian sample doesn't provide significant results. However, including Russia into the Eastern Europe block makes it possible to build logistic and linear regression models on aggregated level. This analysis has been done in the work of Rostgaard and Moberg (2015). The results of their research confirm that, in addition to structural and situational factors, it is crucial to include cultural factors to understand male fertility behaviour. Across

Table 11.3 Attitudes towards importance of fathering for adulthood and towards choice of childlessness, all men (40+)

Countries/Regions	Fathering important for adulthood (1=not important at all, 5=very important)	Individual acceptance of choice of childlessness (1=strongly disapprove, 5=strongly approve)	Perception of societal acceptance of choice of childlessness (1=most people would openly disapprove, 4=most people would approve)
Russia	3.8 (545)	1.8 (520)	2.0 (512)
Scandinavian countries	2.4 (1.082)	3.6 (1.065)	3.2 (1.055)
Continental Europe	2.9 (1.827)	2.8 (1.811)	2.7 (1.790)
Southern Europe	2.7 (623)	2.9 (633)	2.6 (617)
Western Europe	2.4 (559)	3.2 (555)	2.9 (548)
Eastern Europe	3.3 (1.148)	2.0 (1.154)	2.1 (1.105)

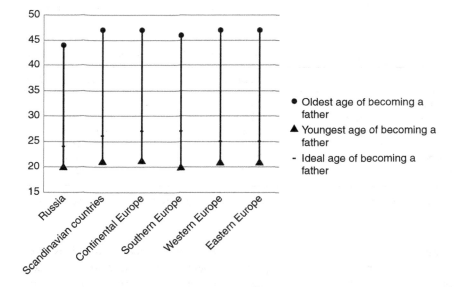

Figure 11.1 Attitudes towards youngest, oldest and ideal age of becoming a father, all men (40+).

all regions, becoming a father is strongly related to whether a man has had a stable partner relationship (e.g. in Russia, only 0.3 per cent of respondents who have never lived with a spouse or partner for more than three months have children). The chance of becoming a father also depends on one's economic position – men who have experienced long periods of unemployment are more likely to remain childless. High tolerance of childlessness is highly associated with actual childlessness, with Scandinavian countries and Eastern Europe being the two extremes in this respect. Men in Eastern European regimes also consider fatherhood to be more important for becoming an adult, while men in Scandinavian countries are more indifferent. Rostgaard's and Moberg's analysis shows that a more relaxed attitude to fatherhood is related to higher odds of not entering into or at least postponing fatherhood (Rostgaard and Moberg 2015). Their other findings confirm the theory of postponement: men who become fathers at a later stage of their lives generally have fewer children. In the case of Eastern Europe, where men become fathers at a younger age but generally have fewer children, ideational factors help to explain male fertility behaviour: men who are more tolerant of voluntary childlessness and those who are more relaxed about the ideal age of fathering have fewer children.

Statistical hindrances: Specifics of Russian sample

It is worth noting, when we speak about ESS sample, that the mortality rate of elderly men in Europe is much lower than that in Russia (Scherbakova 2011). In general, according to 2013 data, Russian men live to 65.5 years. This figure is much lower than in most developed countries. So there are high chances that men over 70 just didn't get into the sample. Besides, in Russia, the birth rate fell below the reproduction level about 5 years earlier than in Europe, so men who had children before the contraception revolution of 1970s and the 1980s couldn't get into the sample because they were likely to have died by then (Figure 11.2). This could be one of the explanations why the number of children per man in Russia is the lowest in Europe.

As far as the average age of becoming a father is concerned, this data is not collected in Russia, even in the census. The Federal State Statistics Service of Russia started gathering data on the birth order for women in 2014, but the results of this recent census haven't been published yet. So, on the basis of the existing census results of 2010 by combination of the data on births with the data on marriages, a very approximate result can be derived: Russian statisticians do not register if it is the second marriage for a man or the first one, and the share of men in their second

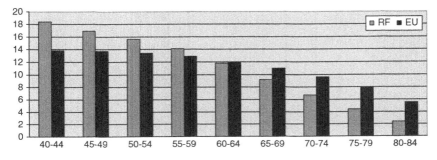

Figure 11.2 Statistical hindrances: male age spread in Russia versus the European Union (men 40+, 2008).

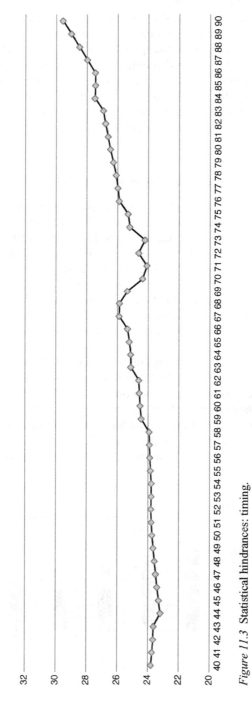

Figure 11.3 Statistical hindrances: timing.
Source: Russian census 2010.

and third marriages is high for the age group 40+. And the higher the age, the higher is the overestimation of the average age at which a man becomes a father for the first time. As can be seen from Figure 11.3, taking the average age difference between husbands and wives in different age groups and adding it to the age at which the wife had her first child gives us a steep increase in the age when the first child was born among the group of elderly men. It can be explained by the fact that this is their second marriage, and these children were born in the previous marriages of their current wives. Still, the picture for men between the ages of 40 and 50 is rather correct, because these men got married in the 1990s, and back then it was common to get married and have a child and then start a professional career, so the average age of becoming a father for this group is about 24 years.

Conclusions

According to some researchers, the model of Russian fatherhood formed in the Soviet past was based on systematic violation of fathers' rights (for example, in most cases children stay with their mother, not father, after a divorce), the impossibility of maintaining the status of the major bread-winner in the family (since women were widely involved in the labour market) and the domination of women in the private sphere (Tartakovskaya 2008). The combination of these factors resulted in the masculinity crisis and men's deprivation of fatherhood. Thus, the type of fatherhood shaped by Soviet gender policy can be considered as a specific parenthood model, which is different from other fatherhood variants ("traditional father," "involved father" etc.) as well as from Soviet motherhood.

Even without taking into account numerous perceptions of masculinity and societal norms concerning "real manhood," it is obvious that men face a lot of strict and rigid demands that are supported by most women as well as most men and that they do not have that many appropriate options of behaviour. A modern woman can claim her right to the traditional male role of a business leader (it will be harder for her to achieve success, but the mere fact of her making an effort is unlikely to face disapproval), but it is still almost impossible for a modern man to work in a kindergarten or just stay at home and look after the children without being considered a total loser.

The results of the ESS show that there is strong correlation between attitudes and behaviour regarding male fertility. Russian society is much less tolerant to childlessness compared to other European countries. Being a father is considered an important part of male identity – a childless man cannot be taken seriously. Thus, the decision to become a father is strongly correlated to the ideals of fatherhood in Russian society. There exists a wide range of ways of "doing masculinity"; still, the notions of what it really means to be a man are deeply embedded in Russian men's consciousness. Men are held responsible for acting according to the cultural ideals of masculinity and behaving in gender-appropriate ways.

Still, demographic data do not give sufficient information on how male and female fertility decisions need and can be separated. Whether they are separated in clear ways to identify gender-specific patterns of fertility decisions is also unclear.

Here we have a variety of situations to deal with: married or cohabitating couples who decide jointly when and how many children to have; couples who do not decide and plan at all how many children and when; couples where the decision is not made jointly, but is that of the dominating partner, be it that of the male or female; couples where the decision is not a decision of one of the partners or both together, but a practice of following traditions, norms and rules that are perceived as "obligatory" by the persons; decisions of individuals, men or women, who decide completely individually when and how many children, without wanting to have a family or partnership and who plan to educate children individually – and then there may be complicated forms of compromises and mixtures of individual and joint decisions and non-decisions. There are the cases that fertility decisions are not decisions of individuals or couples, but "non-decisions," following more the trends and routines. Fertility behaviour becomes dependent on other decisions that are felt to be more important in the life of the persons – decisions that both partners want to work, decisions about the form of partnership. For some people wealth, higher income and hedonism are more important than reproduction and fertility decisions (the phenomenon observed as "DINK – double income, no kids" in rich middle classes in Western countries).

There is a high possibility that structural explanations, situational constraint approaches and cultural approaches require more sorting and differentiation. There may be more and more complex combinations of such approaches that become relevant for explaining the trends observed.

References

Ajzen, I. (1991). The theory of planned behaviour. *Organizational Behavior and Human Decision Processes*, 50(2), pp. 179–211.

Becker, G. S. (1991). *A Treatise on the Family*. Cambridge, MA: Harvard University Press.

Billari, F. C. and Kohler, H. P. (2004). Patterns of low and lowest-low fertility in Europe, *Population Studies*, 58(2), pp. 161–176.

Billari, F. C. and Goisis, A. (2011). Social age deadline for the childbearing of women and men. *Human Reproduction*, 26(3), pp. 616–622.

Blossfeld, H. P. and Timm, A. (2004). *Who Marries Whom? Educational Systems as Marriage Markets in Modern Societies*. Boston, MA and Dordrecht: Kluwer Academic Publishers.

Dowd, N. (2000). *Redefining Fatherhood*. NY: New York University Press.

Gapova, E. (2006). *Vy rozhajte, vy rozhajte, vam zachtetsja [Go on, have a child, you will be rewarded]*, grani.ru (http://grani.ru/Society/m.106127.html).

Hochschild, A. (1997). *The Time Bind*. NY: Henry Holt.

Kon, I. (2009). *Muzhchina v menjajushhemsja mire [A man in a changing world]* Moscow: Vremya.

Koncepcija gosudarstvennoj semejnoj politiki v Rossijskoj Federacii na period do 2025 goda. Rasporjazhenie Pravitel'stva RF ot 25.08.2014 N 1618-r [The concept of state family policy in the Russian Federation for the period till 2025. Edict of Government of Russian Federation of 25.08.14 N 1618-r] (2014) (https://clck.ru/9Ua4L).

Rossier, C. and Bernardi, L. (2009). Social interaction effects on fertility: Intentions and behaviors. *European Journal of Population*, 25(4), pp. 467–485.

Rostgaard, T. and Moberg, R. J. (2015). Fathering: The influence of ideational factors for male fertility behaviour. In Eydal G. B. and Rostgaard T., eds., *Fatherhood in the Nordic Welfare States*. Policy Press, pp. 23–51.

Scherbakova, E. (2011). *Vuslovijah smertnosti 2008 goda do tochnogo vozrasta 65 let v ES-27 dozhivalo 90,5% zhenshhin i 81,3% muzhchin, v Rossii - 78,6% i 48,7% [Under the rate of mortality of 2008 90.5% of women and 81.3% of men lived up to the age of 65 in European Union-27, compared to 78.6% and 48.7% in Russia]* Demoscope Weekly 2011 (http://demoscope.ru/weekly/2011/0487/barom02.php).

Settersten, R. A. (2003). Age structuring and the rhythm of the life course. In Mortimer, J. T. and Shanahan, M. J., eds., *Handbook of the Life Course*. New York: Springer-Verlag, pp. 81–98.

Shadrina, A. (2014). *Ne zamuzhem: seks, ljubov' i sem'ja za predelami braka. [Single: Sex, love and family without marriage]* Moscow: Novoe literaturnoe obozrenie.

Sobotka, T. and Testa, M. R. (2008). Attitudes and intentions towards childlessness in Europe. *People, Population Change and Policies: Lessons from the Population Policy Acceptance Study*, Volume 1. Edited by Hohn Ch. et al. Berlin: Springer, pp. 177–211.

Tartakovskaya, I. (2008). *Maskulinnost': vse muzhiki - svolochi? [Masculinity: are all men bastards?] Gender dlja "chajnikov" [Gender for "dummies"]*. Edited by Alexeeva N. Moscow: Zven'ja, pp. 107–126.

Vovk, E. (2005). *Nezaregistrirovannye intimnye sojuzy: "raznovidnosti" braka ili "al'ternativy" emu? [Unregistered intimate partnerships: "Types" of marriage or its "alternative"?]* Public Opinion Fund database, 2014 (http://bd.fom.ru/report/cat/az/%D0%B5/vovk/gur050103).

12 Well-Being in Married and Cohabiting Families with Children and Social Support during Economic Recession in Europe

Mare Ainsaar

Introduction

Life satisfaction is one of the most popular tools for evaluating one's general life success. Satisfaction with life is interpreted as a cumulative outcome indicator about the personal evaluation of life success (Suldo and Huebner 2004, 2006). Although marriage and children remain an essential part of family life in Europe, the share of never-married persons, cohabitating persons and persons without children increases in Europe (Perelli-Harris and Lyons-Amos 2015; Sobotka and Toulemon 2008; Thomson 2014). At the same time, research about life satisfaction in different family types is limited predominantly to country studies and seldom investigates the total costs or benefits of marriage over cohabitation and the influence of societal support on this.

There is no universal judgement about the value of the different family forms for personal well-being, but analyses of life satisfaction in different family formations can provide some hint about the total costs and benefits of them. Different life satisfaction in family types might, in turn, influence the future demographic behaviour of people.

As family behaviour differs in different regions of Europe, we also assume that the social environment for different families varies and influences the current situation. However, the international comparative analysis on the influence of children and partnership type on life satisfaction are still rare. The European Social Survey (ESS) is a highly standardised database for a large range of European countries and it fits well for this kind of analyses. In this chapter, we compare life satisfaction in six family types: registered partnership with and without children, cohabiting with and without children, and single with and without children. In order to control the selectivity of people into different family types – for example, more optimistic persons find a partner and become parents – we also take into account different individual factors like health, social attitudes, education and religious practices. We assume that personal well-being is also a product of social support.

Influence of children and partnership on life satisfaction

Partnership, money and health explain a substantial proportion of life satisfaction (Margolis and Myrskyla 2013). It is traditionally assumed that marriage is more solid, and therefore a better form of partnership, than cohabitation. At the same time, statistics show a steady increase of cohabiting people in all European countries, although the share of cohabiters in population varies in different regions of Europe (Perelli-Harris and Lyons-Amos 2015). Life and behaviour of cohabiters may be different from the behaviour of married people also because of their individual values, economic situation or life-course stage (Smock et al. 2005; Van der Lippe et al. 2014). Therefore, it is important to take into account individual differences of people in different family types in order to investigate the benefits of partnership types. The country-specific traditions and meaning of traditions of cohabitation might influence the status of cohabiting partners as well, especially when the birth of a child is involved. For example, Perelli-Harris (2014) studied married and cohabiting couples in 15 European countries and reported that women who continued to cohabit after the first birth had significantly lower second conception probability than married women. The only exceptions were women in Eastern European countries. The results indicate some status difference of cohabitation and marriage in different countries. Some other studies (Musick and Bumpass 2012) did not find essential differences in the well-being of married and cohabitation unions over time.

According to the value of children approach, children bring different benefits to their (potential) parents. In developed countries, the value seems to be more related to emotional benefits than utilitarian or normative values (Mayer and Trommsdorff 2010; Nauck 2014). Analysis of childbearing and happiness from the country-comparative perspective has been rather limited so far. Also, previous works had provided controversial results about the influence of children on well-being. The result seems to depend on country, gender and parity of a child. For example, Billari (2008) analysed gender and generations surveys data for France, Germany, Bulgaria, Georgia, Russian and Hungary and found a positive modest effect of children on happiness. Aassve et al. (2012) used ESS data from rounds 1 and 2 and reported a positive and significant association between happiness and childbearing in the case of a new-born child. They also found that additional children after the first-born child did not increase a father's subjective well-being while it increased a mother's subjective well-being, and having children in partnership resulted in higher well-being levels compared with being single. Also Kohler et al., (2005), who used Danish twin registry data, found a positive effect only in the case of the birth of the first child, and Stutzer and Frey (2006) reported about a positive correlation between life satisfaction and having up to three children. On the other hand, Zimmermann and Easterlin (2006) found no significant effect of children on life satisfaction. Vignoli et al. (2014) investigated life satisfaction in Europe. They found that the life-satisfaction levels of couples with children were significantly higher. However, after the socio-economic situation of the family was taken into account, the influence of family status on life satisfaction disappeared almost completely, and the authors concluded that higher life satisfaction can be largely attributed to a better socio-economic position.

Method

For empirical data, we use the ESS data from wave 2010/2011 (ESS Round 5 ... 2010). Twenty-four countries were selected for the analysis: Croatia, Greece, Slovakia, Cyprus, Portugal, Poland, Lithuania, Spain, Ireland, Germany, the Czech Republic, Switzerland, Bulgaria, Slovenia, Great Britain, France, Hungary, Netherlands, Denmark, Belgium, Finland, Estonia, Norway and Sweden. These countries provide a representative overview of different family policy types and social protection regimes in Europe.

Data of respondents aged 20–60 years were selected for analyses because this is the age range of people most likely to have children or who have dependent children in the household. The total number of respondents in the analysis was 28,684. To compare life satisfaction in different types of families, two variables were formed. Firstly, a variable about civil status – married or cohabiting or single – and secondly, a variable about the presence of those aged under 19 in the household. The type of the relationship with the partner was attained on the basis of the questions: "You just told me that you live with your husband/wife/partner. Which one of the descriptions on this card describes your relationship to them?" The answers "legally married" and "in a legally registered civil union" were coded into the category "married." The answers "Living with my partner (cohabiting) – not legally recognised" and "Living with my partner (cohabiting) – legally recognised" were used to detect cohabitation.

The subjective life satisfaction was measured with the question: "All things considered, how satisfied are you with your life on the whole nowadays?" Responses were collected on the scale from 0 to 10, where 0 meant extremely dissatisfied and 10 meant extremely satisfied.

Control variables in the models take into account a respondent's gender, age, years in education, working or unemployment status, evaluation of coping with present income, subjective health status, generalised trust, satisfaction with democracy in the country and attending religious services. The influence of all these indicators is well documented and well known from previous research (Ainsaar 2008; Bradshaw et al. 2007; Drobnic et al. 2010; Gudmundsdottir 2011; Hooghe and Vanhoutte 2011; Groot et al. 2007; Lever et al. 2005; Meer 2014; Ott 2011; Pittau et al. 2010; Suldo and Huebner 2006).

Results

The majority of persons aged 20–60 years in all countries live in some kind of partnership, either in marriage or cohabitation. Cohabitation is more popular in Nordic countries – Sweden, Norway and Estonia – and least popular in Catholic countries. Figure 12.1 shows the distribution of people with children in different European countries. There are essential differences, on one hand in the proportion of people having children in the household and on the other hand in the proportion of married and cohabiting people with children. This diversity is a result of combination of fertility, timing of child birth, emancipation of children and partnership and divorce behaviour. As a result of these demographic differences, there

Well-Being in Families during Recession 217

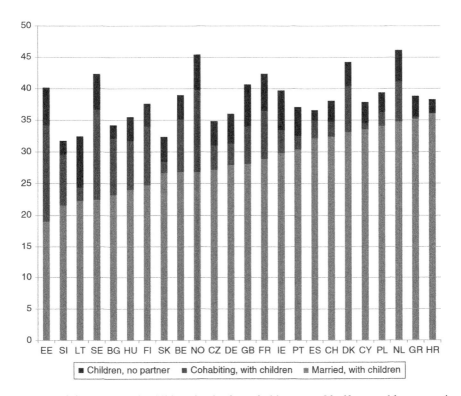

Figure 12.1 People with children in the household among 20–60-year-old persons in different European countries.

Notes: HR – Croatia, GR – Greece, SK – Slovakia, CY – Cyprus, PT – Portugal, PL – Poland, LT – Lithuania, ES – Spain, IE – Ireland, DE – Germany, CZ – Czech Republic, CH – Switzerland, BG – Bulgaria, SI – Slovenia, GB – Great Britain, FR – France, HU – Hungary, NL – Netherlands, DK– Denmark, BE – Belgium, FI – Finland, EE – Estonia, NO – Norway, SE – Sweden.

are child-rich countries like Norway, the Netherlands, Sweden, Denmark and France, and countries with fewer children in the households: Slovenia, Slovakia, Lithuania. The share of single parents with children is marginal in all countries but varies significantly from 2 per cent in Croatia and up to 8 per cent in Lithuania. The tradition of having children in cohabitation varies significantly, but the most "child-rich societies" have more children mainly because of the contribution of cohabiters and single parents in raising children.

Although there are more people living in partnership than with children in the household, the spread of partnerships is associated with a higher share of parents and vice versa (Figure 12.2). In some countries, the rate between partnership and having children in the household is bigger, for example in Bulgaria and Slovakia, while in other countries like Ireland, there are disproportionally more parents compared with all partnered people.

218 Mare Ainsaar

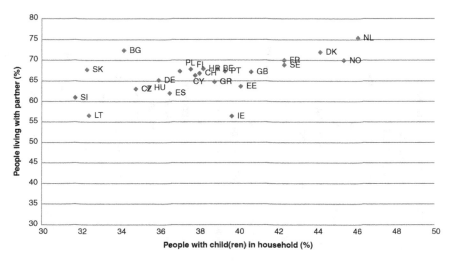

Figure 12.2 People with children in the household and living with a partner (%) among 20–60-year-old persons in different European countries.

The description of people in different family types (Table 12.1) provides some background to understanding the sources of the differences in life satisfaction. Single parents are the most particular group with the highest level of economic difficulties. The single parents are predominantly women; half of them have divorce experience and difficulties with coping economically. Thirty-four per cent of single parents live together with an adult household member who is not their partner. Although they often live together (62 per cent) with another grown-up person who is not their partner, they also experience more health problems than those with partners and are less satisfied with society (democracy) in their country. Those without a partner and children in the household are the youngest group, on average. Only about 60 per cent of this group is employed. They also experience more economic difficulties than other groups, and 17 per cent of them are divorced. Cohabiters with and without children are least religious but are at the same time quite satisfied with the arrangements of democracy and society. Cohabiting persons are a particular group also because of their high experience of divorce or separation. There are rather small differences between cohabiters with and without children in the household.

Officially married groups are the oldest and most conservative (following religious services), which might indicate their higher norm behaviour. The main difference between married people with and without children is age and health conditions. People without children in the household are older and their group probably consists of two subgroups: those who never had children and those whose children had left home.

Life satisfaction among people in different family groups (Figure 12.3) shows that life without a partner is less fulfilling than with a partner. The groups with

Table 12.1 Description of family types in 2010 (all countries, data with weights)

	Married with children N = 8439	Married no children N = 7558	Cohabiting with children N = 1596	Cohabiting no children N = 1932	No partner with children N = 1264	No partner or children N = 8784	Total N = 29573
Female %	54.4	56.5	54.7	52.3	84.8	45.9	53.60
Age, mean (sd)	40.6 (7.4)	50.3 (8.7)	35.9 (7.9)	36.8 (11.9)	39.7 (8.4)	35.1 (13.1)	40.9 (11.7)
Years of education, mean (sd)	14.0 (7.0)	13.2 (8.2)	13.6 (6.4)	14.1 (5.2)	13.7 (7.6)	14.1 (7.7)	13.8 (7.4)
Subjective health status, bad or very bad %	2.8	7.5	3.9	4.1	6.3	6.1	5.3
Never attend religious services %	26.9	29.5	47.3	46.9	37.6	37.2	33.5
Main activity %							
Working	73.9	68.5	68.9	74.2	65.0	57.1	66.9
Unemployed	7.6	8.1	11.8	10.2	12.9	14.9	10.5
Other	18.5	23.4	19.3	15.6	22.1	28.0	22.6
Satisfied more than average how democracy works in the country 6–10 points %	42.2	36.6	43.6	46.5	33.5	38.6	39.7
Ever divorced or civil union dissolved %	6.5	8.4	21.1	21.4	49.5	16.9	13.7
Difficult to cope with income %	28.0	28.5	28.9	21.5	50.0	32.2	29.9

220 *Mare Ainsaar*

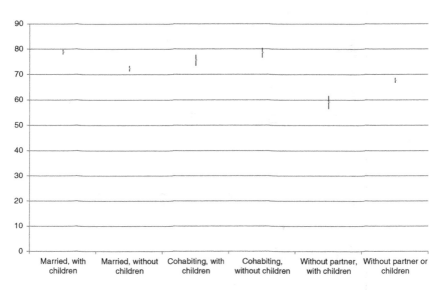

Figure 12.3 Proportion of people satisfied with life in different family types in 2010 (data weighed by design weights, all countries).

the lowest life satisfaction are single parents and individuals without a partner and without children.

The influence of children is less clear. For example, lone parents are much less satisfied compared with single childless people. At the same time, marriage without children in the household is associated with lower life satisfaction than marriage with children in the household. In the group of cohabitants, the presence of children in the household is not associated with life satisfaction differences. However, this situation is quite diverse in different regions of Europe. Table 12.2 presents the diversity of life satisfaction in different families by country. The mean life satisfaction in family groups is compared with the mean life satisfaction of married parents having children in the household. Although the country comparisons are similar in many countries (Figure 12.3), there are also some particularities.

Being married and having children in the household are associated with a highest life satisfaction in all countries, and in the majority of countries, cohabiting couples with or without children have an equally good life as the married couples who have children in the household. Only in several East European countries (Bulgaria, the Czech Republic, Croatia, Hungary, Slovenia and Slovakia) and in Finland, Spain and France, married people without children in the household have a lower level of life satisfaction than married people with children. Single parents are, in the majority of countries, the least satisfied with their life, with the exception of Slovenia, Hungary and Bulgaria, where their life satisfaction level is close to the country average.

Table 12.2 Mean life satisfaction in countries by family type in 2010. All groups are compared with the group of married with children in the household

	Married, with children	Married, without children	Cohabiting, without children	Cohabiting, with children	Without partner, with children	Without partner and children	Average
BE	7.7	7.6	7.6	7.7	6.0**	7.2**	7.5
BG	5.2	4.9*	4.4**	4.2*	4.7	5.0	4.9
CH	8.1	8.3	7.9	7.9	7.3**	7.7**	8.0
CZ	6.7	6.3**	6.1	6.4	5.7**	6.3**	6.4
CY	7.5	7.2	5.9*	8.0	5.7**	6.9**	7.2
DE	7.5	7.4	6.8*	7.4	6.2**	6.8**	7.2
DK	8.5	8.4	8.5	8.3	7.5**	7.7**	8.2
EE	6.8	6.5	6.9	6.5	5.8**	6.2**	6.5
ES	7.6	7.1**	7.3	7.4	6.4**	7.2**	7.3
FI	8.3	7.9**	8.1	8.0*	7.6**	7.3**	7.9
FR	6.6	6.1**	6.6	6.2	5.6**	5.8**	6.2
GB	7.4	7.2	7.1	7.1**	6.0**	6.5**	7.0
GR	5.9	5.6	3.8	5.3*	4.5**	5.7	5.7
HR	6.8	6.3*	3.5	6.9	4.4**	6.5	6.5
HU	6.3	5.5**	5.4*	5.5*	5.9	5.8**	5.8
IE	6.7	6.5	6.3	6.3	5.7**	6.2	6.4
LT	5.3	5.2	4.1	5.5	4.1**	5.1	5.1
NL	7.9	7.8	7.7**	7.9	7.1**	7.4**	7.7
NO	8.1	8.1	7.7	8.2	7.3**	7.4**	7.9
PL	7.3	7.2	6.4	7.3	6.1**	6.6**	7.0
PT	6.2	5.9	6.3	5.8	5.4*	6.2	6.1
SE	8.2	8.0	8.0	8.0	7.2**	7.3**	7.8
SI	7.2	6.8*	7.3	6.8	7.2	7.1	7.0
SK	6.8	6.3**	7.1	7.3	5.3**	6.3**	6.4

Notes: * p<0.05; ** p<0.01, all groups compared to "Married, with children."

Table 12.3 Satisfaction with life in different family types, results of multi-level linear regression models

	Model 1 with family types	Model 2 with family types + personal indicators (no income included)	Model 3 with family types + personal indicators + income
Without partner compared with married people	Lower	Lower	Lower
Cohabiting compared with married people	The same	Lower	Lower
Child in the household	Higher	Lower	The same
Without partner in interaction with having child(ren)	Lower	Lower	Lower
Cohabiting in interaction with having child(ren)	Lower	The same	The same

Notes: Models 2-5 control for age, years of education, generalized trust, subjective health status, attendance of religious services, satisfaction with how democracy works in the country.

As a next step, three models were used to analyse the life satisfaction in different families. In different models, we take into account the influence of individual selectivity and country differences on the overall life satisfaction level and perceived economic coping. The results of the first model (Table 12.3), with only the family type variables and country indicator, proved again that married and cohabiting couples and people with children have the highest life satisfaction. The first simple model also indicated that a child in the household is usually associated with higher life satisfaction for married parents but that a child has a negative effect on life satisfaction for single parents and cohabiting parents.

Variations in life satisfaction can be a result of individual selectivity (Kravdal 2014) of people into some family formations. After adding individual characteristics to the second model in order to control for individual differences, the negative effect of children on life satisfaction of cohabitants disappeared, but persons with children became less satisfied than people without children in the household, and cohabiting persons became less satisfied with life than married persons. The result indicates that cohabitant and parents with children in the household have particular characteristics that make them more satisfied with life. If we take this into account, cohabitation and children in the family are less rewarding than marriage or life without children. In the last stage, we added evaluation of economic coping of a household on a life satisfaction model (Model 3). After taking into account the economic circumstances of families, the life satisfaction of persons with and without children became similar, with the exception of single parents, who remained less satisfied with life.

Life satisfaction and support from society

Because of the importance of economic conditions in life satisfaction of parents, we were also interested in regional differences in economic support for families and their influence on life satisfaction. Economic coping is an essential determinant of life satisfaction of families, and social support might be particularly important during an economic recession period when overall income level is less secure. Vignoli et al. (2014) demonstrated that higher social protection benefit levels in the areas of family and children and of unemployment were associated with higher general levels of life satisfaction. Ainsaar (2008) found that parents were more satisfied with their lives in those societies where family life was considered more important and family policy support was more generous, and Harknett et al. (2014) reported that support for families has a significant positive effect on fertility intentions and behaviour.

We compared the life satisfaction differences in families with children with the fiscal support for families in different countries. All European countries support families with children, but the support level is quite different. Because the family policy is usually targeted to all family types with children, we compared the life satisfaction levels of all families with children with the life satisfaction levels of single persons without children in the country with family policy support from gross domestic product (GDP).

Figure 12.4 demonstrates first that the diversity of support for families and life satisfaction differences were large in Europe in 2010. However, there is a positive link between support for families and life satisfaction of parents compared with non-parents, despite the differences. In those countries where the support is more remarkable, parents with children are more satisfied with life compared

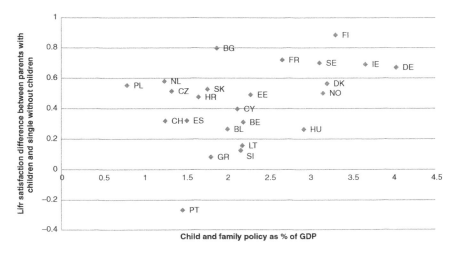

Figure 12.4 Support for families with children and life satisfaction differences between parents with children in the household and single persons without children.

with single childless persons. The only remarkable exception is Portugal, where the families with children are less satisfied with life than single persons without children, and their life satisfaction is disproportionally low. It is mainly the result of the low life satisfaction of single parents.

Conclusions

The aim of the chapter was to investigate how life satisfaction varies in different family types in Europe. The results demonstrated that, although the diversity of family forms increases in Europe, married couples with children have still several life-satisfaction advantages in Europe. We saw the clear benefits of partnership, either marriage or cohabitation, on life satisfaction, but the benefits of children to life satisfaction seems to depend on country differences in economic coping options and support from society.

Country comparisons demonstrated some regional diversity compared with general trends, but marriage and children in the household of married couples were in all countries associated with high life satisfaction, and no difference in life satisfaction of married and cohabiting people in the majority of countries was found.

However, if we take into account that cohabiting persons have specific characteristics more prone to life satisfaction, official marriage seems to be the source of greater life satisfaction than cohabitation in Europe. Also, the group of cohabiting persons is quite diverse.

The influence of children on life satisfaction is more complicated. Despite the hypothesis that children hold some value for their parents and have consequently a positive influence on life satisfaction, we could not see that children in the household always contribute to the increase in life satisfaction. It seems to be true only for officially married people in Europe. Individual (selectivity) characteristics of persons seem to rise, and economic coping difficulties reduce the life satisfaction of parents with children.

Marriage without children in the household lowers the life satisfaction in some countries, compared with married people who had children in the household.

We also found evidence that child and family allocations from government have a positive influence on the life satisfaction of families, compared with single persons without children. In countries with the higher spending on children, the difference of life satisfaction of parents is comparatively higher.

Acknowledgement

The work has been supported by the Estonian Science Council, grant number 93559355.

References

Aassve, A., Goisis, A. and Sironi, M. (2012). Happiness and childbearing across Europe. *Social Indicators Research*, 108(1), 65–86. doi:10.1007/s11205-011-9866-x.

Ainsaar, M. (2008). Ühiskonna toetus, usaldus, tervis ja majanduslik toimetulek kui laste ja lastevanemate rahulolu mõjutavad tegurid Euroopa 13 riigis [Support of society, trust, health and income as factors of life satisfaction for children and parents in 13 countries in Europe]. In M. Ainsaar and D. Kutsar (Eds.), *Eesti Euroopa võrdlustes [Estonia in European Comparisons]* (pp. 49–66). Tallinn: Sotsiaalministeerium.

Billari, F. C. (2008). The happiness commonality: Fertility decisions in low-fertility settings. *How Generations and Gender Shape Demographic Change* (pp. 7–38). New York and Geneva: United Nations.

Bradshaw, J., Hoelscher, P. and Richardson, D. (2007). An index of child well-being in the European Union. *Social Indicators Research*, 80, 133–177.

Drobnic, S., Beham, B. and Präg, P. (2010). Good job, good life? Working conditions and quality of life in Europe. *Social Indicators Research*, 99, 205–225. doi:10.1007/s11205-010-9586-7.

ESS Round 5: European Social Survey Round 5 Data (2010). Data file edition 3.2. Norwegian Social Science Data Services, Norway – Data Archive and distributor of ESS data.

Groot, W., Maassen van den Brink, H. and van Praad, B. (2007). The compensating income variation of social capital. *Social Indicators Research*, 82, 189–207.

Gudmundsdottir, D. G. (2011). The impact of economic crisis on happiness. *Social Indicators Research*, 110(3), 1083–1101. doi:10.1007/s11205-011-9973-8.

Harknett, K., Billari, F. C. and Medalia, C. (2014). Do family support environments influence fertility? Evidence from 20 European countries. *European Journal of Population*, 30(1), 1–33. doi:10.1007/s10680-013-9308-3.

Hooghe, M. and Vanhoutte, B. (2011). Subjective well-being and social capital in Belgian communities. The impact of community characteristics on subjective well-being indicators in Belgium. *Social Indicators Research*, 100, 17–36. doi:10.1007/s11205-010-9600-0.

Kohler, H.-P., Behrman, J. R. and Skytthe, A. (2005). Partner + children = happiness? The effects of partnerships and fertility on well-being. *Population and Development Review*, 31(3), 407–445.

Kravdal, Ø. (2014). The estimation of fertility effects on happiness: Even more difficult than usually acknowledged. *European Journal of Population*, 30(3), 263–290. doi:10.1007/s10680-013-9310-9.

Lever, J. P., Pinol, N. L. and Uralde, J. H. (2005). Poverty, psychological resources and subjective well-being. *Social Indicators Research*, 73, 375–408.

Margolis, R. and Myrskyla, M. (2013). Family, money, and health: Regional differences in the determinants of life satisfaction over the life course. *Advances in Life Course Research*, 18, 115–126.

Mayer, B. and Trommsdorff, G. (2010). Adolescents' value of children and their intentions to have children: A cross-cultural and multilevel analysis. *Journal of Cross-Cultural Psychology*, 41, 671–689. doi:10.1177/0022022110372195.

Meer, P. H. (2014). Gender, unemployment and subjective well-being: Why being unemployed is worse for men than for women. *Social Indicators Research*, 115, 23–44. doi:10.1007/s11205-012-0207-5.

Musick, K. and Bumpass. L. (2012). Re-examining the case for marriage: Union formation and changes in well-being. *Journal of Marriage and Family*, 74, 1–18. doi:10.1111/j.1741-3737.2011.00873.x.

Nauck, B. (2014). Value of children and the social production of welfare. *Demographic Research*, 30(66), 1793–1824. doi:10.4054/DemRes.2014.30.66.

Ott, J. C. (2011). Government and happiness in 130 nations: Good governance fosters higher level and more equality of happiness. *Social Indicators Research*, 102, 3–22.

Perelli-Harris, B. (2014). How similar are cohabiting and married parents? Second conception risks by union type in the United States and across Europe. *European Journal of Population*, 30, 437–464. doi:10.1007/s10680-014-9320-2.

Perelli-Harris, B. and Lyons-Amos, M. (2015). Changes in partnership patterns across the life course: An examination of 14 countries in Europe and the United States. *Demographic Research*, 33. doi:10.4054/DemRes.2015.33.6.

Pittau, M. G., Zelli, R. and Gelman, A. (2010). Economic disparities and life satisfaction in European regions. *Social Indicators Research*, 96, 339–361. doi:10.1007/s11205-009-9481-2.

Smock, P., Manning, W. and Porter, M. (2005). "Everything's there except money": How money shapes decisions to marry among cohabitors. *Journal of Marriage and Family*, 67(3), 680–696.

Sobotka, T. and Toulemon, L. (2008). Changing family and partnership behaviour: Common trends and persistent diversity across Europe. *Demographic Research*, 19(6), 85–138.

Stutzer, A. and Frey, B.S. (2006). Does marriage make people happy, or do happy people get married? *The Journal of Socio-Economics*, 35, 326–347.

Suldo, S. M. and Huebner, E. S. (2004). Does life satisfaction moderate the effects of stressful life events on psychopathological behavior during adolescence? *School Psychology Quarterly*, 19(2), 93–105.

Suldo, S. M. and Huebner, E. S. (2006). Is extremely high life satisfaction during adolescence advantageous? *Social Indicators Research*, 78, 179–203.

Thomson, E. (2014). Family complexity in Europe. *Annals of the American Academy of Political and Social Science*, 654(1), 245–258.

Van der Lippe, T., Voorpostel, M. and Hewitt, B. (2014). Disagreements among cohabiting and married couples in 22 European countries. *Demographic Research*, 31(10), 247–274.

Vignoli, D., Pirani, E. and Salvini, S. (2014). Constellations and life satisfaction in Europe. *Social Indicators Research*, 117, 967–986. doi:10.1007/s11205-013-0372-1.

Zimmermann, A. C. and Easterlin, R. A. (2006). Happily ever after? Cohabitation, marriage, divorce, and happiness in Germany. *Population and Development Review*, 32(3), 511–528.

Appendix

Table 12.4A Number of persons from different families in a sample

	Married, with children	Married, without children	Cohabiting, with children	Cohabiting, without children	No partner, with children	No partner or children
Belgium	298	266	92	99	43	314
Bulgaria	287	447	111	54	36	432
Switzerland	315	224	23	88	32	291
Czech Republic	392	362	56	103	75	597
Cyprus	232	186	7	24	19	212
Germany	494	544	76	135	90	591
Denmark	321	216	71	90	37	236
Estonia	208	219	166	103	65	333
Spain	428	299	39	72	23	472
Finland	279	255	104	127	41	322
France	268	230	81	78	93	363
Great Britain	361	299	84	128	140	480
Greece	576	420	6	50	62	688
Croatia	305	296	2	17	23	317
Hungary	253	256	81	79	40	349
Ireland	445	265	63	108	142	698
Lithuania	189	243	28	48	65	299
Netherlands	344	268	70	103	82	317
Norway	285	193	134	117	59	241
Poland	408	340	27	38	38	354
Portugal	315	316	26	35	66	359
Sweden	201	153	127	135	51	228
Slovenia	193	229	72	52	19	331
Slovakia	289	398	25	29	57	369

13 How to Measure Fathering Practices in a European Comparison?

Ivett Szalma and Judit Takács

Introduction

Changing fatherhood practices, perceptions and ideals have attracted increasing interest from social science scholars in recent decades. This attention is motivated by important social changes that have occurred in many European countries, such as the increasing number of women and mothers entering the labour market and the growing number of working single parents and dual-income families. Fathering practices are not homogenous in Europe: several country-level factors can influence them, including social norms and attitudes as well as parental policies such as shared parental leave and/or father quota provisions that can make it possible and even desirable for fathers to stay at home with their children. Taking into consideration the changes over time is also important, because in some European countries fathers' involvement in childcare started earlier and was more intensive than in other places.

Many social scientific studies on fatherhood apply qualitative methods such as discourse analysis and interviewing (Wall and Arnold 2007; Grbich 1987; Doucet 2004; Merla 2008; Miller 2011; Chesley 2011; Solomon 2014). Qualitative studies on involved fatherhood practices and stay-at-home fathers can provide valuable insights into various ways the concept of involved fathering has been constructed and put into practice in different societies. However, most of these qualitative studies lack the comparative element (with a few exceptions such as Doucet and Merla 2007; Suwada and Plantin 2014) and reflect static pictures based on one-off data-gathering events that cannot realistically reproduce the temporal aspects of the examined situations. Shirani and Henwood (2011) introduced qualitative longitudinal methodology into involved fatherhood research while following men across the first eight years of fatherhood: they returned to their interviewees to measure and explore changes that occurred over the examined time period.

There are also a few studies that examined fatherhood practices on the basis of survey data. For example, Geisler and Kreyenfeld (2011), using German microcensus data from 1999 and 2005, focused on factors that influence whether fathers take parental leave or not, and they found that fathers are more likely to take parental leave if they have a more highly educated or older partner. Puur and his co-authors (2008) used Population Policy Acceptance Study (PPAS) data to show the impact of men's views regarding the male role in their child-bearing preferences in eight European countries.[1] According to their findings, men, including fathers, characterized by more gender-egalitarian views have higher fertility aspirations than more traditionally oriented men.

Hobson and Fahlén (2009) used European Social Survey (ESS) data to highlight the inequalities among European fathers in their ability to achieve work–family balance, and they found that in comparison to Western and Northern European countries, fathers in the examined Central-Eastern European countries had the least capabilities of achieving a work-family balance due to several factors, including low employment protection, lack of father-friendly policies, relatively strong male-breadwinner norms and widespread economic precariousness.

With complete agreement regarding David Morgan's (2002) view about the importance of comparative analysis serving as a valuable corrective against the ethnocentrism that can often get in the way of a critical understanding of fatherhood and fathering, in this article, our central question is how to measure fathering practices in a European comparison. To this end, we will give an overview of fathering-related variable items in freely available international surveys: we will focus on how they have been developing over time, and in two surveys, we will also test the different scale effects.

Measurement tools in European surveys

The possibilities of empirically measuring fathering practices in internationally comparable ways are central issues in the present study. Variables that can potentially be used for measuring various aspects of fathering practices can be found in a few large-scale quantitative cross-national surveys such as the European Value Studies (EVS), the International Social Survey Programme (ISSP), the Eurobarometer (EB) and the ESS. Furthermore, we can also consider the panel surveys of the Generations and Gender Programme (GGS) because data from its first wave in 2004 is available from 19 (mostly European) countries.[2]

The first attempt to measure fathering practices related attitudes in Europe was provided by the first round of the European Values Study in 1981, when the following question was asked: "During the time that you were growing up, were you very close to each other [you and your father], quite close, not very close, or not at all close?" Unfortunately, the former state-socialist Central-Eastern European countries were not involved in the first EVS round: they only joined the second EVS round in 1990. Since then, the following variable became a standard EVS item: "When jobs are scarce, men have more right to a job than women."[3]

The first database to include former state-socialist Central-Eastern European countries was the ISSP: in 1988 in nine countries (Hungary, Australia, Austria, United Kingdom, Ireland, Italy, the Netherlands, the United States and West Germany), the following two items were asked: "Both the man and woman should contribute to the household income" and "A husband's job is to earn money; a wife's job is to look after the home and family." The second variable was modified in the following rounds (1994, 2002, 2004 and 2012) this way: "A man's job is to earn money; a woman's job is to look after the home and family."[4]

Even though the Eurobarometer survey is the oldest one among the others, as it started in 1970, questions about fathering practices related attitudes were asked for the first time in 1993. These were the following: "And in your opinion, is it better for a child if the father is very involved in bringing the child up from an early age, or is it better if the child's education is above all the responsibility of the mother and not of the father?" and "Here is a list of household tasks which may be completed by the father or the mother, or by both. Please tell for each of them, whether you think they should be carried out mainly by the father, mainly by the mother or by both?"[5]

The biannual ESS was launched in 2002 but had items relevant to our present study for the first time only in its second round, in 2004. They included the following variables: "Men should take as much responsibility as women for the home and children" and "When jobs are scarce, men should have more right to a job than women." For a while, it seemed that the second variable could become part of the core module of the survey, but in the latest available round (ESS round 6), there were no relevant items included related to our topic.[6] Table 13.4 in the Appendix provides an overview of all relevant variables of the EVS, ISSP, EB and ESS surveys.

The GGS panel survey is the newest one among the others: it only started in 2004 and differs from the other previously mentioned cross-sectional international surveys as its focus is more specific to family and gender issues. Therefore, it contains relatively many items regarding fathering practices, such as "Children often suffer because their fathers concentrate too much on their work" or "If parents divorce it is better for the child to stay with the mother than with the father." Table 13.5 in the appendix provides an overview of all relevant GGS variables.[7]

Based on availability, for comparison we have chosen one of the most frequently used items: "When jobs are scarce, men have more right to a job than women." Even though this variable does not measure fathering practices directly, by using this item as an indicator, we can draw a more general picture about the different gender orders – referring to a historically constructed pattern of power relations between men and women, as well as definitions of femininity and masculinity (Connell, 1987) – characterizing the examined societies. Previous studies showed that gender roles are related to fathering practices in many ways: for instance, the arrival of the first child pushes couples towards practising traditional gender roles (Grunow et al. 2012; Henchoz and Wernli 2013; Neilson and Stanfors 2014). Even those couples who reported (almost) equal division of labour before having a baby changed their practice after the arrival of their first child. Furthermore, this effect is long term in one's life course because couples tended to maintain this unequal arrangement until children reached secondary school (Kühhirt 2011). These results suggest that the functioning of traditional gender norms can be a main force behind long-term dynamics in couples' household work divisions. However, these norms can be influenced by social policies: for example, by introducing special father quotas within parental leave provisions in the Nordic countries, where state feminism not only provides opportunities for women to combine work and childcare but also "ensures the rights of fathers in relation to their children" (Brandth and Kvande 2001, p. 251).

Data and methods

In this study, we will examine data from the EVS and the ESS. The EVS, a large-scale longitudinal survey research programme, has been conducted every nine years since 1981, following multi-stage probabilistic sampling plans. The EVS provides insights into the ideas, beliefs, preferences, attitudes, values and opinions of citizens all over Europe by applying standardized questionnaires. The ESS is also a large-scale, cross-national longitudinal survey initiated by the European Science Foundation in order to study changing social attitudes and values in Europe. The first round of ESS data collection was completed in 2002. Since ESS is a repeat cross-sectional survey, in each round of data collection, following each other every two years, a core module and two rotating modules (focusing on specific academic and policy concerns, being repeated not in every ESS round but only at certain intervals) are used.

Using data gathered in 2008 (when both EVS and ESS had a data collection round at the same time) we wanted to test the relationship of gender role attitudes with other socio-demographic and attitudinal variables that can be found in both surveys. In 2008, the following 28 European countries took part in both the EVS and the ESS data collection rounds: Belgium, Bulgaria, Croatia, Cyprus, the Czech Republic, Denmark, Estonia, Finland, France, Germany, Greece, Hungary, Ireland, Latvia, Lithuania, Poland, Portugal, Norway, the Netherlands, Romania, Russia, Slovakia, Slovenia, Spain, Sweden, Switzerland, Ukraine and the United Kingdom – thus we have focused only on these countries. This way, we could see whether there are differences between the effects of socio-demographic and other attitudinal determinants regarding gender-role attitudes in the same time period within the same set of countries.

Our dependent variable ("When jobs are scarce, men have more right to a job than women") was included in both surveys – the answer categories, however, were different. It seems to be a general feature that the ESS uses five-point scales (values ranging between 1 and 5) or eleven-point scales (values ranging between 0 and 10) for attitudinal questions, while the EVS applies less consistent methods by using four-, five- or ten-point scales. In social scientific and psychological survey research, the issue of rating scales has generated considerable debate over the optimal number of scale points to be used (Garland 1991; Preston and Colman 2000). The five- and eleven-point scales have neutral points, while four- or ten-point scales do not have neutral points; thus, the latter ones can force respondents to make a choice even if their attitudes are neutral. In the ESS questionnaires, uneven scales (with neutral points) seem to be preferred, while in the EVS questionnaires, there seems to be a preference for the "forced choice" questions. These patterns could be observed in our dependent variables, too: it was measured on a five-point scale in the ESS, where the value of 1 indicated strong agreement while

5 indicated strong disagreement. At the same time, this item was measured on a three-point scale in the EVS, but only the "agree" and the "disagree" categories were offered by the interviewers and the "neither disagree nor agree" category could come up only as a spontaneous choice of the respondent. Figure 13.1 provides an overview of the long-term changes of the dependent variable as measured by the EVS. We have included in Diagram 1 only those countries that participated in all three waves of EVS data gathering in 1990, 1999 and 2008.

We found that in some countries such as Lithuania, Austria, Poland, Malta and Slovakia, the majority of the population agreed with the statement in 1990. Nine years later, there was no country with majority agreement. By 2008, there was only one country left where more than 30 per cent of the respondents agreed with the statement that "When jobs are scarce, men have more right to a job than women," while in the four Nordic countries (Iceland, Denmark, Sweden and Finland) the proportion of those who agreed sank below five per cent. All in all, we can say that regarding traditional gender role attitudes, a significant change happened in Europe, although the Central and Eastern European countries (Slovakia, the Czech Republic, Romania, Bulgaria and Poland), as well as the Southern European ones (like Malta and Portugal) are still lagging behind the Nordic ones.

To check whether we can detect any short-term changes in our dependent variable, we also show how the agreement level changed between 2004 and 2010.[8] We have included in Diagram 2 only those countries that participated in all three waves of ESS data gathering (in 2004, 2008 and 2010) where our dependent variable appeared.

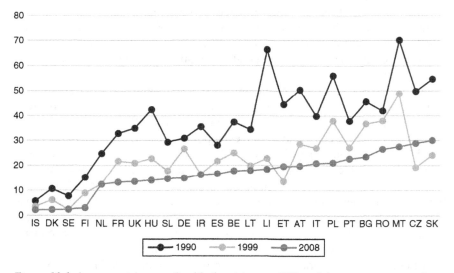

Figure 13.1 Agreement (per cent) with the statement "When jobs are scarce, men have more right to a job than women" in 25 European countries (1990–2008).

Source: EVS 1990, 1999 and 2008 datasets.

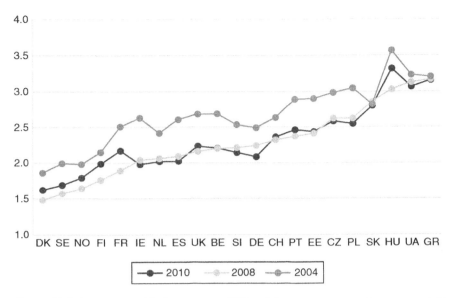

Figure 13.2 Agreement with the statement "When jobs are scarce, men have more right to a job than women": mean values in 21 European countries (2004–2010).

Source: ESS 2004, 2008 and 2010 datasets.
Note: 1 = strongly disagree; 5 = strongly agree.

We can see a clear trend between 2004 and 2008: respondents expressed less traditional views by 2008 in all examined countries, except one, Slovakia. However, we cannot observe such a clear trend between 2008 and 2010: while in the Nordic countries there was a further drop in the mean values, in some other countries, for example Hungary and Portugal, the mean values even slightly increased. When trying to make sense of these very short-term changes, we should also keep in mind the potential effects the recent economic crisis that started around 2007–2008 has caused (Szalma and Takács 2013).

In this study, we have tried to overcome these difficulties by examining the same time frame (2008), the same 28 countries and the same kinds of independent variables within the EVS and the ESS datasets. However, regarding the independent variables – with the exception of gender, age, educational background, belonging to a religious denomination and frequency of attendance at religious services – there are certain differences in the variable categories used by the ESS and the EVS. For example, the settlement type is measured by a five-category variable in the ESS, while the EVS differentiates according to the number of people living in a settlement. Having children is also measured in different ways in the two surveys: in the ESS, the question is about whether the respondents have children living with them in the same household, while in the EVS it is about the actual number of children the respondents have. Table 13.1 provides an overview of all independent variables with all the potential answer categories – from both the ESS and the EVS – that were used in our analyses.

Analytical strategy

Since both dependent variables were measured on an ordered scale, ordered logistic regression was used to study the determinants of social attitudes towards same-sex adoption. To ease interpretation, we reversed the original ESS scale so that higher values indicate stronger agreement, and we recoded EVS dependent variables in the same order. We adjusted the standard error estimates for clustering; that is, we took into account that individuals within the countries cannot be treated as independent observations. This was achieved with the cluster-adjusted robust standard error estimator, which is a standard feature of the statistical software Stata. Estimation of robust standard errors is a good alternative of multi-level modelling, since random effects estimators are computationally demanding.

Hypotheses

I. *Hypotheses regarding the effects of individual level socio-demographic and attitudinal variables on traditional gender role attitudes*

H1.1: Women, younger people, those with higher levels of education and those living in more urbanized environments are less likely to agree with this statement than men, older people, those with lower levels of education and those living in smaller settlements.

H1.2: Concerning religiosity, we assume that those who belong to a religious denomination can manifest more traditional gender views than those who do not belong to any denomination. We also assume that a higher frequency of attending religious services can strengthen traditional gender role attitudes.

H1.3: We expect that marital status and having children can influence attitudes towards gender roles: married people and those having children (or having children in their household) are more likely to agree with the statement than their non-married and/or childless counterparts.

H1.4: We assume that people in full-time employment agree less with traditional gender role attitudes than housewives, unemployed or retired people.

H1.5: Additionally, we assume that having right-wing political attitudes can contribute more to expressing support for traditional gender role attitudes than not having right-wing attitudes.

Table 13.1 Description of the independent variables

Variable	ESS			EVS		
	Scale range	N	%	Scale range	N	%
Gender	Male	24,660	45.4	Male	17,308	43.6
	Female	29,646	54.6	Female	22,393	56.4
Age	Continuous variable					
Settlement type	Big city	13,604	25	Under 2,000	8,059	21
	Suburbs	5,311	9.8	2,000–5,000	3,709	9.8
	Town	16,086	29.6	5,000–10,000	3,694	9.6
	Village	16,224	29.9	10,000–50,000	8,769	228
	Farm	2,843	5.2	50,000–100,000	3,778	9.8
	–	–	–	100,000–500,000	6,389	16.6
	–	–	–	More than 5,000,000	4,071	10.6
Education level	Lower than secondary education	19,325	50.1	Lower than secondary education	11,621	29.5
	Secondary education	11,416	30	Secondary education	18,063	45.9
	Tertiary education	7,355	19.9	Tertiary education	9,713	25.7
Denomination	Not belonging to any denomination	19,171	35.9	Not belonging to any denomination	11,441	29
	Belonging to a denomination	34,188	64.1	Belonging to a denomination	27,975	71
Attendance at religious services	More than once a week	736	1.4	More than once a week	1,272	3.2
	Once a week	13,101	24.6	Once a week	9,178	23.3
	Once a month	11,773	22.1	Once a month	4,017	9.9
	Only on special holy days	10,776	20.2	Only on special holy days	8,850	22.5
	Never	16,516	31	Once a year	7,016	17.8
	–	–	–	Never	13,034	33.1
Family status	Married	27,970	54.1	Married	21,736	55.1
	Widowed	5,403	10.4	Widowed	4,545	11.5
	Divorced	4,938	9.6	Divorced	4,010	10.2
	Never married	13,124	25.4	Never married	9,133	23.2

(continued)

Table 13.1 Continued

Variable	ESS				EVS			
	Scale range		N	%	Scale range		N	%
Employment status	Employed		23,099	43.3	Employed		21,769	53.8
	Retired		12,337	22.1	Retired		10,618	26.2
	"Housewife"[9]		8,913	16.7	"Housewife"		2,577	6.4
	Student		4,182	7.8	Student		2,066	5.1
	Unemployed		2,801	5.3	Unemployed		2,346	5.8
	Disabled		1,133	2.1	Disabled		765	1.9
	Other		894	2.7	Other		342	0.8
Political attitude	Continuous							
Number of children	Not having children		32,821	62	Not having children living in the same household		10,611	26.3
	Having children		20,302	38	Having 1 child		7,861	19.5
					Having 2 children		13,794	34.2
					Having 3 or more children		8,031	20
Employment rate differences between men and women[10]	Continuous variable							
GII (Gender Inequality Index)[11]	Continuous variable							

Source: EVS 2008 dataset and ESS 2008 dataset.

II. *Hypotheses regarding the effects of country-level variables on traditional gender role attitudes*

H2.1: We assume that people in more gender-equal countries – as measured by the Gender Inequality Index (GII) – are less likely to agree with the statement: "When jobs are scarce, men have more right to a job than women."

H2.2: We also expect that people in countries with higher differences between male and female employment rates are more likely to express traditional gender role attitudes than others. In societies where both men and women are in the labour market it is less likely that traditional gender role attitudes are dominant: according to the bargaining theories (Brines, 1993), since women contribute to the household income, they might also be able to achieve a better position regarding the division of household labour.

Results

On the basis of an examination of data from the 2008 EVS and ESS datasets regarding 28 European countries, we found that the levels of acceptance of gender role attitudes differ considerably across Europe. In order to check whether the 28 examined European countries have reached significantly similar order in the two measures (ESS and EVS scales), we have used Kendall's tau test, a non-parametric measure of association based on the number of concordances and discordances in paired observations (Bolboaca and Jantschi 2006). We found that there is no concordance among countries in the two samples.[12]

Table 13.2 provides a detailed overview of the mean values of our dependent variables and shows that in both surveys the lowest levels of support for traditional gender role attitudes could be detected in Sweden, Denmark, Norway and Finland. At the same time, regarding the highest levels of support for traditional gender role attitudes, there were differences between the results of the two surveys: according to the EVS data, the most traditional gender role attitudes were expressed in Cyprus, Greece, Slovakia and Romania, while according to the ESS results, the most traditional gender role attitudes were expressed in Romania, Hungary, Ukraine and Greece.

Estimates of the ordered logistic regressions (summarized in Table 13.3) show that women, younger people and those with higher levels of education were less likely to agree with the statement based on both measurements; these findings support our first hypothesis regarding socio-demographic variables. Regarding the settlement type, we could not find any significant effect in the ESS dataset; at the same time, the settlement size, which was used by the EVS, showed significant effect: those living in settlements with a population of more than 500,000 people were more likely to disagree with the statement that men should have more rights, compared to those living in settlements with fewer than 2000 people. The different effects of settlement size and settlement type can derive from the different settlement sizes as well as the different scales of the dependent variable; however, on the basis of our data, we are not able to determine the cause of this difference.[13]

Table 13.2 Mean values of the dependent variables: agreement with the statement: "When jobs are scarce, men should have more right to a job than women"

EVS		ESS	
Sweden	1.05	Denmark	1.48
Denmark	1.07	Sweden	1.57
Norway	1.09	Norway	1.64
Finland	1.18	Finland	1.76
Netherlands	1.27	France	1.89
France	1.29	Ireland	2.04
Croatia	1.29	Netherlands	2.06
Hungary	1.30	Spain	2.09
Slovenia	1.34	Great Britain	2.16
Great Britain	1.35	Belgium	2.20
Belgium	1.39	Slovenia	2.21
Ireland	1.45	Germany	2.24
Spain	1.46	Switzerland	2.32
Switzerland	1.46	Portugal	2.37
Estonia	1.47	Estonia	2.41
Latvia	1.47	Croatia	2.47
Germany	1.50	Latvia	2.51
Lithuania	1.55	Czech Republic	2.62
Poland	1.56	Poland	2.62
Portugal	1.59	Lithuania	2.69
Bulgaria	1.65	Russian Federation	2.83
Ukraine	1.68	Bulgaria	2.83
Russian Federation	1.69	Slovakia	2.86
Czech Republic	1.69	Cyprus	2.86
Romania	1.70	Romania	2.94
Greece	1.74	Hungary	3.03
Slovakia	1.76	Ukraine	3.13
Cyprus	1.95	Greece	3.17

Notes: ESS: 1 = disagree strongly; 5 = agree strongly; EVS: 1 = disagree, 2 = neither agree or disagree, 3 = agree.

Regarding religiosity, we found similar results in the two surveys: belonging to a denomination seemed not to have significant effect, but very infrequent attendance at religious services increased the disagreement level with the statement that men should have more rights. The less frequently somebody attended religious services, the higher the level of disagreement with the statement was. Probably belonging to a denomination did not have significant effects because it strongly correlates with the frequency of attending religious services. This assumption is supported by the fact that if we include only the belonging to a denomination variable into the models without the other variable (measuring the frequency of attending religious services), we can get a significant effect for denomination, too. Thus we can accept our second hypotheses according to which belonging to a denomination and higher frequency of attending religious services can increase traditional gender role attitudes.

Table 13.3 Estimates of ordered regressions

ESS			EVS		
Gender	Male	Ref.	Gender	Male	Ref.
	Female	−0.62***		Female	−0.56***
Age		0.01***	Age		0.01***
Settlement type	Big city	Ref.	Settlement size	Under 2,000	Ref.
	Suburbs	−0.11		2,000–5000	−0.13
	Town	−0.002		5,000–10000	−0.06
	Village	0.13		10,000–50,000	−0.14
	Farm	−0.14		50,000–100,000	−0.06
	–			100,000–500,000	−0.03
				More than 5,000,000	−0.38**
Education level	Lower than secondary education	0.46***	Education level	Lower than secondary education	0.27***
	Secondary education	Ref.		Secondary education	Ref.
	Tertiary education	−0.4***		Tertiary education	−0.5***
Denomination	Not belonging to any denomination	Ref.	Denomination	Not belonging to any denomination	Ref.
	Belonging to a denomination	0.11		Belonging to a denomination	0.03
Attendance at religious services	More than once a week	Ref.	Attendance at religious services	More than once a week	Ref.
	Once a week	−0.31*		Once a week	−0.15*
	Once a month	−0.42***		Once a month	−0.24**
	Only on special holy days	−0.57***		Only on special holy days	−0.24**
	Never	−0.71***		Once a year	−0.41***
	–			Never	−0.45***
Family status	Married	Ref.	Family status	Married	Ref.

(*continued*)

Table 13.3 Continued

ESS			EVS		
Gender	Male	Ref.	Gender	Male	Ref.
	Widowed	0.21***		Widowed	0.2***
	Divorced	-0.13*		Divorced	-0.07
	Never married	-0.16***		Never married	-0.15*
Employment status	Employed	Ref.	Employment status	Employed	Ref.
	Retired	0.32***		Retired	0.04
	"Housewife"	0.32***		"Housewife"	0.56***
	Student	0.02		Student	-0.12
	Unemployed	0.44***		Unemployed	0.28***
	Disabled	0.16		Disabled	0.16
	Other	-0.13		Other	-0.13
Political attitude		0.04***	Political attitude		0.04***
Number of children	Not having children	Ref.	Number of children	Not having children living in the same household	Ref.
	Having children	0.08**		Having 1 child	-0.12*
				Having 2 children	-0.15*
				Having 3 or more children	-0.17*
Employment rate differences between men and women		0.05	Employment rate differences between men and women		0.05**
GII		6.36***	GII		4.18***

Notes: ***p < 0.01, **p < 0.05, *p < 0.1.

Concerning family status, our results showed that those who never married were less likely to express traditional gender role attitudes than married people, while widowed people were more likely to express such attitudes than married people. These results were supported by both the EVS and the ESS databases. For divorced people, the results coincided with our third hypothesis: they were less likely to express traditional gender role attitudes than married people, but the result was significant only in the ESS database. Regarding the potential effects of having or living with children, we have found contradicting results in the ESS and the EVS: according to the ESS results, people living in a childless household tend to express less traditional views, while the EVS findings indicated that having children can decrease traditional attitudes. These differing findings might be due to the different ways these variables were measured. Thus, on the basis of our findings, we can only partly accept our third hypothesis.

Employment status had significant effects in both databases: unemployed people and those staying at home to do housework and care work were more likely to agree with traditional gender role attitudes than those having full-time jobs. Thus we can accept our fourth hypothesis, but we should also note that there were differences between the two surveys' results because retired people expressed more traditional attitudes in the ESS database but this effect was not significant in the EVS database.

Political attitudes operated in both databases as we expected in our fifth hypothesis: those characterized by stronger right-wing attitudes were also more likely to support traditional gender role attitudes than respondents having less pronounced right wing attitudes.

Regarding the country-level variables, gender inequality measured by the GII seemed to be the strongest indicator of traditional gender role attitudes because it had significant effects in both databases: people in those countries where gender inequality is higher were more likely to agree with the statement that men should have more rights. Thus, we can accept our first country-level hypothesis (H2.1).

Our second country-level variable (measuring employment rate differences between men and women) seemed to work as we expected: higher levels of employment rate differences between the two genders coincided with higher levels of traditional gender role attitudes. However, it had significant effect only in the ESS database.

Conclusion

In order to assess the changes over time and across countries regarding traditional gender role attitudes, we were able to use the freely available international survey datasets such as the ESS and EVS. These surveys allowed us to map the changes over time due to their repeating items regarding fathering practices, and they also made it possible to make comparisons within Europe.[14]

As we could see, there are many international surveys that have items related to fathering practices and attitudes; however, they are not harmonized, and some important features are missing that would be required in order to gain an overall view of fathering practices. For example, if the EVS and the ESS were to use the same measurement scales for the same items, it would allow researchers to follow the changes in more comparable ways. This assumption is supported by our analysis that highlighted that there is no concordance among countries in the ESS and EVS database despite the fact that we examined data from the same countries and the same year (2008).

Despite the different measurement scales of the dependent variable in the EVS and the ESS, most independent variables had the same effects in the two databases. We have found only a few divergent results, such as the effect of settlement size and type and the number of children – but these independent variables were also measured in different ways in the two surveys. Thus, it is not clear whether the differences were due to the different measurements of the dependent or the independent variables or both. However, involving exactly the same two country-level macro variables (the GII and employment rate differences between men and women) brought us a slightly different effect: based on the ESS data, there was no significant effect that might suggest that the deviation is due to the different measurement of the dependent variables.

This study has several limitations. We have used only one measurement that measures just one aspect of gender role attitudes with potential connection to attitudes towards fathering practices. Furthermore, this is only an indirect measurement of attitudes related to fathering practices. Our conclusions are therefore somewhat vague, because besides the scaling effects, other factors, such as different sample design or different sample sizes, could also contribute to the different results. Additionally, we have to point out that attitudes do not necessarily equal actual behaviour – however, we can interpret them as predictors of behaviour. Despite these limitations, this study does contribute to a better understanding of individual and country-level factors that can affect traditional gender role attitudes and also – indirectly – attitudes related to fathering practices.

The possibility of empirically measuring fathering practices in internationally comparable ways was a central issue in the present study. However, if we want to answer the question posed in the title of our article – how to measure fathering practices in a European comparison – we must emphasize the need for more fathering practices–specific variables that are to be used as core variables in numerous waves of many European surveys.

Notes

1. In this study, a "male role index" was constructed from the following three variables: (1) It is not good if the man stays at home and cares for the children and the woman goes out to work; (2) Family life often suffers because men concentrate too much on their work; (3) For a man, the job should be more important than the family (Puur et al. 2008).
2. Australia, Austria, Belgium, Bulgaria, the Czech Republic, Estonia, France, Georgia, Germany, Hungary, Italy, Japan, Lithuania, Netherlands, Norway, Poland, Romania, Russian Federation, Sweden. Source: www.ggp-i.org/data/data-access.html.
3. Source: www.europeanvaluesstudy.eu/.
4. Source: www.issp.org.
5. Source: https://dbk.gesis.org/dbksearch/download.asp?id=5858.

6 Source: www.europeansocialsurvey.org/.
7 Source: www.ggp-i.org/.
8 In our view, the five-point scale measurement can help to detect short-term changes more efficiently than a coarser scale, which would not have revealed these changes.
9 A person characterized by doing housework, looking after children or other persons.
10 We have calculated the differences between male and female employment rates on the basis of OECD (2010) data.
11 The GII (2010) measures gender inequality in a given country by reflecting women's disadvantage in three dimensions: reproductive health, empowerment and the labour market. GII values can range from 0 – indicating that women and men fare equally in a country – to 1, indicating that women fare poorly in all measured dimensions. Source: http://hdr.undp.org/en/statistics/gii/.
12 The applied significance level is $p < 0.05$.
13 When we analysed the different measurements of homophobia based on the same databases (ESS and EVS), we did not find different effects of the same two types of settlement measurements (Takács and Szalma 2013).
14 The research leading to this paper received funding from the European Union's Seventh Framework Programme (FP7/2007-2013) under grant agreement no. 320116 for the research project 'FamiliesAndSocieties'.

References

Bolboaca, S. and Jantschi, L. (2006). Pearson versus Spearman, Kendall's Tau Correlation Analysis on Structure-Activity Relationships of Biologic Active Compounds. *Leonardo Journal of Sciences Issue 9*, July–December 2006 pp. 179–200.

Brandth, B. and Kvande, E. (2001). Flexible work and flexible fathers. *Work, Employment & Society*, 15(2): 251–267.

Brines, J. (1993). The exchange value of housework. *Rationality and Society*, 5(3): 302–340.

Chesley, N. (2011). Stay-at-home fathers and breadwinning mothers: Gender, couple dynamics, and social change. *Gender & Society*, 25: 642–664.

Connell, R.W. (1987). *Gender and Power*. Stanford: Stanford University Press.

Doucet, A. (2004). "It's almost like I have a job, but I don't get paid": Fathers at home reconfiguring work, care, and masculinity. *Fathering*, 2(3): 277–303.

Doucet, A. and Merla, L. (2007). Stay-at-home fathering. A strategy for balancing work and home in Canadian and Belgian families. *Community, Work and Family*, 10(4): 455–473.

Garland, R. (1991). The mid-point on a rating scale: Is it desirable? *Marketing Bulletin*, 2(1): 66–70.

Geisler, E. and Kreyenfeld, M. (2011). Against all odds: Fathers' use of parental leave in Germany. *Journal of European Social Policy*, 21(1): 88–99.

GII (2010) Gender Inequality Index. http://hdr.undp.org/sites/default/files/reports/270/hdr_2010_en_complete_reprint.pdf.

Grbich, C. F. (1987). Primary caregiver fathers. A role study: some preliminary findings, *Australian Journal of Sex, Marriage and Family*, 8(1): 17–26.

Grunow, D., Schulz, F. and Blossfeld, H. P. (2012). What determines change in the division of housework over the course of marriage? *International Sociology*, 27(3): 289–307. doi:10.1177/0268580911423056.

Henchoz, C. and Wernli, B. (2013). Cycle de vie et travaux ménagers en Suisse. L'investissement ménager des hommes et des femmes lors des étapes de la construction familiale. *Swiss Journal of Sociology*, 36 (2): 235–257.

Hobson, B. and Fahlén, S. (2009). Competing scenarios for European fathers: Applying Sen's capabilities and agency framework to work–family balance. *The Annals of the American Academy of Political and Social Science*, 624, 214–233. doi:10.1177/0002716209334435.

Kühhirt, M. (2011). Childbirth and long-term division of labour within couples: How do substitution, bargaining power, and norms affect parents' time allocation in West Germany? *European Sociological Review*. doi:10.1093/esr/jcr026.

Merla, L. (2008). Determinants, costs, and meanings of Belgian stay-at-home fathers: An international comparison. *Fathering*, 6(2): 113–132.

Miller, T. (2011). Falling back into gender? Men's narratives and practices around first-time fatherhood. *Sociology*, 45(6): 1094–1109.

Morgan, D. (2002). Epilogue 273–286. In Hobson, B. (2004), *Making Men into Fathers. Men, Masculinities and the Social Politics of Fatherhood*. Cambridge: Cambridge University Press.

Neilson, J. and Stanfors, M. (2014). It's about time! Gender, parenthood and household division of labour under different welfare regimes. *Journal of Family Issues*, 35(8): 1066–1088.

OECD (2010). *OECD Factbook 2010: Economic, Environmental and Social Statistics*, OECD Publishing, Paris. http://dx.doi.org/10.1787/factbook-2010-en.

Preston, C. C. and Colman, A. M. (2000). Optimal number of response categories in rating scales: Reliability, validity, discriminating power, and respondent preferences. *Acta Psychologica*, 104(1): 1–15.

Puur, A., Oláh, L. S., Tazi-Preve, M. I. and Dorbritz, J. (2008). Men's childbearing desires and views of the male role in Europe at the dawn of the 21st century. *Demographic Research*, 19: 1883–1912. www.demographic-research.org/Volumes/Vol19/56/ doi:10.4054/DemRes.2008.19.56.

Solomon, C. R. (2014). "I feel like a rock star": Fatherhood for stay-at-home fathers. *Fathering*, 12(1): 52–70.

Shirani, F. and Henwood, K. (2011). Continuity and change in a qualitative longitudinal study of fatherhood: Relevance without responsibility. *International Journal of Social Research Methodology*, 14(1): 17–29.

Suwada, K. and Plantin, L. (2014). On fatherhood, masculinities, and family policies in Poland and Sweden—A comparative study. *Polish Sociological Review*, 4(188): 509–524.

Szalma, I. and Takács, J. (2013). Should men have more rights…? Gender role-related attitudes before and during the 2008 crisis. In G. Jónsson and K. Stefánsson (eds.) *Retrenchment and Renewal? Welfare States in Times of Economic Crises*. NordWel Studies in Historical Welfare State Research 6. Helsinki 2013.

Takács, J. and Szalma, I. (2013). How to measure homophobia in an international comparison? *Družboslovne Razprave*, 73(1): 11–42.

Wall, G. and Arnold, S. (2007). How involved is involved fathering? An exploration of the contemporary culture of fatherhood. *Gender & Society*, 21(4): 508–527.

Appendices

Table 13.4A Development of fathering practices related items in freely available international surveys

EVS	1981	1990	1999	2008
And you and your father? During the time that you were growing up, were you very close to each other, quite close, not very close or not at all close?	X			
When jobs are scarce, men have more right to a job than women.		X	X	X
If someone says a child needs a home with both a father and a mother to grow up happily, would you tend to agree or disagree?		X		X
Both the husband and wife should contribute to household income.		X	X	X
A man has to have children in order to be fulfilled.			X	X
In general, fathers are as well suited to look after their children as mothers.			X	X
Men should take as much responsibility as women for the home and children.				X

ISSP	1988	1994	2002	2004	2012
Both the man and woman should contribute to the household income.	X	X	X	X	X
A man's job is to earn money; a woman's job is to look after the home and family.	X[1]	X	X	X	X
A single father can bring up his child as well as a married couple.	X				
It is not good if the man stays at home and cares for the children and the woman goes out to work.		X			
Family life often suffers because men concentrate too much on their work.		X			

Note: [1]In 1988, this version of the variable was asked: The husband's job is to earn money; the wife's job is to look after the home and family.

ISSP	1988	1994	2002	2004	2012
Men ought to do a larger share of childcare than they do now.			X		
Who usually makes/made the decisions about how to bring up your children?			X	X	X
One parent can bring up a child as well as two parents together.				X	X
Still thinking about the same couple, if both are in a similar work situation and are eligible for paid leave, how should this paid leave period be divided between the mother and the father?				X	X
Consider a family with a child under school age. What, in your opinion, is the best way for them to organise their family and work life?				X	X
And, in your opinion, which of these options would be the least desirable?				X	X
A same-sex male couple can bring up a child as well as a male–female couple.					X

EUROBAROMETER	1993	1998	2003	2006	2007	2010
And in your opinion, is it better for a child if the father is very involved in bringing the child up from an early age, or is it better if the child's education is above all the responsibility of the mother and not of the father?	X					
Here is a list of household tasks which may be completed by the father or the mother, or by both. Please tell for each of them, whether you think they should be carried out mainly by the father, mainly by the mother or by both?	X	X	X			
It is more natural for mothers than for fathers to take care of children?			X			
According to you, how important is each of the following in the decision on whether to have or not to have a\another child?						
The working situation of the father				X	X	
The health of the father				X	X	
Childcare for children aged 0–3 can be organised in different ways, by combining several options or by relying on only one option. In your opinion, what is the best way of organising childcare for children aged 0–3?						X
Childcare for children aged 3–6 can be organised in different ways, by combining several options or by relying on only one option. In your opinion, what is the best way of organising childcare for pre-school children aged 3–6?						X

ESS	2002	2004	2006	2008	2010	2012
Men should take as much responsibility as women for the home and children.		X				
When jobs are scarce, men should have more right to a job than women.		X		X	X	
And to be considered an adult, how important is it for a man to have become a father?			X			

Table 13.5A Fathering practices related items in GGS

GGS	2004	2008
How often do you see your father?	X	X
How satisfied are you with the relationship with your father?	X	X
A man has to have children in order to be fulfilled.	X	X
A child needs a home with both a father and a mother to grow up happily.	X	X
If a woman earns more than her partner, it is not good for the relationship.	X	X
Children often suffer because their fathers concentrate too much on their work.	X	X
If parents divorce, it is better for the child to stay with the mother than with the father.	X	X
When jobs are scarce, men should have more right to a job than women.	X	X

Section V
Methodological Issues

14 How Do Reluctant Respondents Assess Governmental Protection Against Poverty?

Helge Baumann

Introduction

Due to decreasing response rates during the past few decades (Schnell 1997, pp. 36ff.; Rao and Pennington 2013, p. 651), a lot of research has been conducted about the issue of non-response bias, which is of particular concern when the missing data mechanism is Missing Not At Random (MNAR) rather than Missing At Random (MAR) (Schafer and Graham 2002, p. 152).[1] When the mechanism is MAR, the cause of nonresponse Z is correlated with the survey variable Y (e.g. attitudes towards poverty), but this correlation can be explained by a vector of characteristics X, which are observable for both respondents and non-respondents (e.g. age and gender of sampled persons). In that case, the non-response bias can be corrected by weighting. When the mechanism is MNAR, the correlation between Y and Z cannot or only partly be explained by X (see Figure 14.1). Thus, correction of non-response bias becomes much more difficult.

When information from register data or at least some "gold-standard" (information from a high-quality survey) is available, it might be possible to evaluate the direction and magnitude of the bias (Hox and De Leeuw, 2002, p. 655). However, in most instances, this is not the case with attitudinal questions.

In the past, most non-response studies have focused on the bias of non-respondents' socio-demographical or geographical characteristics rather than their attitudes, mostly because there is no information on non-respondents' attitudes. In some studies, women and older people are underrepresented. People with average incomes are overrepresented in comparison with both lower and higher incomes (Schräpler 2000, p. 118f; Spitzmüller et al. 2007).

Since more survey agencies have started collecting paradata and interviewer observations in recent years, however, it has been increasingly possible to assess biases of variables and data quality indicators which are unobservable for non-respondents (Couper 1998; Olson 2013; Stinchcombe et al. 1981). This paper tries to expand our knowledge on attitudinal non-response bias by exploiting round six of the Irish and German European Social Survey (ESS) data. Our leading question is: "What are non-respondents' attitudes towards poverty?"

In Section 2, we will discuss our theoretical approach and necessary assumptions. In Section 3, we will explain the data we use and the methods we choose.

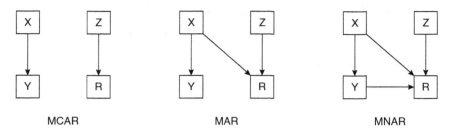

Figure 14.1 Missing data mechanisms.
Source: Schafer and Graham 2002, p. 152.

First, we will estimate response propensities using multilevel logistic regression models. To estimate these models, we will use information on both respondents and non-respondents from contact forms. Second, we will use these response propensities as predictors of attitudes on one question towards governmental action against poverty (question E13 in the questionnaire). Thirdly, we will evaluate whether the relationship between response propensities and attitudes can be explained by using control variables such as age, gender, education and net household income. In Section 4, we will describe and discuss our results before we reflect the limitations of this study and identify needs for further research in Section 5.

Theoretical approach

We want to analyse what non-respondents *would have answered* to a particular attitudinal question *if they had participated* in the ESS. By definition, we do not have any answers from non-respondents. Thus, we need certain assumptions in order to approximate non-respondents' attitudes, which we will explain in this section.

The *continuum of resistance* presumes that the target population of a certain survey is not divided into respondents and non-respondents beforehand (which would be a deterministic approach), but that every sample member can be placed on a scale of "resistance," or non-response likelihood, between 0 and 1. Zero means that the person would participate in any survey at any time and under any circumstances, while 1 means that the person would never participate in any survey regardless of the circumstances (Peress 2010, p. 1419). Among the respondents, there are respondents with lower response probabilities and respondents with higher response probabilities, and also among the non-respondents there are sample members with lower and higher response probabilities. There are even non-respondents with a lower resistance value than some respondents, because situational or interviewer characteristics (age of the interviewer, weather or time of day) prevented their participation in this survey. This leads to a certain overlap on the continuum of resistance between the non-response probabilities between respondents and non-respondents. This is illustrated in Figure 14.2.

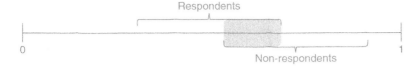

Figure 14.2 The continuum of resistance.
Source: own illustration adapted from Peress 2010.

Next, we assume that respondents with a high resistance (i.e. low response propensity) score are similar to non-respondents and that we can therefore "infer the variables of interest for the non-respondents by extrapolating from the low-propensity respondents" (ibid). This means that, in order to make this theory usable for our research question, we have to estimate the response propensities for *all* sample members first before we can analyse if the propensities of the *actual respondents* influence their answers to the attitude in question. For better understanding of the theoretical assumptions of our study, we would like to summarize them very briefly:

- *Assumption 1: There* is *a continuum of resistance and we can estimate* appropriate *response propensities for both respondents and non-respondents.*
- *Assumption 2: We can* infer *the variables of interest for the non-respondents by* extrapolating *from the low-propensity respondents.*

Data and methods

We will first describe the round of the ESS we use, which countries we will analyse and how our dependent variable is constructed (Section 3.1). In Section 3.2, we will describe our modelling approach. Since this approach consists of two separate steps, Section 3.2 is split into two subsections: one for the response propensity model (Section 3.2.1) and one for the poverty attitudes model (Section 3.2.2).

Data and dependent variable

We will exploit round 6^2 of the German and Irish European Social Survey data. For the response propensity model, we will use contact protocol and interviewer data. For the attitude model, we will use the interview data.[3]

Our dependent variable is question "E13"[4]: "And still thinking generally rather than about [country], how important do you think it is for democracy in general... that the government protects all citizens against poverty?" The categories supplied range from "not at all important for democracy in general" (1) to "extremely important for democracy in general" (10). For analytic purposes, we will treat this scale as a continuous variable even though it technically is a categorical one. We do not use any imputational methods for item non-response (INR), which means that every case with INR on question E13 (42 in Ireland and 17 in Germany) is excluded from our analyses.[5]

Methods

We first estimate response propensities for both respondents and non-respondents by using a multi-level logistic regression model with "participation in the European Social Survey" as a dependent variable. This variable is 1 when a sample member participates and 0 when a sample member does not participate. We estimate different models for both countries, since we assume different response mechanisms in both countries (see Section 3.2.1). Then we match the response probabilities *of the respondents only* to the interview data. We estimate our dependent variable (question E13) by using the response probability as a regressor variable. When this regressor is significant, we can assume that non-respondents' attitudes are different from respondents' attitudes and that the missing data mechanism is at least MAR; (see Section 1). When this regressor is still significant after including a certain set of control variables, we can assume that the missing data mechanism is MNAR and that the non-response bias cannot be corrected by weighting.

Estimating response propensities

We estimate different models for Ireland and Germany since we expect different response mechanisms in both countries. We think that this is the case because both countries have very different response rates (calculated by American Association for Public Opinion Research [AAPOR] standard definitions – AAPOR 2011 – these are 33.9 per cent in Germany compared to 66.3 per cent[6] in Ireland) and because these two countries have different sample designs: In Germany there is an individual person register sample (PRS) and in Ireland there is an address/household register sample (ARS) (ESS 6 Documentation report 2014). It has been shown that different sample designs can be linked to different interviewer behaviour in the European Social Survey, that is, that interviewers in countries with PRS designs are less likely to substitute the target person within a particular household (Menold 2014). It has also been found that there are differences between countries in contacting and cooperation processes, which can only partly be explained by interviewer characteristics (Blom et al. 2011). Between Ireland and Germany, it can be shown that the number of contacts has opposing effects on response likelihood. In Ireland, the response probability for each sample cases *decreases* with additional contacts, while the response probability *increases* for German sample members. We suspect that we are dealing with different doorstep behaviours, which might be the result of different sampling procedures. However, without additional information on interviewer behaviour, this is pure conjecture and further investigation is needed.

We excluded any cases from the analyses that are ineligible by AAPOR standard definitions (AAPOR 2011), e.g. if sample members moved abroad or if the respondent passed away. We also excluded any cases where we found missing values in any independent variable, which led us to 7.847 cases within 185 interviewers[7] in Germany and 3.951 cases within 115 interviewers in Ireland.[8]

We only included independent variables in the response models that were available for both Ireland and Germany,[9] so we could compare the coefficients of both models. These are the number of contacts; the month of the first contact; whether a house is a single-unit home, a multi-unit home or a farm building; if there is an entry phone or a locked gate; the amount of litter or vandalism in the immediate area; and characteristics of the interviewer who established the first contact (age and gender).

The coefficients are estimated with multilevel binary logistic regression models (Hox 2010), because the sample members are clustered within interviewers who established the first contact. Firstly, we estimated an intercept-only model to estimate the contribution of interviewers to respondent participation in the ESS within each country. Secondly, we added individual-level information to this model to see how much of the interviewer information can be explained by composition effects. Thirdly, we added interviewer characteristics in order to explain interviewer variances by their respective age and gender.

Since we expect that the response rates for individual interviewers vary, we included random intercepts. But since we do not expect that different interviewers contribute to different coefficient *slopes*, we did not include random effects for the individual-level variables. Thus, the full response model is a random intercept and fixed slopes binary logistic regression model (Hox 2010).

Estimating the attitude towards governmental protection against poverty

We specified a multiple linear regression model with ordinary least square (OLS) estimators. The answer to the attitudinal question E13 (see above) was our dependent variable. We built the model stepwise (four steps), but in every step we only included cases of the full model. Since we excluded any missing values from our analysis, this led us to 2.365 observations in Germany and 1.894 cases in Ireland. These are considerable deviations from the full samples (2.958 and 2.628, respectively). These deviations are the result of item non-response alone, of which household income non-response accounts for 389 cases in Germany and 693 in Ireland.[10]

In the first model, we introduced the response propensity from our response models as the one and only explanatory variable. Then, we included age and gender of the respondent, followed by level of education (EISCED) and position on a left–right scale. The full model also included deciles of the level of net household income (for analyses on attitudes towards poverty see Hall et al. 2014; Clery et al. 2013; Glatzer and Becker 2009).

Results

By analogy with Section 3, we first present the results of our multi-level response analysis (Section 4.1), because the results of these estimations – the response propensities of the respondents – are required for our subsequent modelling of attitudes towards governmental protection against poverty (Section 4.2).

(Non-)response analysis

The modelling coefficients are presented in Table 14.1. Results of the German model are presented in the first three columns and results from the Irish data in columns four to six.

Firstly, we can compare the explanatory power of both models. The deviance statistic as presented in the last row of Table 14.1 is much lower in the Irish model than in the German model. This holds for the intercept-only model as well as both subsequent models. For the intercept-only model, this means that random intercepts for the interviewers explain the different response propensities of sample members much better in Ireland than in Germany. However, we cannot attribute this explanatory power to the interviewers alone because we are not able to disentangle interviewers and areas in this survey (Schnell and Kreuter 2005). Also, the deviance reduction from Model 1 compared to Model 2 is much larger in the Irish than in the German model, which indicates that the introduction of explanatory variables at the individual level can explain the different response propensities better for the Irish than for the German data. This seems to be mainly the result of the number of contacts, the month of the first contact and the existence of an entry phone.

Secondly, we can compare the variance of random interviewer intercepts. As expected by the deviance statistic in the first models, the interviewer variance (i.e. the performance of interviewers in establishing interviews) is much larger in Ireland than in Germany (0.14 to 1.34, respectively). This means that in Ireland, the performances of interviewers vary much more than in Germany. However, as discussed above, this might be accounted for by area and composition effects, for example, if many interviewers have been assigned only "hard cases" and other interviewers have been assigned many sample members who are easily contacted and willing to cooperate. If this is the case, interviewer variances should diminish when area and sample member characteristics are included as in Model 2. But, as we can see, the variance of random intercepts decreases only slightly in Ireland and in Germany it even *in*creases a little. This means that the performance of German interviewers varies even more if area and sample characteristics are accounted for. In Model 3, we can clearly see that the inclusion of interviewer characteristics cannot explain the variance of interviewers, which is in line with recent research on interviewer effects: differences in interviewer performance can be explained by their respective doorstep behaviours, experience and expectations but not by their socio-demographical characteristics (Hox and de Leeuw 2002, p. 103; Olson and Peytchev 2007; Jäckle et al. 2013). The different interviewer "performances" can be seen in the residual plots, Figure 14.3 (Germany) and Figure 14.4 (Ireland). The interviewers are sorted by their deviation from the fixed intercept (their residuals); that is, interviewers on the left achieved a low response rate (after controlling for individual and interviewer level characteristics) (e.g. Pickery and Loosveldt 2004, p. 83f.). The 95 per cent confidence intervals of the random intercepts are marked so that we can see which interviewers are clearly different from the average interviewer. If the upper bound of the interval of an

Table 14.1 (Non)response modelling coefficients

	Germany			Ireland		
	Model 1	Model 2	Model 3	Model 1	Model 2	Model 3
(Intercept)	−0.63 ***	−1.40 ***	−1.40 ***	0.89 ***	5.89 ***	6.16 ***
log (contacts)		0.58 ***	0.58 ***		−3.34 ***	−3.34 ***
1st cont.: November		−0.09	−0.09		−0.84 *	−0.84 *
1st cont.: December or later		−0.35 .	−0.35 .		−1.93 ***	−1.93 ***
House: Single–unit		0.33 ***	0.33 ***		−0.42 *	−0.42 *
House: Farm		0.50 ***	0.50 ***		−0.07	−0.07
Condition: Good		0.13 *	0.13 *		−0.05	−0.05
Condition: Very good		0.35 ***	0.35 ***		−0.00	−0.00
Entry phone or locked gate		−0.19 **	−0.19 **		−0.92 ***	−0.92 ***
No litter or vandalism		−0.01	−0.01		0.03	0.02
Age of interviewer			0.00			−0.00
Gender of interviewer female			0.03			−0.06
Variance of random intercept	0.14	0.17	0.17	1.34	1.30	1.30
N (observations)	7847	7847	7847	3951	3951	3951
N (interviewers)	185	185	185	115	115	115
Deviance	10133.9	9785.3	9785.2	4508.1	2941.9	2941.8

Source: ESS 6, own calculations.
Notes: ***p < 0.01, **p < 0.05, *p < 0.1.

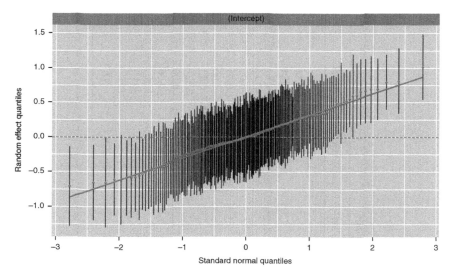

Figure 14.3 Interviewer performance in Germany.
Source: ESS 6, own calculations.

interviewer with a low response rate is below zero or if the lower bound of an interviewer with a high response rate is above zero, we can safely assume that these interviewers perform differently from the average interviewer. As we can clearly see, there are many more such "exceptional" interviewers in Ireland than in Germany. This was expected from the modelling coefficients.

Thirdly, we can compare the coefficient slopes. As stated in Section 3, the effect of the number of contacts is positive in Germany and negative in Ireland. However, the effect is very strong in Ireland, which means that in Ireland a sample member either cooperates very early or a sample member does not cooperate at all. It seems that in Germany, an interviewer needs a certain amount of contacts to make appointments, to find the right target person or to build trust. The strong effect of early contacts in Ireland is also affirmed by the effect of the month of first contact: when target persons are contacted in later months, that is, December or later, it is more difficult for interviewers to gain interviews. However, the reason for this effect could also be that interviewers contact the households they *assume* to be the most resistant at a later stage. The type of house and its overall condition is more important in Germany than in Ireland when response is considered. This could be attributed to the sample design. The existence of an entry phone or a locked gate has a negative effect in Ireland as well as in Germany.

Analysis of reluctant respondents' attitudes

The linear regression models are built step-wise. As in the response models, separate models are estimated for Germany and Ireland. In the first model, the

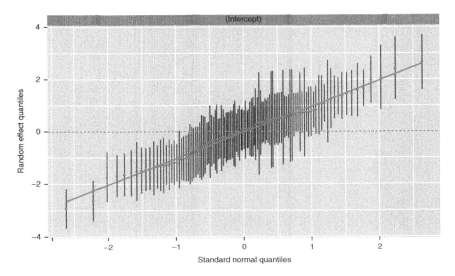

Figure 14.4 Interviewer performance in Ireland.
Source: ESS 6, own calculations.

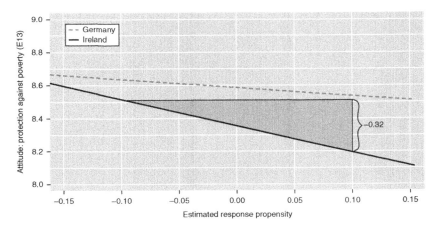

Figure 14.5 The link between response propensity and attitudes towards poverty (full model).
Source: ESS 6, own calculations.

response propensity is the only explanatory variable.[11] In the subsequent models, age and gender, level of education, position on a left–right scale and the household income are included.

In the first model, the response propensity is statistically different from zero in both models with coefficients of −0.89 in the German model and with −1.73 in

Table 14.2 Modelling coefficients of attitudes towards governmental protection against poverty

	Germany					Ireland							
	Model 1		Model 2		Model 3	Model 4		Model 1		Model 2		Model 3	Model 4
(Intercept)	8.59	***	7.89	***	8.10 ***	8.18	***	8.35 ***	8.13 ***	7.46 ***	7.22 ***
Income: 2nd decile						0.10							0.23
Income: 3rd decile						0.09							0.56 ***
Income: 4th decile						0.09							0.44 *
Income: 5th decile						-0.03							0.60 **
Income: 6th decile						0.16							0.55 **
Income: 7th decile						0.02							0.72 **
Income: 8th decile						-0.22							0.59 *
Income: 9th decile						-0.37 .							0.58
Income: 10th decile						-0.65 **							0.47
Left–right scale					0.00	0.00					0.00 .	0.00 *
ES-ISCED II					0.08	0.13					0.09	0.02
ES-ISCED IIIb					0.10	0.16					0.36	0.20
ES-ISCED IIIa					-0.15	-0.09					0.49 **	0.30
ES-ISCED IV					-0.38	-0.27					0.41 *	0.21
ES-ISCED V1					-0.75 *	-0.59 .					0.82 ***	0.59 *
ES-ISCED V2					-0.87 **	-0.62 .					0.72 **	0.45 .
Age of respondent			0.01	***	0.01 ***	0.01	***			0.00	0.01 **	0.01 **
Gender of respondent			0.19	*	0.13	0.12				0.03	0.01	0.02
Response propensity	-0.89	*	-0.80	*	-0.82 *	-0.50		-1.73 ***	-1.76 ***	-1.64 ***	-1.58 ***
N (observations)	2365		2365		2365	2365		1894	1894	1894	1894
R²	0.00		0.02		0.05	0.06		0.03	0.03	0.04	0.05

Source: ESS 6, own calculations.
Notes: ***p < 0.01, **p < 0.05, *p < 0.1.

the Irish model. Since the response propensity ranges from zero to one, this means that for the Irish data the answer to our attitudinal question is 0.173 lower if the response propensity falls by 10 per cent. This result is illustrated in Figure 14.5 (calculated by the 4th model).

In the subsequent models, we see that the direction of the link between response propensity and attitude towards governmental protection against poverty stays the same in the samples for both countries (Table 14.2). However, the magnitude of this effect diminishes slightly. In the German model, after net household income is introduced, the response propensity coefficient is no longer significant, however still moderately large. This means that the link between response propensity and the attitude in question is partly explained by different income groups, so the missing data mechanism (for this particular dependent variable) is MAR rather than MNAR. However, the effect in the Irish model stays highly significant and is still pretty large after including several control variables. This missing data mechanism is most likely MNAR and will not be corrected by weighting with observable characteristics.

Conclusions

In our study, we analysed whether reluctant respondents' attitudes differ significantly from other respondents' attitudes. As an example, we used attitudes towards governmental protection against poverty as a dependent variable. Under the assumption that we can infer non-respondents' answers by extrapolating from respondents with lower response probabilities and under the assumption that we estimated these response probabilities correctly, we can conclude that non-respondents score higher on the attitudinal scale in focus; that is, the average population scores on this particular scale seem to be underestimated. The link between response propensities and attitudes is consistent in Germany and Ireland, although in the Irish model the effect was much stronger. Moreover, the effect could hardly be reduced and remained significant after including several control variables like age, gender, level of education, net household income and even the position on the left–right scale. This makes it difficult to correct this apparent non-response bias by measures of, for example, weighting.

However, this is a case study and there are clearly limitations to our approach. Firstly, we only analysed one particular variable.[12] In future research, more attitudes or groups of attitudinal variables must be examined. Also, theories must be developed in order to explain if and why, for example, certain political groups or people with particular sets of values do participate in surveys more often than others. Secondly, the response propensity models are case based; it would be possible to estimate a multi-level model with every single contact on the first level in order to estimate even more sophisticated response propensities. Thirdly, we just compared two countries. This analysis could be extended to three or more countries.[13] Lastly, random slopes in the response models could be tested; it is conceivable that certain interviewers perform better in dealing with an entry phone or with certain kinds of respondents. All in all, although we demonstrated some reliable results, we have to conclude with the remark that further research is needed.

Notes

1 In theory, there is also the notion of Missing Completely At Random (MCAR) (Schnell et al. 2011), which means that the missing data mechanism is independent of both observable and unobservable characteristics of the respondent. We assume that this mechanism does not occur in survey practice. Thus, we only analyse whether the mechanism leading to missing data is MNAR or MAR.
2 Version 2.1.
3 The SPSS data files "ESS6CFe02.sav", "ESS6INTe02_1.sav" and "ESS6e02_1.sav".
4 In the SPSS data file, this is variable GVCTZPV.
5 As can be seen in Section 3.2, the same holds true for item non-response for the independent variables.
6 The response rates reported in this paper are somewhat different from the response rates documented in the ESS 6 report (33.8 per cent and 67.94 per cent, respectively). This difference might be the results of two different reasons: First, invalid interviews were excluded from the response analysis altogether. However, there are only a small number of invalid interviews. Secondly, the value labels of the variables from the .sav datafile used for calculating the response rates (interval and outnic1 – outnic12) are not identical to the categories used in the ESS 6 documentation. For example, there is no value label for "Address not occupied (not occupied, demolished, not yet built)" (response code N), which holds for 438 Irish cases.
7 Only the interviewer of the first contact is included in this analysis.
8 As for the response rates, the number of cases is not fully identical with the ESS 6 documentation for the same reasons.
9 Because of the different sample designs, this means that we cannot use age and gender of the target person as independent variables in our models, because in Ireland there is only information on households rather than individuals.
10 The dataset allows the distinction between "Don't Know" and "Refusal" item non-response. For each country, ~40 per cent of household income item non-response is "Don't Know" non-response. However, it might be suggested that many "Don't Know" responses are refusals. For disentangling different item non-response categories see Schräpler (2000).
11 We have tested different transformations of the response propensity. However, including it untransformed had the most explanatory power.
12 However, we have tested different attitudinal variables on a bivariate level and there seems to be a general link between response propensities and attitudes.
13 However, for this kind of exploratory study we considered an analysis of only two countries to be much clearer as a starting point for further research.

References

American Association for Public Opinion Research (2011). *Standard Definitions. Final Dispositions of Case Codes and Outcome Rate for Survey*. Revisited Version 2011.

Blom, A., De Leeuw, E. D. and Hox, J. J. (2011). Interviewer effects in the European Social Survey, *Journal of Official Statistics*, 27(2), 359–377.

Clery, E., Lee, L. and Kunz, S. (2013). *Public Attitudes to Poverty and Welfare, 1983–2011. Analysis Using British Social Attitudes Data*, Joseph Rowntree Foundation.

Couper, M. (1998). Measuring survey quality in a CASIC environment. *Proceedings of the Section on Survey Research Methods of the American Statistical Association*.

Glatzer, W. and Becker, J. (2009). *Armut und Reichtumg in Deutschland. Einstellungsmuster der Bevölkerung*, Johann Wolfgang Goethe Universität, Frankfurt.
Hall, S., Leary, K. and Greevy, H. (2014). *Public Attitudes to Poverty*. Joseph Rowntree Foundation.
Hox, J. J. (2010). *Multilevel Analysis*, 2nd edition, Routledge, New York.
Hox, J. J. and De Leeuw, E. D. (2002). The influence of interviewers' attitudes and behavior on household survey nonresponse: An international comparison. In Groves, R. R. M., Dillman, D. A., Eltinge, J. L. and Little, R. J. (eds.), *Survey Nonresponse*, Wiley, New York, 103–120.
Jäckle, A., Lynn, P., Sinibaldi, J. and Tipping, S. (2013). The effect of interviewer experience, attitudes, personality and skills on respondent co-operation with face-to-face surveys. *Survey Research Methods*, 7(1), 1–15.
Menold, N. (2014). The influence of sampling method and interviewers on sample realization in the European Social Survey. *Survey Methodology*, 40(1), 105–123.
Olson, K. (2013). Paradata for nonresponse adjustment. University of Nebraska Sociology Department, *Faculty Publications 203*, Lincoln.
Olson, K. and Peytchev, A. (2007). Effect of interviewer experience on interview pace and interviewer attitudes. University of Nebraska Sociology Department, *Faculty Publications 20*, Lincoln.
Peress, M. (2010). Correcting for survey nonresponse using variable response propensity, *Journal of the American Statistical Association*, 105(492), 1418–1430.
Pickery, J. and Loosveldt, G. (2004). A simultaneous analysis of interviewer effects on various data quality indicators with identification of exceptional interviewers, *Journal of Official Statistics*, 20(1), 77–89.
Rao, K. and Pennington, J. (2013). Should the third reminder be sent? The role of survey response timing on web survey results, International *Journal of Market Research* 55(5), 651–674.
Schafer, J. L. and Graham, J. W. (2002). Missing data. *Our view of the state of the art, Psychological methods*, 7(2), 147–177.
Schnell, R. (1997). *Nonresponse in Bevölkerungsumfragen. Ausmaß, Entwicklung und Ursachen*, Leske + Budrich, Opladen. [in German]
Schnell, R., Hill, P. B. and Esser, E. (2011). *Methoden der empirischen Sozialforschung*, 9th edition, Oldenbourg, München. [in German]
Schnell, R. and Kreuter, F. (2005). Separating interviewer and sampling-point effects, *Journal of Official Statistics,* 21(3), 389–410.
Schräpler, J. (2000). Was kann man am Beispiel des SOEP bezüglich Nonresponse lernen? *ZUMA-Nachrichten* 46, 117–150. [in German]
Spitzmüller, C., Glenn, D. M., Sutton, M., Barr, C. D. and Rogelberg, S. G. (2007). Survey nonrespondents as bad soldiers. Examining the relationship between organizational citizenship and survey response behaviour. *International Journal of Selection and Assessment*, 15(4), 449–459.
Stinchcombe, A. L., Jones, C. and Sheatsley, P. (1981). Nonresponse bias for attitude questions, *Public Opinion Quarterly*, 45(3), 359–375.

15 Combining Multiple Datasets for Simultaneous Analysis on the Basis of Common Identifiers

A Case Study from the European Social Survey and the European Values Study

Brendan Halpin and Michael J. Breen

The problem

We are often faced with the problem of having information (variables) in one large-scale high-quality survey that we want to relate to information not collected in that survey but present in others. This paper explores the question of how well we can combine information from multiple survey datasets to make joint inferences. An early example would be the combination of data on domestic work time (collected in time-use surveys) with good information on household income (collected in household budget surveys) to generate a better estimate of household resources (Gershuny and Halpin 1996).

This problem is in principle amenable to matching or imputation if the two (or more) datasets contain sufficient overlap in variables. Matching and imputation are closely related but conceptually distinct. Matching combines cases from one dataset with very similar cases in the other, based on the common variables, and analyses the synthetic cases. Model-based imputation creates synthetic cases by fitting a predictive (e.g. regression) model in one dataset and using it to predict in the other. Depending on how matching is done, it can be considered as non-parametric imputation. We can thus harness two existing technologies, well-developed for related problems, to this task. These are multiple imputation (MI) (which is normally concerned with imputing missing values in a single dataset) and propensity score (PS) matching (which is normally concerned with matching treated cases with controls). PS matching is in effect imputing a missing (properly, unobservable) variable, that is, what the outcome would have been for the treated cases had they not been treated (the "counterfactual" outcome).

Multiple imputation and matching

It is now well known that single synthetic cases understate variation, even if unbiased, and yield invalid inferences. Donald Rubin (with colleagues) has demonstrated that if a relatively small number of imputations are drawn from the predicted distribution – "multiple imputations" – the results of analysis on the multiple synthetic cases can be combined to yield efficient unbiased inferences

(Rubin 1987). Rubin is also behind PS matching, which solves the problem of matching on many variables by estimating a logit or probit model that predicts whether the observation was "treated" and matches cases (treated) with controls (not treated) which have very similar predicted probability of being treated (Rosenbaum and Rubin 1985). There is a very large programme-evaluation literature in economics using matching (Heckman et al. 1998). PS matching has been used in Ireland on topics such as the effect of active labour market policies (Halpin and Hill 2008), and the effect of family structure on child outcomes (Hannan and Halpin 2014). Other forms of matching seem promising, including King's Coarsened Exact Matching (CEM) (Iacus et al. 2011).

MI and PS matching are typically oriented to a single dataset, but we can extend them to two relatively easily. If dataset 1 has variables $(X, Z1)$ and dataset 2 has $(X, Z2)$, our problem can be described as wanting to use $Z2$ to predict $z \in Z1$. If we combine the datasets, $Z2$ is missing where z is observed. We can proceed by MI, imputing z where it is missing, doing multiple replications of the imputation. This is similar to the normal use of MI, with the exception that usually $Z2$ is not missing in all cases where z is observed. The second important difference is that usually all the data are collected in a single exercise. If we proceed by matching, we assign one dataset as "treated" and match multiple controls to each observation in it. PS matching involves using the common variables X to "predict" membership of the treated group, and matching is done to match controls to cases with very similar probabilities of being "treated." If the distribution of the X variables is not systematically different across the two datasets, the prediction model will not be very discriminating, but the matched cases will be very similar in X. Other methods of matching that do not focus directly on treatment status may also function well. CEM, for example, works by automatically grouping variables and matching within the cells of the cross-classification of the groups. The coarsening in CEM and the use of the predictive model are ways of simplifying the problem of matching on many variables – using more variables is better, but it makes it hard to identify a close match.

One of the strengths of MI is in its methods for analysing the imputed data. For each imputation, we do a single analysis and then effectively average across the results (Rubin 1987). A lot of Rubin's success lies in showing that the averaged result is unbiased, subject to assumptions.

Drawbacks

Neither matching nor imputation cope with unobserved heterogeneity, that is, differences between the observed and missing cases that are not captured by the X variables. Similarly, experience is in using them within datasets and not so much across datasets. Working across datasets gives a strong source of unobserved heterogeneity (different practices, sampling, accidents of survey practice, etc.), and further one that is perfectly aligned with "missingness." Good matching or imputation depends on good variables, so the overlap has to be good, both in the range of variables and in their detailed definition. Identifying and preparing the variables and developing good matching or imputation models will be labour intensive.

Below we report on a trial using MI to combine data from two large multi-national European surveys.

Background to the current study

The authors are involved with multiple European partners in a large-scale project that aims to create a system that allows innovative, high-quality comparative simultaneous analyses of existing social science datasets. Among the objectives of that project are the evaluation and re-consideration of the theoretical and methodological issues and the identification of existing datasets and their "fitness-for-purpose" for simultaneous analysis. This paper is part of the work in examining the feasibility of engaging in high-quality, comparative, simultaneous analysis of existing datasets and uses the European Social Survey (ESS)[1] and the European Values Study (EVS)[2] as exemplars. The ESS is an academically driven cross-national survey that has been conducted every two years across Europe since 2001, measuring the attitudes, beliefs and behaviour patterns of diverse populations in more than 30 nations. The EVS, initiated in 1981, is a large-scale, cross-national and longitudinal survey research program on basic human values that aims to provide insights into the ideas, beliefs, preferences, attitudes, values and opinions of citizens all over Europe – a unique research project on how Europeans think about life, family, work, religion, politics and society.

Case study

The ESS and EVS share certain questions in the area of religiosity. This allows us to use the datasets as a test bed, in which we can both impute missing data and combine data for comparative purposes. Consider Survey #1, which has variables A, B, C and D, which are of interest; and Survey #2, which has A, B, E and F. A and B are identical. Can we relate C and D to E and F through A and B? Can we test imputed values against actual values? In this case study, C is identical to E and D is identical to F. We can compare the outcomes of C directly against E or C+ against E+ where C+ and E+ contain the imputed missing values. Likewise, we can compare the outcomes of D directly against F or D+ against F+ where D+ and F+ contain the imputed missing values.

The data from EVS Round 4 and ESS Round 4 were used, as the two surveys were conducted in 2008. The exercise is limited to the Irish data for both surveys. The EVS has 1013 cases and the ESS has 1764.

In a real exercise, we would be attempting to relate variables observed in only one dataset (i.e. C and D) to variables observed only in the other (i.e. E and F). In this test, we impute values of variables that are actually observed in both sets in order to compare imputed values with real values.

Variables and imputation models

Two religiosity variables in each dataset were recoded to match identically: frequency of attendance at church (ESS_Attend and EVS_Attend) and frequency of prayer

(ESS_Pray and EVS_Pray). The age, sex and years of education variables were matched and combined between the datasets and three new common variables were created: COMBO_Age, COMBO_Sex and COMBO_Edu. This creates a framework where we can impute the missing values of, say, ESS_Attend and compare it with the observed EVS_Attend data. We can impute similarly for ESS_Pray, and also in the opposite direction, that is, impute missing EVS values to compare with ESS observations. In what follows, we do this for the Attend and Pray variables, imputing the missing observations of the ESS variables in the EVS data, since the ESS sample size is larger (results imputing in the opposite direction are broadly similar).

We are thus imputing a religious behaviour variable (or rather, two variables in two parallel exercises) on the basis of a small number of demographic variables (age, sex and education). In practice, it would be necessary to use a much larger pool of variables to generate imputations valid for further analysis, but we work with this limited set for the present exercise. Focusing on imputing a single variable at a time also allows us to use univariate imputation, which is conceptually the simplest version.

The imputed variables are both ordinal. This means we have a choice of approaches to their imputation. While imputation based on a multivariate normal error structure (implying a linear regression imputation model) has the most extensive theoretical support, it is known to produce poor imputations under certain circumstances when the underlying variable is not interval or ratio scale (Allison 2005; van Buuren 2007). However, imputation of ordinal and categorical variables is also well established and quite easy to do with current software. Hence in what follows, we compare imputations using linear, ordinal and nominal models.

As mentioned, we are working with a limited number of imputing variables. While it is desirable to have a wider range of variables, it is also often desirable in imputation to fit very flexible models, with non-linear effects and interactions, so we consider two formulations: a linear predictor of sex, age and education, and a predictor containing a sex by education interaction and a sex by quadratic (i.e. non-linear) age interaction. We used STATA to run the imputations using mi impute regress for the linear model, mi impute ologit for the ordinal model and mi impute mlogit for the nominal model.

Results

In the first pass, we impute frequency of religious attendance using demographic variables only. We generate 100 imputations for each specification, which is high by normal standards but ensures that the conclusions are less affected by random variation.

The first imputation model

We use three imputation models – linear regression, ordinal regression and multinomial regression – and two specifications of the variables. The linear approach is supposed to be robust and is conventionally used to impute ordinal variables by rounding a continuous prediction into the discrete categories. However, this procedure is known to be subject to problems under certain circumstances, and imputation models that deal directly with the categorical nature of the imputed variable are preferred. Given that the variables we are imputing are ordinal, there is good reason to believe the ordinal model would be appropriate, but the multinomial model could work well too, imputing the variable taking account of its categorical nature but without assuming it is ordinal. Similarly, we have a linear specification, where the imputing variables are included in a simple additive structure; and a non-linear specification, where age is given a quadratic form and where age and education are allowed to have separate male and female effects. *A priori*, imputation is likely to be better the less parsimonious it is, and the fewer assumptions it makes, so we might expect the non-linear multinomial format to perform better. To assess this, we have run the 100-imputation models ten times for each of the six combinations and examine the gamma statistic from the resulting table of observed and imputed values (i.e. comparing observed EVS values with values imputed using ESS information). This is reported in Table 15.1.

The gamma statistic is analogous to a correlation coefficient for ordinal variables. Here, the average value is about 0.22, which indicates a modest positive association between the imputed and observed data. Contrary to our expectation, the linear specification performs slightly better. The linear regression is, however, clearly the weakest of the three imputation models, but there is not a clear winner between the other two; treating the variable as ordinal versus nominal does not make a clear difference. If we repeat the exercise imputing frequency of prayer (not shown), the non-linear specification does slightly better, but the weakness of the linear regression imputation model is replicated.

We can get a better view of the adequacy of the imputation by cross-tabulating the imputed ESS attendance variable with the observed EVS variable, where cases are imputed. Table 15.2 reports this cross-tabulation, averaging across the 100 imputations, for the multi-nomial regression–based imputation and the non-linear form of the imputation specification. As we can see, the overall level of agreement between the imputed and observed data is less than perfect, with a high proportion of cases off the diagonal (this is entirely consistent with the gamma values

Table 15.1 Mean Gamma statistics, comparing imputed attendance to observed attendance

	Linear form	Non-linear form	Average
Multinomial	0.226	0.226	0.226
Ordinal	0.227	0.222	0.225
Linear regression	0.204	0.202	0.203
Average	0.219	0.217	0.218

Note: 10 runs of 100 imputations compared for each combination using demographic variables only.

Table 15.2 Imputed religious attendance from ESS data, compared with observed attendance from EVS data, demographic variables only

(ESS)	Weekly	Monthly	Less	Rare/Never	
	Imputed numbers of cases				
Weekly	227.3	44.0	86.6	44.1	402.0
Monthly	60.0	26.3	50.5	24.5	161.2
Less	96.7	40.2	95.2	43.2	275.2
Rare/Never	41.1	19.5	43.7	19.3	123.5
	425.0	130.0	276.0	131.0	962.0
	Pearson Residuals				
Weekly	3.7	−1.4	−2.7	−1.4	
Monthly	−1.3	1.0	0.6	0.5	
Less	−2.3	0.5	1.8	0.9	
Rare/Never	−1.8	0.7	1.4	0.6	

Note: Imputed using multinomial logit, with demographic variables only as predictors, with a non-linear form.

in Table 15.1). The second panel shows the Pearson residuals, which show that there is nonetheless good agreement with regard to weekly attendance. That is, the "demographic" variables of age, sex and education distinguish well between those who attend weekly and those who attend less frequently but not between the three categories of less than weekly attendance. The pattern resulting from imputing frequency of prayer is broadly similar (not shown).

Better models

The performance of the first approach is poor, but the information contained in the imputing variables (age, sex and education) is clearly insufficient to impute religious behaviour in any reliable way. Clearly, people of the same age, gender and educational level will differ greatly in religious behaviour. To carry out a reliable imputation, we would need rather more variables that capture a lot more social differentiation than we have available to us in this initial exercise. For instance, we would like to use marital status, number of children, employment status, region of residence, ethnicity, occupation, social class and so on, as well as measures of attitudes and behaviours, including the religious. However, in the absence of such a set of shared variables, we can at least use one of the two religious behaviour variables to improve the imputation of the other. In using variables that share much more variation with the imputed variable, we should be able to do rather better.

Table 15.3 cross-tabulates the imputed and observed variables using frequency of prayer in addition to the demographic variables to impute frequency of attendance. As we can see, this approach still yields many mis-matching cases, but as the Pearson residuals show, it is much better than the previous model: the off-diagonal cells have negative (or very small positive) residuals, and the diagonal residuals

Table 15.3 Imputed religious attendance from ESS data, compared with observed attendance from EVS data, using also frequency of prayer

(ESS)	Weekly	Monthly	Less	Rare/Never	
	Imputed numbers of cases				
Weekly	250.3	44.5	62.3	22.1	379.2
Monthly	65.4	29.5	46.1	13.7	154.7
Less	80.0	41.0	105.1	45.9	272.0
Rare/Never	23.4	12.9	46.4	46.3	129.1
	419.0	128.0	260.0	128.0	935.0
	Pearson Residuals				
Weekly	6.2	−1.0	−4.2	−4.1	
Monthly	−0.5	1.8	0.5	−1.6	
Less	−3.8	0.6	3.4	1.4	
Rare/Never	−4.5	−1.1	1.8	6.8	

Note: Imputed using multinomial logit, with demographic variables and frequency of prayer as predictors, with a non–linear form.

Table 15.4 Mean Gamma statistics, comparing imputed attendance to observed attendance, using frequency of prayer

	Linear form	Non-linear form	Average
Multinomial	0.496	0.489	0.493
Ordinal	0.485	0.489	0.487
Linear regression	0.464	0.464	0.464
Average	0.482	0.481	0.481

Note: 10 runs of 100 imputations compared for each combination, using demographic variables and frequency of prayer as predictors.

are substantially larger. There is rather more ability to distinguish between all four categories than in the first model. As Table 15.4 shows, the maximum gamma is almost 0.5 (for the multinomial model with the linear specification). If we impute instead the frequency of prayer, the maximum gamma is 0.6 (not shown). Thus, with the addition of a single domain-specific variable, the adequacy of the imputation has increased markedly. We can legitimately expect that the addition of more, relevant variables will further improve the imputation.

Conclusions

We have discussed ways to draw inferences about relationships between variables that are not observed in the same dataset. In the case of two datasets with some shared variables, but with key variables unique to each, we have proposed both matching and MI on the basis of shared variables to permit joint analysis of the unique variables. Of the two methods, we have explored MI in detail and leave matching for future work; both approaches are very similar in that they use the shared variables to create a synthetic dataset that brings the unique variables together.

Our exploration of the application of multiple imputation to the problem has exploited a test case where we impute a variable common to both datasets, thus permitting us to test the correspondence of the imputed values to the observed values. Though we worked with a very restricted set of shared imputing variables, we have shown that this imputations can be generated that show association with the observed data. However, the imputations we produced cannot be said to replicate the observed data well, particularly when we use only generic shared information (age, gender and education) to impute from. But once we include a single domain-specific imputing variable, the performance improves substantially. This promises that imputations carried out with extensive shared variables that have good association with the domain of the imputed variables will produce imputations whose distributions are good estimations of the true unobserved values. However, a lot of painstaking work needs to be done in creating as many variables as possible that match as well as possible, across the two datasets.

We have also considered the role of specification, both in terms of the imputing model (linear, ordinal or multinomial) and of the specification (without and with non-linear forms and interactions between the imputing variables). What emerges clearly is that imputations based on linear regression perform poorly, given our ordinal imputed variables. Across the various tests, there is no clear distinction in effectiveness between ordinal and multinomial forms or between linear and non-linear specifications.

This paper is intended to sketch out some possibilities for increasing the range of inferences that can be drawn from sample-survey datasets by combining datasets that share a good deal of information but have elements of non-overlapping coverage. We have demonstrated one potential route, which promises to provide good results where work is done to integrate the shared variables to the greatest possible degree. The results will never be as good as data where both of the variables of interest are collected together (both the uncertainties of imputation and the possibility of different design effects or other heterogeneity of the two surveys have a bearing on this), but where key variables are not available in the same survey, it permits analysis that would not be possible otherwise and facilitates fuller use of valuable data.

Notes

1   All ESS datasets and documents are open source and are available at www.europeansocialsurvey.org/.
2   All EVS datasets and documents are open source and are available at www.europeanvaluesstudy.eu/.

References

Allison, P. D. (2005). Imputation of categorical variables with PROC MI. In *SUGI 30 Proceedings 2005*, 1–14.

van Buuren, S. 2007. Multiple imputation of discrete and continuous data by fully conditional specification. *Statistical Methods in Medical Research*, 16(3), 219–242.

Gershuny, J. and Halpin, B. (1996). Time use, quality of life, and process benefits. In A. Offer (Ed.), *In Pursuit of the Quality of Life* (pp. 188–210). Oxford: OUP.

Halpin, B. and Hill, J. (2008). *Active Labour Market Programmes and Poverty Dynamics in Ireland*. Combat Poverty Agency. Dublin.

Hannan, C. and Halpin, B. (2014). The influence of family structure on child outcomes: evidence for Ireland. *The Economic and Social Review*, 45(1, Spring). Retrieved from www.esr.ie/article/view/106.

Heckman, J., Ichimura, H., Smith, J. and Todd, P. (1998). Characterizing selection bias using experimental data. *Econometrica*, 66(5), 1017–1098.

Iacus, S. M., King, G. and Porro, G. (2011). Multivariate matching methods that are monotonic imbalance bounding. *Journal of the American Statistical Association*, 106, 345–361.

Rosenbaum, P. R. and Rubin, D. B. (1985). Constructing a control group using multivariate matched sampling methods that incorporate the propensity score. *The American Statistician*, 39(1), 33–38. Retrieved from www.jstor.org/stable/2683903.

Rubin, D. (1987). *Multiple Imputation for Non-Response in Surveys*. New York: John Wiley and Sons.

16 Using Mixed Modes in Survey Research

Evidence from Six Experiments in the ESS

Ana Villar and Rory Fitzgerald

Introduction

Technological advances and increasing access to telephone and the internet mean that it is now possible for people to complete surveys by phone or online rather than face-to-face with an interviewer present. As budgets tighten and the benefits of using other modes (such as speed and flexibility) become more apparent, there has been a debate about whether it is better to use alternatives to face-to-face surveys either exclusively or in combination with in-person interviews. This chapter summarises findings from research conducted under the auspices of the European Social Survey (ESS) over the past 12 years to evaluate the potential effects of mixed-mode data collection on its own cross-national survey estimates.

The ESS is an academically driven cross-national survey that has been conducted every two years since 2001 across large parts of Europe. One of the main aims of the ESS is "to chart stability and change in social structure, conditions and attitudes in Europe" by analysing, combining and comparing data from different countries. In order to be able to ensure meaningful comparisons of survey estimates across countries, it was decided that essential survey conditions, such as mode of data collection, should be as similar as possible across participating countries (Jowell 1998), and that the high standards of scientific rigor would be implemented in all of them (Jowell et al. 2007).

Cross-national surveys like the ESS face challenges not usually encountered in national studies. To ensure data comparability across different countries, these surveys depend on a "principle of equivalence" (Jowell 1998). This principle relies on standardisation of all possible aspects of the survey process: sampling (Lynn et al. 2006), question wording (Harkness 2003; Harkness et al. 2010), response options and coding schema (Jowell et al. 2007), and so on. For this reason, the most ambitious multinational projects tend to require all participating countries to employ the same mode of data collection. In the case of the ESS, the exclusive mode for data collection in the main questionnaire is face-to-face interviewing.

Face-to-face interviewing has been recognised by many as the "gold standard" among data-collection methodologies. Research has shown that face-to-face surveys obtain higher response rates (de Leeuw 1992; Groves et al. 2004; Holbrook et al. 2003), largely because of the effectiveness of in-person contacts at persuading sampled individuals to take part. Face-to-face data collection can also improve data quality, partly because interviewers can help navigate the questionnaire, probe answers to ensure they are recorded correctly and motivate respondents when they feel fatigued. In addition, coverage and familiarity with different modes of data collection varies widely across European countries, whether because of survey traditions or because of differential access to technologies (such as internet or fixed-line telephone coverage). In-person interviewing reduces these gaps and facilitates consistency of survey implementation across countries, thus making it the best-possible single-mode data collection option for a rigorous cross-national survey, especially with the ESS current hour-long questionnaire. For additional details about the goals and initial setup of the ESS and the survey climate at the time, see Jäckle et al. (2006).

However, at the time the ESS was established, there were concerns that face-to-face data collection would not be optimal in all countries. Researchers in a few countries worried that a) an interviewer infrastructure did not exist to carry out large-scale face-to-face surveys, b) costs would be higher than feasible and/or c) participation would be lower or more biased than using a different mode of data collection, given the survey tradition in the country. These concerns were valid and important, but it was not clear from the evidence available how using different modes in different countries would affect survey estimates and data quality, especially in a cross-national context. Therefore, the Core Scientific Team (CST) of the ESS established a programme of methodological research to examine the impact of mixing data collection modes (within and between countries) on the overall quality of survey estimates. At the early stages of the research programme, the most likely alternative mode for the ESS was telephone interviewing, given that the length and complexity of the interview questioned the suitability of using postal self-completion surveys and that large proportions of the population did not have internet access. Thus, the first studies focused on evaluating the suitability of telephone interviews in the ESS. As internet penetration increased across Europe over the life of the ESS mixed-mode research programme, however, attention to the web as an alternative mode has increased, and all studies since 2008 have included web data collection. This chapter summarises findings from the six studies carried out since 2003 under the ESS mixed-mode research programme to evaluate the effects of mixed-mode data collection on survey estimates.

The six studies

Six ESS studies on mixed-mode data collection have been conducted since 2003 (see Table 16.1 for an overview). Of these, three focused solely on assessing the effect of mode on measurement (Studies 1, 2 and 3). The other three investigated the feasibility and practical challenges of implementing different mode designs in cross-national surveys, where all sources of survey error were potentially affected by the mode design (Studies 4, 5 and 6[1]). In this section, we present an overview of the main essential survey features for each study.

Table 16.1 Overview of design characteristics for each study

Study 1: Measurement differences across four modes

Main goal	Mode measurement differences
Modes	F2F vs. Telephone vs Paper SAQ vs Web
Experimental manipulations	Within-respondent re-interview design (different modes)
Sample design	Convenience, hall test
Year	2003
Countries	Hungary

Study 2: Measurement differences: Finding the cause

Main goal	Mode measurement differences
Modes	F2F vs Telephone
Experimental manipulations	Compared questions adapted for telephone (F2F & phone) to standard ESS questions (F2F)
Sample design	Probabilistic, limited to countries[1] capitals
Year	2005
Countries	Hungary and Portugal

Study 3: Measurement differences: F2F vs web

Main goal	Mode measurement differences
Modes	F2F vs Web
Experimental manipulations	Within-respondent re-interview design (different modes)
Sample design	Subsample of ESS respondents
Year	2010
Countries	United Kingdom

Study 4: Feasibility of ESS telephone Interviews

Main goal	Feasibility of alternative mode: telephone
Modes	F2F (if fixed-line at home) vs Telephone
Experimental manipulations	Duration of the survey: 60 minutes vs. 45 minutes vs 30+30 minutes
Sample design	Probabilistic, sometimes different from ESS
Year	2006
Countries	Germany, Poland, Hungary, Cyprus, Switzerland

Study 5: Feasibility of mixed-mode designs: sequential vs concurrent

Main goal	Feasibility of mixed-mode designs
Modes	F2F vs Web-Telephone+F2F
Experimental manipulations	Sequential vs Concurrent mixed-mode designs
Sample design	Probabilistic, same as standard ESS
Year	2008
Countries	Netherlands

Study 6: Feasibility of mixed-mode designs across countries

Main goal	Feasibility of mixed-mode designs
Modes	F2F vs Web-F2F vs Telephone +F2F
Experimental manipulations	Sweden: F2F- Telephone vs Telephone +F2F UK: incentives, respondent selection method
Sample design	Probabilistic, same as standard ESS
Year	2012
Countries	Estonia, Sweden, United Kingdom

Study 1: Measurement differences across four modes. The first study focused on studying measurement differences in estimates by mode, comparing face-to-face interviews, telephone interviews, self-completion paper-and-pencil questionnaires and web-based self-completion questionnaires. The study took place in May and June 2003 in Hungary, where a convenience sample of participants were approached on the street and invited to participate in a "hall test." Those agreeing to take part were randomly assigned to one of the four modes of data collection. Participants were re-interviewed in a different randomly-assigned mode,[2] either 20 minutes later at the same venue or a few days later at home. Cooperation rates to the second interview for those completing at home were 73 per cent for telephone and 48 per cent for mailed questionnaires. All participants received the same 25 questions from the ESS and the Eurobarometer in both interviews, making it possible to examine differences in responses both between and within the same participants.

Study 2: Measurement differences: Finding the cause. The second study aimed to investigate the causes of measurement differences between telephone and face-to-face data collection observed in Study 1. The experiment was designed to isolate the effect of mode from the effect of question changes related to adaptation of the questionnaire for a different interview setting (i.e. a telephone interview). Three experimental groups were compared: (1) a group interviewed face-to-face using 44 ESS standard questions including showcards; (2) a group interviewed by telephone (fixed or mobile) using the same 44 questions, adapted for telephone implementation and without showcards; and (3) a group interviewed face-to-face using the 44 telephone-adapted questions without showcards.

Gallup Europe carried out the experiment using random samples from Hungary and Portugal starting in July 2005. Fieldwork was concentrated in Budapest and Lisbon, where suitable sampling frames were available that included telephone numbers *and* addresses, thereby holding error from sampling and coverage constant between modes. Respondents answered questions about their interview experience, and interviewers answered six questions to describe the respondents' engagement and effort during the interview process. The response rate was 32 per cent in both modes.

Study 3: Measurement differences: F2F versus web. This study intended to evaluate measurement differences between face-to-face and web data collection, using a within respondent re-interview design. The goal was to evaluate how open-ended questions, complex questions and seemingly mode-sensitive questions compared across the two modes. The study was carried out in two waves: the first wave was the main stage of Round 5 of the ESS in the United Kingdom (September–November 2010), and the second was a follow-up web survey of a subsample of the same face-to-face respondents (October 2010–January 2011). The sampling design for the face-to-face stage was a clustered, stratified, three-stage random probability design using a frame of addresses. At the end of the interview, UK ESS respondents were invited to participate later on in a web survey; the survey included a subset of 32 of the questions they had answered during the face-to-face interview. Of all respondents invited to the follow-up study,[3] 43 per cent said they were willing to be contacted. Invitations were sent about three weeks after the face-to-face interview to 927 respondents, of whom 613 completed the web survey, for a completion rate of 66 per cent and a cumulative response rate (Callegaro and DiSogra 2008) of 29 per cent. Comparisons between responses given to the face-to-face interview and web survey by the same respondents can provide insights about measurement differences across the two modes. There was, however, no face-to-face control group due to limited funding availability. In addition to the implications for mode differences in measurement, this study is relevant to the current ESS pilot to establish a cross-national probability based panel as part of the Synergies for Europe's Research Infrastructures in the Social Sciences (SERISS) project (see www.seriss.eu).

Study 4: Feasibility of ESS telephone interviews. In 2006, a study was designed to examine a) the practical challenges and feasibility of using telephone as a mode of data collection in the ESS and b) the effect of inviting respondents to participate in telephone interviews of different lengths on their willingness to participate in the survey. It was the first study to implement the full ESS interview in an alternative mode. Sample members, selected using probability sampling methods, were randomly assigned to one of three treatment groups, which varied according to the length and design of the questionnaire: (A) 60 minutes, (B) 45 minutes, and (C) 30 minutes (and a further 30-minute interview offered at the end of the first 30 minutes). The target population in the telephone samples were households with fixed-line telephones; for this reason, all analyses comparing the telephone and face-to-face samples in Study 4 excluded respondents from the standard ESS who did not have a fixed-line at home. Response rates varied widely across different countries and interview lengths (see Section 4.1 on outcome rates). The experiment was carried out in five countries: Cyprus, Germany, Hungary, Poland and Switzerland. The selection of countries was based on pragmatic considerations and the available budget, but within those constraints, countries with divergent traditions of survey practice and facing different challenges in their data collection efforts were chosen. Countries were encouraged to use fieldwork procedures as similar as possible to the standard ESS in their countries, but some features varied due to budget constraints (e.g. incentives, pre-notification letters).

Study 5: Feasibility of mixed-mode designs: sequential versus concurrent. Study 5 also intended to investigate the feasibility of alternative mode designs, including for the first time the web mode as a way to increase cost efficiency. The study was conducted in the Netherlands in 2008, parallel to Round 4 of the standard ESS, and it was the first ESS study to use within-country, across respondents mixed-mode data collection. A random sample of 2500 addresses was selected, using the same postal sample frame and probability-based design as in the standard Dutch ESS. The sample of addresses was matched with information about the name and telephone number of people living at the address for 70 per cent of the sampled units using a commercial database. The sample for which a telephone number was available was then randomly allocated to one of the two mixed-mode designs: a "concurrent" design, where respondents were contacted by telephone and offered three modes to choose from; and a "sequential" design, where respondents first received a telephone request to complete the survey using the web (without mention of other modes if they had internet access). Those who had not completed the survey after a certain period were offered a telephone interview or, finally, a face-to-face interview. For addresses for which telephone contact was not available, the design was different: an interviewer visited the household and offered an in-person interview; those who refused were invited during the same visit to complete a web survey.

Study 6: Feasibility of mixed-mode designs across countries. In this study, countries were invited to select the ideal mixed-mode design given the country's survey environment. The Estonian experiment compared the standard ESS survey to a sample of 1050 units selected from the same population register from which the main ESS sample was drawn. An invitation was mailed to each sample unit (named individual) asking them to participate in the ESS by completing a web survey. An interviewer visited those who did not complete the web survey after two reminders, to try to complete a face-to-face interview. Similarly, the United Kingdom tested a mixed-mode data collection design where invitations to a web survey were mailed to a random sample of UK addresses; if no response was obtained from the address after one reminder, an interviewer visited the selected address and tried to complete a face-to-face interview.[4] However, the United Kingdom lacks a sample frame of individuals, so additional procedures were implemented to try and randomly select a household member by enclosing instructions for a household member to carry out the selection. The UK experiment compared the main ESS survey of about 4500 respondents to a sample of 2000 households selected from the same address sample frame from which the main ESS sample was drawn.

The Swedish experiments compared the main ESS survey to two samples of 300 respondents selected from the same population register from which the main ESS sample was drawn. The proposal focused on the comparison of two mixed-mode designs: (a) a *sequential, response-enhancing design* where individuals who refused to make an appointment for an in-person interview would be re-contacted and offered the possibility of completing it over the telephone and (b) a *sequential, cost-effective design* where sampled individuals were first offered to respond to a telephone survey, and those who refused were re-contacted by telephone and invited to make an appointment for an in-person interview.

Sampling and coverage in the ESS mixed-mode studies

When survey programmes consider new designs of data collection, this may have consequences for their sampling procedures. In this section, we consider the implications of different mode designs for sampling frames, sampling designs and fieldwork procedures. The measurement studies in general did not involve large-scale probability-based sampling; therefore, this section focuses on the feasibility studies (Studies 4 through 6).

Survey sampling involves defining a target population and deciding on an approach (the sampling design) to randomly select the final units of research from a list of units (the sample frame). As with the standard ESS, sample designs were allowed to vary cross-nationally (see Table 16.2. for an overview), depending on the availability and quality of sampling frames in each country (Lynn et al. 2007)

Table 16.2 Overview of design characteristics for each study: sampling

	Year	Location	Sample design	Sampling frame	Realised sample size
Study 1	2003	Hungary	Convenience sample	Street recruitment	1,987 respondents. Interviews: 402 web 1,109 F2F, 1,189 Telephone 1,259 Paper self-administered
Study 2	2005	Budapest/Lisbon	Simple random sample	Database with telephones and addresses	515 F2F with showcards 518 F2F without showcards 887 Telephone
Study 3	2010	United Kingdom	All UK ESS Round 5 respondents who were interviewed before 11 November 2010 were invited	ESS respondents	2,422 ESS 613 Web
Study 4*	2006	Cyprus, Germany, Hungary, Poland, Switzerland	Random sample (varied)	RDD, population register + matched telephone data	Cyprus: 918 ESS, 83 Telephone Germany: 2,663 ESS; 369 Telephone Hungary: 855 ESS; 252 Telephone Poland: 1,218 ESS; 339 Telephone Switzerland: 1,776 ESS; 342 Telephone
Study 5	2008	The Netherlands	Systematic sampling of households, last birthday method for respondents	Population register + matched telephone data	1,778 ESS 198 Web 123 Telephone 187 F2F
Study 6	2012	Sweden, Estonia, United Kingdom	For each country, same as in ESS Round 6	For each country, same as in ESS Round 6	Estonia: 2,380 ESS; 356 Web, 230 F2F UK: 2,286 ESS; 389 Web, 64 F2F Sweden: 1,847 ESS; 185 phone, 187 F2F

Note: *ESS sample sizes in study 4 represent respondents with fixed telephone lines at home.

but this "flexibility assumes probability selection methods: known probabilities of selection for all population elements" (Kish 1994, p. 173). In Section 3.1, we discuss the sampling frames used in the three feasibility studies, and we evaluate challenges faced and solutions applied in the context of conducting these studies. In Section 3.2, two self-administered approaches to within-household random selection of respondents are compared, addressing one of the biggest obstacles for surveying the general population when sampling frames of individuals are not available and an interviewer is not present.

Sampling frames and sampling designs

The use of different modes for data collection can affect the choice of sample frame and sample design. For simplicity, one could choose sample frames with contact information best suited for the mode of data collection: addresses for in-person and mail surveys, telephone numbers for telephone surveys and email addresses for online surveys. However, such sampling frames are not always available or do not have adequate quality, especially when conducting surveys among the general population. Telephone lists often suffer from under-coverage problems – excluding certain parts of the population – as well as over-coverage problems when members of the population can be linked to more than one telephone number. Email lists are hardly available. Therefore, researchers often face the decision of choosing between a high-quality frame that does not contain contact information for the desired mode of data collection and a lower quality frame with the contact details.

Choosing the sampling frame with the highest quality might mean changing mode from recruitment stages to the actual data collection. For example, in Study 6, the ESS used sampling frames containing addresses to recruit respondents for an online survey in Estonia and the United Kingdom. Given that these sampling frames did not include email addresses or other online contact information for population units, the invitation mode had to be different from the mode of data collection. In both countries, it was decided that a mailed invitation was the most cost-effective approach.

Study 4 – Feasibility of ESS telephone interviews. Participating fieldwork agencies were instructed to use the best possible probability sample design available containing telephone contact information that would support telephone interviewing (Roberts et al. 2009). The sampling frames that countries were using for the standard ESS did not include telephone contact information, so alternative sampling frames were used for the telephone surveys. The main sampling challenge posed by using telephone as the survey mode stemmed from the fact that available sampling frames included only households with fixed-line phones, which resulted in exclusion from the sample of households with mobile telephones only and households without telephone access. Therefore, the frames led to under-coverage of the intended ESS population (residential adults aged 15+). The proportion of households without a fixed-line varies across Europe (surpassing 5 per cent of the general population in most countries and rising in many), which would lead to different coverage error levels across countries, potentially jeopardising comparability and introducing bias.

Study 5 – Feasibility of mixed-mode designs: sequential versus concurrent. In Study 5, the mode design involved telephone contact to invite respondents to participate using different modes of data collection (Eva et al. 2010). The goal was to reduce fieldwork costs by not having interviewers travel to the households. Ideally, target respondents would be selected from a sampling frame containing telephone contact information. However, before interviewers called households, a pre-notification letter was to be sent, as research has shown that this is an effective way to increase response rates (de Leeuw et al. 2007). Therefore, address contact information was also necessary. The only possible sampling frame with telephone and address data available were telephone directories, but using a telephone directory would have excluded members of the population who did not have fixed-line telephones and those with "unlisted" numbers. These groups comprised about 12 per cent of the population in 1987, but the number has considerably increased since then, which may explain why only 70 per cent of the addresses selected for Study 5 could be matched to a telephone number. Furthermore, unlisted households differ significantly from those found in telephone directories (Beukenhorst 2012). Therefore, a sampling frame of addresses was chosen for Study 4. The research team selected 2500 address from a list of postal addresses (Martin and Lynn 2011). For the addresses where no telephone could be matched, contact with the household took place in person. This increased both the complexity of the fieldwork management and the costs, reducing the overall benefits of the design. The last stage of the sampling procedure where the target respondent was identified matched the standard ESS sampling procedure in the Netherlands, so no additional challenges were met in relation to this procedure. However, this study shows the complex relationship between different error sources, which multiplies exponentially when adding modes of data collection and countries.

Study 6 – Feasibility of mixed-mode designs across countries. Sampling in the ESS mixed-mode designs followed the same design procedures that were agreed for the main stage in Round 6 (Villar et al. 2014). In Estonia, there were no differences across mode designs in how the sampling design was implemented: a random sample of individuals was drawn from the same population register used for the main ESS, with explicit stratification by region and implicit stratification by age and gender. Instead of an interviewer visiting the address available from the sampling frame, a letter was addressed to the named respondent with an invitation to take part in a web survey. The challenge was that a considerable proportion of the population had a different address from the one in the register. Addresses are easier to update when an interviewer visits the address than by just sending a letter, which suggests that a web survey alone could lead to higher non-response rates than a face-to-face survey amongst a rather specific group of the population due to non-contact. This raises the question of whether those for whom address information is incorrect differ systematically from those with correct information, creating a potential for non-response bias. In Sweden, the sampling frame, sampling design and first-contact attempts were conducted identically in all mode designs, given that telephone contact is used in the standard Swedish ESS to make appointments for face-to-face interviews. The design was a simple random sample without replacement using a population register as sampling frame, which includes all individuals living in Sweden together with their contact information, including address and telephone number. Finally, in the United Kingdom, the sample design for the selection of addresses was identical across all mode designs: a stratified, clustered, random sample, drawn using the Postcode Address File (PAF). However, selection of the final respondent in households with more than one individual aged 15 or older differed. In the standard ESS, selection of the final respondent was done by the interviewer using a Kish grid (Kish 1949), whereas in the mixed-mode sample this step was left to the target household themselves. Section 3.2 discusses in detail the implications of these approaches.

Within-household random selection of individuals

Some ESS countries have access to population registers that provide information about individuals and contact information, whereas others have to resort to using samples of addresses or area probability sampling. When sampling frames that contain addresses are used, contact with the final respondent cannot take place until the selection of a person within the household has been carried out; sometimes, the sampled address contains more than one household, and two selection procedures are necessary. Face-to-face data collection is especially useful for obtaining a random sample in countries using sampling frames of addresses or areas, because interviewers can be trained to implement these random selection methods. When interviewers are not involved, selection of the individual has to rely on the person in the household that receives the instructions. Research suggests that compliance from these individuals is less than perfect, because people are sometimes unable and other times unwilling to follow these instructions (Olson and Smyth, 2014; Olson et al. 2014). Therefore, in many countries, a change in mode of data collection can affect whether the final sample is actually a random sample of the population.

In Study 6 (*Feasibility of mixed-mode designs across countries*), recruitment of UK respondents started by sending an initial invitation to "the resident." Two approaches were considered to complete the sampling frame and carry out within-household selection of the respondent: (a) an interviewer-based within household selection procedure. Sampled addresses would be sent a letter with a description of the study and a free toll number to call if they were interested in participating in the online study. During the call, the interviewer would ask the household informant to describe the household composition, apply random selection procedures to identify the final sample unit, and ask the selected person to complete the web survey. (b) A respondent-based selection procedure. Sampled addresses would be sent a letter with a description of the study, an explanation of why random selection is important and how to apply the procedure. In the end, the respondent-based approach was chosen, because we expected that very few household informants would actually call the toll-free number to go through the selection procedure. Two respondent-based selection procedures were tested: (a) the last/next birthday method, where the eligible household member with the last (or next) birthday is invited to participate, a procedure that has been described as "quasi-random" (Gaziano 2005); and b) the household roster method, which consisted of a few steps: first, a household informant followed the survey link provided in the letter; second, the informant was asked to list all household members aged 15 or older; third, a built-in algorithm carried out the random selection of one of the household members and this was communicated to the informant; last, if the selected member was someone other than the person completing the roster, the informant was asked to pass on the letter to that member. The household roster method is more intrusive than the birthday method, but it is truly random if instructions are followed correctly.

After fieldwork was completed, we evaluated both approaches. The goals were to find out whether household members who received the invitation letter complied with the instructions and to test the impact of the two different methods on response rates. To assess compliance, we asked respondents to provide the month of birth of all household members, and we asked those who completed a household roster to provide their name or alias at the end of the survey so that the promised incentive could be sent to them. Compliance with the birthday method was evaluated by checking whether the respondent had the birthday closest to the month of interview in the household, whereas compliance with the household roster method was evaluated by comparing the name provided at the end of the survey to the name or initials of the respondent selected from the household roster. Compliance tests proved to be challenging. In many instances, compliance could not be assessed because the necessary information had not been provided (e.g. month of birth for one of the household members or the initials at the end of the survey) or because it could not be determined with certainty (e.g. two household members were born in the sample month or two household members had the same initials). The birthday method led to noncompliance levels of 23 per cent of the total sample. About a third of households only had one adult (therefore, no selection was necessary), in 17 per cent of cases it was not possible to determine compliance, and 27 per cent of cases were identified as compliant. Unfortunately, we could not appropriately evaluate compliance of the household roster method. Of those households with more than one adult, more than half did not provide either name or initials. Of the remaining respondents (n = 93), two-thirds provided names that matched the selected respondent and one third provided a different name, but that may just signify that the name in the first instance was just a pseudonym or fake name.

We found no evidence of an association between the within-household selection method and response rates (39 per cent with the birthday method, 37 per cent with random selection; $\chi^2 (2) = 3.37; p = 0.19$).

Summary

Sampling in the existing cross-national face-to-face survey is already rather complex, with a mixture of samples of individuals, samples of households or addresses and area probability sampling (including random routes procedures) all being used. However, all these sampling frames are followed by visits to the address where, if necessary, an interviewer can complete the sampling process by applying procedures to randomly select a respondent from among all household members. Based on these ESS experimental studies, it seems that cross-national surveys switching to mixed-mode designs may need to either use new frames (and accept lower coverage in most cases) or use the existing frames and allow households to do their own selection. This could not only jeopardise quality or lead to reduced cost savings, but it may also introduce even greater differences in sampling design across countries, potentially reducing comparability of the collected data.

Survey participation: response rates, non-response bias, and sample composition in the ESS mid-mode studies

One of the expected advantages of adopting a mixed-mode data collection design rests on improving survey participation, either because more potential respondents end up taking part or because the final make-up of the realised sample of respondents is more similar to the target population than the respondents to the alternative single-mode design would have been. Different mechanisms for these differences in sample composition can be hypothesised (de Leeuw 2005; Martin 2011):

- Sample units and target respondents might be easier to contact via some modes. In many European countries, letters and telephone calls are generally easier (or more tempting) to disregard nowadays than a personal visit to an address, due to the volume of contact attempts received through those channels of communication. Perhaps the same could be said of email and pop on-line survey requests. At the same time, in certain populations, a personal visit may not be appropriate or well received.
- Sample units may also be more likely to agree to participate depending on the mode of data collection. Some may prefer to complete the survey at their own time and pace or without an interviewer present and thus be more likely to agree to complete a self-administered questionnaire but others may prefer to have the personal interaction with the interviewer. Many may find it easier to refuse (ignore) a mailed or telephone request than an in-person request by an interviewer.
- Some modes may be more accessible to certain populations than others. For instance, self-administered modes may not be appropriate for populations with low literacy levels (de Leeuw 2005), on-line surveys might not be accessible to the elderly or those on low incomes and modes relying on telecommunications may not reach the entire target population in war zones.

Therefore, depending on the target population and the single mode to which we are comparing the mixed-mode design, survey participation may increase or improve when allowing respondents to complete the survey in an alternative mode. Given baseline levels of response rates, web and telephone surveys have the greatest potential for improved survey participation, and mail and face-to-face surveys have the least potential because they generally achieve high rates for that mode of completion, following well-established response maximisation strategies. In fact, there is no empirical evidence suggesting that mixed-mode designs can reduce non-response error with respect to face-to-face surveys (Dillman et al. 2009; Lynn et al. 2010; Martin 2011). Surveys with high response rates around the world tend to be conducted face to face, like the Labour Force Survey and the European Quality of Life Survey in many European countries, the National Health Interview Survey in the United States and the British Crime Survey in the United Kingdom. Mandatory mixed-mode surveys can achieve response rates as high as face-to-face surveys (e.g. the American Community Survey in the United States or the Labour Force Survey in some European countries), but these are exceptional cases because, unlike most surveys, they are not voluntary. Therefore, we have no grounds to expect that more people will agree to participate in the ESS if mixed-mode data collection is allowed. However, if response rates were not damaged substantially, measurement differences between modes were minimal, non-response bias did not increase and costs were reduced, mixed-mode data collection might be preferable on the grounds of cost effectiveness. Therefore, it was still worth testing whether mixed-mode designs could be effectively implemented in the ESS to improve cost efficiency. In addition, response rates to face-to-face surveys might see substantial droops in the future and this become prohibitively expensive in certain countries. This is what has made assessing the possible implications of introducing mixed-mode data collection so critically important. Four of the studies in the ESS mixed-mode programme of research (Studies 2, 3, 4 and 6) evaluated the impact of mixed-modes on survey participation; we summarise their findings in this section.

Outcome rates

Survey participation can be measured using different outcome rates. Final response rates are a general way to assess and compare survey participation across studies; in addition, analysing different non-response components (e.g. refusals, non-contacts) provides insight into the mechanisms that explain the differences in survey participation across modes. We start this section discussing overall response rates and then focus on noncontact and refusal rates, comparing outcomes from the face-to-face standard main stage ESS to each alternative mode design. All outcome rates below assume that cases where eligibility could not be determined during fieldwork would have been eligible for participation[5] in the survey (yielding rates similar to the American Association for Public Opinion Research Response Rate 1).

Response rates

The percentage of all selected sample units that participated in the survey was lower in all mixed-mode designs compared to the main stage face-to-face ESS. Some of these differences were rather striking; for most countries in Study 4 (*Feasibility of ESS telephone interviews*), for example, response rates were two to three times higher for the face-to-face survey than for the alternative telephone design (see Figure 16.1). Even though these differences might in part be attributed to variation in the invitation protocol between the two mode designs (e.g. sample units assigned to the alternative mode received lower incentives or did not receive a pre-notification letter), it is unlikely that the large differences in response are entirely (or even mainly) due to those design differences.

The mixed-mode data collection designs of studies 5 (*Feasibility of mixed-mode designs: sequential versus concurrent*) and 6 (*Feasibility of mixed-mode designs across countries*) did better than the single alternative mode from Study 4 (*Feasibility of ESS telephone interviews*), but response rates were still lower than for the face-to-face standard ESS sample. In Study 5, the response rate in the standard ESS in the Netherlands was 52 per cent but was somewhat lower for the two alternative designs: 43 per cent for the sequential design and 44 per cent for the concurrent design (see Figure 16.1), even though the recruitment process was carried out by interviewers, either by telephone or in person (Eva et al., 2010).

In the United Kingdom, the web + face-to-face design implemented in Study 6 resulted in a response rate loss of 17 percentage points compared to the standard ESS (55 per cent, see Figure 16.1),[6] in spite of the additional monetary incentive offered to web respondents conditional on completion (£15/£35 pounds, depending on the experimental condition).

The loss was much lower in Estonia, where the mixed-mode design achieved a response rate of 64 per cent, only 4 percentage points lower than the standard

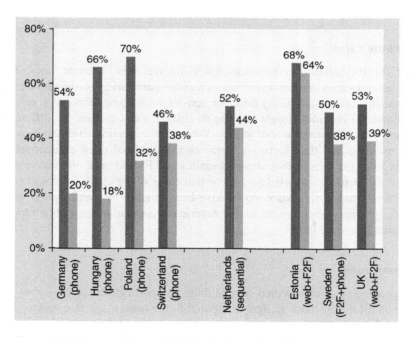

Figure 16.1 Response Rates (RR1) for Studies 3, 4, and 6.

Using Mixed Modes in Survey Research 287

ESS (68 per cent, see Figure 16.1). This is particularly striking as respondents completed the almost 1-hour-long ESS survey, which suggests the length of the questionnaire on-line is not a barrier for web implementation, in Estonia at least. The response rate in the Swedish response-enhancing design (38 per cent) was much lower than in the standard ESS design (50 per cent). However, compared to the mixed-mode sample, additional resources (extra incentives and visits) were allocated to the standard ESS sample to try to achieve the highest possible response rate; therefore, the lower response rates may be partly due to this difference.

Overall, there were no apparent advantages from offering additional modes of data collection to respondents in terms of response rates. Response rates were low in all mixed-mode designs compared to the face-to-face design, although the Estonian experiment rates were similar to the face-to-face rate. However, the Estonian mixed-mode survey benefitted from a large internet penetration rate and a sampling frame with named individuals to whom a mailed invitation could be sent. It is doubtful whether these findings could be replicated in countries without these features.

Refusal rates

Results were mixed within and across studies when it came to refusal rates. Respondents were more likely to refuse to participate in the telephone survey than in the standard face-to-face ESS in Germany and Hungary and to a lesser extent in Poland (Study 4, see Figure 16.2). However, they were less likely to refuse telephone invitations compared to face-to-face invitations in Switzerland (Study 4) and Sweden (Study 6), both countries where telephone surveys are generally more prevalent than in other ESS countries. Similarly, the web + face-to-face

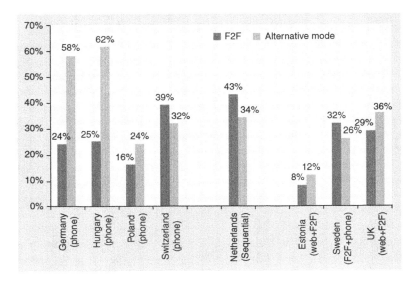

Figure 16.2 Refusal rates for Studies 4, 5 and 6.

designs led to higher refusal rates in Estonia and the United Kingdom (Study 6) but not in the Netherlands (Study 5), where refusal rates for the face-to-face sample were quite high (43 per cent) compared to only (34 per cent) in the sequential mixed-mode approach. This suggests that, in some countries, offering additional modes of data collection can persuade sampled individuals who would otherwise have actually refused to take part.

The lower refusal rates in Switzerland may be related to the survey tradition in this country. Since the early 1980s, high-quality surveys in Switzerland have been carried out by telephone (Ernst Staehli 2012). Therefore, Swiss target respondents may have assigned less importance and legitimacy to face-to-face requests than they did to the telephone request. Unfortunately, it is not possible to test this hypothesis with the existing data.

Noncontact rates

In most countries and studies, differences in contact rates across modes were a lot smaller than refusal rates, with the exception of Germany and Poland (Study 4), where reaching sample units was considerably more difficult when contact was made via telephone than in the standard ESS (see Figure 16.3). Contact rates were also slightly lower for the alternative mode design in Hungary (Study 4), the Netherlands (Study 5) and Estonia (Study 6), but no differences were observed in Switzerland (Study 4) or Sweden (Study 6). Therefore, among the countries that participated in these studies, increased refusal to participate played a larger role in the lower response rates than lack of contact with respondents.

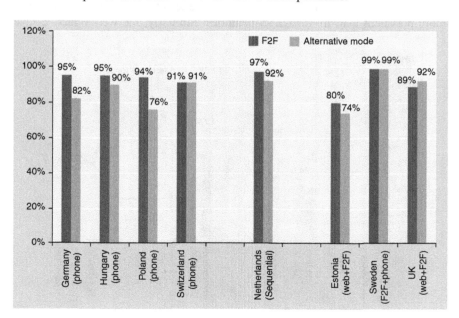

Figure 16.3 Household contact rates for Studies 4, 5 and 6.

Sociodemographic composition of realised samples and non-response bias

Outcome rates can help a researcher to understand why certain sample units are not part of the final, realised sample. However, non-response bias analysis is necessary to assess the extent to which non-response affects survey estimates. To assess non-response bias, one would ideally compare respondents to non-respondents with respect to the variables of interest. However, this information is typically unavailable. For the ESS studies, we used an alternative approach where we compared the sample of respondents obtained with each mode design to estimates from the population with respect to a few socio-demographic variables, providing an assessment of the extent of non-response bias for those variables.[7]

In Study 2 (*Measurement differences: Finding the cause*), the face-to-face and telephone samples were compared with respect to five variables: age, gender, education, having a paid job and occupation (Jäckle et al. 2006). Telephone respondents included significantly fewer males (33 per cent versus 40 per cent), fewer manual workers (25 per cent versus 36 per cent) and fewer individuals with lower education (48 per cent versus 55 per cent) than face-to-face respondents did. No differences were found for the age or in the proportion of respondents having a paid job. Population estimates for Lisbon and Budapest were not available, but on the basis that most populations in the world have a nearly even divide in the proportion of males and females, it could be argued that the gender proportion in the telephone sample is probably more biased than in the face-to-face sample.

In Study 4 (*Feasibility of ESS telephone interviews*), we compared face-to-face samples to telephone samples in six socio-demographic variables: gender, age, education, being in paid work, occupation and area of residence (Roberts et al. 2009). Countries differed on how similar the realised sample in the telephone survey was to the realised sample in the standard ESS survey. Respondents to the German telephone survey were less likely to be in paid work than respondents to the German face-to-face survey (42 per cent versus 53 per cent), but the opposite was found in Hungary (65 per cent versus 42 per cent). Years in education and paid work differed significantly in almost all countries. In Germany, Poland and Hungary, the telephone sample showed higher educational attainment than the face-to-face survey. The Hungarian samples showed the largest number of differences for five of the six variables. The Swiss samples only differed significantly in percentage of the sample that was in paid work, but the difference was striking: 34 per cent in the telephone survey compared to 62 per cent in the face-to-face survey. Of particular concern here are the cross-national differences in how mode impacts the sample composition.

In Study 5 (*Feasibility of mixed-mode designs: sequential versus concurrent*), samples were compared with respect to age, gender, urbanisation, size of household, occupation and educational level (Eva et al. 2010). In addition, data were compared to population estimates from Statistics Netherlands[8] in the first four of those variables. There were few differences between the composition of the face-to-face realised sample and the mixed-mode alternatives: the mixed-mode samples included fewer women with low educational level (20.4 per cent) than the face-to-face sample (23.4 per cent), and more women of middle educational level, 21.4 per cent in the sequential deign compared to 17.1 per cent in the face-to-face sample. However, these differences were rather modest.

Differences were larger when comparing the ESS standard and experimental samples to the population estimates. All ESS samples under-represented males under 45, females over 75, single-person households and people living in urbanised areas. The face-to-face sample was closer to the population values with respect to age and gender, and the concurrent sample differed most from the population estimates for all variables.

Comparing the face-to-face sample to those respondents from the sequential design that completed the web survey (the "web sample") can provide a simulation of what would happen if the ESS were implemented as a web survey. In terms of sample composition, the web sample included fewer respondents over 65, especially among females (4.6 per cent compared to 12.3 per cent in the face-to-face sample), fewer men with higher education, fewer respondents from highly urbanised locations, fewer one-person households and fewer retired respondents. Therefore, the web sample exacerbated the non-response bias observed in the face-to-face sample as compared to the population estimates rather than reducing it.

Study 6 – Feasibility of mixed-mode designs across countries. Comparing the profiles of the responding samples in each mode design with external population data, we found broadly similar distributions between the 2011 census data in Estonia and the United Kingdom and the ESS samples, both from the face-to-face and mixed-mode designs (Villar et al. 2014). However, the mixed-mode sample showed greater bias relative to census statistics than the face-to-face sample. In the United Kingdom, all samples attracted fewer respondents from the youngest and oldest age groups and more people looking after the home or family compared to the UK census data, but the difference was larger in the mixed-mode sample. In Estonia, only the mixed-mode sample under-represented people in paid work and those born outside Estonia, whereas the computer-assisted personal interviewing (CAPI)-only face-to-face sample was not problematic.

Summary

In line with previous research, evidence from these four studies suggests that mixed-mode data collection designs are unlikely to increase response rates or reduce non-response bias in survey estimates compared to data collected face to face. In fact, overall they suggest that response rates would decrease and non-response bias would probably increase. Participation was lower for the mixed-mode designs mostly because of higher refusal rates rather than because of lower non-contact rates, which suggests that respondents can be contacted using different channels but may still be unwilling to take part in an hour-long survey over the telephone or on the web or find it more difficult to refuse an in-person request from a persuasive interviewer. When there were differences in the composition of the realised sample, the socio-demographic profile of the face-to-face survey design was usually closer to the population estimates than the mixed-mode design.

Measurement error in the ESS mixed-mode studies

Multiple studies have found that collecting data in different modes can lead to measurement differences (e.g. Christian et al. 2006; de Leeuw 1992); the same respondent answering the same question may give different answers depending on whether the question is asked in person, over the telephone, on a web browser or on paper. In fact, in-person surveys sometimes switch to self-administered modes for sections asking sensitive questions (Couper 1998; Tourangeau and Smith 1996), on the grounds that reporting will be more accurate that way. However, it is less clear whether data collected from respondents who answer in different modes should be combined to compute survey estimates. If modes can attract respondents with different characteristics (e.g. a survey conducted via SMS may attract younger people compared to a face-to-face survey), any observed differences between those groups could be due to measurement differences related to mode rather than to actual differences related to the variable of interest. This could in turn affect interpretation of survey findings. Similarly, if countries in a cross-national survey collect data using different modes, differences in survey estimates for each country could be related to actual differences in those estimates or to differences in how respondents answered to the specific mode of data collection. Therefore, the question of measurement differences across modes is of the utmost importance for cross-national research.

Multiple factors can help explain measurement differences across data collection modes (de Leeuw 2005; Tourangeau et al. 2000). From the start, the ESS mixed-mode research programme paid special attention to measurement effects to better understand these mechanisms. Three of the ESS studies investigated the effect of mode on estimates by designing experiments that allowed these effects to be disentangled from the other sources of error like non-response, coverage or processing. Observed differences in estimates can thus be attributed to the effect of mode on measurement. In the feasibility studies, observed effects can be due to differences in the composition of the realised sample or to differences in measurement. However, applying different approaches, one can try to account for selection effects and gain insight by comparing survey estimates across modes in those studies. In addition, measurement effects may also be assessed by observing respondent behaviour across groups of items. For example, item non-response, acquiescence (the tendency to agree with survey statements), and non-differentiation of response options have often been used to assess measurement effects (e.g. Schuman and Presser 1981). In this section, we will evaluate the effects of mode on univariate estimates, on multivariate estimates, on response behaviours and on data quality. Survey errors are item- and statistic- specific (Groves 1989); mode effects might be found in univariate estimates of one variable (such as averages and percentages) and yet leave estimates of other variables or multivariate estimates including that variable unaffected. For a survey programme like the

ESS, an important concern was the effect that switching mode designs would have across different questions, estimates and multivariate analyses that data users may want to carry out. Furthermore, it is important to evaluate how mode effects could affect the interpretation of changes observed across time.

Effect of mode on univariate estimates

Effect of mode on univariate estimates: Measurement studies

In two of the studies (1 and 3), respondents answered the same set of questions in two different modes. In both studies, the percentage of respondents who gave the same answer on both occasions was relatively low. In Study 1, the percentage of identical answers ranged from 52 per cent for the income question to 76 per cent for self-reported belonging to a discriminated group. In Study 3, the average matching percentage across all attitudinal questions was 52 per cent, ranging from 28 per cent in a question about the effect of immigrants on cultural life of a country to 70 per cent matching for questions about perception of different types of crime. Behavioural questions led to higher levels of matching, ranging from 38 per cent to 98 per cent. Attitudinal questions (which are prevalent in the ESS) showed lower average consistency than behavioural questions, in line with previous research. Nonetheless, some of the differences between attitudinal and behavioural questions could be related to other formal differences between the questions like the number of response options. For example, 4 out of the 11 attitudinal questions had 11-point answer scales. It would be reasonable to expect that the larger the number of response options, the easier it will be for respondents to provide a different answer on two occasions, partly because the meaning of the two scale points may become closer. Questions with more response options indeed exhibited lower consistency across the two modes, and this was true both for attitudinal and behavioural questions (Jäckle et al. 2006).

Study 2 (*Measurement differences: Finding the cause*) investigated the mechanism behind measurement differences between telephone and face-to-face data collection. When response distributions of 33 items across the three experimental groups (telephone, face-to-face with showcards and face-to-face without showcards) were compared, it was found that 17 of the 33 items were affected by mode of interviewing after controlling for differences in sample composition due to age, gender, educational qualification and occupation. In 12 cases, telephone estimates were different to face-to-face estimates, but no differences were observed between the two face-to-face versions (with vs. without showcards), implying that mode differences were not driven by the questionnaire adaptation for telephone mode related to the sensory channel through which the response options were conveyed, but to other mechanisms related to mode (Jäckle et al. 2006). In all but one case (household income), the observed mode effects were comparatively small (no greater than one standard error) and would be unlikely to affect the conclusions of analysts using mixed-mode data.

Effect of mode design on univariate estimates: Feasibility studies

For each feasibility study, large numbers of items were compared across mode designs. The goal was to estimate the proportion of ESS questions that would be affected if mixed-mode designs were allowed. The proportion of significant differences varied across studies,[9] but in all cases and mode designs it was higher than what would be expected by chance alone. Out of the 43 well-being variables analysed in Study 4, 31 (72 per cent) showed statistically significant differences across the two samples, and a further four were marginally significant. This finding was replicated when each country was analysed separately, although fewer of the differences were significant given the smaller sample sizes. In the feasibility study conducted in the Netherlands (Study 5), we compared estimates for 230 items as measured using the standard ESS face-to-face approach to the mixed-mode sequential design and the mixed-mode concurrent design. The concurrent mixed-mode sample featured differing distributions in 25 items (11 per cent), whereas in the sequential mixed-mode sample 38 items (17 per cent) had distributions significantly different from the face-to-face sample. Finally, in Study 6, we compared distributions of 128 questions across mode designs. Mode effects were present in numerous questions for all countries and across all mode comparisons. Effects were larger when comparing web and face-to-face in Estonia (63 per cent) and the United Kingdom (83 per cent) than when comparing telephone to face-to-face data in Sweden (32 per cent, see Figure 16.4). This may be partly due to the smaller Swedish sample, but differences between face-to-face and the alternative mode (telephone) were smaller overall in Sweden than in the other countries.

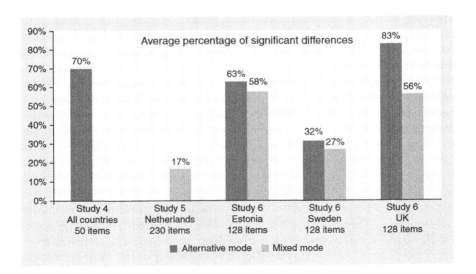

Figure 16.4 Percentage of variables showing significant differences across modes.

Significant differences were more common when comparing respondents to two single different modes (e.g. web vs. face-to-face) than when comparing mixed-mode designs to face-to-face (see Figure 16.4). Differences were also largest for estimates of personal well-being, followed by questions from the core ESS questionnaire about political attitudes, political participation and attitudes towards immigrants. These are some of the most frequently used items on the ESS according to ESS user statistics (www.europeansocialsurvey.org /about/user_statistics.html) and bibliographic studies (Malnar 2015).

To estimate the size of the differences, the average absolute difference between mode designs was computed for different sections of the questionnaire and different types of questions in Study 6 (see c).[10] Differences between the face-to-face data and the alternative mode designs were moderate but non-ignorable, ranging from 2.1 to 8.3 percentage points for categorical variables. The smallest difference was found when comparing estimates on questions about well-being in Sweden, in striking contrast to the large differences in these questions between web and face-to-face in the United Kingdom and Estonia (see row 7 in Table 16.3). Coincidentally, these comparisons also reflected the smallest and largest differences for the quantitative questions.

Effect of mode on multivariate estimates

Effect of mode design on multivariate estimates: Feasibility studies

A number of statistical models involving political attitudes were tested in Study 5 (Martin and Lynn 2011). In all the models tested, some model parameters differed across mode designs: when looking at political interest, just two out of 16 examined variables showed a significant interaction effect with data collection design. However, when political interest is used as a predictor variable, there were significant differences in several models. The study suggested caution when comparing models from surveys carried out with different data collection designs (Martin and Lynn 2011).

In Study 6, bivariate correlations were compared between 30 items about perception of democracy. Out of 435 correlations, we considered how many were significantly different in the two mode designs (see Table 16.4). As with univariate estimates, differences were smaller when comparing the mixed-mode sample to the face-to-face than when comparing the web sample to the face-to-face. In Estonia, 13.1 per cent of the correlations were significantly different, whereas in the United Kingdom it was almost a third (32.3 per cent). Larger differences in correlations ($p < .001$) represented only 2.5 per cent of the 30 variables in Estonia but 9.7 per cent in the United Kingdom. Overall, substantive conclusions in Estonia would be relatively close but could lead to different relationships across the 30 variables studied and may cause problems when comparing statistical models in these countries. In the United Kingdom, depending on the variables studied, the substantive conclusions might be impacted.

Finally, using Studies 5 and 6, data quality for each mode design was compared using sets of questions measuring various concepts (Revilla 2010, 2013). Overall,

Table 16.3 Average absolute error by section, mode and country

	Estonia		United Kingdom		Sweden	
	F2F vs web	F2F vs MM	F2F vs web	F2F vs MM	F2F vs phone	F2F vs MM
Section A (5 quantitative)	0.3	0.3	0.3	0.3	0.4	0.2
Section B (20 quantitative)	0.3	0.3	0.6	0.6	0.3	0.1
Section B (15 qualitative)	6.5%	3.0	5.9%	5.2%	4.4%	2.2%
Section C (6 quantitative)	0.2	0.2	0.6	0.5	0.2	0.2
Section C (13 qualitative)	5.0%	2.8%	3.7%	2.9%	4.1%	2.5%
Section D (24 quantitative)	0.4	0.2	0.8	0.7	0.1	0.1
Section D (15 qualitative)	6.8%	4.4%	8.3%	5.7%	4.1%	2.1%
Section E (30 quantitative)	0.2	0.2	0.5	0.3	0.2	0.1
Average absolute error quantitative questions	0.3	0.2	0.6	0.5	0.2	0.2
Average absolute error qualitative questions	6.1%	4.4%	8.3%	5.7%	4.1%	2.3%

Table 16.4 Significance of the difference in correlations across mode designs

	Estonia (n = 435)	UK (n = 435)
	%	%
$p < .001$	2.53	9.66
$.001 \leq p < .01$	2.76	10.34
$.01 \leq p < .05$	7.82	12.18
$.05 \leq p < .10$	5.75	7.59
$p \geq .10$	81.15	60.23
Total	100.00	100.00

there were small differences across the three mode designs in terms of reliability and validity, and those differences did not show any one mode having consistently higher quality. The largest difference was found in the quality of the political trust concept, where the face-to-face survey showed higher validity than the mixed-mode designs.

Effect of mode on response behaviours: Item non-response, acquiescence, non-differentiation and other response behaviours

In this section, we review findings from the measurement studies about the impact of mode on how respondents answer questions. A variety of response behaviours have been used as measures of data quality: item non-response, response styles such as acquiescence and tendencies to select the same response option regardless of the real answer (e.g. extreme response style, non-differentiation).

Effect of mode on response behaviours: Measurement studies

Item non-response. In Study 1 *(Measurement differences across four modes)*, significant differences in item non-response were found for half of the 38 questions analysed. Item non-response rates were highest for self-completion (paper) mode in 12 questions. For the remaining 7 questions, item non-response was significantly higher among telephone respondents compared to other modes. In Study 2 *(Measurement differences: Finding the cause)*, item non-response rates were similar across the three groups; however, respondents interviewed face-to-face without showcards had higher overall item non-response rates and significantly higher item non-response to the income question, with almost double the proportion of refusals than the telephone group. In Study 3, item non-response was again low in both modes, but selecting "don't know" or choosing refusal or providing no answer to the 35 analysed questions was more likely on the web than face-to-face, even though the web survey was much shorter than the face-to-face interview.

Non-differentiation, extreme response style, acquiescence and order effects. In Study 1, *(Measurement differences across four modes)*, for three out of five questions, there were significant mode differences in the tendency to select answer scale endpoints (extreme response style), but there was no obvious pattern;

sometimes web mode obtained the highest proportion of extreme responses, sometimes face-to-face did. No differences were observed when comparing acquiescence response style across modes.

In Study 2 (*Measurement differences: Finding the cause*), telephone respondents were just as likely as face-to-face respondents to acquiesce, repeat the same response option across questions and select the first or last options. This suggests that showcards had little effect on data quality. Similarly, there was no evidence of increased non-differentiation or increased acquiescence among telephone respondents compared to the face-to-face respondents who were not given showcards. However, when comparing face-to-face interviews with showcards to telephone interviews, non-differentiation is significantly higher in the latter; potentially, not having the interviewer be physically present and not having showcards has a cumulative effect, leading to higher non-differentiation (Jäckle et al. 2006).

Effect of mode on response behaviours: Feasibility studies

Item non-response. Across all feasibility studies, item non-response was generally low in all modes as it was in the standard ESS conducted face-to-face. Study 4 (*Feasibility of ESS telephone interviews*) found that item non-response was significantly higher in the standard face-to-face survey than in the telephone survey, although this difference was small. In Study 5 (*Feasibility of mixed-mode designs: sequential versus concurrent*), item non-response was very low in all groups and all modes, but slightly higher in face-to-face (4.3 "don't knows" and 4.7 refusals per interview on average) than telephone (2.8 "don't knows" and 2.9 refusals per interview on average) and web (0.1 "don't knows" and 0.2 refusals per interview on average). In Study 6 (*Feasibility of mixed-mode designs across countries*), there was higher item non-response in the mixed-mode design than in the standard ESS but showed opposite directions in the United Kingdom (higher for web respondents) and Estonia (higher for face-to-face respondents). The differences across countries in efficiency of the different mode designs underline how mixing modes in different ways could be problematic for cross-national comparisons. Furthermore, changes over time within a country could also cause difficulties.

Non-differentiation, acquiescence, response option positional preferences. In Study 6 (*Feasibility of mixed-mode designs across countries*), the proportion of respondents who selected the same response option in sets of items that shared the same answer scale was, in general, similar or lower in the overall mixed-mode design than in the standard ESS. When looking at respondents by mode, there was reassuringly no evidence of higher straight-lining among web respondents.

Mode, interview length and interview experience

In Study 2, interviews conducted by telephone were significantly (although slightly) shorter than those conducted in person (15.3 vs. 17.5 minutes). In Study 4, actual duration was about 8 minutes shorter by telephone than face to face for all countries but Poland, where, interestingly, it was 4 minutes longer.

Regardless of telephone surveys being seemingly shorter than face-to-face surveys, previous research (e.g. de Leeuw 1992; Holbrook et al. 2003) and common sense suggested that an invitation to carry out the hour-long ESS survey would yield lower response rates than a face-to-face request for several reasons (see Groves 1990 for a review of the possible mechanisms behind this difference). Therefore, Study 4 tested the feasibility of conducting the ESS over the telephone and whether shorter versions (45 and 30 minutes long) of the survey could help improve the expected low response rates. Response rates differed depending on the duration communicated during the invitation to participate: cooperation was higher for the 45-minute interview than for the 1-hour interview, increasing response rates by 5 percentage points in Germany and Poland, 4 in Hungary and 2 in Switzerland. When respondents were first invited to a 30-minute interview followed by an additional 30-minute interview, response rates were highest for the 30-minute interview but were significantly lower if we consider the total number of respondents who completed both 30-minute interviews. In addition, the 30-minute interview led to a response rate lower than the 45-minute interview in Poland (50.5 per cent vs. 55.6 per cent). More importantly, response rates for the standard ESS face-to-face surveys were higher than for any of the three versions of the telephone survey in all countries. Even when considering only the 30-minute interview, cooperation rates were better in the face-to-face design than the telephone design in all countries except Switzerland.

In Study 2, 69 per cent of respondents when asked whether they would be willing to continue the interview for longer, telephone respondents were more likely to be willing (69 per cent) than face-to-face respondents (60 per cent). It is not clear whether that willingness would turn into higher or lower response rates if the interview indeed continued, especially when less than half of the respondents to the 30-minute interview in Study 4 completed the second part of the survey.

A number of questions were asked in Study 2 to evaluate respondents' perception of the survey experience. Face-to-face respondents were more likely than telephone respondents to report that they had felt uneasy about answering certain topics. However, respondents who felt uneasy were also more likely to report having answered truthfully. Based on answers recorded by the interviewer, telephone respondents were less likely to ask for clarification, less likely to be reluctant to answer, more likely to answer questions to the best of their ability and more likely to have understood the questions. It is unclear how accurate these interviewer perceptions were, especially when telephone interviewers had considerably fewer cues on which to base their assessments.

Summary

This section highlights that mode does indeed have some impact on how respondents answer questions. It is not always clear which mode is best in terms of quality, but the differences between modes have the potential to damage comparability. Mode-related differences in a country's estimates across time could confound comparisons within and across countries. The ESS, as well as other cross-national projects, has built a time series using face-to-face data collection, and this single-mode design is likely to continue in some countries where other mode designs would not be optimal (or even possible). This has implications for the usage of ESS data, which are publicly and freely available. Advanced data users familiar with the ESS may quickly note and try and account for these changes, but few reliable methods are available to allow for mode-difference correction (Vandenplas et al. 2014). Data users less acquainted with the ESS procedures and history may miss the switch in mode design altogether and thus proceed to analyse the data as if no mode effects were present.

The possibility of shortening the ESS questionnaire to facilitate completion in other modes has been discussed during the mixed-mode methodology programme. Offering a 45-minute questionnaire rather than one of 60 minutes could be beneficial for the telephone mode, while administering two 30-minute sections would be damaging to the response rate. However, contrary to expectation, the 60-minute web survey did not appear to be a problem in Estonia in Study 6. The large web participation levels in Estonia and moderate participation levels in the United Kingdom suggest that long surveys can be conducted using self-administered modes. Nonetheless, the one-hour standard ESS face-to-face survey gets the highest cooperation compared to any single mode and to most mixed-mode designs.

Costs in the ESS mixed-mode studies

The ESS studies have shown that switching to mixed-mode data collection is unlikely to produce increases in response rates or improvements in data quality. In fact, reductions in response rates seem likely, and additional mode effects could be introduced with each new mode permitted. However, one of the key advantages of a switch to mixed modes is the possibility of substantially reducing *fieldwork* costs. Alternative modes may lead to reduced efforts to engage respondents, where fewer contact attempts are necessary to obtain a response from sampled units. In addition, certain modes with a lower cost per respondent contact attempt could lead to an overall lower cost per respondent. At the same time, these potential savings need to be weighed against any potential increased *fixed setup costs*, which, in a cross-national context, include central coordination costs as well as country-level costs. This section summarises the evidence gathered in the ESS research programme regarding the effect of mixed-mode designs on overall costs.

Like many publicly funded cross-national social survey programmes, the ESS has a rather complex funding structure. There are two distinct budget streams, one to cover each country's own national survey and coordination costs, and one to cover central coordination and dissemination costs. Central costs were historically met by the European Commission but have been funded collectively by participating countries since the ESS was established as a European Research Infrastructure Consortium (ESS ERIC) in 2013. Currently, it is not possible to transfer funds between these two different funding sources: costs for design of questionnaire and other fieldwork instruments, central quality control and data archiving and dissemination are met from the central budget, whilst all translation and data collection costs are met nationally. Consequently, different researchers are in direct control of each budget, and overarching changes to the design of the survey become more complex than they would be for a single budget study like that of many single nation survey projects.

In a complex budgetary context like the ESS's, mixed-mode data collection would likely lead to cost savings at the national level, where data-collection agencies would reduce the amount they charge to national funders. However, one would expect higher costs for development of questionnaire instruments, quality control, fieldwork monitoring and data processing in multiple modes. Some of this investment might reduce fieldwork savings. Thus, central ESS costs could increase, as source instruments and other materials (such as instructions and invitation letters) would have to be designed and tested for multiple modes. If it proves feasible in the future, the production of correction factors for mode differences would also need to be funded. The ESS mixed-mode methodology programme was not designed to simulate all of these different interactions, but it is important to remember them when assessing the available evidence.

Unfortunately, there are many other difficulties of isolating costs differences by mode from the work conducted in the ESS mixed-mode methodology programme. As Villar and colleagues (2014) commented:

> Comparing the actual costs incurred to carry out the survey in each mode is fraught with difficulties. Some of the costs in a split-run experimental design are inevitably shared between the mode designs and any allocation of costs to each design will be arbitrary. Furthermore, the costs will be shaped by a variety of contextual factors that could differ greatly in a different situation (market buoyancy, relevant experience of the survey organisation and the interviewers, etc). And then there is the additional difficulty of comparing costs cross-nationally (page 3).

It is therefore helpful that general information about data collection costs was collated during the mixed-mode methodology programme. In all ESS countries, face-to-face fieldwork was the most expensive mode (see Figure 16.5). Information was collected by asking national statistical institutes in ESS countries to provide information about the relative costs of different data collection modes (Roberts et al. 2008). In addition, countries reported that face-to-face fieldwork costs were increasing, even simply to maintain the same response rates. Often in the most expensive fieldwork countries for ESS fieldwork, the difference between face-to-face and the next most expensive mode is particularly large (see Table 16.5). In Germany, for example, reported costs for web interviewing were almost six times cheaper than those for face-to-face interviewing, whereas in Switzerland they were almost 20 times cheaper (Roberts et al. 2008).

Fieldwork costs and efforts

The mapping exercise carried out before Study 4 (see Figure 16.5), showed that in countries where face-to-face was highest, the gap with respect to the next most

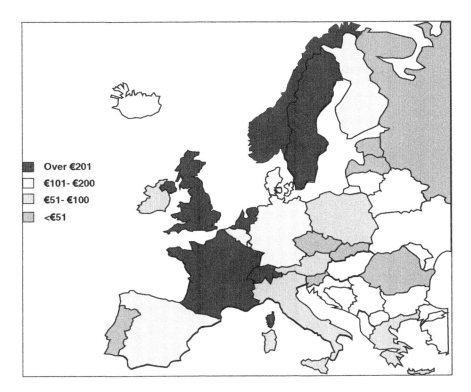

Figure 16.5 Mean costs per successful interview.
Source: Based on ESS Round 3 2006 figures.

expensive mode also tended to be larger – thus, the potential for cost savings using a different mode was larger. Conversely, in countries where face-to-face fieldwork was not as expensive, the difference in cost by mode was smaller (Roberts et al. 2008). As a result, it was expected that those countries where data collection was the most expensive would be more interested in switching to an alternative, cheaper, mode. Indeed, countries such as Netherlands and Switzerland have been the most eager to see mixed-mode data collection on the ESS. However, there has not been such pressure from countries where there is no sampling frame of individuals that would allow mixed-mode data collection without sending an interviewer to do initial respondent selection. For instance, there has been no real pressure from Germany and the United Kingdom to switch modes thus far despite face-to-face data collection costs being particularly high in these nations.

Three studies in the ESS mixed-mode methodology programme directly addressed the costs issue: Study 4 (*Feasibility of ESS telephone interviews*), Study 5 (*Feasibility of mixed-mode designs: sequential versus concurrent*) and Study 6 (*Feasibility of mixed-mode designs across countries*). Survey costs depend on a range of factors. In the ESS, various elements that would affect cost

Table 16.5 Relative costs of fieldwork using different modes

Country	ESS Field Agencies (~=National Statistics Institute)			
	F2F	Tel.	Postal	Web
Austria~	100	30	25	–
Belgium	100	70	–	25
Belgium~	100	80	83	62
Cyprus	100	50	–	–
Cyprus~	100	80	50	40
Denmark	100	35	25	25
Finland~	100	50	35	–
Germany	100	43	20	15
Hungary	100	80	60	50
Iceland	100	40	25	15
Ireland	100	65	50	*
Italy	100	60	70	50
Norway~	100	50	25	20
Poland	100	–	40	–
Portugal	100	75	50	–
Romania~	100	60	–	–
Russia	100	63	–	–
Slovakia	100	85	35	65
Slovenia	100	30	25	20
Spain	100	60–70	30	30
Sweden	100	60	30	–
Switzerland	100	50	–	–
Switzerland~	100	40	20	5
Ukraine	100	60	50	40

Note: Question phrasing was: "To help give us an idea of the relative costs of fieldwork using different modes of data collection, please estimate the average cost of conducting a survey of a random probability sample of the population using the modes listed below. (Assume 1,000 achieved interviews and a 20–minute questionnaire.) You do not need to give the actual cost estimate. Simply describe the relative costs of modes b, c, and d (below) as a percentage of the cost of mode a (a survey using face–to–face interviewing). Please enter your answers below."

are fixed, such as length of questionnaire or sample size. Other factors will differ by country – such as the size of the country, the population density, mode coverage and available sampling frame – and by survey agency, such as interviewer experience and training and the available software.

The cost findings from these studies demonstrate that mixed-mode or alternative-mode data collection have the potential to save costs. The telephone studies suggest that cost savings might be extensive in countries where face-to-face fieldwork is most expensive (like the United Kingdom and Switzerland) but non-existent in countries like Poland, where there would be no savings at all (Roberts et al. 2009). However, as we approach the end of the ESS mixed-mode methodology programme, it appears that telephone is largely seen as a mode of the past rather than the future. Therefore, the real focus now is on whether web surveys or mixed-mode web and face-to-face surveys can save money.

The evidence from the ESS studies in the programme suggested that a web + face-to-face mixed-mode design has the potential to save field-data collection costs without harming the survey response rate in Estonia. However, the equivalent results from the United Kingdom suggest that it may prove impossible to realise this potential in all or probably most ESS countries in the near future since extensive face-to-face activity would still be required to achieve an acceptable response rate. The differences between Estonia and the United Kingdom in this respect are really striking. In Estonia, effectively the same response rate as the main single-mode face-to-face ESS was achieved at a substantially lower cost. In the United Kingdom, a significantly lower response rate was achieved despite extensive field efforts that resulted in very little, if any, cost savings (Villar et al. 2014). It seems quite likely that such variability in experiences with mixed-mode data collection would also be observed between other ESS countries. The experiment in the Netherlands is somewhere between the two, showing that substantial cost savings are possible but once again at the cost of a substantial drop in the response rate (Eva et al. 2010).

For a cross-national survey like the ESS, there are the additional development and coordination costs that would be incurred at a central level if more modes were allowed. A switch to mixed-mode interviewing would save money in some countries, and in a small group, these savings could be rather substantial. However, a switch would only be possible in some countries, would only save money in some countries where a switch was possible, would lead to a loss of quality in most countries where a switch took place, would undermine cross-nationally and longitudinal comparability and would increase the central costs.

Implementation challenges in the ESS drawing on the mixed-mode studies

The ESS, like many cross-national social surveys, has a complex organisational and implementation structure. On the one hand, it can be seen as one survey in multiple countries in the sense that each country contracts and carries out their own fieldwork. On the other hand, the ESS is more like a single survey across countries. The project is a compendium of national surveys conducted under a common framework, where the CST specifies how the survey should be conducted, sets targets, provides key documents like the questionnaire and contact forms and supports and monitors the work of ESS national teams. The CST harmonises the datasets before making the data and documentation available and providing supporting tools such as data-analysis platforms and weights. As noted earlier, the ESS also operates an input harmonised model of data collection, trying to keep all essential survey conditions the same and organising necessary variation in a way that is equivalent across countries.

Introducing mixed-mode data collection would require designing future ESS questions in a uni-mode manner, so that the same exact question can be used in all modes. Questions from previous rounds would have to be re-drafted and adapted to allow collection in new modes. Taking into account more than one mode during the question-design process would increase the intricacy of an already complex process where potential language and cultural effects are being considered. In addition, the existing core questionnaire would have to be reviewed and parts of it rewritten to make it suitable for use in, say, a web survey. This would mean that the time series that the ESS has been creating since 2002 would have to be disrupted, with the extent varying between countries and different questionnaire items.

Further decisions would likely ensue from a change to mixed mode. If web data collection were allowed, the ESS would need to decide how to handle web survey programing efficiently. A central programming tool would be most convenient but may have implications related to data protection issues associated with collecting data across borders. For efficient management of data collected with different modes, such a web survey tool should preferably be compatible with the CAPI system used for face-to-face data collection. Therefore, a decision to select a central web tool could entail all countries adopting the same CAPI system, whereas current procedures allow countries to use their preferred system. Even though this unifying approach may indeed provide advantages, the CST would need to make an investment to evaluate, select and prepare training materials for the tool.

The ESS also harmonises and makes data from interviews and data about interviewer efforts to contact respondents publicly available. Additional steps would be needed to prepare and process data files from different modes. Survey agencies and national teams involved with some of the experimental studies in the ESS mixed-mode programme reported that the additional complexity caused difficulties and required additional resources. Problems with sample management were experienced on at least one of the ESS experiments, highlighting the overall issue that mixed-mode data collection increases the likelihood of implementation error simply because it involves more instruments.

Whereas none of the issues identified in this section are insurmountable and some would be helpful innovations in their own right, they would require additional coordination time and resources for the ESS CST, who would need to carefully evaluate and plan for such a change.

Strengths and limitations

The ESS mixed-mode methodology programme has been one of the most extensive exercises looking at the potential impact of introducing such a change on a single survey and certainly for a cross-national survey. That said, experiments were only conducted in ten countries across the years, and data collection designs differed across these. Therefore, the results may not be generalizable to the whole of the ESS. In addition, implementation errors were identified in some of the studies that may impact the conclusions drawn. The individual reports for each of the studies, cited throughout this chapter, provide more details on these issues.

Conclusion

The face-to-face standard ESS mode design fared better than all the alternative designs we tested in terms of survey participation and net sample representativeness.

So while it remains the most expensive mode, face-to-face is still the highest quality mode in these respects. The findings relating to data quality are more complex due to the lack of external record data or population benchmarks for most variables, and to the difficulty of disentangling 'selection effects' from 'measurement effects' (Vannieuwenhuyze and Loosveldt 2013; Vannieuwenhuyze et al. 2010, 2014). However, numerous differences between mixed-mode and the standard ESS face-to-face survey were observed, and these differences remained even after controlling for demographics. Therefore, using mixed-mode designs in some countries while others continue using a face-to-face design would introduce alternative explanations to differences not present in the current data collection model. Furthermore, if the proportion of respondents participating in each mode varies over time – which would be likely unless carefully controlled – cross-time comparisons could also be jeopardised, further complicating comparability of the ESS datasets.

In recent years, there has been increasing evidence of differential interviewer effects across countries leading to questions about the gold standard status of face-to-face interviewing (Beullens and Loosveldt 2014). In addition, whilst there were many differences between the mixed-mode designs and the standard ESS face-to-face survey, initial analyses of effect size suggest that these were relatively small (less than 5 percentage points), although some larger differences were noted in questions about personal well-being and income. At the same time, some of the larger differences may be reducible using careful question design (Dillman et al. 2009) although this would require disrupting the time series for repeat items. In addition, one of the key challenges remains that there is no cost-effective way to correct for measurement differences arising from data collection mode (Vandenplas et al. 2014).

Like with all survey design decisions, it is necessary to accept some trade-offs between different sources of survey error. As the underlying goal of the ESS is to keep measurement as similar as possible across countries and rounds, countries using a single mode different from face-to-face would potentially jeopardise comparability to a larger extent than countries using mixed-mode designs that include face-to-face data collection. As recently as 2011, no country appeared ready to switch to a single alternative mode of data collection than face-to-face (Martin 2011), and there is no indication that has changed.

In the current context of the ESS, the limited cost saving available in terms of fieldwork itself cannot justify a switch to mixed-mode data collection that, in most countries and on many key quality dimensions, would reduce quality. Until the time comes when more countries have access to named person samples, more people are willing to take part in surveys without being persuaded by an interviewer and cost-effective mechanisms are developed to allow mode differences to be corrected, a high quality cross-national survey like the ESS would be unwise to make such a switch. In fact, on the advice of the ESS ERIC Methods Advisory Board, the ESS CST has rejected such a switch for the near future. Instead, preparations are focused on the possibility of recruiting ESS face-to-face respondents to a probability-based web panel, which could overcome many of the serious problems that mixed-mode data collection poses.

Acknowledgements

The authors would like to thank Lorna Ryan, Willem Saris, the ESS ERIC CST, the ESS ERIC Methods Advisory Board and the ESS ERIC Scientific Advisory Board for their guidance and support.

Notes

1. It is worth noting that all studies intended to evaluate feasibility and compare alternative modes to the standard ESS face-to-face data collection (studies 4, 5 and 6) used fieldwork procedures as close as possible to those applied in the country for the corresponding ESS round.
2. The experimental design was not fully crossed: those interviewed by web in the first wave of data collection were re-interviewed in the same mode.
3. Invitations were issued during the first two months of fieldwork; 2,144 ESS respondents were invited.
4. To reduce costs, only one-fourth of those who did not complete the web interview were contacted for a face-to-face interview.
5. Eligible sample units in the ESS are 'all persons aged 15 and over (no upper age limit) resident within private households in each country, regardless of their nationality, citizenship or language' (for further details on how eligibility of sample units is determined in the ESS see section 10.4 in the ESS Round 8 Survey Specification, www.europeansocialsurvey.org/docs/round8/ESS8_project_specification.pdf).
6. Note that the mixed-mode experiment was conducted by a different fieldwork agency (NatCen) than the standard ESS (IPSOS). NatCen had conducted the ESS before and since but achieved a substantially lower response rate for the standard ESS in Round 7 than IPSOS achieved in Round 6.
7. This comparison is not a "pure" measure of non-response bias, given that the sampling frame and sampling design can also affect the final response composition and that the socio-demographic variables were measured using different modes and somewhat different wording. Based on the rigorous sampling procedures followed in the ESS and on the simplicity of some of the demographic questions we use, we assume here that most of the differences between the realised sample and the population estimates are due to non-response effects.
8. Results based on calculations by the authors using non-public microdata from Statistics Netherlands.
9. In each study, an appropriate regression model was fitted for each item, with the survey item as the dependent variable and a dummy variable "survey design" as the independent variable, where "survey design" was coded "1" for cases from the mixed-mode sample and "0" for cases from the face-to-face survey. The regression model differed depending on the measurement level of the item: for questions with 6-point-scales, 11-point questions or ratio-scale measurement, we used ordinary least squares regression; for questions with 4- or 5-point scales and other ordinal scales, we used ordinal logit regression; for dichotomous items, we used logistic regression; and for nominal items, we used multinomial regression. Data were weighted using weights inversely proportional to selection probability, and the "svy setup" command in STATA was used to compute appropriate standard errors in each regression model.
10. For questions with 6-point, 11-point or ratio answer scales, the difference between the means was compared; for ordinal and categorical questions, the absolute difference for the category with the highest proportion of respondents (modal category) was computed.

References

Beukenhorst, D. (2012). The Netherlands. In *Telephone Surveys in Europe: Research and Practice* (1st ed., pp. 17–24). Berlin: Springer-Verlag.

Beullens, K. and Loosveldt, G. (2014). Interviewer effects on latent constructs in survey research. *Journal of Survey Statistics and Methodology*, 2(4), 433–458. http://doi.org/10.1093/jssam/smu019.

Callegaro, M. and DiSogra, C. (2008). Computing response metrics for online panels. *Public Opinion Quarterly*, 72(5), 1008–1032.

Christian, L. M., Dillman, D. A. and Smyth, J. D. (2006). The effects of mode and format on answers to scalar questions in telephone and web surveys. In *2nd International Conference on Telephone Survey Methodology*. Miami, Florida.

Couper, M. P., Tourangeau, R. and Smith, T. W. (1998). Collecting sensitive information with different modes of data collection. In M. P. Couper, R. P. Baker, J. Bethlehem, C. Z. F. Clark, J. Martin, W. L. Nicholls II and J. M. O'Reilly (Eds.), *Computer Assisted Survey Information Collection* (pp. 431–454). New York: Wiley.

de Leeuw, E. (2005). To mix or not to mix? Data collection modes in surveys. *Journal of Official Statistics*, 21(2), 1–23.

de Leeuw, E., Callegaro, M., Joop, H., Korendijk, E. and Lensvelt-Mulders, G. (2007). The influence of advance letters on response in telephone surveys: A meta-analysis. *Public Opinion Quarterly*, 71(3), 413–43.

de Leeuw, E. D. (1992). *Data Quality in Mail, Telephone and Face To Face Surveys*. ERIC. Retrieved from http://eric.ed.gov/?id=ED374136.

Dillman, D. A., Smyth, J. D. and Christian, L. M. (2009). *Internet, Mail, and Mixed Mode Surveys: The Tailored Design Method*. Hoboken, NJ: John Wiley and Sons.

Ernst Staehli, M. (2012). Switzerland. In *Telephone Surveys in Europe: Research and Practice* (1st ed., pp. 25–36). Berlin, Heidelberg: Springer-Verlag.

Eva, G., Loosveldt, G., Lynn, P., Martin, P., Revilla, M., Saris, W. E. and Vannieuwenhuyze, J. T. A. (2010). *ESSPrep WP6 – Mixed Mode Experiment. Deliverable 21 Final Mode Report* (No. 21).

Gaziano, C. (2005). Comparative analysis of within-household respondent selection techniques. *Public Opinion Quarterly*, 69(1), 124–157.

Groves, R. M. (1989). *Survey Errors and Survey Costs*. New York: Wiley-Interscience.

Groves, R. M. (1990). Theories and methods of telephone surveys. *Annual Review of Sociology*, 16, 221–240.

Groves, R. M., Fowler, F. J., Couper, M. P., Lepkowski, J. M., Singer, E. and Tourangeau, R. (2004). *Survey Methodology* (1st ed.). John Wiley and Sons.

Harkness, J. A. (2003). Questionnaire translation. In J. A. Harkness, F. J. Van de Vijver and P. P. Mohler (Eds.), *Cross-Cultural Survey Methods*. Hoboken, NJ: John Wiley and Sons.

Harkness, J. A., Villar, A., and Edwards, B. (2010). Translation, adaptation, and design. In J. A. Harkness, M. Braun, B. Edwards, T. P. Johnson, L. Lyberg, P. P. Mohler, ... T. Smith (Eds.), *Survey Methods in Multinational, Multiregional, and Multicultural Contexts* (pp. 115–140). Hoboken, NJ: John Wiley and Sons.

Holbrook, A. L., Green, M. C. and Krosnick, J. A. (2003). Telephone versus face-to-face interviewing of national probability samples with long questionnaires: Comparisons of respondent satisficing and social desirability response bias. *Public Opinion Quarterly*, 67(1), 79–125. http://doi.org/10.1086/346010.

Jäckle, A., Roberts, C. and Lynn, P. (2006). Telephone versus face-to-face interviewing: mode effects on data quality and likely causes: Report on phase II of the ESS-Gallup mixed mode methodology project (ISER Working Paper Series No. 2006-41). Institute for Social and Economic Research. Retrieved from https://ideas.repec.org/p/ese/iserwp/2006-41.html.

Jowell, R. (1998). How comparative is comparative research? *American Behavioral Scientist*, 42(2), 168–177. http://doi.org/10.1177/0002764298042002004.

Jowell, R., Roberts, C., Fitzgerald, R. and Eva, G. (2007). *Measuring Attitudes Cross-Nationally: Lessons from the European Social Survey*. SAGE.

Kish, L. (1949). A procedure for objective respondent selection within the household. *Journal of the American Statistical Association*, 44(247), 380–387. http://doi.org/10.1080/01621459.1949.10483314.

Kish, L. (1994). Multipopulation survey designs: Five types with seven shared aspects. *International Statistical Review/Revue Internationale de Statistique*, 62(2), 167–186. http://doi.org/10.2307/1403507.

Lynn, P., Haeder, S., Gabler, S. and Laaksonen, S. (2007). Methods for achieving equivalence of samples in cross-national surveys: The European Social Survey experience. *Journal of Official Statistics*, 23(1), 107–124.

Lynn, P., Japec, L. and Lyberg, L. (2006). What's so special about cross-national surveys? *Conducting Cross-National and Cross-Cultural Surveys*, 7.

Lynn, P., Uhrig, N. and Burton, J. (2010). Lessons from a randomised experiment with mixed mode designs for a household panel survey. Working paper, Colchester, UK. Retrieved from http://research.understandingsociety.org.uk/publications/working-paper/2010-03.

Malnar, B. (2015). *Science Communication and Monitoring. Task 9.1: Promoting ESS to User Communities* (Unpublished deliverable). Ljubljana, Slovenia: University of Ljubljana.

Martin, P. (2011). What makes a good mix? Chances and challenges of mixed mode data collection in the ESS. Working Paper, London. Retrieved from www.city.ac.uk/__data/assets/pdf_file/0015/125133/CCSS-Working-Paper-No-02.pdf.

Martin, P. and Lynn, P. (2011). The effects of mixed mode survey designs on simple and complex analyses. Working paper, Centre for Comparative Social Surveys, London.

Olson, K. and Smyth, J. D. (2014). Accuracy of within-household selection in web and mail surveys of the general population. *Field Methods*, 26(1), 56–69. http://doi.org/10.1177/1525822X13507865.

Olson, K., Stange, M. and Smyth, J. (2014). Assessing within-household selection methods in household mail surveys. *Public Opinion Quarterly*. http://doi.org/10.1093/poq/nfu022.

Revilla, M. (2010). Quality in unimode and mixed-mode designs: A multitrait–multimethod approach. *Survey Research Methods*, 4(3), 151–164.

Revilla, M. (2013). Measurement invariance and quality of composite scores in a face-to-face and a web survey. *Survey Research Methods*, 7, 17–28.

Roberts, C., Eva, G., Lynn, P. and Johnson, J. (2009). Measuring the effect of interview length on response propensity and response quality in a telephone survey. Final report of the ESS CATI experiment (Unpublished).

Roberts, C., Eva, G. and Widdop, S. (2008). *Assessing the Demand and Capacity for Mixing Modes of Data Collection on the European Social Survey: Final Report on the Mapping Exercise*. London: Centre for Comparative Social Surveys.

Schuman, H., and Presser, S. (1981). *Question and Answers in Attitude Surveys. Experiments on Question Form, Wording, and Context*. San Diego, CA: Academic Press.

Tourangeau, R., Rips, L. J. and Rasinski, K. A. (2000). *The Psychology of Survey Response*. Cambridge: Cambridge University Press.

Tourangeau, R. and Smith, T. (1996). Asking sensitive questions. The impact of data collection mode, question format and question context. *Public*, 60(2), 275–304.

Vandenplas, C., Loosveldt, G., Beullens, K. and Vannieuwenhuyze, J. T. A. (2014). Protocols and tools for correcting mode differences in the data (http://cordis.europa.eu/result/rcn/168963_en.html).

Vannieuwenhuyze, J. T. A. and Loosveldt, G. (2013). Evaluating relative mode effects in mixed-mode surveys: Three methods to disentangle selection and measurement effects. *Sociological Methods and Research*, 42(1), 82–104. http://doi.org/10.1177/0049124112464868.

Vannieuwenhuyze, J. T. A., Loosveldt, G., and Molenberghs, G. (2010). A method for evaluating mode effects in mixed-mode surveys. *Public Opinion Quarterly*, 74(5), 1027–1045. http://doi.org/10.1093/poq/nfq059.

Vannieuwenhuyze, J. T. A. Loosveldt, G., and Molenberghs, G. (2014). Evaluating mode effects in mixed-mode survey data using covariate adjustment models. *Journal of Official Statistics*, 30(1), 1–21.

Villar, A., Winstone, L., Prestage, Y. and Lynn, P. (2014). Deliverable 7.4 Feasibility report – Costs, response rates, design effects and quality of alternative data collection (Unpublished ESS DACE Deliverable No. 7.4). London: City University London.

Appendix

Table 16.6A Research teams for each study

Study 1 researchers	Roger Jowell Caroline Bryson Ruth O'Shea	
Study 2 researchers	Caroline Roberts Annette Jäckle Peter Lynn	
Study 3 researchers	Rory Fitzgerald Roger Jowell Peter Martin	Gideon Skinner Ana Villar Lizzy Winstone
Study 4 researchers	Gillian Eva Roger Jowell Caroline Roberts	
Study 5 researchers	Gillian Eva Dirk Heerwegh Roger Jowell Willem Saris	Peter Lynn Peter Martin Melanie Revilla Geert Loosveldt
Study 6 researchers	Mare Ainsaar Rory Fitzgerald Mikael Hjerm Alun Humphrey Roger Jowell Kaur Lumiste Peter Martin	Hideko Matsuo Allison Park Yvette Prestage Melanie Revilla Jorre Vannieuwenhuyze Ana Villar Lizzy Winstone

Index

address/household register sample (ARS) 254
American Association for Public Opinion Research (AAPOR) 254
attitudinal questions 251; *see also* reluctant respondents, attitudes of towards poverty

birth-rate studies 10

capitalism: defense of 21; Protestantism and 146; varieties of 100, 119; welfare 106; work organisation in 101; "worlds" 102
Catholic Church 41, 42
citizen involvement and democracy, attitudes towards (Ireland) 184–95; Biggs outlines 185–7; challenges in current higher education 191–2; characteristics of democratic mind-set in social sciences education 187–8; current Irish context (higher education) 189–90; "cycles of institutional reviews" 191; facilitating change 191; how educators conceptualise and facilitate democracy 188–9; inquiry-based learning 186; mind-set, encouragement of 187; modifying out mind-set 193; plans for the future 193; status quo, flipping of 191–2
Coarsened Exact Matching (CEM) 265
cohabiting families *see* married and cohabitating families with children (well-being of during economic recession)
Cold War (United States) 20
computer-assisted personal interviewing (CAPI) 290
corruption (cross-national comparison) 143–57; causes of corruption 145–7; Corruption Perception Index (CPI) 150; countries with communist past 153–4; countries with no experience of communism 152; dependent variable 150; Europe, corruption in 144–5; "free-riding" 149; income inequality 154–6; independent variables 151; measurement of corruption 147–50; methodology 150; opinion polls 149; results 151–2
Cronbach's Alpha 168, 182

democratic mind-set 184; *see also* citizen involvement and democracy, attitudes towards (Ireland)
deprovincialisation 128
direct democracy 163
dual-earner family 77

Eastern Orthodox churches 42
economic crisis *see* work–life conflict before and during the crisis in 18 European countries
economic recession *see* married and cohabitating families with children (well-being of during economic recession)
educational homogeny 204
electoral participation *see* youth political participation, changing tendencies of
equality *see* societal-level equality and well-being
Eurobarometer (EB) 229, 246
European Research Infrastructures Consortium (ERIC) 2
European Social Survey (ESS) 100; analysis of corruption 143; case study *see* multiple datasets, combining of for simultaneous analysis on the basis of

common identifiers; life satisfaction analysis 214; measurement of fathering practices 229; secularization data 23; *see also* welfare attitudes, prediction of by work regime (using the European Social Survey and the European Working Conditions Survey)

European Social Survey (ESS), religion and values in 58–73; analysis (individual level) 66–7; analysis (multi-level) 68–72; data and variables 63–4; hypotheses 61–3; openness-to-change values 72; overview of religion and values in Europe 64–6; societal value orientations 59; socio-demographic variables 62; theoretical overview 58–61

European Social Survey (ESS), significance of 1–13; birth-rate studies 10; challenge for the future 12–13; Descartes Prize 2–3; ESS scholarship 5–12; European Research Infrastructures Consortium 2–3; European Strategy Forum on Research Infrastructures 2–3; European Working Conditions Survey 8; face-to-face interviewing 11; history of European Social Survey 1–2; life satisfaction 10; research output and impact 4–5; social well-being, measures of 9; survey themes 3–4

European Strategy Forum on Research Infrastructures (ESFRI) 2–3

European Values Study (EVS) 11; case study *see* multiple datasets, combining of for simultaneous analysis on the basis of common identifiers; data 22, 23; variables found in 229

European Working Conditions Survey (EWCS) 8, 100; *see also* welfare attitudes, prediction of by work regime (using the European Social Survey and the European Working Conditions Survey)

face-to-face interviewing 11, 273
fatherhood in Russia 201–12; data and methods 206–9; educational homogeny 204; fatherhood crisis in Russia 201–2; fertility decisions and their possible explanations 202–6; gendered differential 201; ideational factors 204; "living-apart-together" relationships 203; mothers' "second shift" 201; power crisis 202; "second demographic transition" 203; social age deadline 204; statistical hindrances 209–11; "theory of planned behaviour" 204

fathering practices, measurement of in European comparison 228–42; analytical strategy 234; data and methods 231–4; dependent variables 238; employment status 236, 240, 241; estimates of ordered regressions 239–40; Gender Inequality Index 237; hypotheses 234–7; independent variables 235–6; measurement tools in European surveys 229–31; results 237–41

financial crisis *see* work–life conflict before and during the crisis in 18 European countries

"free-riding" 149

Gender Inequality Index (GII) 237
General Social Survey (GSS) data 19
Generations and Gender Programme (GGS) 229
Gini coefficient 152
Good Friday agreement 17
Google Ngram Viewer 20
governmental protection against poverty, estimating the attitude towards 255; *see also* reluctant respondents, attitudes of towards poverty
gross domestic product (GDP) 120; corruption and 146, 151; growth rate of 85, 86; individualism and 9; Protestantism and 153, 157; ratio of investment to 143

income inequality, corruption and 146, 154–6
inquiry-based learning (IBL) 186
International Social Survey Programme (ISSP) 229
International Standard Classification of Occupations (ISCO) codes 85
Ireland *see* citizen involvement and democracy, attitudes towards (Ireland); religion, declining significance of
item non-response (INR) 253

life satisfaction 10; *see also* married and cohabitating families with children (well-being of during economic recession)
"living-apart-together" (LAT) relationships 203

male breadwinner family 77
married and cohabitating families with children (well-being of during economic recession) 214–24; influence of children and partnership on life satisfaction 214–15; life satisfaction and support from society 223–4; method 216; results 216–22
Missing At Random (MAR) 251
Missing Not At Random (MNAR) 251
mixed modes in survey research, use of 273–305; compliance tests 283; computer-assisted personal interviewing 290; costs 299–300; ESS implementation challenges 303–4; face-to-face interviewing 273; fieldwork costs and efforts 300–4; interviewer effects 305; measurement error 291–300; mixed-mode designs 278; mode, interview length and interview experience 297–8; multivariate estimates, effect of mode on 294–6; noncontact rates 288; outcome rates 285–8; refusal rates 287–8; research teams 310; response behaviours, effect of mode on 296–7; response rates 285–7; sampling and coverage in the ESS mixed-mode studies 278–80; sampling frames and sampling designs 280–2; sociodemographic composition of realised samples and non-response bias 289–90; studies 274–8; summary 283–4, 290–1; survey participation 284–5; univariate estimates, effect of mode on 292; web sample 290; within-household random selection of individuals 282–3
multiple datasets, combining of for simultaneous analysis on the basis of common identifiers 264–71; background to current study 266; better models 269–70; case study 266; Coarsened Exact Matching 265; drawbacks 265–6; multiple imputation (MI) and matching 264–5; problem 264; propensity score matching 264; religiosity variables 266–7; results 267–9; variables and imputation models 266–7

non-electoral participation *see* youth political participation, changing tendencies of
non-governmental organisations (NGOs) 45

non-response studies *see* reluctant respondents, attitudes of towards poverty

openness-to-change values 72
opinion polls 149
ordinary least square (OLS): estimators 255; regression analysis 150; regression models 85
Orthodox political theology 42

paradata 251
political participation *see* religiosity and political participation across Europe; youth political participation, changing tendencies of
Population Policy Acceptance Study (PPAS) 228
Postcode Address File (PAF) 282
post-communist heritage, effect of on political participation 163–4
power crisis (fatherhood in Russia) 202
propensity score (PS) matching 264
Protestantism: capitalism and 146; GDP and 153, 157; individualism and 9

religion, declining significance of 17–31; beginning of secularization in Ireland 22–6; ESS data 23; General Social Survey data 19; Good Friday agreement 17; Google Ngram data 20; mechanisms of secularization 26–31; propaganda 21; United States and the Cold War 18–22
religiosity and political participation across Europe 36–50; behaviour and beliefs, religiosity as 42–5; control variables 46; degree of political activism 49; dependent variable 45; discussion 48–50; empirical analysis 45–6; hypothesis, data and methods 45–6; non-governmental organisations 45; political participation index 37, 49; previous church–state relations and political participation 41–2; propaganda campaigns 21; religion as affiliation 39–41; results 46–8; tables 52–7; theoretical framework 39
religiosity variables, multiple datasets 266–7
reluctant respondents, attitudes of towards poverty 251–62; address/household register sample 254; analysis of reluctant respondents' attitudes 258–61; data and dependent

variable 253; data and methods 253; governmental protection against poverty, estimating the attitude towards 255; item non-response 253; methods 254; (non-)response analysis 256–8; ordinary least square estimators 255; paradata 251; response propensities, estimating 254–5; results 255; theoretical approach 252–3
Russia *see* fatherhood in Russia
Russian Orthodox Church 42

"second demographic transition" 203
social age deadline 204
social well-being 8, 9
societal-level equality and well-being 127–38; competition 128; deprovincialisation 128; discussion 135–8; economic growth 132; equality as presented in intergroup relations research 127–31; measures 133–4; method and data 133; results 134–5; societal health 131–2; subjective well-being 132–3; trust and fairness as mediators 135
societal value orientations 59
"socio-political logics" 120

"theory of planned behaviour" 204

voting age, lowering of 162–3, 166

web sample 290
welfare attitudes, prediction of by work regime (using the European Social Survey and the European Working Conditions Survey) 100–26; comparing datasets in the analysis of workplace regimes 107–16; Europe's workplace regimes 104–7; EWCS and ESS variables 123–5; "socio-political logics" 120; understanding work organisation and welfare attitudes 100–4; varieties of capitalism approach 100; work regimes and welfare attitudes 116–20
welfare capitalism 106
well-being *see* societal-level equality and well-being
work–life conflict before and during the crisis in 18 European countries 77–96; analytical procedure 85–6; data and sample 81–3; descriptive analysis 87; determinants 79–81; directions of work–life conflict 78; dual-earner family 77; male breadwinner family 77; measurement 83–5; multivariate analysis 87–94; research questions 81; results 87–94
World Bank (WB) 143

youth political participation, changing tendencies of 160–77; aim of study 161; compulsory voting 162, 176; control variables 168; Cronbach's Alpha 168; data and methods 168; dependent variables 168; difference in non-electoral participation 170; direct democracy 163; hypotheses 166–8; institutional level (hypothesis) 167–8; methodology 169; non-electoral participation logistic binary model 172; perspectives 162–4; "political participation-panic" 169; post-communist heritage 163–4; results 169–76; systemic level (hypothesis) 166–7; variable in analysis 181–2; view on the European landscape 164–6; voting age, lowering of 162–3